1985

University of St. Francis

S0-BMV-376

3 0301 00080081 9

second edition

Organizational Behavior

W. Jack Duncan

University of Alabama in Birmingham

LIBRARY
College of St. Francis
JOLIET, ILL.

Houghton Mifflin Company   Boston
Dallas   Geneva, Illinois   Hopewell, New Jersey   Palo Alto   London

To Judy who gives me happiness and Lyn who gives me hope.

Copyright © 1981, 1978 by Houghton Mifflin Company.
All rights reserved. No part of this work may be reproduced or
transmitted in any form or by any means, electronic or
mechanical, including photocopying and recording, or by any
information storage or retrieval system, without permission in
writing from the publisher.

Printed in the U.S.A.

Library of Congress Catalog Card Number: 80-82460

ISBN: 0-395-29640-4

658.0019
'D921
2 ed.

Contents

Preface   xxii

part I
Historical and Scientific Foundations   1

chapter 1
Organizational Behavior: Defining the Field   3

Organizations and Organizational Behavior   4
Organizations   5
Organizational Behavior   7

Organizational Behavior and the Behavioral Sciences   8
The Behavioral Sciences   9
Management and the Behavioral Sciences   10

Alternative Views of Organizations   11
The Closed System   12
The Open System   12

A Strategy for Analyzing Organizational Behavior   13
The Approach   13
The Method of Discussion   14

Summary   15

Questions for Discussion   16

118,013

Exercise: Classifying Organizations   16

Suggested Readings   17

chapter 2
Historical Perspective   **18**

Emergence of Behavioral Science   19
The Nature of Human Behavior in Organizations   19
Road to Human Understanding   20
Machiavelli and Practical Administration   21

Behavioral Foundations of Systematic Management   22
Weber and Bureaucracy   22
Administrative Theory and Practice   26
Scientific Management   26
Some Observations   28
Behavioral Criticisms of Early Thought   28

Human Relations: The Move from Structure to People   31
The Hawthorne Studies   32
Criticisms of the Hawthorne Studies and the Move to
Behavioral Science   36

What History Tells Us About Organizational Behavior:
Implications for Managers   38

Summary   39

Questions for Discussion   43

Case: Administrative Systems, Inc.   43

Suggested Readings   44

chapter 3
Research Methods in Organizational Behavior   **45**

Essential Elements of Science and Philosophy   45
Philosophy and the Philosophy of Science   46
Elements of Scientific Inquiry   46

Approaches to Understanding Organizational Behavior   48

Models of Knowledge Development   48
Deductive Model   49
Inductive Model   50
Behavioral Measurement   61
Reliability and Validity   64

Why Managers Need to Understand Research
Methods   67

Summary   68

Questions for Discussion   68

Exercise: Selecting a Research Technique   69

Suggested Readings   69

part II
Individual Behavior in Organizations   71

chapter 4
Understanding Individual Employees   73

Personality Development: Three Approaches   74
Psychoanalytical Theory   75
Trait Theory   76
Needs Theory   77

Human Behavior: A Systems View   81
Inputs, Transformations, and Outputs   81
Interaction of Heredity and Environment   82

The Environment   84
Culture   84
Social Class and Work Values   88
Implications for Management   90

Attitudes   90
Behavior and Attitudes   92
Measuring Attitudes   95
Attitude Change   98

What Managers Need to Know About Individual
Employees   100

Summary   101

Questions for Discussion   101

Exercise: What Do You Expect from a Job?   102

Case: Tony Howard's Participant Management Plan   103

Suggested Readings   104

chapter 5
Perception, Learning, and Problem Solving in   106
Organizational Behavior

Perception: Providing the Link   109
Nature of Perception   109
Some Implications for Management   113

Extrasensory Perception: Some Developing Insights   116

Learning: Models and Implications   116
Two Learning Models   117
Measuring Learning   121
Implications of Learning for Management   123

Problem Solving   123
Acquiring Information   124
Action in Decision Making   126
Cognitive Dissonance   126

Modern Trends in Decision Theory   128
Normative Decision Making   128
Behavioral Decision Theory   129
A Critique of Decision Theory   131

What Managers Need to Know About Cognitive
Processes   132

Summary   133

Questions for Discussion   133

Exercise: Academic Stereotypes   134

Case: Management Practice and Management Theory   135

Suggested Readings   135

chapter 6

Motivating Human Performance   137

A Definition of Motivation   138
Job Satisfaction and Motivation   139
Three Cases   140

Selected Theories of Motivation   141
Instrumental Theories of Motivation   141
Content Theories of Motivation   151

What Managers Need to Know About Motivation   157

Summary   158

Questions for Discussion   158

Case: Two Approaches to Motivation   159

Case: Cork Manufacturing Company   160

Suggested Readings   161

part III

Groups in Organizations   163

chapter 7

Social Behavior in Groups   166

Groups in Organizations   167
Types of Groups   168

Person-to-Person Communication   172
Barriers to Communication   173
Nonverbal Communication   175

Patterns of Group Communication   177

Status Structures and Group Behavior   179
Nature of Status Relationships   179
Some Research Findings   180
Status and Patterns of Interaction   183

What Managers Should Know About Social Behavior in
Groups   184

Summary   185

Questions for Discussion   186

Exercise: Sizing Up Those Around You   186

Case: Status in the Senate   188

Suggested Readings   188

chapter 8
Work Groups in Organizations

Work Groups in Organizations   190

Normative Behavior in Groups   191

Norms and Conformity   192
Conformity, Compliance, and Acceptance   192
Studies of Conformity   194

Conformity and Cohesiveness   197

Group Problem Solving   199
Are Groups Superior?   199
Groups and Risk   202

Role Relationships and Behavior in Groups   203
Role Ambiguity   204
Effects of Ambiguity   205

From Ambiguity to Conflict   205
Some Examples of Role Conflict   206
A More General Framework   207

What Managers Should Know About Work Groups   208

Summary   209

Questions for Discussion   210

Case: Janice Yeager, R.N.   210

Case: Role Relations in Bravo Platoon   211

Suggested Readings   212

chapter 9
Power and Leadership in Groups   214

Power   215
Sources of Power   216
Power and the Source of Leadership   217

Styles of Leadership   221
A Leadership Classification   221
Selected Research Findings   224
Measuring Leadership Styles   225

Contingency Theory   228
Elements of the Theory   228

Path-Goal Theory   235

What Managers Should Know About Power and
Leadership   236

Summary   237

Questions for Discussion   238

Exercise: Classifying the Sources of Power   238

Case: Good Leader in Hard Times   239

Suggested Readings   240

part IV

Foundations of Organizational Design

243

chapter 10

Coordinating Intergroup Relations

245

Intergroup Behavior	246
Uniqueness of Intergroup Analysis	246
Conflict and Control	246
Coordination in Historical Perspective	249
The Traditional Argument	250
Behavioral Alterations	253
A Closer Look at Conflict and Conflict Resolution	254
Conflict	254
Competition	256
Coordination	259
Managing Intergroup Relations	260
Coalitions of Groups	262
Coalitions and Organizations	265
Managing Horizontal Relationships in Organizations	266
What Managers Need to Know About Coordinating Groups	269
Summary	269
Questions for Discussion	271
Case: Maryville Hospital	271
Case: Subscribers' Services	273
Suggested Readings	274

chapter 11

Perspectives on Organizational Design

275

Structural Design Theory	276
Rationality Versus Irrationality: Weberian Logic Applied	276

Roles, Not Personalities: Perrow's Sociology   279

Behavioral Theories of Organizational Design   281
Structure and Personality: Argyris's Hypothesis   281
Democracy and Change: Bennis on Bureaucracy   284

Situational Design Theory   286
Joan Woodward's South Essex Studies   287
The Lawrence and Lorsch Studies   288

What Managers Need to Know About Principles of
Organizational Design   290

Summary: The Three Perspectives Compared   291

Questions for Discussion   293

Exercise: What Goes Wrong in Organizations?   293

Case: Clarkville University   294

Suggested Readings   295

chapter 12

Designing Modern Organizations: Environment, Structure, and Behavior

Designing Modern Organizations: Environment,
Structure, and Behavior   297

Open and Closed Organizational Systems   298
Environment and Organizational Design   298
The Closed System   299
Opening the System   300

Framework for Viewing Behavior in Organizations   302

Responding to Contingencies   304
Task Force or Project Groups   304
Leadership Behavior in Temporary Groups   309
From Project Structure to Matrix Organization   311

Collegial Organizations   313
The Professionalized Hierarchy   314
The Organic-Adaptive (Ad Hoc) Structure   316

What Managers Need to Know About Designing
Modern Organizations   319

Summary   319

Questions for Discussion   320

Exercise: Recognizing Organizational Designs   320

Case: Morningview Hospital   322

Suggested Readings   323

part V
Changing Organizations   325

chapter 13
Boundary-Spanning Behavior   327

Managing Interorganizational Behavior   328
Organizational Systems and Boundaries   328
Interorganizational Issues   330
Two Views of Interorganizational Relations   332

Spanning Organizational Boundaries   334
Environmental Influences on Boundary-Spanning Behavior   335
Behavioral Demands on Boundary Spanners   337
Boundary Behavior and Systems Coupling   338

Innovation in Organizations   340

What Managers Need to Know About Boundary
Spanning   341

Summary   342

Questions for Discussion   343

Exercise: Recognizing Organizational Roles   343

Case: A Managerial Debate   344

Suggested Readings   345

chapter 14
Performance Evaluation and Organizational Effectiveness   347

Some Basics of Organizational Control   348

A Closer Look at Performance Evaluation   350
Some Behavioral Assumptions   350
The Criteria Issue: Setting Goals   351
Implementing and Using the System   352

Some Specific Issues   353
Validity of the Appraisal Instrument   353
Appraisal Methods   356
Who Should Evaluate?   360
Assessment Centers   364

Examining Organizational Effectiveness   366
Evaluation of Effectiveness Models   366
A Descriptive Measure of Effectiveness   369

A Model of Organizational Effectiveness   370

What Managers Should Know About Performance Evaluation and Organizational Effectiveness   372

Summary   373

Questions for Discussion   374

Exercise: You, the Executive   374

Case: Employees Saving and Loan   375

Suggested Readings   376

chapter 15
Planned Change and Organization Development   377

Change as a Social Phenomenon   378
Types of Change   379
Agents of Planned Change   379

Planned Change   381
Unfreezing the System   381
Initiating the Change: The Action Plan   382
Stabilizing and Refreezing   384

Resistance to Change   385
Why People Resist Change   386
How Managers Can Ease Change   387

Essentials of Organization Development   387
Organization Development: A Definition   387
Organization Development and Human Nature   389
Organization Development and Management
Development   389

Some OD Techniques   391
Intra- and Interpersonal Analysis   392
Integrating Individuals and Organizations   394
The Confrontation Meeting   396

What Managers Should Know About Planned Change
and Organization Development   398

Summary   398

Questions for Discussion   400

Case: Management Development at Bayer Bindery   400

Case: Sally Washington's Battle to the Top   401

Suggested Readings   402

chapter 16

Using Behavioral Knowledge to Improve Organizational Performance

Organizational Performance   404

The Knowledge-Flow System   405
Developing Behavioral Knowledge: Research Subsystem   405
Applying Management Knowledge: Practice Subsystem   406

Linking Management Theory to Practice   407
Barriers to Knowledge Flow   407

Linking Agents: Overcoming Barriers 409
Action Research 410

Ethical Issues in the Use of Behavioral Knowledge 413

Why Managers Should Understand Knowledge
Transfer 417

Prospects for the Future: Some Speculations 418

Questions for Discussion 419

Case: The Little Red Schoolhouse 419

Suggested Readings 421

Chapter Notes 422

Important Terms 449

Index 458

Preface

WRITING THE PREFACE of a book is like visiting with a former student after the passage of some time. Defenses can be lowered, informality can be encouraged, and one can reflect openly on things yet to come.

The preface to the first edition of *Organizational Behavior* was written in Leysin, Switzerland, a small, beautiful village in the Alps, while I was serving as a visiting professor of management studies at the International Business Institute. My perspective today is somewhat different than it was at that time, and the change is probably reflected in this revision.

This book continues to be an introductory text on organizational behavior. Since it is an introduction, it does not assume any prior knowledge on the part of readers. An introductory course in psychology, sociology, or management would be helpful but not essential. An effort is made to define terms and develop concepts in a way that will allow the book to stand on its own.

Although substantial changes have been made in this revision, the basic approach to the subject matter remains the same. I continue to believe that organizational behavior can be understood accurately by examining the inputs into the organizational system, the processes performed on them, and the outputs from the system to the larger environment. I hope no change can be found in the accuracy of the discussions. As in the first edition, I have carefully developed and documented the topics covered, using up-to-date, relevant sources. If there are any unintentional omissions and oversights, I apologize and sincerely trust no serious damage has been done.

This edition remains primarily cognitive in orientation. My aim continues to be the development of a sound, relatively comprehensive, research-based approach to organizational behavior. I believe this approach will be the most useful to prospective managers.

The real change, I believe, is that this edition is much better written. Every effort has been made to say things in a better way, to sharpen key points, and to improve the presentation. Toward this end, more cases and involvement exercises have been added to each chapter, and more real-world examples have been integrated throughout the text.

The approach used in this revision can best be understood by viewing an organization as an input-output system. In the accompanying figure, the organization is at the center of a large social, political, and technological environment. It is from this environment that organizations acquire the informational, individual, and group inputs to the organizational system. It is also into this environment that organization outputs ultimately flow. Therefore, some of the cultural and social forces discussed in Parts I through III are considered again in the concluding Part V.

As shown in the figure, the first three parts of the book deal with various inputs into the organizational system. Part I defines the subject of organizational behavior, goes into the history of the field, and explores the systematic nature of the discipline. The justification for Chapters 1 and 2 is self-evident. The reasons for including Chapter 3 require some explanation.

The methodology of studying organizational behavior often appears abstract and sometimes meaningless. It need not be so. In a research-based book I continue to believe that the subject of methodology must be introduced if the contemporary state of research and practice is to be appreciated adequately. Methodological procedures in the social and behavioral sciences are not familiar to most prospective managers, yet the validity of the tools and techniques they ultimately will employ rests on the value of the theory underlying all practice. Therefore, I hope you will look upon the history and methodology chapters not as a necessary hurdle to jump before getting to the real content of the book, but as information that can make the content more useful.

Part III examines the importance of groups in organizations. A variety of group characteristics is analyzed by developing three general categories of groups. Social groups give the organization a

Inputs into the organizational process

A. Informational
  1. Definition of the field
  2. Historical perspective
  3. Methodological considerations
B. Individual
  1. Attitudes and personality
  2. Cognitive processes
  3. Motivation
  4. Problem solving and decision making
C. Group
  1. Power and leadership
  2. Conflict and conflict resolutions
  3. Group dynamics
  4. Intergroup relations

Sociopolitical institutions

Organizational-structural processes

A. Structural design
  1. Bureaucracy
  2. Contingency alterations
B. Individual-organizational interface
  1. Goal formation
  2. Conflict relations
  3. Emergent social structures
  4. Political dynamics
C. Emerging designs
  1. Project structures
  2. Professional bureaucracies
  3. Ad hocracy

Legal rules and regulations

Outputs of organizational processes

A. Boundary-spanning behavior
B. Performance results
  1. Evaluation
  2. Corrective strategies
C. Planned change and organizational development
  1. Recognizing need for change
  2. Understanding change strategies
  3. Implementing change through the use of behavioral knowledge

Cultural forces

Environment

Economic system

Technology

type of personality and satisfy social needs of individuals. Work groups are designed to accomplish organizational goals. Power-oriented groups emerge because of the politics involved in human interaction.

Part IV develops the logical foundations of classical and contingency organization design. The importance of intergroup relations is examined from the perspective of structuring group performance. In this revision more attention is directed toward alternative designs such as the matrix organization, the professional bureaucracy, and "ad hocracy."

Finally, Part V looks at the real issues involved in implementing change in organizations. Expanded treatment is given to boundary-spanning behavior, organizational effectiveness, and planned change. Throughout the concluding chapters, the importance of the organization's interaction with its various environments is stressed. The book concludes with an analysis of how and why behavioral science is important to the effective and efficient management of organizational behavior.

Detailed coverage of all aspects of organizational behavior is impossible in a relatively short book such as this one. As Thomas Kuhn points out in *The Structure of Scientific Revolutions,* one function of a textbook is to address the articulated body of data and theory to which the discipline is committed at a given time. Reality demands a degree of selectivity, and I have tried to present the most important theories and issues of today. My hope is that, for each topic, the foundations have been provided for further research and reading.

Most important to me personally is the hope that I have remained true to two groups of people—those who had the faith to encourage me along the way and those who have the faith that what is contained in these pages will benefit them in the future. With respect to the first group, it has been my good fortune to receive the advice, criticism, and encouragement of many. Dean William D. Geer of Samford University was the first to encourage me to follow an academic career. Professors Raymond V. Lesikar and Herbert G. Hicks, both formerly of Louisiana State University, kept the commitment alive by devoting much of their own time to ensuring my progress. University Professor Dalton E. McFarland and Dean M. Gene Newport of the University of Alabama in Birmingham continue to sacrifice many of their own personal pursuits in order to counsel and encourage me. Professor J. Leslie Jankovich of California State University at San José is also due a word of sincere appreciation because of his enthusiasm and support during the formative days of this book, while I was at the International Business Institute in Switzerland.

Again, Donna K. Pruet has managed to complete the typing and retyping of the manuscript in spite of numerous other responsibilities. During the five years it has been my pleasure to work with her, Donna has completely typed several drafts of at least four book-length manuscripts and numerous articles, papers, reports, letters, and memoranda. Not once in all this time has she shown impatience with me, although surely she must have thought some terrible things. For keeping them to herself and remaining predictably kind and considerate, I thank her once again.

Numerous reviewers have carefully read the manuscript at various stages of the first edition and this revision and have offered many helpful comments and suggestions. I am indebted to Professors David J. Cherrington of Brigham Young University, Michael E. McGill of Southern Methodist University, Tai K. Oh of California State University at Fullerton, Robert G. Roe of the University of Wyoming, Larry E. Short of Drake University, David D. Van Fleet of Texas A&M University, and Donald D. White of the University of Arkansas.

Finally, and most of all, my sincere thanks and deepest love to Judy and Lyn, my wife and daughter, for unfailing encouragement. It is customary for authors to thank their families for understanding them through the trying times of a book's development. However, for me, writing a book is full of excitement, opportunity, and challenge. Most of the trials fall on family and friends. Therefore, Judy and Lyn have my thanks for bearing the hardships while I merrily proceeded to pursue my interests. That, I believe, is the one thing families do for one another better and more faithfully than anything else. I hope I reciprocate by allowing them freedom to pursue their interests without making unreasonable demands. Although these and numerous others have contributed uniquely and significantly to this book, I alone remain responsible for its content.

W. J. D.

part I

Historical and Scientific Foundations

WE HAVE THREE MAIN GOALS in Part I: (1) to define the field of organizational behavior, (2) to survey briefly its historical evolution, and (3) to present the scientific foundations of the behavioral sciences.

Much is involved in defining organizational behavior. In Chapter 1, we define it from a managerial perspective. Our goal is to apply the behavioral sciences to the challenge of managing organizations.

Chapter 2 presents a historical survey that focuses on how the behavioral sciences pertain to problems of management. True, a science of human behavior has a long, evolutionary history. By contrast, applying the behavioral sciences to practical problems of administrative organization is a relatively recent development. Chapter 2, therefore, focuses mostly on recent developments in the field.

Chapter 3 deals with the research methods in the foundations of application of the behavioral sciences to organizational behavior. The philosophy underlying the behavioral sciences is not very familiar to many of us, which is unfortunate. The management pioneer Henri Fayol stated, in his famous *General and Industrial Administration,* that "without theory no teaching is possible." We might add that without a philosophical basis, no theory is possible.

Philosophy has practical relevance. Philosophical understanding leads to good theory, which leads to a systematic field that can be taught and learned. Through teaching and learning, management practice can be improved. To this end, Part 1 introduces the field of organizational behavior in its historical and philosophical settings.

In a sense, these first three chapters are important inputs into the study of organizational systems. By defining organizational behavior, exploring its roots, and seeing how it is studied, we prepare ourselves for the substantive findings discussed in later chapters. The issues covered in this book are many and varied, but they are all included for a single reason: to provide a comprehensive understanding of human behavior in organizations.

Organizational Behavior: Defining the Field

> Organizations are so familiar that their presence among us is either accepted uncritically, ignored or mindlessly despised.
>
> William G. Scott and David K. Hart,
> *Organizational America*

Mayor Betty Harrison is the chief administrative officer in the municipal government of the city of Bakersburg. She is a successful attorney who clearly understands the political process. Little of her time, however, is spent on political processes. As chief administrative officer of the city, Mayor Harrison has been preoccupied with trying to prevent a strike by the police and fire departments. She has also been working with the city's personnel department to develop a new system for evaluating employees, and she is trying to organize a new community development department. Mayor Harrison is convinced she needs a course in organizational behavior.

Barry Perkins, R.N., was just promoted to supervisor of the nurses' unit in the "B" wing of General Hospital. He has a graduate degree in nursing but really provides little direct patient care. In the first month in his new position, Perkins has handled a grievance concerning a scheduling problem, has recommended salary increases for two nurses who completed their six-month probation, and has tried to explain to hospital administrators why the nurses' jobs should be re-evaluated and upgraded. Perkins, too, feels he needs a course in organizational behavior.

Rachel Stein is a nationally known sociologist with an outstanding reputation for her research on voluntary groups such as social and civic clubs. She resigned her job as head of a sociology department to become academic vice president at City University. Although she has not written anything recently, Dr. Stein has been meeting with leaders of the faculty senate about some proposed changes in fringe benefits. She also has proposed a plan for changing the academic calendar and has recommended a new committee structure for the institution. Dr. Stein, like the others, could use a course in organizational behavior.

Benjamin Coals has always been a good chemical engineer. Recently he was promoted to manager of compensation and recruitment at True Engineering Company. He is responsible for developing and overseeing all wage and salary policies, for planning a long-range recruiting strategy for engineering personnel, and for evaluating the large-scale uses of project structures in True Engineering. Coals is comfortable with engineering problems, but right now he needs a course in organizational behavior.

These four people—in government, health care, education, and business—are experiencing similar problems. As managers, they must know something about the people and processes that operate within their organizations. This is the main purpose in studying organizational behavior. Even major corporations like American Telephone and Telegraph Company (AT&T) that have pioneered much of the theory and practice of organizational behavior need to understand and apply it. For example, June 15, 1979, was designated "job pressures day" by the Communication Workers of America to emphasize that workers at AT&T are "people not machines." In this way, employees pointed to many of the pressures leading to their dissatisfaction on the job.[1]

The goal of this chapter is to introduce the field of organizational behavior. We will present some basic definitions and will show how this field of study can help in solving real problems. Then we will examine how organizational behavior relates to the broader field of management and will outline a plan for the remainder of the book.

Organizations and Organizational Behavior

When we hear the term *organization,* most of us think of business firms like General Motors and Standard Oil; or government agencies like the Department of Health and Human Services; or some other collection of individuals and economic resources. To be sure, all these are organizations. In this book, however, we are concerned mostly with the general characteristics of organizations, rather than with a particular group. Because organizations are human creations, we first must define some terms and relate them to human behavior in organizations.

Organizations

An *organization* is a collection of interacting and interdependent individuals who work toward common goals and whose relationships are determined according to a certain structure. This definition is broad and includes many ideas that we must investigate more closely.

For example, a family is an organization. All its members interact and are interdependent in their efforts to achieve household goals. A structure also is apparent in a family, for the parents usually have authority over the children. Similarly, the production department in a steel mill is an organization. Its interrelated individuals work in structured groups under appropriate supervisors while striving toward production goals.

In our discussion, however, we need to define an organization more specifically. Although families and production departments are organizations, we must add another factor to describe the kinds of things managers attempt to manage. Someone must be responsible for coordinating different people and groups. The family and the work group often have an unusual element of spirit when compared with more complex structures like General Motors. They also display a more limited perspective in approaching the accomplishment of their goals.

Since our aim is to study organizational behavior from a management perspective, our analysis should include not only naturally unified groups but also groups with diverse interests that a manager coordinates and directs toward common goals. Managers of modern organizations face the problem of coordinating dissimilar departments, such as sales and production, to accomplish the firm's profit goal. This does not mean that the management of a subunit such as, say, a production group is not important. To be sure it is. We are simply starting with the more complex or more diversified structure.

Figure 1.1 Structured and Less Structured Organizations

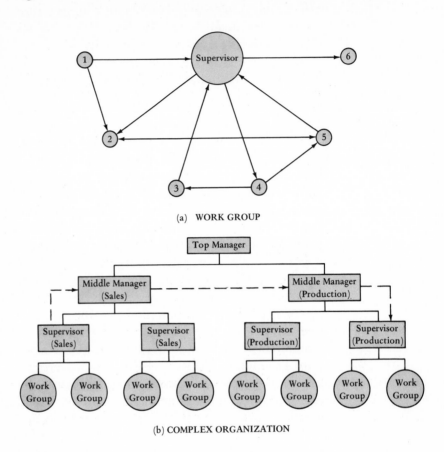

(a) WORK GROUP

(b) COMPLEX ORGANIZATION

Then we will look at groups within this larger organizational framework.

Figure 1.1 illustrates the difference between what happens in more and less structured groups. In Figure 1.1a, the supervisor in a typical work group is unquestionably the boss. Even so, interaction and communication among group members are free and relatively unstructured. The diagram shows that each member has access to the supervisor and to other members of the group. If a problem arises, there is little formality required in reporting it: one of the workers simply approaches the supervisor and defines the problem. The supervisor responds in a similarly informal way. Each member of the group is familiar with what everyone else is doing and with what the unit as a whole is attempting to accomplish.

The complex structure in Figure 1.1b is quite different. In this case, each work group under a given sales or production supervisor is doing a specialized task. The group understands exactly what its own task is and how it must be done, but it may know little about the work of another unit. Thus each sales supervisor must coordinate two sales groups to accomplish a higher-level goal of the entire sales department. These sales goals must then be coordinated with production goals to accomplish the organizational goal. The middle manager in charge of sales then must coordinate the two sales supervisors to work toward departmental objectives. The same system applies to people working in production. Finally, top management must coordinate these various sales and production efforts to meet the organization's goals.

In this more complex structure, relationships are clearly more formal. Not every person and every unit can relate directly to higher-level objectives. If communication is necessary between a sales supervisor and a production supervisor, it must occur along formal lines. As illustrated by the arrows in Figure 1.1b, communication flows up through the sales manager, over to the production manager, and then down to the production supervisor. In this way all relevant personnel are informed, and coordination is achieved. Such formality may influence everyone's behavior within the organizational structure, as it increases efficiency and facilitates communication.

Organizational Behavior

Organizational behavior, as a field of study, concerns all aspects of human action in an organizational or group setting. It includes the effects of organizations on human beings as well as the effects of human beings on organizations. Our practical purpose in studying it is to determine *how* behavior affects the accomplishment of organizational goals.

Any definition of organizational behavior must include more than the purely psychological aspects of individual action. Other important aspects include the following:

1. The study of organizational behavior includes relevant parts of all behavioral sciences that attempt to explain human action in organizations. Thus since money is part of anyone's reason for joining a work organization, certain aspects of economics are relevant. And since attitudes influence performance, psychology is also relevant. Sociology, too, helps us understand the influence of groups on individual behavior.
2. Organizational behavior as a discipline recognizes that individuals are influenced by how the work is organized and who is responsible for seeing that it is done. Therefore, we must consider the impact of organizational structure on individual behavior.
3. Although recognizing the uniqueness of the individual, organizational behavior focuses on the manager's need to ensure that the total task is performed. As a result, it proposes ways to ensure that individual efforts are coordinated toward accomplishing an overall goal.[2]

These observations tell us several important things about organizational behavior. First, it is interdisciplinary and draws freely from the knowledge generated by a variety of sources. At the same time, it maintains its own identity by concentrating on behavior that takes place in an organizational setting. Finally, it provides prescriptive guidelines, or directives, for accomplishing goals effectively and efficiently. Whereas psychology and sociology seek only to understand and describe the actions of individuals and groups, organizational behavior is an applied field of study. It seeks to use knowledge about behavior to accomplish desired results.

Organizational Behavior and the Behavioral Sciences

Engineering managers and market research supervisors obviously need to know something about engineering and market research. They also must understand human behavior.

If managers are to be supportive of employees, they must recognize the uniqueness and complexity of the people they supervise. If they are to build teamwork, they must understand group relations and the nature of small groups. If they are to coordinate groups, they must understand how organizations develop and function as well as how the external environment influences an organization. In other words, managers must be well informed about the behavioral sciences as well as their own specialized areas of expertise. Let us consider some of the behavioral sciences that apply to management.

The Behavioral Sciences

We learn about human behavior in many ways. We come to understand some aspects of behavior through our personal experiences. We also learn about behavior by viewing it historically and through the insights provided by philosophy and theology.

Although history, philosophy, and theology help us understand human behavior, they are not considered behavioral sciences. The term *behavioral sciences* is reserved for disciplines that build knowledge through the application of scientific methods.[3] The primary emphasis of this text is on systematic findings and research in the behavorial sciences. The fields on which we rely most in developing our understanding of organizational behavior are psychology, sociology, and social psychology.

Psychology   Psychology is concerned with numerous aspects of individual behavior. A few of the most important areas include the thinking processes of learning, perception, and problem solving as well as personality formation, attitude development, and motivation theory. We will examine all these topics.

The practical implications of psychological research are countless. Particularly important are applications of learning theory to training and development, motivation research, and decision making.[4]

Sociology   Sociology has been defined as the scientific study of human interaction.[5] Sociological research focuses on groups. It reaches into many areas ranging from the emergence of social institutions (such as religion, education, and business) to the design of complex organizations.

Because we are concerned with human behavior in organizations, we will concentrate on the sociological research that has examined group interaction. We also will pay attention to the theory of organizational design.[6]

Social Psychology Social psychology is closely related to both psychology and sociology. If we conceive of psychology as the study of individuals, and sociology as the analysis of institutions and organizations, we can think of social psychology as the study of behavior in small groups.[7]

Organizational behavior draws heavily on social psychology because of its insights into such areas as group relations and research methods, and such specific concepts as conformity and group cohesiveness.

Other Disciplines Several other disciplines contribute significantly to our understanding of human behavior in organizations. Economics, for example, provides a framework for analyzing human choice when constrained by limited resources. One area of increasing importance is economic psychology, which analyzes human choice and the effects of attitudes and motives on economic behavior.

Certain areas of political science also are relevant because of their concern for the scientific study of political behavior. In particular, researchers have obtained impressive results in the areas of political psychology and voter behavior.

Management and the Behavioral Sciences

Does anyone really use the knowledge generated by the behavioral sciences? This is a logical question to ask before going further. Fortunately data have been gathered that can help us answer this important question.

More and more colleges and universities are including behavioral science concepts in their management curricula. The research interests of business school faculty members also frequently include behavioral science topics. For example, a survey of the professional interests of members of the Academy of Management reveals that well over half the membership is researching behavioral topics such as organization theory, executive training, leadership, and motivation.[8]

Even more impressive, perhaps, is a survey of over three hundred business firms in which about 80 percent of the respondents showed some interest in the use of behavioral science concepts.[9] Behavioral science research has been applied most frequently in the fields of communications, performance evaluation, selection and placement, motivation, and training and development. Although interest in the behavioral sciences is great, the ideas and theories that influence researchers and managers vary widely.

In one study, two hundred business people were asked to look at a list of thirty-three well-known works of behavioral scientists and to indicate which works they had heard of, read, and actually used. At the same time, a panel of behavioral scientists was asked to study the same list and indicate which works represented significant contributions to the field. In general, the works found most useful by business executives were different from the works ranked as significant by the panel.[10]

It seems reasonable to conclude that there now is strong managerial interest in the behavioral sciences and in specific applied areas, such as organizational behavior. Certainly, such interest encourages further study in the area. Yet we must recognize that what managers actually use and what behavioral scientists consider valuable sometimes differ. Perhaps this difference reflects the divergent value systems of the two groups. Regardless, the behavioral sciences are being applied more and more to the everyday problems of practicing managers.

The behavioral sciences in general, and organizational behavior in particular, are dynamic and exciting fields of study. These fields have much to offer in helping practicing managers accomplish organizational goals. At the same time, some managers and researchers disagree about what actually constitutes significant research in the field. This conflict, perhaps, is the key to the excitement that surrounds behavioral research in management. The possibilities are great, as is the challenge of realizing them. In this book, we will accept the challenge. We will collect, analyze, and evaluate the masses of organizational research and illustrate their implications for the practice of management.

Alternative Views of Organizations

We can think of organizations in different ways. The specific view we adopt in turn influences how we approach the study of behavior within organizations. One writer has classified the various views as either open or closed systems.[11] We will briefly look at the general characteristics of each.

The Closed System

The *closed-systems view* of organizations evolved from the need to predict accurately the outcome of organizational performance and thus do away with uncertainty. As we will see in Chapter 2, the major thrust of classical organization theory was to search for ways to increase efficiency. It is not surprising, therefore, that efforts were made to simplify the task by ignoring factors that increased uncertainty. Emphasis was placed on designing organizations that promised efficient goal accomplishment and there was little regard for complicating external forces, such as technology and social values. In the closed-systems view, people in the organization and their interactions are seen as components or parts of a complex organizational machine.[12]

This view of organizations often is too simple, however, for it fails to account adequately for important environmental factors that influence behavior. At the same time, when viewed properly, the closed-systems perspective can help us understand how organizations *might* behave in the absence of complicating factors such as competitors, changing value systems, and technology.[13] In reality, however, we need to consider other views as well to develop an accurate picture of organizational behavior.

The Open System

The *open-systems view* captures more accurately the dynamics of organizational life. Early organizational research acknowledged that social forces (such as sentiments, group norms, and attitudes) can and do have important effects on individual behavior. More recent arguments have specifically illustrated the importance of environmental forces on organizational design and behavior. This open-systems view concentrates both on the elements of organizations (such as individuals and small groups) and on outside environmental forces. This more realistic view introduces uncertainty. As a result, organizational analysis becomes more complex.

In accepting the open-systems view, we face a problem. Should we begin by looking at the context within which behavior occurs and then look at environments, goals, and structure to learn about the characteristics of small groups and individual behavior? That approach is followed in much of modern systems theory, but it risks developing an overly simple model of human behavior. On the other hand, we might begin with the elements of organizations, analyzing individuals and small groups first before learning about structure and environments. The risk of this approach is that we might fail to recognize the complexity of the overall organizational system.

The only practical solution is to make a choice. We will begin with the individual, seeking to understand his or her behavior, and then build on this information to examine small groups, organizations, and environmental forces.[14]

A Strategy for Analyzing Organizational Behavior

The Approach

The complexity of the field of organizational behavior becomes awesome when one attempts to plan a strategy for analyzing it. The topics to be discussed defy all attempts to make a completely defensible and clear-cut method of presentation. In this book, we divide the field into categories and parts to make our study manageable. Unfortunately, this sometimes makes topics and concepts artificially simplistic, because we must not lose sight of their interrelationships.

This book includes five parts. Part I deals with the nature of organizational behavior. It defines the field, surveys its history briefly, and then introduces some unique problems in studying it.

Part II concentrates on the individual. It examines attitudes and such thinking processes as perception, learning, and problem solving. An analysis of motivation theory and research concludes this section.

Part III focuses on behavior in small groups. We will pay particular attention to social behavior and human interaction in work groups. In addition, we will examine power processes and leadership.

Next, in Part IV, we will explore organizational design. After investigating the basic framework of classical organizational design, we will review some emerging organizational structures. Boundary-spanning behavior will be discussed as a means of illustrating the relationship between an organization and its environment.

Part V concludes the book by examining some outputs of the organizational system. We will study how organizational effectiveness and performance are appraised. Then we will investigate planned change and organizational development. Together these subjects provide a useful framework for understanding the problems of measuring and evaluating organizational behavior.

The Method of Discussion

The behavioral sciences are rich with systematic findings that have implications for human behavior in organizations. Not all the findings are consistent, of course, but they all contribute to our knowledge of organizational behavior. Some findings are conflicting and paradoxical. These differences are opportunities for further study and are essential parts of a relatively new and challenging field of study.

In our discussion, we will use a *dialectical approach*. That is, we will present and examine contradictory views with the goal of resolving them. First we will present a statement or thesis, then we will examine an alternative view and attempt to synthesize the two. This approach is particularly useful in analyzing the findings of behavioral science research.

For example, existing research points to the need for structure in achieving order and efficiency in organizational behavior. Max Weber, the German sociologist, cites many cases of how the hierarchical, or pyramid, structure leads to organizational efficiency through the coordination of individual and group effort.[15] In contrast, Warren Bennis argues convincingly that highly structured organizations can lead to dysfunctional behavior in modern, rapidly changing societies.[16] Thus we have a conflict.[17] How do we reconcile the two views?

Fortunately, research has resolved the issue. Paul Lawrence and Jay Lorsch illustrate how some organizations, such as those characterized by stable environments, are effective by emphasizing order and structure. Organizations operating in rapidly changing environments (such as the electronics industry) are most effective when they develop more flexible structures.[18] We can formulate a synthesis of the two points in the form of a proposition.

Proposition 1.1

> Structure and adaptability are both important aspects of organizational design. The relative importance depends on the dynamics of the environment within which the organization exists.

Summary

Organizations are collections of interacting and interrelated human and nonhuman resources working toward a common goal or set of goals within the framework of structured relationships. Organizational behavior is concerned with all aspects of how organizations influence the behavior of individuals and how individuals in turn influence organizations.

Organizational behavior is an interdisciplinary field that draws freely from other behavioral sciences, including psychology, sociology, and many others. The unique mission of organizational behavior is to apply the concepts of the behavioral sciences to the pressing problems of management and, more generally, to administrative theory and practice.

In approaching organizational behavior, we can use many strategies. Historically, the study of management and organizations took a closed-systems view. The chief aim of this view is to maximize the efficiency of internal operations. In doing so, the uncertainty of uncontrollable and external environmental factors often were ignored. This traditional closed-systems view of organizations made substantial contributions to the theory of organizational design. At the same time, for analytical reasons, organizations came to be viewed as precise and complex machines. In this framework, human beings were reduced to components of the organizational machine.

More recently, the study of organizations and the behavior of human beings within them has assumed an open-systems perspective.

Factors such as human sentiments and attitudes, as well as technological and sociological forces originating outside the organizations, have assumed greater importance in analyzing organizational behavior.

This book adopts the open-systems perspective because it is a contemporary and more complete way to view organizations and the human behavior within them. After discussing some preliminary issues, we will begin with an examination of the individual. Then we will move from the individual to the small group, to the complex organization, and finally to some environmental factors important in organizational change.

Questions for Discussion

1. Is the term *organizational behavior* really meaningful or is all behavior really individual behavior? Explain your response.
2. What are some distinguishing characteristics of the behavioral sciences? What disciplines usually are included in this field?
3. What implications for management do you think the behavioral sciences have? Are all management phenomena behavioral?
4. What is the difference between open and closed systems? Why is this difference important for organizational behavior?
5. What is an organization? In what ways do organizations display characteristics of closed systems? Of open systems?

Exercise: Classifying Organizations

Following is a list of real-world organizations and a brief description of each. Classify each organization as an informal (less structured) or a formal group (structured), and justify your classifications.

Midtown Pool Hall   The Midtown Pool Hall is the gathering place for almost all the college students at City University. At any time of the day or night you can enter the hall and find friends and acquaintances. The crowd changes, but the routine is the same: some people are shooting pool, some are watching, and others are walking around talking to one another.

Engine Company Four   Fire Station Number Six of the Municipal Fire Department has several truck crews, but the best by far is Engine Company Four. This company is composed of a crew chief, driver, and three linespeople who have worked together for three months. The crew chief is in charge and carefully coordinates an efficient interaction between the other members of the crew.

Literary Forum   The Literary Forum meets the second Wednesday of every month at the public library. The group sits in a circle, and any member can begin the session by proposing an idea or controversy related to some recent reading he or she has done. The group then discusses the idea and extends the discussion into any area that seems to be logical or interesting.

Suggested Readings

Daft, R. L., and J. C. Wiginton. "Language and Organization." *Academy of Management Review* 4 (1979): 179–192.

Dowling, William, ed. *Effective Management and the Behavioral Sciences.* New York: AMACOM, 1978.

Gibbons, C. C. "Marks of a Mature Manager." *Business Horizons* 19 (October 1975): 54–56.

Hackman, J. R., and J. L. Suttle. *Improving Life at Work.* Santa Monica, Calif.: Goodyear, 1977.

Hershey, Robert. "Executive Miscalculations." *University of Michigan Business Review* 31 (September 1979). 1–7.

Humphreys, L. W., and W. A. Shrode. "Decision Making Profiles of Female and Male Managers." *Michigan State University Business Topics* 26 (Autumn 1978): 45–52.

Katz, D., and R. L. Kahn. *The Social Psychology of Organizations,* 2nd ed. New York: Wiley, 1978.

Nehrbass, R. G. "Ideology and the Decline of Management Theory." *Academy of Management Review* 4 (1979): 427–432.

Scott, W. G., and D. K. Hart. *Organizational America.* Boston: Houghton Mifflin, 1979.

Weick, K. E. *The Social Psychology of Organizing,* 2nd ed. Reading, Mass.: Addison-Wesley, 1979.

chapter 2

Historical Perspective

To those of us who study history not merely as a warning
reminder of man's follies and crimes, but also as an encouraging
remembrance of generative souls, the past ceases to be a
depressing chamber of horrors; it becomes a celestial city, a
spacious country of the mind.

Will and Ariel Durant,
The Lessons of History

Chapter 1 introduced organizational behavior and its relationship to the behavioral sciences. We emphasized that behavioral inquiry is systematic and sometimes scientific in describing human behavior in organizations. Although we will look primarily at this type of analysis, not all human behavior can be explained scientifically. Much can be learned from other disciplines. We would be in error to ignore the insights they can provide.

Because the broader field of management has shown concern for the human aspects of organization, this chapter deals with the evolution of the behavioral aspects of management that relate specifically to organizational behavior. Our goal is to enlarge this analysis by describing the development of behavioral science applications to management. Our survey of the behavioral sciences in management makes no claims at scientific explanation. We do, however, defend the usefulness of historical analysis in providing the framework for a systematic examination of organizational behavior. This examination, in turn, is necessary in developing a comprehensive understanding of human behavior.

Emergence of Behavioral Science

Interest in human behavior can be traced to early periods in history. Speculations about the psychic makeup of human beings, for example, can be found throughout the writings of early Greek philosophers. Plato often referred to the human soul, which, he believed, was divided into three parts. One part, the "philosophic," was the means of gaining knowledge and understanding. Another, the "spirited" aspect, sought power and was ambitious. The third part of the soul Plato called the "appetite," because of its desire for food, drink, sex, and money. Plato believed that any of these parts could dominate behavior, and so he classified human beings into three types: the philosophic, the ambitious, and the lovers of gain.[1] Although Plato's interest in human behavior was philosophical, his analysis had great impact on political organization. Indeed, his thinking influenced many later political scientists in defining the assumptions on which present-day governments are built.

It is tempting to trace society's interest in human behavior from the ancient Greeks to the present. Such an analysis would provide valuable insights into organizational behavior. Unfortunately, such an investigation is beyond the scope of a single chapter or, for that matter, a complete book. Therefore, we must be content with a brief survey of selected contributions, so that we may proceed directly to our subject—the history of behavioral inquiry as it relates to management and organizational behavior. We will move quickly into the twentieth century by briefly mentioning only three issues. These relate to (1) the evolution of our view of human behavior, (2) the appropriate way of learning about behavior, and (3) the purpose for which human action is analyzed.

Human Behavior in Organizations

Any field is influenced by the way the researchers view the subject. For example, a sociologist who has trust and confidence in human beings is likely to view criminal behavior sympathetically. Someone who maintains a different view may be more harsh and may demand severe punishments for crimes. Take alcoholism, for example. A researcher or manager who believes that alcoholism is an illness will stress the need for removing punishments and will insist on rehabilitation. But someone who views alcoholism as arising from a character weakness will be inclined to punish alcoholics and to protect those who may be harmed by them.

Similarly, behavioral scientists and organizational managers differ in their view of human beings at work. Hart and Scott state that "the rules of organizational behavior are rooted in some *a priori* assumption about innate human nature."[2] That is, behavioral scientists hold certain preconceptions about human behavior in groups. Indeed these same writers argue that our self-image as human beings has suffered greatly because of our increasing knowledge about human behavior and the universe around us.

To illustrate, before Copernicus proved that the sun was the center of the solar system, most people believed that everything rotated around the earth. Human beings, as masters of the earth, must surely be central to the universe. However, Darwin's theory of natural selection and survival of the fittest reduced human beings to a lower biological state. In fact, Darwin suggested that human life may have evolved from a lower form of life and therefore could not be unique. Freud supported this suspicion when he argued that human beings often are controlled by unconscious factors and frequently are not the thinking, rational demigods we thought. Finally, B. F. Skinner, in modern times, completed the argument by suggesting that people are not really free, self-controlled beings but are environmentally determined in much the same way as laboratory pigeons and rats.[3]

Human beings thus have been reduced in the minds of some to the level of lower animal forms.[4] The development of this view provided the foundations for accepting the time-tested scientific method as the appropriate way to analyze behavioral as well as natural phenomena.

Road to Human Understanding

As Europe emerged from the Dark Ages in the fifteenth century, serious thought was directed toward the natural world and all the things in it, including art and culture. By the seventeenth century, modern science was taking shape. Francis Bacon refined the inductive method (reasoning from specific cases to the general class) and illustrated its usefulness in understanding natural processes. John

Locke, George Berkeley, and David Hume followed with major eighteenth-century works on human understanding. New insights were provided into behavioral processes such as perception and learning. Although systematic science remained limited to natural and physical phenomena, the inductive method was firmly established as "true" science and was adopted by many behavioral scientists in later years. This inductive approach will be discussed more fully in Chapter 3, which deals with research methods.

In the discipline of organizational behavior, however, we are interested in more than ideas. We are also interested in action. This practical concern existed centuries ago, even in early political institutions.

Machiavelli and Practical Administration

Niccolo Machiavelli, a sixteenth-century Italian statesman, was well known for his practical politics. His view of organizational behavior and its management was equally practical. Machiavelli, for example, was quick to advise political administrators such as the territorial prince to enslave conquered people and thus reduce the potential for revolution. According to him, it was better to be feared than loved. Although his advice was harsh, many of today's managers find Machiavelli's authoritarian views logical, practical, and supportive of pre-existing ideas about leadership.[5] Yet research has discovered no connection between authoritarianism and success. In fact, one study shows that a manager's Machiavellianism led to job stress, reduced job satisfaction, and limited promotions.[6] Thus we propose a synthesis (proposition) to resolve the conflict between what we think is observed in organizations and what the research actually reveals.

Proposition 2.1

> The practical orientation of Machiavellianism is frequently thought to contribute to executive success. Experience and research suggest that this success is probably short range. Managers who become Machiavellian become suspect. Their upward mobility becomes limited and the likelihood of job stress increases.

Thus there developed an authoritarian philosophy of administration that was to emerge in later management thought. Although significant humanistic contributions were made during the centuries dividing medieval states from modern organizations, one important factor probably led to the preservation of the power approach. This factor was its *practicality*. Much historical evidence suggests that when humanistic ideals conflict with practical reality, the latter prevails.

Numerous contributions in psychology, sociology, anthropology, and other relevant fields occurred before the late nineteenth century. However, since we are concerned primarily with the behavioral sciences as they relate generally to management and specifically to organizational behavior, we will move to the period when systematic thinking about management began to occur.

Behavioral Foundations of Systematic Management

By the beginning of the twentieth century, concern about the management of organizations was gaining momentum. Because this concern arose in various settings, it is difficult to explain completely what forces shaped organizational behavior as a field of study. It is possible, however, to identify three individuals who generated these new ideas. In Germany, Max Weber, the well-known sociologist, formalized the notion of bureaucracy and devised his model of a rational organization structure. In France, Henri Fayol, an executive with long experience, introduced his principles of administration. In the United States, Frederick Taylor, an engineer, pioneered the analysis of work at the shop level. Figure 2.1 clarifies our historical perspective by showing when the various schools of thought came together. The figure also identifies the spokesman for each school and the main problem each man sought to solve.

Weber and Bureaucracy

Max Weber was a social scientist. Because of this orientation, he was more concerned with describing organizations than with developing

Figure 2.1   The Emergence of Modern Administrative Thought

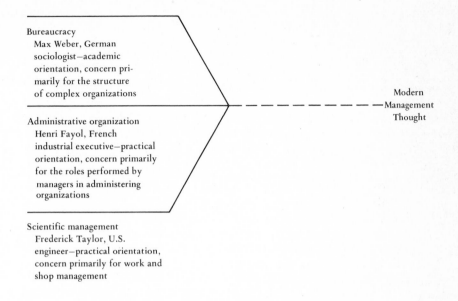

principles that could be used to accomplish practical ends. Two aspects of Weber's work are relevant here. First, as a sociologist, Weber was interested in explaining his perceptions of the growth of large organizations. Second, he was impressed with the frailty of human beings and with the unreliability of human judgment and emotions.[7] Both these aspects of bureaucracy require further examination.

The Ideal Bureaucracy   To Weber *bureaucracy* was an ideal, in that it was a model for theorizing about organizations. This sense of bureaucracy is much like the concept of perfect competition in economic theory. No one proposes that such a market structure ever has existed or should exist. The structure is simply a model and to some extent a standard of reference against which reality can be measured. The same is true of the ideal bureaucracy.

Theoretically, a bureaucracy has various characteristics that distinguish it from other patterns of organization.[8] A few of the more important characteristics are:

Figure 2.2   The Bureaucratic Structure

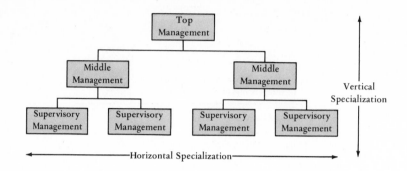

1. Specialization, or division of labor
2. A developed hierarchy
3. A system of procedures and rules
4. Impersonality of group relations
5. Promotion and tenure based on competence

Bringing these characteristics together produces a structure like the one shown in Figure 2.2. Specialization of labor is evident along the two dimensions of the organization. Horizontally, the organization is divided functionally into such specialized areas as sales and production units. Vertically, the organization is specialized by levels of management, ranging from lowest (supervisory management) to highest (top management). This vertical specialization provides the hierarchy. Within the theoretical bureaucracy, decision making is programmed and made automatic through procedures and rules that guide the behavior of organization members. Relationships are based on positions rather than on personalities, and membership and promotion depend primarily on technical competence.

We can illustrate bureaucratic organization by considering almost any business firm. Even better, think of the college or university you attend. The work is specialized in that the institution employs instructors in the sciences, business, humanities, and so on. It also has secretaries, maintenance crews, and counselors. Each person is expected to specialize in one or more tasks. Thus the institution clearly maintains a specialization of labor. And since a university also distinguishes among faculty members, department heads, deans, vice presidents, and so on, a hierarchy is established.

If you carefully read your institution's catalog, student handbook, and employee manual, you will find numerous procedures and rules regarding admission, tuition payments, faculty promotions, and vacation days. You also might find procedures designed to ensure fairness in disciplinary actions. For example, appeals procedures might be available for questioning grades or challenging campus parking tickets. Such procedures are attempts to ensure that interpersonal relations remain objective and are not based on prejudices or personality conflicts.

Finally, although all organizations eventually promote people who seem unqualified, your institution probably has well-conceived checks and balances to ensure that competence is rewarded. Certainly, most organizations are bound less to tradition today than in Weber's day. Few jobs now require a person to be born into a certain social class or to belong to some "old-line aristocracy" before being eligible to compete.

Thus Weber's concept of organization led to the views of today's structural sociologists. Modern supporters of the structural view, who may not accept the mainstream of organizational thought, still emphasize that the pattern of organization determines behavior and such processes as leadership. They further believe that behavior and leadership, in turn, influence structure.[9]

Behavioral Assumptions   One reason for Weber's emphasis on structure was his distrust of the individual's ability to make rational, well-informed, objective decisions. His apparent behavioral premise was that individuals require assistance in arriving at sound judgments. Structure was the answer. By ordering the relationships within an organization and by specifying procedures and rules, decisions would be made consistently and systematically.

The element holding the organization together and ensuring that procedures were followed was the authority of officials responsible for management. For this reason, Weber was interested in how officials got their authority, and he identified the following sources:

1. Rational-legal authority, which is established by the rank or position the person holds in the hierarchy
2. Traditional authority, which is established by social class or custom
3. Charismatic authority, which is established by the appeal of the official's personality[10]

College of St. Francis Library
Joliet, Illinois

118,013

Weber's view that bureaucracy is built on rational-legal authority was, to a certain extent, a reaction against traditionalism and emotionalism. Weber thus gave management a structural context within which we can examine organizational behavior.

Administrative Theory and Practice

Henri Fayol published his famous *General and Industrial Administration* in 1919 and immediately influenced management thinking in Europe. The impact of the book was not evident in the thinking of American managers, however, until some thirty years later, probably because of difficulties in the translation.[11]

Fayol's view came to be thought of as *administrative organization.* He viewed all business organizations as composed of the following units or subsystems: (1) the technical and commercial aspects of purchasing, production, and sales; (2) the financial operations dealing with acquiring and controlling capital; (3) the security or protection units; (4) the accounting function; and (5) the administrative functions of planning, organizing, commanding, coordinating, and controlling.[12] This functional systems orientation was successful in establishing boundaries that were to focus management research for years to come. The administrative theory proposed by Fayol is commonly referred to as the *functional approach.*

This functional orientation to management behavior dominates much modern administrative thought. Some people have been especially impressed with the simplicity and practicality of the approach, although it presently is the subject of considerable criticism. It is said that a past president of Mars Candy Company passed out copies of Fayol's book to all managers.[13] The book was required reading for all prospective executives.

Fayol looked inside Weber's bureaucracy and dealt with how it might be directed toward goal accomplishment. He also identified many of the processes such as organizing, controlling, and so on that behavioral scientists later examined from a human orientation.

Scientific Management

The final tradition of early management thinking to be discussed here is the *scientific management* movement, which emerged in the

United States and was championed by Frederick W. Taylor. In his introduction to *Principles of Scientific Management*, Taylor proposed three objectives:

1. To point out, through simple examples, the great loss the country is suffering through inefficiency in almost all of its daily acts
2. To try to convince the readers that the cure lies in systematic management rather than searching for unusual people
3. To prove that the best management is a true science based on clearly defined laws, rules and principles, and to show that the principles of scientific management are applicable to all forms of human activities[14]

To accomplish these goals, Taylor built his system on a series of elements that made up the mechanism of scientific management. One element was time study, which was designed to determine exactly how much time was needed for each aspect of a person's work. Another was the differential piece-rate system, in which workers were rewarded if they exceeded standards of performance based on time studies. Taylor also proposed the use of a planning department to explain how work should be done, and a series of functional supervisors to instruct workers in the most precise methods of work. Cost systems, standardization of tools, and various other elements thus gave scientific management a mechanism.[15] More important, however, was the fact that it had a philosophy. Managers and workers needed to undergo a mental revolution to use this new philosophy. They had to move from rules of thumb to the systematic analysis and conduct of work.

Early applications of scientific management were quite successful. For example, Ford Motor Company introduced it in 1908. During that year, the company successfully assembled and inspected an automobile in fourteen minutes.[16] From a behavioral science viewpoint, however, the performance of scientific management has been mixed. It certainly employs a systematic experimental technique; yet it also exhibits mechanistic assumptions about organizational behavior that remain open to criticism. To Taylor, human behavior was just one component of a large productive machine. Only those individuals who could act like machines had a place in his productive system.

Some Observations

It may seem strange that our discussion of the emergence of modern management has paid so little attention to early twentieth-century behavioral scientists. In fairness, we should note that several psychologists were involved in the problems of industry during this period. However, the problems they chose to study were similar to the topics discussed by engineers and business executives.[17] These psychologists limited their attention mostly to fatigue, rest periods, efficiency, and so on.

Two early psychologists, Hugo Munsterberg and Walter Dill Scott, are of particular interest. Although these two writers were more aware of the complexities of human behavior than Taylor was, they constantly dealt with topics revolving around the mechanistic model of men and women at work.

For example, Scott noted at one point that "almost without exception the interests of workers center around wages."[18] Like Taylor, Munsterberg was concerned with the scientific selection of employees, and he viewed society as the primary culprit and victim of haphazard selection and placement policies.[19] Both these psychologists provided detailed analyses of fatigue and motion economy and the effects of these factors on worker productivity.

In other words, during the early evolution of management history, psychologists were interested in industry's management problems. However, their concerns and methods were not significantly unique. Therefore, we have little reason to single out significant contributions made by behavioral scientists during this period.

Behavioral Criticisms of Early Thought

Today's managers and behavioral scientists have found much valuable material in the works of Weber, Fayol, and Taylor. At the same time, they have detected various problems with these writers' approaches to management. Following is a brief critique of the early traditions we have discussed.

Bureaucracy Behavioral scientists are critical of the mechanical model of organizational behavior implied in Weber's structuralism. Numerous studies—including one of a federal agency and one of a public unemployment agency—have shown that organizations are more than formal rules, procedures, and complex structural arrangements. Rather than exhibiting the precise nature suggested by Weber's ideal, organizational behavior takes on a social dimension and deviates from the impersonal set of relationships illustrated on an organization chart.[20] Employees in sales do communicate formally through the chain of command with people in production. Yet they also interact on coffee breaks and in informal gatherings during and after working hours.

It is also argued that bureaucratic structures demand excessive conformity and allow inadequately for personal growth. Moreover, the emphasis on control and on the rigidity of relationships discourages creativity and ignores the reality of informal relationships. Because of this, Warren Bennis has suggested that the bureaucratic mentality must be replaced by a new concept based on our increased understanding of human needs, on collaboration and reason, and on humanistic-democratic values.[21] Only in this manner can organizations deal with the demands of an unprecedented knowledge-based society.[22] These findings lead to the following observation.

Proposition 2.2

> The ideal bureaucracy is a theoretical model that proposes a rational basis for decision making and a structural context for organizational behavior. In reality, however, human behavior in organizations is more than a system of formal relationships. There is also a social dimension to behavior that provides need satisfaction and the basis for change. A comprehensive theory of organizational behavior must include the social as well as the formal dimensions of organizations.

Administrative Theory Administrative theory has problems like those of bureaucracy. One writer argues that the guidelines and rules of classical administrative thought have survived and remain influential because they support the authoritarian views of managers and ease decision making. The principles add certainty to managerial action and justify decisions that are made.[23]

Behavioral scientists, however, question the validity of the principles proposed. Herbert Simon, for example, states that the principles emerging from early thought "are little more than ambiguous and mutually contradictory proverbs."[24] Much administrative theory is said to suffer from a promanagement bias and a concern more with what managers *should* do than with a general understanding of managerial behavior.[25]

Proposition 2.3

> Administrative theory provides a practical and simplistic view of organizational behavior. Like bureaucracy, it gives little recognition to the social relationships in organizations. More important, administrative theory is based more on casual observation than on systematic analysis. It tends to be promanagement and prescriptive, rather than offering a satisfactory description of organizational behavior.

Scientific Management   Scientific management also has received its share of criticism. This approach was limited at first because it chose to study work at the shop level. It had limited applicability to the more general problems of organizational management.

Scientific management went to great lengths to develop systematic approaches to observation. In fact, so much emphasis was placed on science that the doctrine of efficiency became something of a dogma. Because Taylor and his followers were obsessed with scientific methods, they tended to overlook or deny the individual and the qualitative aspects of human behavior.

Proposition 2.4

> Scientific management, although systematic and analytical, has limited value to the theory of organizational behavior because it fails to consider the qualitative nature of human action. Taylor viewed people as being motivated by economics. The assumptions of scientific management are too simplistic to deal with the complexities of human behavior in organizations.

Having made this survey and summary, we will leave the period in which management first became a systematic discipline and will move to a time when social scientists clearly became interested in industrial problems. This period is the late 1920s, generally referred to as the human relations period in management thought.

Human Relations: The Move from Structure to People

Between 1900 and 1930 many changes were taking place in American society. Economically, the real wages of production workers increased 25 percent, yet by 1930 the Great Depression was beginning to take its toll in unemployment. Sociologically, conditions were being created that would steadily increase social consciousness and result in such legislation as the Social Security Act (1935) and the Wage and Hour Act (1938). Intellectually, also the times were changing, as can be seen in the management philosophy of the day. Again three writers stand out as having made important contributions.

Mary Parker Follett was a political philosopher who became interested in the problems of business organizations. Her main concern was attainment of unified action or coordination among people and groups. This, of course, was no different from the concerns of Weber, Fayol, and Taylor. However Follett was distinguished by her ideas about how the coordination should be achieved. She argued that consent or consensus (general agreement) was better than authority and direction as a means of government. This idea applied to nations as well as to business firms. Follett led in the shift of management focus from the individual to the group.[26]

Chester Barnard, a former president of New Jersey Bell Telephone Company, supported the consensus view in his book *The Functions of the Executive.* In fact, Barnard's acceptance theory of authority was based on the idea that managers have authority only when employees accept it.[27] The idea that authority depended on acceptance was clearly at odds with Weber's legalism and Taylor's authoritarianism. It was, however, consistent with Follett's idea of consent.

Finally, Henry Dennison has been acknowledged as an important figure in the transition from early structural thought to human relations. John Mee, a well-known management writer, maintains that

Dennison's book *Organization Engineering* was a forerunner of modern behavioral views in business.[28] Much of the book deals with human problems, and Dennison explicitly acknowledged the uniqueness of the individual personality.[29] Moreover, he was a theorist who put his beliefs into action. At Dennison Manufacturing Company, he formed an employee representation system that demonstrated large-scale participative management long before that idea became popular.

In the writings of Follett, Barnard, and Dennison, we can detect a trend toward a new philosophy of management oriented toward the behavioral sciences. This revolution in thought culminated in an event that left a lasting mark on management and the behavioral sciences. This event was the now-famous Hawthorne Studies.

The Hawthorne Studies

In 1924 Western Electric Company initiated a series of studies at its Hawthorne Works outside Chicago. The studies were conducted in cooperation with the National Research Council of the National Academy of Sciences. In 1927 Elton Mayo and the Harvard Business School were invited to participate. These studies, which became known as the *Hawthorne Studies*, were extremely important to the development of behavioral science interest in the problems of industry. We will look first at their research objectives and then outline the findings of the successive stages of the investigations. Finally, we will note some of the more important limitations of the findings.

First, let us look at the overall goals. The research began with an experiment involving five workers and was expanded to include more than twenty thousand. The initial objective was to determine the relationship between physical working conditions and worker productivity. Specifically, the goal was to obtain precise knowledge about the effects of such factors as temperature, humidity, and lighting on worker fatigue and monotony.[30] The research was conducted in a series of phases.

Phase 1 Lighting experiments were conducted between 1924 and 1927, before the involvement of the Harvard Business School. In this phase, various work groups were subjected to increases and decreases in the amount of lighting in the work place. It was observed that as these changes occurred, output varied among the groups. In some groups output increased, in some it decreased, and in others it remained constant. In no case was the change in output proportionate to the change in illumination. Other experiments were conducted to clear up some of the confusion, but they were, unfortunately, unsuccessful in achieving clarification.

In general, two major findings resulted from the illumination experiments. First, lighting was only one of several factors influencing output, and its effect obviously was small. Second, because of the number of influential factors present, some factors had not been controlled properly.

Phase 2　After the Harvard researchers joined the study, the relay-assembly test-room experiments were initiated. In this phase, attempts were made to work with smaller groups in more isolated settings in an effort to overcome the effects of variations in worker attitudes and performance when individuals knew they were being observed. In other words, an attempt was made to reduce what has been called the *Hawthorne Effect*, or changes in behavior resulting from the knowledge that one is being observed.

In this phase of the studies, a manual, repetitive, standardized job was selected for observation. All subjects were experienced, thereby reducing the effects of learning or improvements simply because practice was acquired on the job. The subjects also were people who were willing to cooperate. An observer was placed in the test room throughout the experiment, and numerous records about production, attendance, and other factors were collected.

During the test period many variables—such as rest periods, shorter workdays, and shorter work weeks—were introduced. Again, however, the results of this long period of experimentation were confusing. Output increased throughout the period, in spite of numerous changes in working hours. Morale and attendance in the test group also improved, even though both had worsened in the regular (nonexperimental) department.

The researchers speculated that the improved performance had resulted from one or more of the following factors: a reduction of fatigue because of rest periods, a reduction of monotony, an increased wage incentive, or an improvement in the test group's social relations and resulting reduction of close supervision. After the data were examined more closely, the first two possibilities were eliminated. Then a second relay-assembly group was developed to test the effects of incentive wage payments.

When the second group was formed and placed on a wage incentive, its output increased to a point below that of the first group, and then output leveled off. This experiment was discontinued after about two months because of complaints from the rest of the department (workers outside the experimental group).

Phase 3　In this phase of the study, efforts were made to vary working conditions (hours of work and rest periods) without changing the incentive system. Initially, output increased with the introduction of rest periods. When overtime was eliminated, output increased for a while and then began to decline.

The effects of the Depression made it necessary to end these experiments prematurely. Given the complexities of the relationship between wage incentives and productivity, the researchers concluded that the wage changes were not the determinants of the productivity changes. According to the researchers, wages were tied so closely to other factors that it was impossible to infer that wage changes caused the output variations.

Phase 4　This phase of the study, which took place between 1928 and 1930, was designed to gain insights into employee attitudes toward jobs, supervisors, and working conditions. In the beginning, the interviewers asked specific questions but noticed that the workers had a tendency to stray from the subject. It was concluded that the best thing to do was to move from the interview structure and simply state the purpose of the interview, thereby allowing participants to respond in any way they desired.

After the results of the interviews were compiled, the benefits were listed. First, the researchers identified a large number of working conditions with which workers were dissatisfied. This data could be included in management training programs. Insights into worker attitudes, in general, also were useful for supervisory training purposes. In-depth analysis of worker attitudes provided many useful insights into the conditions and value systems behind many complaints and explained a great deal about worker motivation. Finally, it was noted that open-ended interviews, in which workers could "get things off their chests," improved attitudes.

All this information suggested to the researchers that the work place really is a complex social system and that informal relationships and attitudes are important parts of this environment. Thus the researchers developed one final experiment to examine how social relationships and attitudes influence worker behavior.

Phase 5 The goals of this phase of the study were (a) to supplement the information obtained in the interviews with actual observation of a work group and (b) to study a group intensively under normal working conditions. Fourteen workers were selected and observed by two researchers. The first observer was in the test room but remained as detached as possible. The other observer interviewed the workers off the job to understand better their attitudes and emotions.

It became evident to the observers almost immediately that workers were restricting output and falsifying performance records. Interviews revealed that employee ideas about a fair day's output was different from the standards established by the engineers. Few workers seriously believed that their earnings would be increased through higher productivity.

To explain these findings, the researchers developed an extensive analysis of the social relationships within the group. Such factors as supervisory relations, position status, and the relationship of the group to the total organization were considered influential. A few of the important aspects were analyzed in a symposium commemorating the fiftieth anniversary of the studies (see Frame 2.1). The studies concluded that the work place is a complex social system that influences the behavior of individuals within it.[31] With this conclusion, the validity of social and behavioral scientists' interest in industry was established. Many of the mechanistic assumptions of early management thought were rejected. The social nature of the work place was recognized, and management has never been quite the same since.

Frame 2.1

One More Look at the Hawthorne Studies

In November 1974, a select group of leaders from the academic, business, and government sectors gathered outside Chicago to commemorate the fiftieth anniversary of the Hawthorne Studies.

After the Studies were reviewed and some of the important findings were itemized, the research was related to various topics of interest to modern behavioral scientists and managers.

One writer noted and reaffirmed the notion that individuals differ. This fact places greater responsibility on managers to match individuals with jobs and to redesign tasks so as to use human resources better.

The importance of participation in management decisions also was examined. The dangers of "false participation" were pointed out, and the importance of real participation in improving the quality of decisions was analyzed. Specific examples were cited to show how participation in reward systems can have positive effects. These effects resulted because employees had better and more information about their pay and how it compared with that of others. They felt that they were part of the incentive system, and they thus developed feelings of justice and trust.

The topic of leadership also was examined by outstanding researchers in the field. Of particular significance was the observation that the way a manager leads is related to the situation he or she faces. In fact, some people would argue that the situational view of management was the primary lesson learned at Hawthorne. In other words, it takes different kinds of people and organizations to successfully perform different tasks.

Adapted from "Hawthorne Revisited," *Sigma* 2 (1975): 16–25.

Criticisms of the Hawthorne Studies and the Move to Behavioral Science

Modern behavioral scientists, although interested in the same problems as the Hawthorne Studies, have been critical of the experiments and the *human relations* movement they generated. The human relations movement was the approach that related satisfaction and group dynamics to productivity. Daniel Bell, for example, refers to the Hawthorne researchers as "cow sociologists," because of their contention that the most satisfied workers are most productive, in the same sense that the most contented cows give the most milk.[32] Bell also questions the ethics of the researchers (or "ambulatory confessors," as he calls them) in conducting in-depth interviews into worker attitudes and motives. Such interviews, he argues, subjected workers to increasing manipulation by managers.

Other writers have rejected the researchers' assumptions— especially Mayo's—about the cooperative rather than the competitive nature of human beings.[33] Because of this assumed inherent good in human nature, the basic management problem was to eliminate conflict and to keep everyone happy and productive. Later researchers came to question the possibility, or even the desirability, of a conflict-free work place. The challenge, according to the contemporary viewpoint, is to provide healthy methods of conflict resolution and not to assume away the reality of conflict.[34]

Perhaps the most damaging criticism of the Hawthorne Studies comes from Alex Carey. He claims that the research is worthless and that the researchers were at best naive, and perhaps totally unjustified, in drawing their conclusions from an extremely questionable research design.[35] In reviewing the data generated in phases 2 and 3, Carey argues that different computational techniques were used to justify the researchers' conclusion that supervision, not the wage incentive, accounted for the production increase. Had this alteration not been made, the importance of the wage variable would have been much greater.

Further, the selection of cooperative participants, and the removal of two uncooperative participants, may have biased the results in favor of the effects of friendly supervision. These facts, along with the absence of control groups and small samples, caused Carey to maintain that the Hawthorne Studies actually validated, rather than disproved, the assumption that workers are motivated by economic concerns.

Not everyone agrees that Carey is entirely accurate or fair in his criticisms of the Hawthorne researchers. John Sheppard maintains, for example, that if the Hawthorne researchers went too far in emphasizing group dynamics and disregarding incentives, Carey did the same thing by overemphasizing the influence of money as a motivator.[36] Certainly, the scientific criticisms have not worried most business people, who continually adopt lessons—valid or not—from the studies.[37]

Organizational managers and behavioral scientists are not always in agreement about the merits of research. Managers may find the human relations approach useful even though researchers may find it scientifically questionable. This is no surprise, since behavioral scientists place great importance on the scientific method and on objective handling of data. Chapter 3 will discuss the methods of behavioral science in more detail. For now we simply note that, to be acceptable within the behavioral sciences, research must have the following characteristics:

1. Data must be collected objectively and must be publicly testable by competent behavioral scientists.
2. Experimentation must be conducted in a way that allows cause and effect to be distinguished from chance occurrences.
3. Facts must be related within a systematic and meaningful framework.
4. The findings of science always must remain open to question. Nothing should be accepted as unquestioned fact.[38]

Although numerous variations can be found in what behavioral scientists study (acts, individuals, groups, and so on), all behavioral scientists use the same scientific method. This is the hallmark of modern behavioral science and can be referred to as the *modern behavioral science view*.

What History Tells Us About Organizational Behavior: Implications for Managers

Today's managers are the benefactors of the years of experience of all previous managers. The typical personnel manager, hospital administrator, or production superintendent does not sit around reflecting on the theories of Max Weber, Henri Fayol, or Frederick Taylor. Even the most devoted, employee-oriented manager may know little about the details of the Hawthorne Studies. Each day, however, these managers freely use the administrative knowledge passed down through several generations.

The organization chart on the wall, the job descriptions and wage and salary guidelines in the company's procedures manual, and the retirement plan providing security for the manager and the employees reflect the best concepts of previous days. Moreover, the way the manager relates to employees may result from how he or she is taught, based on the best existing management theory and practice of the time. History is important to managers, because today's history leads to tomorrow's management theory.

Managers need to know about the historical roots of organizational behavior for other reasons as well. First, it keeps them from constantly "reinventing the wheel." A manager who must organize a company may save considerable time, energy, and expense by reviewing what is already known about organizations. This review can reduce the number of options available by illustrating the advantages and disadvantages of various structures. Second, a knowledge of history helps one to speculate about the future. A manager who has studied the past will be in a better position to plan for the future. Finally, a knowledge of history engenders pride and confidence among practitioners. Those involved with medicine, law, education, and the ministry can look back with pride on the great accomplishments of their fields. So it should be with the discipline of organizational behavior. Managers need to appreciate their forerunners if they are to feel confident about the art they practice.

Summary

This chapter has briefly surveyed management history. We have taken care to stress the events that are most relevant to our behavioral science perspective. Table 2.1 highlights some of the important elements we have discussed.

In looking at the table, we see a variety of interesting trends. For example, Machiavelli saw humanity as basically evil but capable of being manipulated toward the desired ends of rulers. The English philosophers adopted essentially the same view but placed more emphasis on the interests of the state (or organization) and less emphasis on the personal aspirations of individuals in power. Weber avoided moralistic assumptions about the degree of good or evil in human nature and chose to view people as irrational and emotional. Taylor looked upon human beings as lazy and motivated by self-interest. Any of these premises leads to the conclusion that con-

Table 2.1 Evolution of the Behavioral Sciences in Management

	Machiavelli	English Philosophers	Weber	Taylor	Mayo	Modern Behavioral Scientists
1. Basic assumption about human nature	Human nature is basically evil and subordinate to the demands of the ruler and the state.	Human nature basically requires strong state if inherent desires are to be kept within boundaries.	Human beings are primarily irrational and subject to emotion, which makes for suboptimum decision.	Human beings are fundamentally lazy and must be carefully controlled to avoid waste.	Human beings are social creatures desiring association with others. The tendency is toward cooperation, not competition and conflict.	Human beings are neither good nor evil. Some argue that people possess a uniqueness in terms of purposeful behavior. Others view human behavior as being orderly in much the same way as inorganic objects.
2. Approach to analyzing human behavior	Historical analogy and observation of behavior in total environment.	Basically a philosophical rather than scientific view. All believed that experience was source of understanding and they accepted the inductive method as refined by Francis Bacon.	A rational approach that was logical and deductive. Began with well-founded premises and progressed to conclusions.	Experimental and extremely scientific. Used an approach that began with small elements of work and emerged to a theory of management.	Basically experimental but also philosophical. Took considerable liberty in supplementing fact with philosophical insights.	Fundamentally experimental. Places emphasis on closely controlled observation and the generation of data.

3. Predominant value sought	Power and practical political methods for goal accomplishment.	Order and the means to achieve functional government.	Rationality and logic in organizational decisions.	Justice and a fair day's work for a fair day's pay.	Mental health and satisfaction in organizational relationships.	Scientific understanding with a comprehensive description of human behavior.
4. Primary beneficiary of prescriptions	The ruler or the politician.	The society through viable government.	The organization as a rational and efficient entity.	Managers of organizations and workers through increased pay.	Management and workers through increased satisfaction and mental health.	The scientific community through increased understanding of human behavior. Value to management in that the understanding may lead to improved performance.
5. Appeal to modern management	Practical and expedient.	Idealistic in the concept of order.	Promising in its support of rational, well-informed decision making.	Compelling in its simplistic view of economic man.	Attractive in its picture of social man.	Compelling in its objectivity and systematic structure.

trol of human behavior is necessary, as evidenced by the concern for authority in early administrative and political thought.

Mayo and the Hawthorne Studies, however, assumed a cooperative and social human being. The emphasis in management thought moved away from the control philosophy. Behavioral scientists today assume that human beings are neither good nor evil. They place more emphasis on describing behavior as it exists under different conditions. No clear-cut prescription for any authority orientation can be applied to all cases.

With regard to the methods employed in understanding behavior, Machiavelli relied on historical analogy and observation. The English philosophers advocated inductive logic, whereas Weber approached the subject deductively. Taylor was extremely experimental and scientific; Mayo mixed experiments with philosophy. Behavioral scientists today are almost completely experimental.

Machiavelli sought a practical theory of power; the philosophers sought order. Weber's quest was for rationality; Taylor championed justice. Mayo's preoccupation was with the mental and emotional health of workers. Today's behavioral scientists are concerned primarily with understanding behavior for its own sake.

The person in power, or aspiring to be in power, would be the benefactor of Machiavellianism, whereas a society with a stable system of government would benefit from the guidelines proposed by the English philosophers. Weber's bureaucracy was designed to add rationality to decision making. Both managers and workers conceivably could benefit from the systems proposed by Taylor and Mayo, although the benefits derived would be different. Modern science would be served best, as would workers and managers, by contemporary behavioral scientists applying their scientific knowledge.

Finally, Machiavelli's appeal lies in his practical, objective approach to reality. The philosophers are appealing because of their ideal of order. Weber and Taylor find support from business because their ideas offer rationality and economic efficiency. Mayo is attractive because he enhances our self-image as unique beings unlike all others. Behavioral science today is compelling because of its objectivity and systematic structure.

The basic interest in human behavior in organizations can be traced to distant origins. The interest goes back even further than we have noted, perhaps even to Biblical times, and contributions to the field have come from a variety of sources. Political and moral philosophy have made contributions, as have economics, psychology, engineering, and sociology. Systematic administrative thought, which concerns itself with practical matters relating to organizational management, is properly viewed as a product of the twentieth century. From the mechanistic views of Weber, Fayol, and Taylor came the humanistic interest of Mayo and others in the 1920s and 1930s. This human relations view has been refined even more by modern behavioral scientists.

Questions for Discussion

1. What implications can you see for Taylor's scientific management in the study of organizational behavior?
2. What similarities do you detect in the theories of Mary Parker Follett, Chester Barnard, and Henry Dennison? Why are these theories important for understanding organizational behavior?
3. What is your image of the behavioral sciences? How are they different from more humanistic disciplines such as history and philosophy?
4. Why are the Hawthorne Studies generally recognized as an important contribution to management history? What was the primary finding of these studies?
5. Why do you think social and behavioral scientists were so late in developing an interest in industrial problems? Explain.

Case: Administrative Systems, Inc.

Administrative Systems, Inc., is a management consulting firm founded by Peter E. Slovick. Dr. Slovick, who holds a doctoral degree in psychology, specializes in developing and implementing performance evaluation systems in large corporations. He also does pre-employment testing for companies who hire him to report on a prospective employee's suitability for a particular job.

The firm is very successful and the list of Dr. Slovick's clients is long and impressive. Recently, he wrote a letter to the local state university, expressing his interest in a teaching position on the psychology or business faculty. The university's response was a surprise.

The chairperson of a faculty screening committee indicated that they were unimpressed with Dr. Slovick's credentials. The committee was particularly concerned that Dr. Slovick had no record of applying scientific methods to organizational problems and certainly did not present any evidence of published scholarship. The chairperson specifically noted that although Dr. Slovick's work was human relations work it was not hard behavioral science.

Dr. Slovic was outraged! The business community apparently appreciated his work even if it was not impressive to the "eggheads at the university."

1. What do you think is the primary difference between what the chairperson calls human relations and hard behavioral science?
2. Do you think that most business people do not care about the scientific rigor of consultants? Why or why not?

Suggested Readings

Bennett, J. T., and M. H. Johnson. "Laws of Committee Organization and Management in Bureaucracies." *The Bureaucrat* 8 (Fall 1979): 50–55.

Denhardt, R. B., and H. S. Dugan. "Managerial Intuition: Lessons from Barnard and Jung." *Business and Society* 19 (Spring 1978): 26–30.

Divine, D. R. "A Political Theory of Bureaucracy." *Public Administration* 57 (Summer 1979): 143–158.

Ireland, R. D., and P. M. Van Auken. "A View of Management History as Prologue to Future Management Philosophy." *Akron Business and Economic Review* 10 (Fall 1979): 7–12.

Leavitt, H., W. R. Dill, and H. B. Eyring. *The Organizational World*. New York: Harcourt, Brace, Jovanovich, 1973.

Posner, B. Z., and J. M. Munson. "The Importance of Values in Understanding Organizational Behavior." *Human Resources Management* 18 (Fall 1979): 9–14.

Pugh, D. S., D. J. Hickson, C. R. Hinings. *Writers on Organization*. 2nd ed. Baltimore: Penguin, 1971.

Scott, W. G. "Organization Theory: A Reassessment." *Academy of Management Journal* 17 (1974): 242–254.

Wieland, G. F. "The Contributions of Organizational Sociology to the Practice of Management: A Book Review Essay." *Academy of Management Journal* 17 (1974): 334–338.

Wren, D. A. *The Evolution of Management Thought*. 2nd ed. New York: Wiley, 1979

Research Methods in Organizational Behavior

> One of the reasons why normal science seems to progress so rapidly is that its practitioners concentrate on problems that only their own lack of ingenuity should keep them from solving.
>
> Thomas Kuhn,
> *The Structure of Scientific Revolutions,* 2nd ed.

Chapter 1 introduced the field of organizational behavior, and Chapter 2 traced the development of behavioral scientists' interest in the problems of organizations. We distinguished organizational behavior from other fields that analyze human affairs by its adherence to systematic behavioral science methods.

Now we will examine these methods in more detail. We will look first at science in general and specifically at the behavioral sciences. Next we will illustrate various approaches to developing valid behavioral knowledge. Finally, we will discuss some unique methods in behavioral inquiry that have important implications for organizational behavior.

Essential Elements of Science and Philosophy

To introduce and discuss adequately the methods used in analyzing organizational behavior, we first must define some terms. A few of these terms relate to philosophy or, more specifically, to the philosophy of science. Other terms deal with the elements of scientific inquiry.

Philosophy and the Philosophy of Science

Philosophy involves an examination of the ultimate nature of things; it has no practical purpose other than the discovery of truth.[1] Although philosophy is made up of various subspecialties, our concern is with obtaining meaningful knowledge about organizational behavior.

More generally, we will be concerned with selected issues in the behavioral sciences that attempt to examine the development, validity, and use of scientific research.[2] Our purpose is not to become philosophical, but to recognize some important issues in organizational behavior that are essentially philosophical. Once we understand the importance of these issues, we will better understand human behavior in organizations.

Elements of Scientific Inquiry

This section briefly reviews some of the terms used in any discussion of scientific analysis. Most of these terms are common. However, we need to present some basic definitions to avoid confusion as our discussion progresses.

Science   Science often is equated with the use of the scientific method, which is a precisely developed process for conducting experiments. Although this method is certainly part of science, the two terms do not mean the same thing.

The objective of science is to describe real-world events. It is hoped that the description will lead to explanation and eventually to prediction. Science stops with description and has no goal except understanding. Often the knowledge gained through science is used to control various aspects of reality, such as production processes and sometimes even human behavior.

The essential nature of science lies in one's attitude. The "scientific mentality" is the tendency to suspend belief until appropriate evidence is produced and then to believe or accept findings only to the extent justified by available evidence.[3] Herbert Simon illustrates this point by stating that "propositions are scientific only if truth or falsehood, in a factual sense, can be predicted from them. If such predictions can be made the proposition is scientific."[4]

Scientific analysis requires a knowledge of the elements of science. The scientific mentality, therefore, insists on certain procedures if it is to accept the outcome of research. Let us briefly define several key terms relating to scientific inquiry.

Premise   Scientific inquiry usually begins with one or more premises, or assumptions. A *premise* is an assumption about the state of nature that is under consideration. In a study of decision makers, for example, we may assume (make the premise) that the quantity of information known by the decision maker is related to the quality of the resulting decision. That is, we can say that when x is true (decision maker has more knowledge), then y (better decisions) will follow.

Hypothesis   A *hypothesis* is a precisely stated proposition that can be tested logically. We usually insist that a hypothesis be stated in measurable form. For example, we may want to learn whether or not absenteeism is related to job satisfaction, as tested by some specific measurement. We therefore propose a relationship between absenteeism and job satisfaction stating that absenteeism increases as job satisfaction decreases. We test this hypothesis through experimentation and, finally, either accept or reject it.

Theory   Once we have collected data, we have to explain the relationships that develop among them. Data collection alone is not science. Thus we propose a *theory* to associate and integrate in a comprehensive explanation the data collected through experimentation and observation. Theorizing, in other words, is systematically organizing reality within a logical framework.

Through theory building, we learn about organizational behavior. However, since we are exposed to theories that are basically different, we must examine some possible approaches to developing behavioral knowledge.

Approaches to Understanding Organizational Behavior

We have suggested that valid knowledge can be obtained in several ways. Historically, the most appropriate path to valid knowledge has been a key issue in organizational behavior.

In general, knowledge can be obtained through reason, sense perception, intuition, authority, and revelation.[5] We will organize our analysis around the first three categories and ignore the last two. We choose to ignore authority, because in organizational behavior there is no group, such as the Church, nor any specific dogma capable of imposing "truth" on researchers and practitioners. Revelation also will be ignored, not because we reject the possibility of divinely inspired knowledge, but, as C. West Churchman argues, one simply has no way of ensuring that any individual is sufficiently in touch with divine truth to act as a translator of such insights.[6] Thus we will look only at sources of knowledge that are within the realm of human experience.

Behavioral processes have certain unique characteristics when compared to the natural or physical sciences. For one thing, human behavior is more complex than the behavior of inorganic objects because every human personality is unique. Human behavior is also less repeatable and, therefore, more difficult to isolate and control effectively under experimental conditions. In other words, human behavior is caused by a complex set of forces that scientists can seldom duplicate. Absolute cause-and-effect relationships are difficult to establish.

Finally, much human behavior is caused by factors that cannot be observed directly or measured precisely. Attitudes and emotions often require an indirect measurement technique. Despite these problems, we must generate knowledge concerning human behavior in organizations if we are to understand it.

Models of Knowledge Development

Two models of knowledge development are important in organizational behavior. These models are probably familiar, since they are

Figure 3.1 The Deductive Model

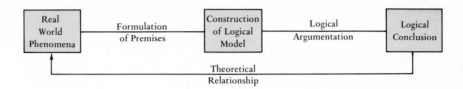

basic to the scientific approach. To illustrate the models, we will use examples from the field of motivation theory.

Deductive Model

Figure 3.1 represents the *deductive model* of knowledge development. Basically, this approach moves logically from the general aspects of broad descriptive premises to specific conclusions about the phenomenon under examination. For example, we may state certain premises about all human beings and then draw specific conclusions about a particular individual.

A conclusion is developed logically from this model through reason with little reference to the real world. Of course, the real world is important as a source of premises and as a means of checking conclusions against actual occurrences. But the reasoning itself is based on logic, not on observation.

In organizational behavior, Abraham Maslow's needs hierarchy is a good example of deductive reasoning. We will examine Maslow's needs hierarchy in detail in Chapter 4. For now, it is enough to note that Maslow began with certain assumptions: that human beings are animals whose wants are never satisfied; that a satisfied need does not motivate human behavior; and that human needs are arranged in a hierarchy, or levels of importance.[7] None of these premises is directly observable in reality.

How then do we observe that human beings are never satisfied or that satisfied needs never motivate human behavior? Moreover, who has ever seen a needs hierarchy and can say for sure that it takes a triangular shape and is divided into five layers? (Look ahead to Figure 4.1.) Obviously, no one has ever directly observed any of these phenomena. However, few people would deny that all these assumptions are intuitively accurate. For this reason, we refer to such statements as *a priori* truths, meaning that we know them to be true without actually experiencing or observing them.

Logically progressing from Maslow's premises, we can draw many conclusions vital to modern motivational theory. For example, the theory helps explain why employees begin to seek noneconomic benefits (such as improved work conditions and participation in decision making) after they reach a certain level of income. Once biological needs are satisfied, higher-level needs become the motivating forces. But the validity of such deductive explanations depends on the validity of the premises that sparked the investigation. If the premises are inaccurate, the conclusions will be invalid.

Proposition 3.1

> Insights into organizational behavior can be obtained through the use of deductive arguments. The validity of conclusions drawn depends on the accuracy of the premises upon which the argument is based.

Inductive Model

The *inductive model* is perhaps the most commonly used method in modern behavioral science. It moves from specific observations of actual events to inferences about the larger populations. Figure 3.2 illustrates this method.

In using the inductive model, researchers make a specific observation about one or more parts of the organization they want to understand. For example, if they want to know about job satisfaction among production workers in an industry, they may select one firm for study. They then observe and measure the sample and finally generalize the results to the larger industry.

Empirical studies in organizational behavior can be conducted in several ways. These include actual observations of behavior by an outside observer (or by an inside observer when the researcher actually becomes a member of the group being observed). For exam-

Figure 3.2   The Inductive Model

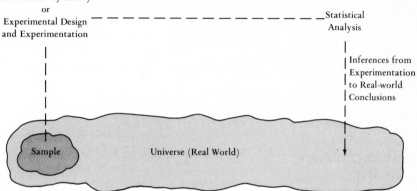

ple, a behavioral scientist interested in human behavior in penal institutions might visit a prison and observe the inmates at work, play, and rest. Then the researcher might be placed in a cell to observe the institution as an inmate.

Besides the observational method, researchers in organizational behavior may use field studies and experiments, laboratory experiments, and survey questionnaires. *Field studies* preserve the "natural setting" and usually involve only observation. When a behavioral scientist is placed in a prison cell, he or she is conducting a field study. The researcher remains unidentified and does nothing to influence the day-to-day circumstances of the prison environment. Field studies offer the advantage of enabling a researcher to observe behavior as it actually occurs. The disadvantage is that the researcher cannot control the circumstances under which observations are made. As a result, cause-and-effect relationships are rarely found using this approach.

Field experiments are like field studies except that the researchers introduce changes into the natural setting. For example, to study the effects of job enrichment or satisfaction, researchers first would select two groups of employees who have similar characteristics. Then jobs of one group would be redesigned or enriched, while the other group's work would not be changed. The effects of the change

Figure 3.3   The Basic Experimental Model

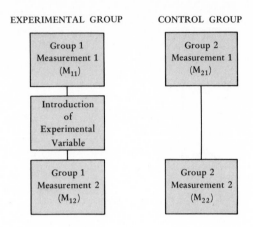

would be calculated by comparing the outcomes (measured satisfaction) in the two groups. Again, however, although much of the natural setting would be preserved, researchers could not achieve complete and precise control over the experimental environment.

We must now give more attention to two remaining research methods: laboratory experiments and survey questionnaires. These approaches illustrate many of the issues that arise in behavioral research. We will begin by looking at the problems of experimental design.

Experimental Design   Experimentation is an important research method because it allows researchers to introduce and manipulate variables within an environment. In this way, they can determine cause-and-effect relationships. Figure 3.3 illustrates basic experimental design.

One experimental research design is a "before-and-after" test that uses a control group. To illustrate, consider the following study by a behavioral scientist. The researcher wanted to determine how group interaction influenced problem solving. First, a test was devised and refined to measure the quality of problem solving. A score of 100 was considered perfect; 70 was average; and anything below 50 was poor. Next, two groups of managers were selected randomly from the two hundred managers of a local company. Ten managers were placed in each group, and the two groups were compared to ensure that no obvious differences existed.

The members of each group were then given the test. In Figure 3.3, the label M_{11} indicates the average first test score for group 1, and the label M_{21} is the average first test score for group 2. The average score obtained by group 1 was 72; group 2 averaged a score of 70. After the first test, or pretest, the members of group 1 (the experimental group) were allowed to interact and talk about the test. This interaction was the *experimental variable,* the introduced change. Members of group 2 (the control group) were isolated from one another and could not discuss the test.

After a specified length of time, both groups were retested (the post-test). The average post-test score for group 1 was 84, whereas the average score for group 2 was 76. The differences (D) in the average scores were calculated in the following manner:

$$D_1 = M_{12} - M_{11} = 84 - 72 = 12$$

$$D_2 = M_{22} - M_{21} = 76 - 70 = 6$$

Since the score for group 1 increased twice as much as the score for group 2, it is tempting to assume that the experimental variable of group interaction resulted in an increase of six points ($D_1 - D_2 = 12 - 6 = 6$). Perhaps it did. But perhaps other experimental factors—or even errors—could have accounted for part of the difference. In fact, such a research design allows for several errors, so we must look at possible explanations for the difference in scores. Not that errors occur in all experimental research, but we should be aware of the following common problems.[8]

Testing Error. Some of the difference in scores could result because the pretest prepared respondents for the post-test. Subjects may have remembered some questions, thought about them, and changed their responses on the post-test. This could account for the six-point increase in the score of group 2, even though its members were not allowed to interact.

History Error. Events that occur between the time of the pretest and the post-test could change the results. For example, some subjects may have attended a management lecture about problem solving, which could lead to higher scores on the posttest even without direct interaction.

Maturity Error. In some experiments, uncontrollable factors may cause original members to leave either group and be replaced by other subjects who score differently. Thus the group's average score on the post-test could be affected.

Instrument Decay Error. Any experimental situation in which time passes between the pretest and the post-test may cause group members to become tired, bored, too hot, too cold. All such factors may influence performance on the post-test.

Mortality Error. This is like maturity error, in which some of the original subjects may drop out of the experiment. Mortality error often becomes serious, as when classes are tested at the beginning and end of a school term to measure learning. Those who drop or add the course can influence its outcome. Similarly, the difference in pretest and post-test scores can reflect mortality error.

Selection Error. If group members are not selected and assigned randomly, a bias can be introduced. For example, if all males are placed in one group, or if all middle managers make up a group, test results will be biased. Scores will reflect only how males or middle managers might perform. The research thus will not represent the sample population.

Interactive Errors. Two or more of the previous errors may work together to pollute the research. For example, maturity error and selection error could interact to produce an even more serious experimental error.

With these errors in mind, we will look at some experimental designs that are useful in identifying cause-and-effect relationships. In using experimental designs, we are interested mainly in the validity of the results. *Validity* refers to whether or not we are measuring what we think we are measuring.[9] If researchers are conducting an experiment on job satisfaction, they must be sure that the measuring instrument does, in fact, measure job satisfaction in an accurate manner.

The validity of an experimental design, however, has a more exact meaning and can be divided into two categories. First, we must achieve *internal validity*. Our experiment has internal validity when we are reasonably certain that the experimental treatment caused the results. Experimental conditions must be controlled closely. According to most behavioral researchers, internal validity is the minimum requirement of a good experimental design.[10] Without internal validity, an experimental design has little value.

Let us examine some designs that lead to internally valid experimentation. Notice that all the following designs use randomly selected samples (to overcome selection errors) as well as control groups.[11] In diagramming the designs, we will use the following symbolic notations:

$S_{r,m}$ = This signifies the subjects used in the study. The subscripted r illustrates that the subjects are randomly selected; the m tells us that the subjects in two or more groups are matched, or similar in nature.

O = This is the measurement or observation procedure.

X = This is the experimental variable.

D = This is the difference in the measurement among groups.

The first experimental design is the classical experiment we discussed involving two groups. It appears as follows:

$$S_{r,m} \begin{cases} O_{11} \underline{\quad} X \underline{\quad} O_{12} \longrightarrow \text{Experimental group} \\ O_{21} \underline{\qquad\qquad} O_{22} \longrightarrow \text{Control group} \end{cases} D$$

As stated previously, this experimental design is referred to as the "before-and-after" test with a control group. In this case, we have ensured randomly selected groups. If the difference (D) is greater between O_{11} and O_{12} than between O_{21} and O_{22}, if the groups are randomly selected and matched, and if we can assume that all errors are accounted for, the resulting D is assumed to be the result of the experimental treatment.

Another useful experimental design involves three groups that are manipulated in the following manner:[12]

$$S_{r,m} \begin{cases} O_{11} \underline{\quad} X \underline{\quad} O_{12} \\ O_{21} \underline{\qquad\qquad} O_{22} \end{cases} D_1 \\ \underline{\qquad} X \underline{\quad} O_{31} \end{cases} D_2 \Bigg\} D_3 \quad \begin{matrix} \text{Experimental group} \\ \text{Control group 1} \\ \text{Control group 2} \end{matrix}$$

The main improvement offered by this design is that it provides a means of isolating the influence of testing error that results from the pretest. Although control group 2 receives the experimental treatment, it acts as a control. Here we can measure the overall effect of the experimental treatment by D_1. We also can measure the effect of testing sensitivity by D_3 ($O_{12} - O_{31}$). The disadvantage of this design is a practical one. It may be difficult and expensive to select three identical groups randomly.

The final design we will discuss is called the "Solomon four-group" design. It appears as follows:

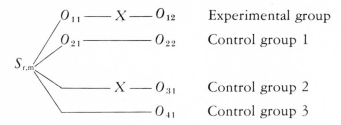

This design establishes control by means of the experimental group and three control groups. The randomly selected matched groups eliminate selection error. We also control history error by means of the experimental group and control group 1. Finally, control group 3 is valuable in isolating numerous possible interactions. With this systematic design, internal validity is established. The design, in fact, is so powerful that it has been called ideal for behavioral research.[13] Its limiting factor again is the difficulty in finding four similar groups.

External validity relates to whether the design has generality. For example, critics of research on job enrichment feel the idea that work should be meaningful is built on a middle-class assumption. Evidence suggests that some workers, such as urban blue-collar employees, actually may be put off by efforts to enrich jobs.[14] Thus an experiment is externally valid when its design relates to the general population and is not bound by a specific group of subjects.

Questions about the external validity of experimental research also have been raised because of timing factors, variations among organizational settings, and cultural differences. Frederick Hayek notes that experimental investigations do not allow enough time for analyzing changing conditions. According to him, it is useless to think that observed behavior at a given moment will yield anything of value beyond that particular time and place.[15]

Consider the evolution of management thought with regard to motivation theory. In the early 1900s, Frederick Taylor concluded that wage incentives could increase performance. Recently, monetary incentives have been considered less important. No doubt the object of study has changed during seventy-five years. Human beings are, in general, relatively affluent and have become engaged in the quest for higher-level need satisfaction. Scientific management prescriptions have become less applicable in the present.

In analyzing organizational settings, Ernest Dale raises additional difficulties about external validity by pointing to the problems of designing research in the face of our countless economic, social, and religious organizations.[16] Comparative researchers might agree that Frederick Herzberg's original research on two hundred accountants and engineers in Pittsburgh tells us much about the motivation of professional workers. However, what does it tell us about skilled workers in a midwestern steel mill or about west coast dockworkers? Fortunately, Herzberg and others have expanded their research to include such a variety of occupations that many of the reservations concerning external validity have been reduced.

Finally, as behavioral interest has expanded to the international level, cultural variations present additional problems.[17] Are there, for example, sufficient differences among Japanese decision makers' modes of operation to negate the value of modern decision theory in predicting their behavior? Research conducted in various cultural settings may reveal significant differences.

Proposition 3.2

> Experimental designs can discover cause-and-effect relationships only when experimental errors are controlled in a way that isolates the experimental variable. Internal validity is necessary for an acceptable design; external validity is highly desirable.

Recent Variations in Experimental Design   Not all problems in organizational behavior lend themselves to the accepted practices of experimental researchers. Sometimes control groups may not be available, making other methods of analysis necessary. Or it may not be possible to select participants randomly. Facing such problems, researchers may use a quasi-experimental design. One such design is time-series analysis, in which a researcher uses repeated measures on

Figure 3.4   Time-Series Data for Implementation of an MBO Program

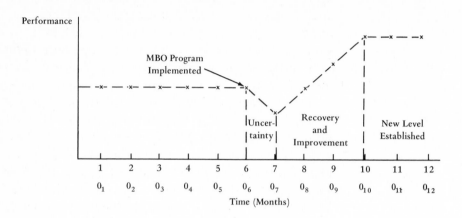

the same group. Consider the example of a behavioral scientist who is hired as a consultant to design and implement a management-by-objectives (MBO) program for a firm. Since the organization is small, it is not possible to experiment with one department while controlling for the errors with another. Therefore, the consultant decides to collect performance data about the firm for six months before the MBO program is implemented and for six months after it is in operation. The implementation itself is the change (the experimental variable). The results are shown in Figure 3.4.

In this illustration, the repeated measures are shown as the months on the horizontal axis (0_1 through 0_{12}). The MBO program is implemented in 0_6. Note that the productivity measure on the vertical axis remains constant in 0_1 through 0_6. A difference appears immediately after the implementation in 0_6. This suggests that the experimental variable (the MBO program) does have an impact. Unfortunately, however, productivity falls off, rather than improving. This result is not uncommon in behavioral experiments, for the variable (change) may cause insecurity and uncertainty among subjects or may require them to learn new ways of doing things. Productivity recovers and improves in 0_7 through 0_{12}. Then the new level is established (0_{10} to 0_{12}).

Because of the quasi-experimental nature of time-series analysis, we can never be completely sure that the experimental change caused the change in productivity. However, the similarity of the period from 0_1 to 0_6 and the drastic change in 0_7 suggests that the MBO program has a substantial impact. The leveling off of performance in 0_{10} to 0_{12} further suggests that—after initial uncertainty —productivity will climb to a higher level.

When it is not possible to select research subjects randomly, nonequivalent groups sometimes can be used effectively.[18] Pretests are needed to determine the basic differences between comparison groups (not control groups); then the experimental variable is introduced. Moreover, if maturity error affects one group, it can be offset by making changes in the other group. Again, however, such an approach is not desirable unless required by uncontrollable factors. When necessary, quasi-experimental techniques can be used. Some writers even have suggested that such research designs overcome the tendency of stricter experiments to be mechanical and less creative.[19]

Lawler, for example, suggests the use of adaptive experiments. These cannot provide the control and precision that traditional experiments do. Yet they require data collection before the experimental change is introduced as well as comparison groups, time-series or longitudinal information, and objective evaluation of controls.[20] Others have agreed by arguing that, although control groups are the ideal, comparison groups can be used as long as before-and-after measures are obtained, efforts are made to control testing areas, and time-series measurements are acquired. Evans even argues that "unequivocal experimental inferences" can be made with quasi-experimental approaches if the comparison groups, before-and-after measures, and time-series data are presented.[21]

The trend today seems to be toward using designs that can trade off between experimental control and organizational reality. Now we will extend the discussion to another empirical method—the mail survey.

Survey Research   The basic difference between a survey and an experiment is that the former collects data as they exist in reality, whereas the latter manipulates selected variables (independent variables) and records the results.[22] In addition, surveys allow respondents to provide their own perceptions rather than the recorded data of an objective observer.

Behavioral scientists classify survey research in several ways. Surveys may be administered personally through an interview or over the telephone. A face-to-face interview allows probing questions, but the geographical diversity of respondents is restricted. A telephone survey covers a larger geographical area, but it is unlikely to yield a random sample since not everyone has a telephone.

Regardless of the survey technique used, the selection of the sample is critical. In most cases it is impossible or impractical or both to survey the entire population. Thus a sample must be developed. Unless there is some compelling reason to divide the sample on some basis such as sex, age group, or geographical distribution, the random sample is used. A random sample results when the researcher selects participants in a way that ensures that each member of the population has an equal chance of being included.

To illustrate some issues involved in survey research, we will consider a mail survey. This technique is by no means perfect, but it is relatively inexpensive and can offer many advantages. The most serious limitation of a mail survey is that the subjects selected often refuse to respond. If a substantial portion of the sample does not respond, the value of the results is negated. In other words, a randomly selected sample may ensure that a representative group receives the questionnaire, but the researcher cannot control who actually returns the form.

Fortunately, much research has been done concerning methods for improving responses to mail surveys.[23] Table 3.1 (pages 62–63) summarizes techniques used to improve response rates and describes how each technique influences responses. Notice that response rates increase only with the following inducement techniques: prenotification of respondents, personalization of the cover letter, monetary incentives, follow-up, and stamps on the return envelope. These findings are based on an extensive review of recent research literature. Such information can be very useful to managers or researchers planning a mail survey.

Thus these are advantages and disadvantages to alternative research methods. The essential concerns are summarized in the following proposition.

Proposition 3.3

> Survey research can provide important information from geographically dispersed individuals. The key points to remember when using mail surveys are to select a random sample and to use inducement techniques that ensure representative responses.

Behavioral Measurement

Regardless of the data-gathering technique used, it is necessary to develop a measurement scheme. In a survey, for example, it may be necessary to measure attitudes or other behavioral phenomena. Measurement is one of the most difficult and controversial issues in organizational behavior because quantifying behavioral data has unique problems. The issue is so complex, in fact, that we can look only briefly at selected concerns. We will first examine the levels of measurement in behavioral inquiry, and then we will look at the problems of reliability and validity.

Levels of Measurement   In discussing measurement problems, we again must define some specific terms. In the natural sciences as well as the behavioral sciences, one hopes to measure objects that exist in reality. Rarely, however, can we measure behavioral objects directly. We actually measure properties or characteristics of objects. For example, if we wish to measure the temperature of a certain liquid, we develop some indicator of heat, such as the expansion of mercury in a tube. The same is true for attitudes, such as an individual's inclination toward Machiavellianism. Researchers may wish to measure the degree of Machiavellianism displayed by various groups of managers. When researchers are developing an indicator, they actually are devising some way to measure one property of an individual's management style. When they devise a test to accomplish such a measurement, they develop the stages necessary to measure a *construct,* which is another name for the property, or characteristic, being examined.

In establishing a measurement scheme, we first must define the population (*P*) under examination. We then divide the population into subsets such as males and females, blacks and whites, or age groups. This division must result in sets that are mutually exclusive (subsets are completely independent) and collectively exhaustive (all subsets account for the entire population).[24]

When we measure, we assign numbers to the degree of a certain property some object possesses. To do this, we must consider such factors as the order or magnitude of the numbers, the distance between numbers, and the origin of a series of numbers (such as zero).[25] We can easily establish a series of levels of measurement based on the characteristics of order, distance, and origin. We thus

Table 3.1 Mail-Survey Response Rates

Inducement	Influence	Comments
1. **Prenotification —** **letting potential** **participants know** **the questionnaire** **is on the way**	Consistent increase in response rate	Precontact by telephone is most effective but expensive. There is no difference in the impact of postcard and letter prenotification.
2. **Personalization —** **using a personal** **address and** **greeting**	Consistent increase in response rate	Personal letter and greeting influence respondent positively.
3. **Monetary incentive — offering** **payment for returning questionnaire**	Consistent increase in response rate	Researchers enclose small payment such as $.25 in the envelope.
4. **Follow-up — reminding nonrespondents to** **return the form**	Consistent increase in response rate	Follow-up is most effective when sent by certified mail or special delivery with a replacement questionnaire.
5. **Return postage —** **type of stamps** **used on return envelope**	Consistent increase in response rate	Researchers put stamps on the return envelope rather than a business reply permit.
6. **Sponsorship of** **survey — official** **sanction by some** **organization**	Inconsistent increase in response rate (depends on situation)	Some samples (such as physicians) may respond more when the survey is sponsored by a professional group.
7. **Type of appeal in** **cover letter — emphasizing the social value of research, and so on**	Inconsistent increase in response rate (depends on situation)	Some groups (such as professors) may respond to an appeal that emphasizes the scientific value of the research.

Table 3.1 *(cont.)*

Inducement	Influence	Comments
8. Specification of a deadline — request for a response by a specific date	No influence on response rate	May accelerate the rate of return but will not increase the overall rate.
9. Mimeograph vs. printed form of varying color and length	No influence on response rate	Different colors, length, and methods of printing have no influence.
10. Interaction of factors 1 to 5 — extent of additive effect of successful inducements	No interaction	Seems to be no evidence of additive increase.

Source: Adapted from W. Jack Duncan, "Mail Questionnaires in Survey Research: A Review of Response Inducement Techniques," *Journal of Management* 5 (1979): 52. Used by permission.

classify a variety of scales. Stevens has presented such a scheme that provides four scales: nominal, ordinal, interval, and ratio.[26]

Nominal Scale   The nominal scale is the lowest order or least powerful measurement. A scale of this type can be used for classification only. In the most simple case, one might assign a value of 1 to all males in a sample and 2 to all females. The requirement for nominal scaling is that all elements in the population must fall into one or another mutually exclusive subset.

With a nominal scale, no arithmetic operations can be performed. If the number 1 designates satisfied workers and 2 identifies dissatisfied workers, $1 + 2$, $1 - 2$, and $1 \div 2$ are meaningless. When working with these data, measures of central tendency such as the mode and the median can be used. But the mean cannot be used, since an average of 1.2 would require that we know something about the interval between 1 and 2.

Ordinal Scale   With the ordinal scale, it is possible to rank items relative to one another. We can state, for example, that A is greater than, less than, or equal to B. We cannot, however, say *how much* greater or less A is relative to B. In a true ordinal scale, if $A > B$ and $B > C$, then $A > C$.

Interval Scale   The interval scale has the properties of both the nominal and ordinal scales. In addition, it possesses a meaningful measurement of distance. Not only can we say that $A > B$, but it is also possible to state the magnitude of the difference. We know, for example, that the difference between points 1 and 2 on an interval scale is equal to the difference between points 2 and 3 and so on.

In the interval scale, measurements such as the mean become useful and enable us to use more powerful statistical analyses. We can use almost any type of statistical analysis with interval data (except analyses that assume that we know a true origin or zero point). Simply stated, it is possible to say that the difference between a test score of 50 and 10 is eight times as great as the difference between a score of 20 and 15. We cannot say, however, that a score of 50 is exactly twice that of 25, because we do not know the origin or zero point of the measurement.

Ratio Scale   The ratio scale is the same as an interval scale with a natural origin or true zero point. This scale is rarely found in the behavioral sciences. Numerous physical measurements such as length, time, and so on have this quality. For example, we know that the difference between 6 inches and 3 inches is exactly equal to the difference between 9 inches and 6 inches. We also know that 6 inches is exactly twice as long as 3 inches.

Most of the measurements we encounter in studying organizational behavior will be ordinal. Students not familiar with behavioral measurement often have difficulty interpreting original research and analyzing data because of the techniques employed in obtaining those measurements. Throughout our discussion in later chapters, we will emphasize the hard findings of the behavioral sciences as they apply to human behavior in organizations. However, we will avoid reference to specific methods and will focus instead on the results and implications of the research.

Reliability and Validity

Two final aspects of measurement are concerned with the instruments used. *Reliability* is the consistency of a measurement instrument. A test or questionnaire is reliable if the same results are obtained from repeated measures of the same or comparable phenomena. There are several ways of testing reliability. One of the simplest methods is the test-retest approach, in which the same test is given twice to the same group. A correlation then is calculated between the results of the tests to see how the two scores are associated with one another. Again, we should recognize that testing errors can arise with this technique, although experimental designs like those mentioned earlier can be used to control the testing error that might develop from the first test.

If we have equivalent tests (tests that are constructed the same and are designed to measure the same thing), we can give both to the sample population and then correlate the results to obtain a measure of reliability. This equivalent-forms procedure overcomes the problems of testing error.

A final procedure, the split-half technique, is probably the best test of reliability, because it does not require that subjects be tested twice. The researcher randomly divides the test into two parts by doing such things as using all even-numbered questions as one test. The results then are correlated as a measure of reliability. The hope, of course, is for as high a measure of reliability as possible.

Reliability can be illustrated by a rifle that is bolted to a frame and fired at a target. If the repeated shots cluster around a single point, the gun's performance is reliable. The cluster may be well outside the bull's eye, even in an extreme corner. However, if the shots hit around the same spot, the gun is reliable even if it is not accurate. The upper-right corner in Figure 3.5 shows a reliable pattern.

Validity of a measuring instrument relates to whether or not it measures what it is designed to measure. In this sense, validity is more important than reliability. It does us little good to measure something consistently if we are not measuring the correct thing. Several types of validity are of interest to behavioral researchers.

First, researchers are concerned with *content validity,* or how well the scales or measurements reflect the actual properties of the object being measured. If researchers want to examine the tendency of a decision maker to make well-informed decisions, they may ask questions about the information used in selecting alternatives. These factors can be tested by subjective reasoning or by more systematic techniques such as discussions among panels of experts.

Figure 3.5 Reliability and Validity Illustrated

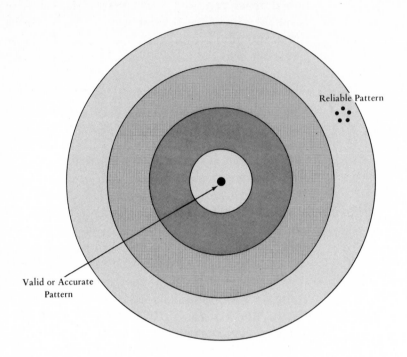

Reliable Pattern

Valid or Accurate
Pattern

Researchers also are concerned with *construct validity*. (This will be important to our discussion of performance appraisal in Chapter 13.) It refers to what factors or constructs account for the measurements obtained.[27] Finally, researchers want to know something about predictive validity and the associated issue of concurrent validity. The difference between these two criteria is only with regard to time. Both are concerned with the practical problem of how well a test predicts an outcome. An entrance test for graduate school has concurrent validity if it predicts the degree of success of current students. It has predictive validity if it continues to be an indicator of success for future students.

The center of Figure 3.5 (the bull's eye) represents validity. If a testing instrument measures exactly what it is designed to test, it is accurate, or valid.

Proposition 3.4

> A testing instrument is said to be valid if it measures what it is designed to measure (for example, morale, satisfaction, and so on). A test is reliable if it measures consistently. Reliability and validity are both highly desirable characteristics of data-gathering instruments.

Why Managers Need to Understand Research Methods

Managers make numerous decisions every day. Sometimes they have enough accurate information to make a decision. At other times, they have plenty of information but do not know how it was developed or analyzed. Consequently, they must have faith in those who collected and presented the data. Such faith or trust in specialists is a necessary part of every manager's job. However, it is the manager who ultimately is accountable for the success or failure of the decision—not the staff specialists. For this reason, managers are well advised to question the data presented for decision making. The following factors should be considered:

1. *Sample Selection.* How was the sample selected? Was it random and representative, or did the specialist or consultant simply interview the first fifty respondents?
2. *Data Collection.* How was the information gathered? If a mail survey was used, what was the response rate? If behavior was observed, what bias-reducing controls were used?
3. *Instrument Construction.* What, exactly, is known about the validity and reliability of the data-gathering instrument?
4. *Data Analysis.* How were the data analyzed? Are the results descriptive or statistical in nature?
5. *Relationship to Conventional Wisdom.* What has been written about the problem under consideration? Are the research results generally supportive of what is already known? If the results are conflicting, how can the differences be explained?

If the consultant or staff specialist cannot answer such questions to the manager's satisfaction, care should be taken in using the data.

Questions like these do not require a manager to be an expert researcher. But they do suggest that managers should know enough about research in organizational behavior to be able to ask the right questions.

Summary

This chapter has looked closely at various methods for collecting valid knowledge in organizational behavior. We emphasized the requirements for an acceptable deductive argument as well as for an accurate analysis of observations. We also looked at some problems of behavioral measurement.

Rather than repeating our arguments here, we will simply review the necessity of devoting a chapter to the selected philosophical problems of the inexact sciences. Such discussions sometimes seem boring and tiresome. However, methodological issues are especially pressing in organizational behavior. As we continue our analysis in the remainder of this text, we will make frequent reference to issues of knowledge generation, measurement, and associated topics. We must remember that it is the method that unites science. If we are to develop a systematic understanding of organizational behavior, we first must appreciate the methods used in formulating them.

It is hoped that this chapter has provided a useful introduction to the methodology of the behavioral sciences. Especially important is the recognition that although organizational behavior is scientific, it deals with human beings. People are not inanimate objects. To be sure, organizational behavior is an empirical discipline. All by itself, however, the inductive method fails to account for many uniquely human qualities. Our goal is to be as scientific as possible while remaining open to the realities of human behavior.

Questions for Discussion

1. Compare and contrast the deductive and inductive methods of inquiry. Which do you think is more important in gaining valid knowledge of organizational behavior? Why?

2. Compare and contrast the advantages and disadvantages of the following research methods: mail questionnaires, field studies, field experiments, and laboratory experiments.
3. Why do we consider random samples so important in experimental design? Are there cases in which nonrandom samples may be preferred? Explain.
4. What is the difference between reliability and validity in measuring instruments? Which is more important? Why?
5. How are nominal data different from interval data? From ordinal data? Why do we say behavioral measurement rarely achieves more than ordinal-level data?

Exercise: Selecting a Research Technique

You just walked into your first course in organizational behavior, and what a surprise! Your professor introduced the course and stated that 30 percent of your grade will be determined by performance on a research project. You will be required to design a study, collect and analyze data, and write up the report.

Your immediate problem is to formulate the study and design a methodology. After discussing the idea with several people, you decide to investigate the following question: Is there a consistent relationship between job satisfaction and employee performance?

Now you must decide how to study this question. List and compare the advantages and disadvantages of using a field experiment or a mail questionnaire.

Suggested Readings

Behling, Orlando. "Some Problems in the Philosophy of Science of Organizations." *Academy of Management Review* 3 (1978): 193–201.

Berlin, V. N. "Administrative Experimentation: A Methodology for More Rigorous 'Muddling Through'." *Management Science* 24 (1978): 789–799.

Connor, P. E., and B. W. Becker. "Value Biases in Organizational Research." *Academy of Management Review* 2 (1977): 421–430.

Cummings, T. G., E. S. Molloy, and Roy Glen. "A Methodological Critique of Fifty-eight Selected Work Experiments." *Human Relations* 30 (1977): 675–708.

DeVall, Mark, Cheryl Bolas, and T. S. Kang. "Applied Social Research in Industrial Organizations." *Journal of Applied Behavioral Science* 12 (1976): 158–177.

Kramer, H. E. "The Philosophical Foundations of Management Rediscovered." *Management International Review* 15 (1975): 47–54.

Levi, A. M., and J. A. Benjamin. "A Constructive Method of Developing Complex Applied Models." *Human Relations* 31 (1978): 353–362.

Motomedi, K. M. "Toward Explicating Philosophical Orientations in Organizational Behavior (OB)." *Academy of Management Review* 3 (1978): 354–360.

Ramos, A. G. "Misplacement of Concepts and Administrative Theory." *Public Administration Review* 38 (1978): 550–557.

Tsatsos, H. E. C. "Methodology and Teleology." *Management Science* 24 (1978): 709–711.

Individual Behavior in Organizations

INDIVIDUALS—people—are the central resource and the only indispensable elements of organizations. You can purchase desks, tables, buildings, supplies, computers, and even books, but without people you cannot have a university. Nor is it the operating rooms or clean hallways that make a hospital. Rather, it is the doctors, nurses, patients, and maintenance personnel who make up the organization.

We often say that organizations make profits, cure diseases, pass laws, or develop a person's intelligence. But organizations cannot do any of these things. Only people can work, solve problems, or teach. Yet individuals frequently can be effective only *when* they form an organization. For this reason we must understand individual behavior to examine organizational behavior adequately. In his book *The Sociology of Organizational Change,* E. A. Johns states that the successful manager of the future must be a "do-it-yourself behavioral scientist."

Part II focuses on the individual by looking first at personality and attitude development. In Chapter 4, we will investigate how our culture, social environment, friends, and family influence the way we feel toward organizations, work, and many other things. We also will note the problems in measuring attitudes and will propose practical guidelines for changing job attitudes.

Next, in Chapter 5, we will look at how individuals use information, how they relate it to prior experience, and how they make decisions. To do so, we examine the cognitive (thinking) processes of perception, learning, and problem solving. Perception allows employees to take in information presented by a supervisor. Through learning, individuals make meaningful comparisons between present and past experiences. Finally, since many responses to a situation are always possible, decisions must be made. Selecting a desirable course of action requires problem solving.

Understanding these three processes—perception, learning, problem solving—is essential for understanding motivation. In Chapter 6, we will analyze and evaluate selection theories of motivation. Substantial attention is devoted to this issue because it is the basis of organizational efficiency.

The following diagram illustrates the sequence of topics discussed in Part II.

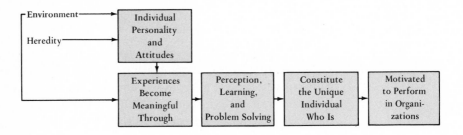

chapter 4

Understanding Individual Employees

The workers' dependence upon their managers for continued employment and income can inhibit or disguise their real feelings.

Randall B. Dunham and Frank J. Smith,
Organizational Surveys

Kyocera International, a California subsidiary of Kyoto Ceramic Company of Japan, is an unusual organization. Ten years ago the firm had only ten employees. Today it employs about fifteen hundred people. The parent company, Kyoto Ceramic, was only established in 1959. Its motto is "Respect the Divine and Respect People."

The company takes its motto seriously. It emphasizes teamwork between management and employees, encouraging open communication and the participation of all groups in decision making. More than anything, perhaps, Kyoto Ceramic and its subsidiaries look to the future; they minimize concern for short-run market fluctuations and temporary hardships. Nowhere is this more evident than in the company's "no layoff responsibilities." Kyoto acknowledges that layoffs result in waste and inefficiency. Yet management points out that employees must demonstrate faith and trust by high productivity—even in slow times—if the policy is to work. By American standards, this policy is unusual to say the least. Apparently, it is not at all uncommon in Japan.*

*Special thanks to Professor Tai K. Oh of California State University at Fullerton for pointing out the details of this example.

How can we explain this difference in American and Japanese management philosophy? The difference is cultural. Japanese business looks at the long run and is less concerned with the periodic ups and downs of economic conditions. Kyoto Ceramic believes that profitability will be enhanced by maintaining stability over the long run. Reacting to the recurring booms and busts simply creates insecurity and poor morale among employees.

All businesses have to be interested in employee attitudes. An understanding of attitudes, however, requires that we look at all aspects of individual behavior. We will begin by examining human personality, hoping to gain insights into why American and Japanese businesses approach management from a different perspective. First, we will study some approaches that managers can use in getting to know employees. For example, a personnel manager might try to understand an employee's low performance record by probing into the individual's mind, looking for evidence of conflict or frustration. Or the manager might choose to concentrate on certain observable traits, such as competitiveness or size. The manager also could direct attention toward the needs that the employee hopes to satisfy, such as achievement or recognition. Each of these approaches provides insights into a person's total *personality,* the unique character, behavior, and temperament of that individual. Therefore, it is important that managers be familiar with various approaches to personality development.

Personality Development: Three Approaches

Assume that you work in the data processing department of an insurance company and have a programmer reporting to you named Helen Parks. Helen has all the qualifications needed by an outstanding employee, and she does a satisfactory job. However, you know she is not working up to her potential. Furthermore, she complicates your job because of her constant involvement in group conflicts. Every major issue somehow seems related to Helen. When raises are given, she complains about inequities. When work schedules are posted, she suggests that one person or another is working too much on the day shift or the night shift. In short, Helen Parks is a troublemaker. To deal with the problems she causes, you conclude you must try to understand Helen Parks. The following theories of personality development provide three approaches you might take.

Psychoanalytical Theory

The psychoanalytical approach to understanding behavior and, therefore, Helen's personality was developed by Sigmund Freud. Emphasis is placed on the intrapsychic: one looks inside the individual for possible clues to behavior. This view assumes that something causes Helen to behave as she does. Perhaps she is insecure or jealous and desires attention. It also assumes that the cause of behavior has developed over time and is continuing to develop. Maybe Helen was reared in a large family and had to compete with brothers and sisters for attention. Finally, if we support Freud's view, we assign a structure to Helen's personality.[1] It includes an id, or pleasure-seeking part, which encourages Helen to do what is necessary to satisfy her desires—regardless of the effects on herself and others. Helen also has a superego, which is idealistic and noble, providing her with a conscience or quest for goodness. Somewhere in between lies Helen's ego, which attempts to find a compromise between the selfish demands of her id and the noble requirements of her superego. It is the ego that establishes a realistic behavior pattern. Thus the psychoanalytical explanation is founded on a conflict view: the id and the superego are in conflict and constantly compromised by the ego. Behavioral patterns are considered defensive and can be predicted on the basis of how the id and the superego are compromised.

Following are descriptions of the more frequently encountered *defense mechanisms.* These defensive patterns of behavior are designed to reduce an individual's anxiety over the extreme demands of the id and superego.[2]

Aggression When Helen is angry with a fellow employee about the work schedule, her initial impulse may be to attack the coworker physically. Her conscience tells her, however, that such behavior is not acceptable. Therefore, instead of striking the other person, Helen settles for verbal abuse. Although this may not be as satisfying, neither will it result in punishment. If Helen is angry at you, her supervisor, she even may displace her aggression by taking out frustrations on a coworker or on someone in her family. Then there is no danger of her being charged with insubordination.

Avoidance   If Helen needs her job to earn a living but does not like the people with whom she works, she will experience anxiety. She may withdraw socially from the group and become a loner. She will also be sure to use all her sick leave and will be absent from the job as much as possible—without, of course, jeopardizing her employment.

Other Defenses   An employee like Helen may do many other things to reduce her anxiety. She may rationalize her behavior by excusing it or blaming it on others. (If other people would only leave her alone, perhaps she could do more work!) Or she may compensate for all the conflict she causes by periodically doing nice things, like remembering your birthday or bringing donuts for morning break.

Only extremely defensive behavior is unproductive. A reasonable amount of aggression may reduce stress; some avoidance may give conflict time to go away; and compensation actually may improve performance in certain areas. In the extreme, however, defensive behavior can reduce satisfaction and harm group performance.

Many behavioral scientists and managers have doubts about the psychoanalytical approach to understanding personality. It always involves guessing about human action, and it often relies on an accurate account of unconscious motivation. From a practical viewpoint, managers or researchers can never be quite sure that they have discovered the real explanation.[3]

Trait Theory

Trait theory is one of the earliest theories of personality. Simply put, it assumes that there are identifiable, stable, and lasting personality traits that can be used in predicting behavior.

Traits have been defined as distinguishable and enduring ways in which one person differs from all others.[4] The objective of trait theory is to discover the traits and to use them in predicting human action. The trait theory of personality assumes that traits exist, are uniquely distributed among individuals, are stable over time, can be measured quantitatively, and can be used to predict how people will act.[5]

Traits can be analyzed from many perspectives. Some people take a strictly biological approach by arguing that if genetic factors can and do account for differences among species, then they also might account for differences within a species.[6] For example, people's eyes and hair and even body structures are different.

Other researchers have examined the variations among psychological traits. Rather than belaboring the example of Helen Parks, consider some recent attempts by business researchers to predict the motivation to manage. Efforts have been made to identify psychological traits useful for management success. Research has shown, for example, that managers score rather high on such psychological characteristics as competitiveness and assertiveness. Attempts to measure these psychological traits from the early 1960s until the present reveal that college students have scored consistently lower on these characteristics over time. This trend has led some researchers to predict shortages of managerial talent in the 1980s. Students seem to be losing the will to manage, and many will likely choose careers that avoid the necessity of managing others.[7] Such a conclusion, of course, is speculative and may or may not occur during this decade. The research, however, illustrates how future behavior is predicted on the basis of selected psychological traits.

Needs Theory

It has been argued that all theories of personality are motivational, because they must account for human actions and the variety of goals toward which these actions are directed.[8] But some theories explicitly strive to identify and measure the motives or needs giving rise to human action. We will examine two such theories now.

Maslow's Needs Hierarchy   Abraham Maslow is among the best-known psychologists of modern times. According to Colin Wilson, Maslow noted that most psychologists devoted the majority of their efforts to studying psychologically ill people. Maslow chose instead to examine the psychologically healthy.[9] From this early interest, he constructed his theory of a needs hierarchy.

Maslow presents a deductive theory of human needs. As we would expect from our discussion in Chapter 3, his argument is based on three basic assumptions that are not subject to direct observation but generally are considered to require no such proof. The assumptions are as follows:

1. People are wanting animals. Their desires are never completely satisfied.
2. A satisfied need is not a motivator of human behavior.
3. Human needs are arranged in a hierarchy of importance.[10]

These assumptions see the human being as constantly in quest of some unsatisfied goal or objective. Once a need is satisfied, it no longer motivates action. Once hungry people have eaten, they no longer direct their behavior toward securing food. In addition, the hierarchy suggests which needs will motivate behavior after one need has been satisfied. The result is a deductive theory that argues that once our needs for survival and safety are satisfied, we will strive to satisfy needs of belongingness, esteem, and self-actualization—in that order.

Consider Figure 4.1 and recall the problems created by Helen Parks. In the figure, human needs are arranged from the very basic biological necessities of food, clothing, and shelter to the highest level of self-actualization. In between are safety, belongingness, and esteem needs. Since the biological needs are understood easily, let us look more closely at the other categories of needs.

1. *Safety needs* relate to ensuring security. After employees earn enough money to satisfy their biological needs, they will want to acquire retirement programs, hospitalization insurance, and disability protection.
2. *Belongingness needs* reflect peoples' desire to be accepted by others. Once biological and safety needs are taken care of, employees probably will exhibit a need to be accepted and respected by others. Status symbols such as private offices and social lunch gatherings help an employee to satisfy belongingness needs.
3. *Esteem needs* relate to an individual's self-image. A person can be accepted and respected by others and still not have self-esteem. For example, a community leader may be respected by others but may lack self-esteem because he or she is dishonest in paying income taxes. Thus esteem needs relate to how "at peace" a person is with one's self.
4. *Self-actualization needs* relate to our ability to realize our greatest

Figure 4.1 The Hierarchy of Needs

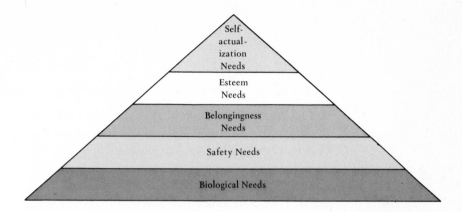

Source: Data for diagram based on Hierarchy of Needs in "A Theory of Human Motivation," in *Motivation and Personality,* 2nd Edition, by Abraham H. Maslow. Copyright © 1970 by Abraham H. Maslow. By permission of Harper & Row, Publishers, Inc.

potential. Maslow said that self-actualizing people develop an identity with the callings they pursue. Some managers as well as physicians, professors, and ministers self-actualize in their work.

But what about Helen Parks? How does Maslow's hierarchy help explain her disruptive behavior? As her supervisor, you might suspect that Helen is trying to satisfy belongingness needs. Even though she annoys some people with her complaints, she may feel that such behavior will help her gain acceptance among other complainers.

Maslow's theory, though widely quoted, has not escaped criticism. Although this popular psychologist has admitted that his theory is not based on factual data and that the needs cannot be viewed independently, as the hierarchy sometimes implies, he has been criticized on both scores.[11] Efforts have been made to uncover causal relationships suggested by the hierarchy. Some studies support the idea that needs have less influence on behavior once they are satisfied.[12] Other studies find problems in the several levels of Maslow's concept and suggest other methods of characterizing needs.[13]

Of particular significance is the existence-relatedness-growth theory (ERG) proposed by Clayton Alderfer.[14] Essentially, this theory reduces Maslow's five-level hierarchy to only three levels. Existence needs include biological as well as certain safety needs.

Relatedness needs include safety needs as well as belongingness and esteem needs. Growth needs include esteem needs and self-actualization needs.

The ERG theory is relatively new, but it has strong research support. Even though it was developed specifically as a motivation concept, it probably will take a long time for this view to approach the popularity enjoyed by Maslow's hierarchy.

McClelland's Achievement Motive   Another needs theory of personality was developed by David McClelland. This theory is unlike Maslow's because it looks at only a single need, and it is based on a good deal of research.

McClelland focuses on the *achievement motive,* or *n Ach,* as it is called. The basic assumption of achievement theory is that all needs are learned; thus, personality develops as one learns.[15] In line with this, one's early environment and experiences are considered important to personality development. For example, people who are encouraged to be independent and self-sufficient from childhood on tend to develop a stronger need for achievement and to experience less anxiety than others.

To support these claims, McClelland examined the content of children's readers written in different countries during the 1920s. He found a high association between the achievement motive found in children's readers and the country's economic development as measured by changes in the use of electrical power.[16] The implication is that a society's *n Ach* and its economic development go hand in hand.

For management, the implication is that high achievers must be assisted in making their greatest possible contribution to the organization. A manager who is sensitive to personality theory is better equipped to recognize achievers and to understand how they can be motivated to achieve their highest performance.

Proposition 4.1

> Numerous theories of personality development are available, and all provide valuable information for understanding behavior in organizations. These theories range from Freud's psychoanalytical approach to the familiar concept of Maslow's needs hierarchy.

Human Behavior: A Systems View

Human behavior is extremely complex. It is also the most fundamental topic in the study of organizational behavior.

One effective way to view human behavior is as an input-output system. This view is illustrated in the following diagram. The input-output concept is valuable because it fits in with the open-systems view of behavior, which sees the individual not as an isolated being but as living within an environment.

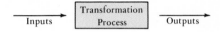

Inputs, Transformations, and Outputs

In the input-output diagram, we see the individual as a being who takes inputs from the environment, performs certain processes on them (transformations), and behaves in a manner that sends outputs back to the environment.

On the surface, this explanation presents an unrealistically simple image of human action. It would be useful to rethink the input-output model in behavioral terms, as in Figure 4.2. This figure illustrates that behavior begins with an event originating outside the individual. The individual perceives the event and responds to it.

Figure 4.2 The Process of Human Behavior

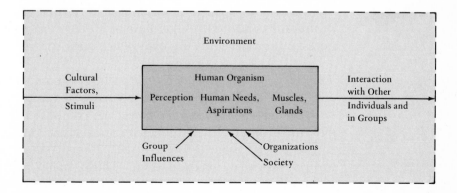

In this view, the combination of one's environment and one's inborn characteristics causes needs and motives to emerge.[17] Consider the athlete who is born with unusual physical strength and is reared in a family that instills the need for achievement in the child. By the age of twenty, this young man or woman may feel a great need to become a professional athlete, for heredity has provided the potential and experience has shaped the skills to attain such a goal. Someone with less biological potential or who was raised in a less supportive environment may feel no such need.

Since human actions are determined by both environmental (experience-based) and hereditary (inborn) factors, it is worth our while to examine that interaction briefly.

Interaction of Heredity and Environment

It is generally accepted by behavioral scientists that human action is caused, motivated, and goal directed. Behavior is neither without cause nor random.[18] The question is: What causes human action and defines the goals toward which it is directed?

Kurt Lewin, another famous psychologist, provides a simple yet useful explanation that can be expressed as follows:[19]

$$P = f(H,E)$$

This expression states that personality (P) is a function of heredity (H) and experience (E).

Remember Helen Parks? As her supervisor, you might be able to explain her behavior with this equation. Helen's unhappy childhood could be part of her personality problem. She also may have some unattractive (or attractive) physical features that cause her to be resentful (or conceited). Regardless of Helen's exact problem, we can bet that both heredity and experience have contributed to it.

The Biological Being   The human body is composed of billions of cells, each containing a nucleus, which, in turn, contains pairs of chromosomes. The chromosomes are composed of genes, which determine the hereditary characteristics of each unique individual.

The genetic characteristics of the parents combine in the child to form a variety of physical traits. These, many people argue, can influence our behavior. Traits such as the color of eyes are stable predictable traits. Others, such as skin color, are complex but predictable. Still other traits, such as the general development of the nervous system, are less predictable.

In spite of the impressive results of genetic research, most psychologists assign less importance to heredity than to experience in determining behavior.

Experience Human beings are exposed to countless environmental influences from the moment of birth. Some children are born into deprived families and thus have limited educational opportunities. Others have the best of everything from the beginning and thus develop differently.

An interesting body of research has developed recently concerning the effects of motivational programs used in organizations. One motivational program, known as job enrichment, is built on the distinctly middle-class assumption that jobs *should* be satisfying. Employees from rural backgrounds and those with both rural and urban backgrounds who have attained managerial positions seem to be more receptive to job-enrichment efforts than are lower-level employees with urban backgrounds.[20]

This finding suggests that other experiments may be limited to specific samples and that environmental influences can determine work values. It may be true, and probably is, that some workers have never been exposed to the middle-class value that job satisfaction is desirable. Thus psychologists are quite insistent that family influences, group interactions, and similar factors influence behavior much more than heredity does. In fact, one researcher states clearly that "psychological development is fully dependent on stimulation from the environment."[21]

A Synthesis The story is told that Abraham Maslow, early in his career, had the opportunity to work with the great psychologist E. L. Thorndike at Columbia University. One of Maslow's first assignments as Thorndike's assistant was to work out the percentage of human behavior resulting from heredity and the percentage resulting from experience. Because he knew that behavior is caused by an interaction of both factors and was unable to work on anything that bored him, Maslow thought the project was silly. He wrote Thorndike a note saying that he could not do the research because it was not worth doing.[22]

Other people have experienced the same reaction, although few have been so bold in expressing their views. However, Theodosius Dobzhansky argues specifically that all important traits are the result of the interaction of heredity and experience, so that any attempt to deal with them independently is unworkable.[23] This view of nature and nurture as a synthesis, or blending, leads us to a second proposition.

Proposition
4.2

> Personality is functionally related to hereditary and environmental factors. The interaction of heredity and experience is so intimate that, with regard to all important traits, any attempt to specify which patterns of behavior are biologically caused and which are environmentally caused is meaningless.

From the perspective of the behavioral sciences, little can be done to change biological properties. More success can be obtained in examining and understanding the environment. This will be our major focus throughout the rest of the chapter.

The Environment

When we suggest that experience—and the environmental forces contributing to it—influence behavior, we are admitting the importance of learning in the development of human behavior. A discussion of learning, however, requires an analysis of several other cognitive processes, such as perception and problem solving. These processes will be examined in detail in Chapter 5. Here it is enough simply to acknowledge that the human organism receives information from various environmental forces as illustrated in Figure 4.2.

Culture

Before looking at specific aspects of the environment, consider again the example of Kyoto Ceramic that opened this chapter. Recall that the key question was: How can American and Japanese management philosophies be so different? The long-run orientation of the Japanese culture partly accounts for the difference. For example, in late 1979, as the energy crisis intensified, Trans World Airlines announced some immediate layoffs because of increasing fuel costs. From August to September 1979, TWA reduced its work force at its Kansas City headquarters by 2.5 percent. Kyoto Ceramic probably would have found another option and absorbed the loss.

This underscores the importance of the cultural environment, even to institutions involved with education, government, and business. Customs and traditions evolve over time and have significant impact on business behavior. Let us look at some of the forces which make up culture.

Culture is the broadest category of forces that influence behavior. To some extent, it includes all other factors in the environment. Culture is the "complex whole which includes knowledge, belief, art, morals, law, custom, and any other capabilities and habits acquired by man as a member of society."[24] Bernard Berelson and Gary Steiner itemize the following characteristics of culture.

1. Culture is learned behavior. One acquires culture through exposure over time. Thus, Americans learn to respect success and money because of the values to which they are exposed.
2. Culture is shared with others. In a given society, all members are exposed to similar values.
3. Culture influences the way in which needs are satisfied. All people require shelter. However, in a primitive society the shelter may be a cave, whereas modern men and women live in high-rise apartments.
4. Culture is consistent. All parts of the culture fit together in certain important ways. The American economic system is constructed and changed to reflect the values of American society.[25]

Anthropologists use a specialized vocabulary to discuss various aspects of culture. For example, enculturation is the process by which a culture molds a person. A person who leaves a native culture and adapts to a new culture undergoes acculturation. When a person is integrated into a new culture, assimilation takes place. If people are not completely integrated into the culture, they may accommodate themselves on important matters to avoid conflict.[26]

Studies have tried to determine which factors of culture are influential and how they actually influence us. We will look briefly at the more significant influences on human behavior.

Some Cultural Influences   Barry Richman has described several cultural factors and how they influence organizational behavior. Two important factors are sociological constraints (attitudes toward authority, the perceived value of achievement, and so on) and educational constraints (literacy levels, attitudes toward education, amount of formal education, and so on). Although Richman suggests that over time cultures may lose their uniqueness, differences certainly exist in the short run. Cultural factors are sure to remain important influences on managerial behavior and the attainment of organizational goals.[27]

More specifically, some researchers have examined the manner in which culture can influence how people perceive reality. For example, natives of Western societies are more familiar with three-dimensional structures that have straight lines and right angles than are natives of other cultures.[28]

Some useful insights have also been gained regarding a culture's view of authority and family structure. In Germany, where the father is the dominant figure in the family, management practices tend to be more authoritarian. In England, the more cooperative attitudes within and between organizations are associated with the mother's primary position in the family. Finally, in America, where the family is more child oriented, the responsibility of organizations for individual needs has been emphasized.[29]

All this illustrates one important point: cultural factors result in different behavioral patterns. Culture is instrumental in forming concepts of what should and should not be done in a given situation. It determines to a great extent the values held by a group of people. Cultural values influence behavior in organizations in specific ways.

Implications for Organizations   Perhaps the most obvious cultural influences on organizational behavior relate to motivational problems and challenges. Particularly significant are insights that could lead managers to redesign how work is done. For example, a typist's job might be improved by allowing the employee to prepare the working draft and to distribute final copies, thus making the task less routine and perhaps satisfying the typist's higher-level needs. Similarly, a manager's knowledge about a person's cultural background might be useful in motivating that employee to improve performance. Consider your own concepts of various cultures, such as Swiss, German, Japanese, and Mexican. What might you say about the motivating needs of these national groups? You probably have some definite opinions about these cultures. Most people are aware of cultural differences.

We have mentioned the relationship between a society's achievement motivation and its economic development (as detected in David McClelland's studies). This idea is closely related to the work of Max Weber, who described the emergence of capitalism and its emphasis on the individual. Weber seemed convinced that John Calvin's teachings about the importance of good works in attaining spiritual salvation and the heightened reputation of those who pursued economic rewards provided the incentives needed for the emergence of capitalism.[30]

Even within a culture, various subcultures may reflect how managers can coordinate people's behavior to accomplish organizational goals. One thoroughly discussed, little understood, but highly important subculture in the United States is made up of youth and their relationship with older generations.

The most interesting thing about the values of the younger generation is the manner in which they have changed in less than a decade. In 1968, for example, Daniel Yankelovich conducted a survey of 718 young men and women between the ages of eighteen and twenty-four. Some attended college; others did not. Of those in college, one group was classified as "practical minded," whereas another group was labeled "forerunners." The first group attended college for practical or career-oriented reasons. The other students wished to change things rather than simply to exist within the present system. This survey speculated that the forerunners would become increasingly influential and would continue their push to change existing educational, economic, and religious organizations. The noncollege group appeared extremely conservative and was oriented toward maintaining the status quo.[31]

In 1973, Yankelovich conducted a follow-up study and got different results. The second survey exposed a "new conservatism" among college students. These young people seemed to be less concerned about social issues and change, and seemed more obsessed with their own personal success. The noncollege group, however, had grown much more dissatisfied.[32]

No recent data describe youth values since 1973. However, *Parade* magazine wrote that the recently renewed popularity of college fraternities confirms the trend: compared with students of the late 1960s, today's students are "more traditional, less political, more interested in remunerative occupations than idealistic projects" (September 9, 1979, p. 20). James McConnell, a well-known psychologist, agrees that today's students may be like those of the 1950s—with two exceptions. First, today's students have a better grasp of reality; second, they do not mind letting you know it.[33]

Thus we see a notable change in youth values from the days of student activism to the present. This change should not imply that motivational problems no longer exist. It simply may mean that even though young people are more content today with traditional organizations, they may be looking for different things within them. One thing appears quite certain: managers in the future must motivate employees who are less oriented toward authority, who are less competitive, and who desire more meaningful or enriching work.

Proposition 4.3

> Culture influences the values of a group of people and thus influences the group's behavior. Whereas cultural influences and their potential results are usually stable over time, values—especially those of important subcultures—may be variable and changing. This situation requires constant monitoring by managers to detect significant changes that may require administrative action.

Culture is clearly an important influence in an individual's environment. Yet other smaller factors, such as social class and work values, also influence an individual's behavior within an organization. These, too, require our understanding.

Social Class and Work Values

Socialization is the process through which a society bestows its values on an individual or group. This experience begins at birth and continues until death. The family is probably the first source of socialization, and its values are related to a variety of factors.

Social class has long been recognized as an important influence on work values. Research has demonstrated how social class can affect one's orientation toward work. Leonard Pearlin and Melvin Kohn argue that individuals in a high social class develop greater self-direction, whereas those in lower social positions conform to established traditions and norms.[34] Self-direction is consistent with our belief that we can accomplish what we desire.

In this view, individuals conform to society because the occupational system emphasizes the dangers of stepping out of line.[35] People from the higher social classes probably feel less need to conform. They have the resources needed for independence. They can take risks and can deviate in how they make decisions because if they fail not all is lost. People from the lower social classes, on the other hand, have to conform to the "rules of the game" if they want to get ahead. If they take a chance on success by risky decision making, they may lose their opportunities forever. Thus it seems that a person's social class significantly influences how one relates to the authority structure of organizations.

Societies also may influence the alienation, or isolation, one may experience on a job. One study illustrates how conflicts can develop between a person's orientation toward an organization and the requirements of a given job situation. Some feel that ultimate loyalty should be directed toward society; others are oriented more toward individuals and friends.[36] The results of this study illustrate how the second outlook, displayed by Mexicans, resulted in alienation of employees when they were exposed to a work environment in a bank that expected loyalty to the organization.[37] People from a middle-class American background, on the other hand, were not alienated in such a setting, which was consistent with their social value system.

Proposition 4.4

Work values evolve through socialization, and they influence both an individual's needs for work and the alienation experienced in the work place.

Implications for Management

Cultural factors in the environment and socialization (through which the factors become meaningful) influence the behavior of individuals at work. Managers of organizations, therefore, must be aware of the unique cultural and social factors affecting the people they manage.

Again, the example of Kyoto Ceramic Company is relevant. First, Japanese culture clearly values different job characteristics from many American culture values. The Japanese appear to encourage interaction and communication between managers and employees. In contrast, American organizations seem to discourage close interaction, emphasizing instead rank and position. Second, the managerial approach at Kyoto Ceramic reveals a concern for lower-level biological and safety needs. Not that American firms are more interested in higher-level needs, but at times they seem less concerned with lower-level ones. Obviously, the two cultures have evolved significantly different approaches to management. These different approaches apply to national as well as to multinational organizations.

It should be no surprise that new generations of employees behave differently from older generations and are motivated by different needs and desires. An administrator who insists on dealing with all employees in exactly the same manner is not likely to enjoy success. Similarly, a manager who is responsible for supervising employees from deprived backgrounds must realize that such people are likely to behave differently from employees with advantaged backgrounds.

Managers must recognize the uniqueness of each individual. A good place to start is with attitudes, the measurable aspects of individual differences.

Attitudes

John Palmer, supervisor of the casting department at Grayiron, has received a list of four new trainees assigned to his third shift. In checking the list, he notes that William Greene was employed under a minority hiring program. He passes the list to George Nelson, the shift supervisor, and tells George to pay special attention to Greene, who "is not likely to make it because of his previous difficulty in

Figure 4.3 Attitude Development

holding a job." As it happens, Greene's work record is better than that of two other trainees who were *not* hired under the minority program.

John Palmer has displayed his prejudice about the minority hiring program. A prejudice is a negative opinion that is formed without regard for facts. Prejudice is a frequently encountered attitude, an individual's feeling that is directed toward an object or thing (in this case, the minority training program). An *attitude* is a predisposition to react in some manner to an individual or a situation. Attitudes frequently are equated with opinions, but an *opinion* can be defined more specifically as an expression of an evaluation or judgment with regard to a situation.

Attitudes develop as illustrated in Figure 4.3. It is easy to see from the diagram that attitudes evolve from one's past experience and from the forces of one's present environment. Of course, these two factors are not completely independent. For the environment surrounding past experiences may be quite similar to forces operating in the present. Attitudes then become important aspects of past experiences.

Besides prejudices, which are directed toward groups of people, a person may hold attitudes toward many things, particularly work. For example, a person may be more favorably inclined to perform one task than another because it seems more challenging. Favorable and unfavorable attitudes may be directed toward geographical locations, such as the South or the Midwest; toward people, such as the nation's president or the company's janitor; or toward academic subjects, such as statistics, economics, or organizational behavior. However, the basic questions about attitudes in relation to organizational behavior are: How do attitudes influence human action? How can we measure these important forces?

Behavior and Attitudes

Discussions about attitudes revolve around three components. The first is the cognitive component. Cognition is the perceptual process through which attitude objects (persons, places, things, and so on) are made known to individuals. Cognition is the subject of Chapter 5. In this chapter, our emphasis has been on the second, or affective, component, which relates to the reasons behind a person's feelings of good and bad, likes and dislikes, and so on. Now we will look briefly at the third, or behavioral, component, which is a person's interaction with a person or thing.

Several early studies in the behavioral sciences raised questions about the existence of any causal relationship between attitudes and behavior. One study illustrated how innkeepers' apparent attitudes toward Orientals vary substantially from their actions. The researcher was consistently refused reservations when he wrote letters stating that Orientals would be in the visiting party. However, when he actually appeared with Orientals and asked for accommodations, he was not refused.[38]

Another study, of white coal miners, revealed interesting differences about reactions toward blacks on and off the job. Of the coal miners studied, about 20 percent were free from prejudice on and off the job: this group interacted with blacks in the mine and in the community. Another 20 percent were prejudiced in both situations. The remaining 60 percent displayed an obvious inconsistency and rarely interacted with blacks. In the mine, they acted as though they were free from prejudice. After work, however, their behavior in the community appeared to be motivated by distinct race consciousness.[39]

On the basis of these studies, we could conclude that there is no consistent relationship between attitudes and action. Other research, however, shows something quite different. Sherif and Hovland illustrated how people who joined certain organizations (such as advocates of prohibition) displayed significantly different attitudes from those of members of other organizations. Thus membership in specific organizations appears quite consistent with attitudes.[40] Attitudes about participation in student political activities were related closely to whether or not the participants actually voted in a student election shortly before the survey was taken.[41]

The contradictions in this research are explained by one social psychologist on methodological grounds. His points are important enough to review briefly.

1. *Environmental Influences.* The response one makes to an attitude object is related to attitudes and environmental forces. Sometimes environmental forces actually may overcome the behavioral patterns evoked by attitudes. For example, a person who is prejudiced against college students may react in a nonprejudiced way to a college group in which all members are dressed and groomed as that person would like them to be. Thus a group's appearance (dress) may override the prejudice. The greater the influence of environmental factors that encourage behavioral actions inconsistent with attitudes, the lower the association between measured attitudes and observed behavior.

2. *Design Problems.* Although behavioral scientists try to control the effects of nonexperimental factors through careful design of the study, they are seldom completely successful. Participants commonly behave, for example, in a way that they feel will please the observer. Thus a supervisor who normally would respond negatively to a handicapped employee may act in another way if he or she knows the act will be observed. The result, once again, is a weakened association between attitudes and action.

3. *Measurement Errors.* In recording attitudes or actions, errors often are made that can reduce the association between attitudes and observed behavior. The observer may fail to notice certain acts. Or items on questionnaires may fail to discriminate precisely. For example, a test designed to measure job attitudes may be capable of classifying a group under one of only two categories—satisfied and dissatisfied. In analyzing data, the researcher cannot distinguish intermediate degrees of satisfaction. The result is an inaccurate conclusion.

4. *Generality and Specificity.* Attitude tests often ask respondents to react to a general class of people or things, while their actions toward a specific object are observed. The supervisor may display a prejudice toward handicapped workers in general but may act in a nonprejudiced manner toward a specific individual. A person

may dislike cats and yet love the family pet. The result is a loss of the association between attitudes and action.[42]

Here we see that at least one behavioral scientist explains the failure of some researchers to observe close associations between attitudes and behavior. On this basis, he concludes that these two factors are correlated, thus attitudes may be useful in predicting behavior. Certainly, the general literature of management supports the proposition (see Frame 4.1).

Proposition 4.5

> Although research is inconsistent with regard to the association between attitude and behavior, the lack of association can be explained in methodological terms. Therefore, we conclude that attitudes are important determinants of human action.

Frame 4.1

> **Attitudes and Action**
>
> Attitudes enable the release of human potential, which includes talent, education, and motivation. This is what Howard Westphall, of J. W. Newman Corporation, believes. He defines attitudes as how individuals feel about themselves and the world around them. Consistent with this definition, Newman Corporation has developed several attitude patterns observed in high-performing people. The patterns of thinking are
>
> *Self-esteem.* The high performers perceive themselves as valuable, important, and capable of achievement.
>
> *Responsibility.* The high performer accepts responsibility for the outcomes of actions. When one is successful, one is proud. When one is unsuccessful, accountability is acknowledged and mistakes are corrected.
>
> *Optimism.* Achievers expect things to be better because they are convinced that they influence the course of events.
>
> *Goal Orientation.* A sense of goal direction is important to high performers. The goal is constantly directing behavior.
>
> *Imaginativeness.* High performers are not bound by the past.

Their imagination is full of all the good things they will cause to happen.

Communicativeness. Emphasis is placed on getting the message through to others.

Growth Orientation. The emphasis is always on pushing ahead and meeting the world of change head on, rather than on standing still.

Positive Response to Pressure. The achiever functions best in a time of crisis. The reality of pressure is accepted as a challenge.

Trust. The achiever believes others want to achieve and is willing to provide opportunities for responsible action.

Joyfulness. The high performer experiences a genuine enjoyment in what he or she does.

Risk Taking. Achievers appreciate the reality of uncertainty and expect nothing better. The objective is excellence, not perfection.

Nowness. High performers make decisions and engage in actions in the present because they want to and enjoy doing so.

Adapted from "Attitudes: The Secret of Superperformers," *Industry Week,* 21 January 1974, pp. 36–38.

Measuring Attitudes

If we agree that attitudes can influence behavior, it becomes extremely important for us to have an *attitude scale,* or some means of measuring attitudes. By far, the attitude measure used most often in management is the Likert scale. This is usually a five-point scale ranging from "strongly agree" to "strongly disagree." Customarily, a general statement is presented, and respondents are asked to check the point on the scale that best describes their reaction. A Likert scale appears as follows:

Statement: I find my job challenging and rewarding.

Strongly Agree	Agree	Undecided	Disagree	Strongly Disagree
(5)	(4)	(3)	(2)	(1)

The responses are assigned numerical values ranging from 5 (strongly agree) to 1 (strongly disagree).

The Likert scale is called a summed-rating measure because several statements are collected in an attitude area (such as one's attitude about a job), and the scales then are added up to obtain a person's attitude toward the job. The summed-rating scale provides a means of measuring the intensity of one's attitude toward a particular attitude object.

Table 4.1 is an evaluation questionnaire that students can use in rating faculty members. The form uses a standard five-value Likert

Table 4.1 Student Form for the Evaluation of Teaching

	SA	A	U	D	SD
My instructor displays a clear understanding of course topics.	—	—	—	—	—
My instructor is able to simplify difficult materials.	—	—	—	—	—
My instructor has an effective style of presentation.	—	—	—	—	—
My instructor seems well prepared for class.	—	—	—	—	—
My instructor speaks audibly and clearly.	—	—	—	—	—
My instructor writes legibly on the blackboard.	—	—	—	—	—
My instructor displays enthusiasm when teaching.	—	—	—	—	—
My instructor emphasizes relationships between and among topics.	—	—	—	—	—
My instructor emphasizes conceptual understanding of material.	—	—	—	—	—
My instructor makes good use of examples and illustrations.	—	—	—	—	—
This course builds understanding of concepts and principles.	—	—	—	—	—
My instructor's explanations and comments are always helpful.	—	—	—	—	—

My instructor returns papers quickly enough to benefit me. — — — — —

I am free to express and explain my own views in class. — — — — —

I feel free to ask questions in class. — — — — —

I understand what is expected of me in this course. — — — — —

There is sufficient time in class for questions and discussions. — — — — —

Exams stress important points of the lectures/text. — — — — —

I know how I stand on exams relative to others in the class. — — — — —

Grades are assigned fairly and impartially. — — — — —

Course topics are dealt with in sufficient depth. — — — — —

The format of this course is appropriate to course purposes. — — — — —

Class lectures contain information not covered in the textbook. — — — — —

I would enjoy taking another course from this instructor. — — — — —

Frequent attendance in this class is essential to good learning. — — — — —

My instructor motivates me to do my best work. — — — — —

My instructor explains difficult material clearly. — — — — —

Course assignments are interesting and stimulating. — — — — —

Overall, this course is among the best I have ever taken. — — — — —

Overall, this instructor is among the best teachers I have known. — — — — —

Source: Used with permission of Purdue University.

scale. After students complete the form, teachers can obtain a great deal of useful information. The scores on the various questions can be compared with those of other faculty members or with the scores of the same teacher in different classes. Instructors can also use this scale in tracking their scores from one academic term or year to another.

Various other attitude scales can be used by researchers or managers. The Likert scale was selected for special attention because it is used widely and is familiar to most people, and because it is relatively easy to understand and analyze. Still one must be careful with the analysis. As we noted in Chapter 3, most data generated by the Likert scale achieves only the ordinal level of measurement. Thus only appropriate techniques of analysis should be used.

Attitude Change

Although present attitudes relate to past experiences, we should recognize that a recurring problem in management is the future dimension of attitudes. The individual, the people around the individual, and the environment are in a constant state of flux. This means that attitudes supporting one's personality development and well-being in the present may require alteration if they are to perform the same function in the future.

Attitude change can be classified in two ways. The first can be called *congruent change,* which is a change in the intensity but not in the direction of an existing attitude. To illustrate, consider on a Likert scale the following change relating to work satisfaction. Here we see that an initially unfavorable attitude toward work (X_1) has become an even less favorable attitude toward work $(X_2 - X_1)$.

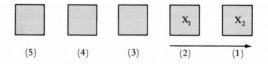

Generally speaking, congruent changes are easier to effect than *incongruent changes,* which represent changes in direction. This change appears as follows:

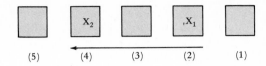

In this case, the unfavorable attitude toward work (X_1) has changed to a favorable response (X_2).

It is sometimes a key administrative function to trigger attitude change. For example, everyone probably has witnessed a situation in which the general morale (or in this case, attitudes toward the work and the organization) of a group becomes unfavorable to effective and efficient goal accomplishment. Such a reduction in morale may be evidenced by a decline in job performance among group members, by absenteeism, and by conflict. If managers are to change these attitudes, they must understand the important factors involved in attitude change. Although we cannot examine all the influential factors, we can look briefly at the more important ones.

Communicator credibility and source attractiveness are, no doubt, among the most important factors influencing an individual's predisposition toward attitude change. A nice-looking, clean doctor probably can change your attitudes—even about nonmedical issues—more easily than can an ill-kempt person with no educational training. One study examined the differences in attitude change resulting when ideas were presented by a recognized authority (high credibility source) and by a high school sophomore (low credibility source). The high credibility source produced greater attitude change than the high school student did.[43]

The implication of such research seems clear from a behavioral viewpoint. Employees are more receptive and are inclined toward attitude change when they receive information from sources they perceive to be credible. This correlation makes it all the more important for managers to maintain their credibility, and it suggests certain strategies for implementing change. For example, working with a respected group member might be appropriate when a manager is attempting to make a significant change in a job or task.

Situational factors are also important. Research has shown, for example, that certain media—such as films, public and private statements, and group discussion—can influence the direction and extent of attitude change.[44] Thus we arrive at our final proposition.

Proposition 4.6

> Attitude change is easier when the intensity rather than the direction is altered. The expertise and appearance of the person changing the attitude has an important influence on success.

What Managers Need to Know About Individual Employees

Managers do not have to be psychologists, but a knowledge of psychology is useful. If an employee is not working up to capacity, it would be helpful to know something about his or her personality and needs. The employee may be trying to acquire acceptance in a group and to satisfy some social need. Since the group generally does not work to capacity, the employee is "following suit."

Managers will also benefit from knowing how important the employee's environmemt has been in developing work values. The employee may not be working to capacity because he or she grew up in a family in which the importance of work was not emphasized. Perhaps the father was unskilled and unemployed during the employee's early childhood. The presence of the father at home, the pressures caused by unemployment, and the bitterness and resentment resulting from the father's state of poverty simply did not impress the child with the value of work.

So we might concede that we know or have an idea why the employee is not working hard. How does this solve the problem? Obviously, it does not. It does, however, suggest that the environment must be changed to provide stimulation and incentive for hard work. Perhaps placing him or her under a respected and skilled worker will enrich the work environment and encourage higher performance.

Finally, any successful manager will need to appreciate the importance of attitudes and the necessity of understanding attitude change. When work attitudes are unsatisfactory, reversal will be more easily achieved by a high-status or highly respected employee or manager. Perceived expertise is very important in effecting constructive attitude change.

Summary

This chapter briefly examined personality development by exploring the contributions and limitations of psychoanalytical theory, trait theory, and the needs theories of Maslow and McClelland. All these concepts provide useful information about the behavior of individuals in organizations.

Next a systems view of human behavior was proposed to illustrate how cognitive processes and needs act on forces from the environment. This tendency results in actions that once again are subjected to the influence of environmental forces. We reviewed the complex problem of how heredity (nature) and experience (nurture) interact in determining human behavior. The most important aspects of behavior are determined neither genetically nor environmentally, but result instead from interaction between the two.

We also examined the relationship between culture and behavior. Culture includes all learned behavior, but we limited our analysis to the influences of youth values, social classes, and work groups on behavior.

Finally, the chapter examined attitudes and attitude change. We analyzed attitude formation and the relationship between attitudes and behavior. Although some studies question any causal association between the two, most discrepancies can be explained on methodological grounds.

With regard to attitude change, we noted that congruent changes (changes in intensity rather than direction) are easier to effect than incongruent changes (changes in direction). Such factors as communicator credibility and attractiveness strongly affect the ease with which changes are made.

Questions for Discussion

1. Compare and contrast the psychoanalytical theory and the trait theory of personality development. How does each compare with the needs theories in their usefulness for management? Defend your answer.
2. Referring to Chapter 3, what level of measurement is obtained by Likert's attitude scale? Why and how did you reach your conclusion?

3. What do you consider to be the three factors in the environment that influence attitude development most? Why? Give specific examples showing how these factors influence organizational behavior.
4. Explain briefly the causal link between attitudes and behavior. How can we explain the studies that fail to observe a causal link?
5. Why is attitude change an important subject for practicing managers? Try to list five specific situations in which managers may be called on to act as agents of change.

Exercise: What Do You Expect from a Job?

Instructions: Rank the items listed below in order of their importance to you in evaluating a job offer. (5 = most important; 1 = least important.)

	5	4	3	2	1
Geographical location	___	___	___	___	___
Money	___	___	___	___	___
Recognition	___	___	___	___	___
Forty-hour work week	___	___	___	___	___
Company reputation	___	___	___	___	___
Fringe benefits					
Insurance	___	___	___	___	___
Sick pay	___	___	___	___	___
Paid vacation	___	___	___	___	___
Pension	___	___	___	___	___
Responsibility	___	___	___	___	___
Achievement	___	___	___	___	___

After you complete the ranking, review the items you consider most important. For comparison, the table below shows how several groups of college students rated these employment factors.

| | Group Ranks | | |
| | | | |
Items	All business majors*	Accounting	Economics	Management
Geographical location	9	3	8	7
Money	5	2†	3	3
Recognition	3	2†	6	6
Forty-hour work week	11	8	10	8
Company reputation	10	6	9	9
Insurance	4	5	1	5
Sick pay	8	7	4	2†
Paid vacation	6	4†	5	2†
Pension	7	4†	7	4
Responsibility	2	1†	2†	1†
Achievement	1	1†	2†	1†

*Includes the composite group.
†Indicates tied rankings.

1. How did your ranking compare with those of the other groups?
2. What can you theorize about the employment values of the various groups?
3. Describe in two or three words your impression of the groups, based on their rankings of the various items.
4. How do you think your parents would rank the eleven job characteristics? How would their rankings be similar to or different from yours?

Case: Tony Howard's Participant Management Plan

Tony Howard is the supervisor of a group of structural engineers employed by Rayburn Engineering Company. Most engineers in Tony's group are young and have recently graduated from college. Typically, Rayburn puts the young engineers in Tony's group until they gain the experience to move on to greater responsibilities.

Tony Howard has been a supervisor for many years. When he first began the job about fifteen years ago, he believed that most engineers wanted to be left alone to do their jobs with as little interference as possible. As a result, he developed a philosophy of making decisions with little input from group members. No one seemed to object to this mode of operation and so he continued this procedure until the late 1960s.

Around 1968, Tony began to notice changes in the young employees he supervised. Several outstanding performers suggested to him that they had ideas about how things could be improved and how organizational effectiveness could be increased. Tony then began to involve group members in decision making, and once again everyone seemed happy.

During the past two years, Tony has made additional observations. According to him, the new employees seem more like those of the early 1960s than of the early 1970s. They want to be left alone to do their work, leaving administration to the supervisor. This characteristic does not mean they never suggest that input is good. However, when attempts are made to involve employees in meaningful decision making, they fail to participate and complain that they were not hired as managers. Tony is beginning to wonder whether he once again should become the primary decision maker.

1. Given existing youth values, how would you explain Tony Howard's dilemma?
2. What might Tony do to deal more effectively with the motivational problem he currently faces?
3. How would you explain the extreme changes in the values of youth that appear to have taken place in recent years?

Suggested Readings

Bem, D. J., and A. Allen. "On Predicting Some of the People Some of the Time: The Search for Cross-situational Consistencies in Behavior." *Psychological Review* 81 (1974): 506–520.

Brief, A. P., and R. J. Aldag. "Employee Reactions to Job Characteristics: A Constructive Replication." *Journal of Applied Psychology* 60 (1975): 182–186.

Dowling, William. *Effective Management and the Behavioral Sciences.* [1] (New York: Amacon, 1978).

Kobayashi, M. K., and W. W. Burke. "Organizational Development in Japan." *Columbia Journal of World Business* 11 (Summer 1976): 113–123.

Kraar, L. A. "Japanese Are Coming with Their Own Style of Management." *Fortune* 91 (March 1975): 116–121.

Pedalino, E., and V. Gamboa. "Behavior Modification and Absenteeism: Intervention in One Industrial Setting." *Journal of Applied Psychology* 59 (1974): 694–698.

Porter, L. W. "Turning Work to Nonwork: The Rewarding Environment." In *Work and Nonwork in the Year 2001,* edited by M. D. Dunnette. Belmont, Calif.: Wadsworth, 1973.

Porter, L. W., and R. M. Steers. "Organizational, Work, and Personal Factors in Employee Turnover and Absenteeism." *Psychological Bulletin* 80 (1973): 151–176.

Waters, L. K., and D. Roach. "Job Attitudes as Predictors of Termination and Absenteeism: Consistency over Time and Across Organizational Units." *Journal of Applied Psychology* 57 (1973): 341–342.

Yang, C. Y. "Management Styles: American vis-à-vis Japanese." *Columbia Journal of World Business* 12 (Fall 1977): 23–31.

Perception, Learning, and Problem Solving in Organizational Behavior

> The importance of deciding how to decide is not trivial. There are no pat solutions to this problem, but there is a methodology to help decision makers.
>
> David W. Miller and Martin K. Starr,
> *The Structure of Human Decisions*

Have you ever heard that movie makers insert pictures of popcorn, soft drinks, and candy bars into the frames of a film so that viewers will pick up the message and buy more of those products? When toy makers began inserting messages like "Get it" into television commercials to increase children's desire for a product, the Federal Trade Commission issued a warning for the manufacturers to stop the practice immediately.

When people are exposed to and pick up a message without being aware of it, they experience subliminal perception. Movie makers produce great effects this way. A frame or two of a skull and the word blood at key points in a horror movie can increase the viewer's fear. In fact, Warner Brothers is being sued because one viewer of *The Exorcist* claims that frame flashes of a death mask throughout the movie scared him so much that he fainted and broke several teeth.

The use of subliminal messages is becoming big business. A firm in Louisiana produces a system for use in department stores so that messages like "I am honest" can be mixed softly with music to reduce shoplifting. Not surprisingly, the American Civil Liberties Union objects to such devices because they could be used to manipulate behavior in undesirable ways.

Without raising ethical questions about subliminal messages, let us consider how communication influences human behavior. First, if a message is to influence our actions, it must be received. This reception is *perception*. An individual receives the message by hearing, seeing, or feeling relevant information.

When a message is received, we evaluate the information by comparing it with past experiences and relating it to our own needs and desires. If the information changes our behavior, we *learn* certain types of responses. A compulsive shoplifter who has heard the honest message often enough to go straight has learned to behave in a different way when confronted with a tempting situation.

Finally, when we receive a message such as a subliminal picture of popcorn and soda, we must solve a problem. We know that our goal is to be happy and that there are several ways to obtain happiness. Therefore, through *problem solving* we choose either to eat the tempting foods or to save our money for something else.

These three aspects of human behavior are the basic *cognitive,* or thinking, *processes*—perception, learning, and problem solving. They link us with our environment. Through these processes, we sense or perceive what is happening in the environment, receive and evaluate information, and choose one course of action over all others. Cognitive processes are the means by which such subtle information as the facial expressions, words, and actions of a supervisor are received by employees. Then employees analyze the information and convert it into observable behavior ranging from improved performance to absenteeism. The results of perception, learning, and problem solving are real. If they were not, businesses would not spend thousands of dollars on subliminal perception techniques, and the American Civil Liberties Union would not be concerned about devices that carefully interrupt music with the spoken word.

This chapter examines perception, learning, and problem solving and illustrates their importance to managers in organizations. We will consider these processes not only in abstract psychological terms but also in practical ones. After all, these processes are real and managers must deal with them whenever they come into contact with people.

Figure 5.1   The Behavioral Process

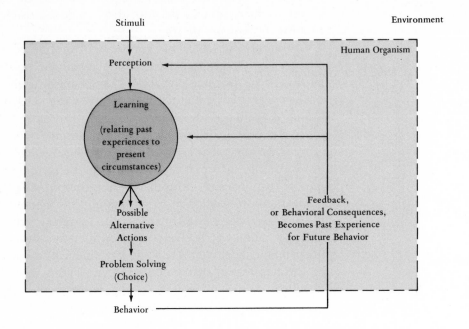

The three cognitive processes of perception, learning, and problem solving form a direct link between the receipt of an external stimulus (or stimuli) and the resulting behavior. This link is illustrated in Figure 5.1. The process begins with the perception of stimuli in the environment. The perceived stimuli are assigned meaning through learning, when the individual's past experience is combined with the present situation and possible responses are considered. One or more alternatives are selected and behavior results. This behavior may be something that is observable—an action—or it may be something invisible, such as an attitude. In any case, the learned behavior is retained, and it influences future perception and learning. Thus perception, learning, and problem solving are the basic determinants of behavior. Perception provides the link between the individual and the environment. Learning assists in providing meaning to unique as well as familiar stimuli and problem solving is instrumental in determining which action the individual will take. The rest of the chapter will examine these important processes in detail.

Perception: Providing the Link

Perception has been defined in various ways. In the behavioral sciences, particularly psychology, the term is used to mean more than simply hearing, seeing, or tasting something. The significance of perception is expanded beyond the five senses and becomes an important element in the behavioral adjustment of human beings.

Nature of Perception

Each time a person is confronted with a familiar stimulus, the information is assembled and compared with existing data. How any person interprets the stimulus depends on his or her personality and aspirations.[1] For example, a psychologically insecure employee may perceive a manager's advice as criticism. The mature and psychologically secure person may perceive the advice as an opportunity to learn from another's experience.

Past experiences with people and things in the environment influence our perception. For example, cultural factors certainly influence the way we perceive objects and situations. Individuals exposed to a particular religious tradition may perceive a certain food as "unclean," or not appropriate for consumption. Individuals from other traditions may accept the same food as a basic part of their diet. With regard to job factors, a person from a deprived environment may have difficulty adjusting to a clearly structured time schedule because he or she has not been exposed to the requirements of rigidly structured tasks. Another person may adjust quite easily to the regimentation of a timeclock.

Perception is an extremely personal thing. However, certain characteristics are found in all perceptual processes. As shown in Figure 5.2, perceptual variations usually result from selectivity and closure.

Selectivity Human beings are not capable of sensing all the stimuli surrounding them. In Figure 5.2, the individual is exposed to a variety of stimuli in the environment. However, he or she receives only a small portion of all the possible sounds, smells, and other stimuli. Selective perception can be compared to a beam of light focused on

Figure 5.2   Characteristics of Perception

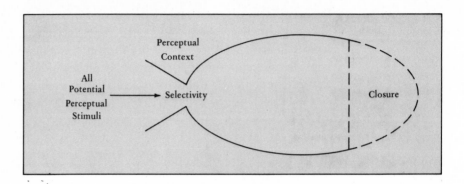

incoming sources of information. Personality factors influence how the beam appears. A very anxious person might focus a narrow beam over a range of possibilities, not holding too long at any single point. The less anxious person might focus less intensely on a larger number of alternatives.[2]

Usually, we perceive those things that already match our own value systems. For example, a class that scores very low on a test will be viewed in several ways. The professor will be sure that no one studied; the students will feel that the exam was unfair; and the dean may conclude that admission standards have been reduced to the point where students cannot do the work expected of them.

A situation that occurred in a large textile firm is even more interesting. A high percentage of employees voluntarily quit their jobs after nine months' employment, and another group quit after eighteen months. Upon further investigation, it was discovered that the employees thought the company had broken its contract to give them raises at nine-month intervals. The company contended that the intervals were for merit-increase reviews, not automatic raises. It was speculated that the employees "heard" only what they wanted to. The same could be said of the company.[3]

Another study illustrates a similar point. When a sample of executives were given a case study, production managers emphasized the manufacturing aspects of the case, sales executives selected the marketing problems, and so on.[4] Thus the executives selectively perceived those parts of the problem that were most consistent with their experience and interest.

Proposition 5.1

> Perception is selective. No one is capable of receiving all the stimuli in a particular circumstance. People select for perception those things that are most interesting and relevant to them, things that already match their experience.

Closure Although people perceive objects and situations selectively, they fill in the gaps and act as if they understand the entire situation. For example, one study showed how groups of subjects were conditioned to view double-digit numbers, capital letters, and a combination of the two. The subjects then were shown a capital *B* that was separated so that it could also appear as the number *13*. The subjects who were conditioned to perceive capital letters saw the figure as a *B*, whereas those people who were conditioned to perceive numbers saw a *13*.[5]

Other studies have shown that managers sometimes judge employees and develop procedures based on limited characteristics, such as a person's leadership ability.[6] More specifically, one's preconception or expectation about a person can determine an entire behavioral pattern. An employee who has a conflict with one supervisor may be transferred to another shift. If, however, the old supervisor tells the new shift leader what a troublemaker the employee is, it is likely that conflict also will emerge on the new shift. If a supervisor expects someone to make trouble, the person's other important traits may be overlooked. Sure enough, in time, that employee behaves just as expected.

Proposition 5.2

> Perception is selective, but human beings fill in gaps and behave as though they have complete knowledge of a situation, person, or event. The result is often a failure to recognize the complexity of the entire situation. Inaccurate evaluations may result through such processes as stereotyping and halo effects.

Closure, the tendency to assume that you perceive a total situation, is an important part of the perceptual process and leads to some well-defined and predictable results. One such behavior is called

Figure 5.3   The Perceptual Context

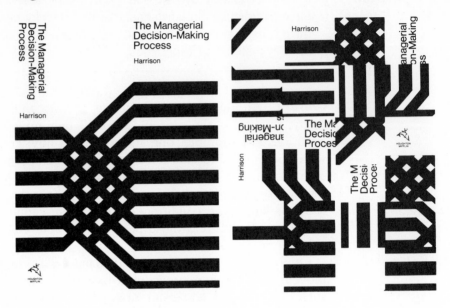

Source: From E. Frank Harrison, *The Managerial Decision-Making Process.* Copyright © 1975 by Houghton Mifflin Company. Used by permission.

stereotyping.[7] For example, a college student may be considered to be like all other college students, or stereotyped, because he or she shares the one characteristic of attending a college. In all other ways, the individual may be clearly different from all fellow students.

Another pattern is known as the halo effect. In this case a person is evaluated on the basis of a single trait. For example, the star of the company tennis team may be given higher performance evaluations on the job than work behavior justifies.

Context   Perception occurs in a setting, or a *context*. This context is made up of physical factors, such as the amount of lighting or noise. It also relates to emotional and social environments. Research indicates that it is not uncommon for supervisors' evaluations of employees to be influenced by factors unrelated to the job, such as the perceived value systems of employees. For example, managers may rank subordinates higher when they share common values with regard to work, religion, and so on.[8] Consider how perception is affected when familiar real-world scenes are distorted. Figure 5.3 illustrates the importance of context.

This figure shows the familiar front and side covers of a college textbook. (Figure 5.3, left). If asked to identify the author, we automatically respond to the context, drawing on past experience, and find the author's name. We can do this easily, because in the past we have noted that an author's name usually appears above or below the title. Thus we quickly find what we are looking for. However, the problem is different in the second picture (Figure 5.3, right). The same book cover has been distorted; it has been cut and rearranged randomly. Our context is thus distorted, and it is more difficult to locate the author's name. We have no point of reference, as we did in the first picture.

Proposition 5.3

> The perceptual context is important because it gives a point of reference. This context includes a number of elements within the environment, such as attitudes, emotions, and physical properties. When distortions occur, perceptual accuracy is reduced.

Some Implications for Management

Managers can draw many implications from what they know about perception. Since perception is always selective, a manager never has all the information needed to make decisions. Individuals with supervisory responsibilities should be more aware of the limits of the information on which they operate. This awareness would encourage them to seek more information and to view it objectively. Open-minded people seek more information before making evaluations.

Closure also has important implications for management. No one is free from the dangers of stereotyping. It is tempting to select a few characteristics of a person or group and to evaluate the entire situation on the basis of limited information. This, however, leads to inaccurate evaluations.

With closure as well as selectivity, the best "cure" is to understand the dangers. Then, and only then, are we able to deal more objectively with the reality around us.

Context is important in another sense. It sometimes can be controlled and changed directly. When managers are asked to evaluate decisions in a tense and stress-oriented environment, distortions are likely to occur. Therefore, when perceptual accuracy is especially important, extra care must be taken to develop as stress-free a context as possible. Zalkind and Costello provide a useful summary of the behavioral results of perception by stating:

1. People are influenced by things (stimuli) they do not consciously perceive. Thus, individuals may behave on the basis of prejudices that they are not consciously aware of possessing.
2. When abstract factors are being considered, irrelevant stimuli may influence behavior. A loan officer may judge a person's credit worthiness or wealth on the basis of physical appearance.
3. Emotions influence perception and behavior. A judge who dislikes teenagers may "throw the book" at a young driver who runs a traffic light.
4. People often evaluate the importance of perceived stimuli based on personal factors. Information from a fellow worker may be valued more than an official memo from management.[9]

What do the users of subliminal-perception technology hope to accomplish? First, they obviously know that people perceive things even when they are unaware of it. Since we selectively perceive those things which are most consistent with our values, it is important to relate the subliminal stimuli to what interests people, such as food, toys, and so on. Next, the users always employ messages that can be "closed" in a way that accomplishes their goals (usually to increase profits). Finally, the context surrounding the stimulus is important. If the goal is to sell popcorn, a movie theater is the ideal place. If the objective is to sell toys, Saturday morning cartoons will do the job. The person who wants to avoid such manipulation had better learn how perception works. Frame 5.1 presents an example of the importance of the perceptual process to management.

Frame 5.1

Guesswork at General Motors

In the early 1970s, the General Motors Vega plant in Lordstown, Ohio, became the focus of much management research. The Vegas produced at Lordstown often came off the assembly line with assorted dents, broken windows, and other strange "redesigns."

General Motors, with the help of behavioral scientists, concluded that the workers belonged to a new generation that could not adjust to the routine of assembly lines. These new, better educated, more independent workers were frustrated and dissatisfied by the structure and specialization they found on the job. As a result, many businesses began to redesign and "enrich" jobs to make them more challenging and satisfying. Management was confident a new concept in motivation had been developed.

Not so, says British behavioral scientist John Child. Writing in *Management Review,* Professor Child says that the Lordstown problem was nothing more than a typical labor-management dispute over traditional issues such as seniority, job security, and control over the speed of the assembly line. Actually, General Motors management was worried about falling profits, and so jobs were reorganized to increase efficiency. This led to the workers' fears of a layoff. In fact, the motivation to redesign had little to do with the dehumanizing effects of the assembly line.

How could managers and researchers miss the real problems at Lordstown? Perhaps we can explain the situation in terms of perception.

Selectivity   Management's emphasis at Lordstown was on the obvious problems, such as the destruction of cars by workers during the production process. Since such destruction was unusual, management sought equally unusual solutions. Surely, if workers had reached the point where they were ruining the results of their own labor, the solution could not lie in traditional motivation theory.

Context   The late 1960s was a time of great social change. Government leaders, educators, and business managers were convinced that the turmoil would continue and that the changes would affect all areas of life. Everyone seemed to expect that workers, organizations, managers, and management techniques would have to change as well.

Closure   In a context built on the expectation of social change and with a large, although limited, amount of information indicating great dissatisfaction, managers and researchers had to explain the decline in the quality of Vegas produced at Lordstown. What a perfect chance to promote the cause of the quality of working life. Pieces of the motivation puzzle were missing, and the idea of job enrichment made everything fall into place.

Extrasensory Perception: Some Developing Insights

Extrasensory perception, or ESP, is not usually considered an appropriate topic in the study of organizational behavior. As recently as 1967, Bernard Berelson and Gary Steiner noted that only about 5 percent of all psychologists believed ESP to be an established fact, whereas about one-third of them looked on it as an unknown quality. The remainder displayed various degrees of doubt.[10] However, there appears to be growing interest in ESP and management decision making in recent years.

There are four major areas of interest concerning ESP. The first is precognition, or an unusual ability to see into the future. As the word implies, knowledge is prior to experience. Another area of interest is telepathy, which involves sending and receiving messages without the use of the five senses. Clairvoyance is the ability to perceive objects or events not normally perceived, and psychokinesis is the ability to move or control physical objects without touching them.

What has all this got to do with management? In 1971, an article reported that unusually successful chief executives seem to possess higher degrees of ESP than other individuals do. The article also revealed that the samples of business people in this study believed in the existence of ESP by a three-to-one margin.[11] In spite of this belief, business has seldom used ESP for practical purposes.

There are, of course, a number of possible uses for ESP. Any executive would be overjoyed to know what will happen in the future or to be able to transmit and receive messages without using the five senses. But the research is far from conclusive. Students of organizational behavior should be acquainted with ESP because of its potential, but excessive enthusiasm seems unwarranted.

Learning: Models and Implications

Henri Cartier drives a truck in Quebec. Throughout his career, he has been considered a minimally satisfactory driver. He likes to talk to people, drink coffee, and read magazines. As often as not, he does all three on company time, when he should be driving. As a result, Henri is always behind schedule.

Most of Henri's past supervisors knew about the problem and tried to correct it. Henri was told that he should not talk to people when he made deliveries, and so he sometimes insulted good customers by saying the boss would not let him talk or be friendly. He began carrying coffee and magazines in the truck, and increased his already large number of minor accidents because he was drinking coffee or reading when he should have been paying attention to the road. Henri had learned how to respond to the supervisor's threats of punishment. Unfortunately, his performance was still low.

Benjamin Lyon has been in charge of Henri's shift for three months, and there has been a surprising improvement in all truck drivers' performances. Ben seldom threatens employees. Instead, he accentuates the positive. When Ben first came to work, Henri was surprised to be complimented for the deliveries he made on schedule; he was used to complaints about the deliveries that were late.

Ben even held a meeting and asked the drivers to help set goals for making deliveries on schedule. Drivers who met or exceeded these goals were treated to lunch. And each month the driver with the best record of on-schedule deliveries was allowed to load from the first dock, at which was posted a conspicuous sign: "Driver of the Month." As a result of these changes, Henri and the other drivers learned to react differently to below-satisfactory performance. Now they work to improve their performance rather than making excuses for delays.

Learning is the process through which perceptual information is made meaningful. It is a change in behavior based on previous experience. Learning theory has many uses in organizational behavior. For example, employees learn how to respond to others, to perform their tasks, and how to do their jobs. All this takes place within an organizational context. Therefore, to understand individuals and groups, we must appreciate the process and complexity of the adjustments people make in responding to the demands of everyday life.

Two Learning Models

There are two basic types of learning: classical conditioning and operant conditioning.

Classical Conditioning Classical conditioning is associated with the pioneering work of Ivan Pavlov, a Russian psychologist.[12] Pavlov's discoveries grew out of experiments on the digestive system of dogs. He observed that saliva in the dogs' mouths and gastric juice in the dogs' stomachs increased when the animals observed food as well as when they held food in their mouths. When food was in a dog's mouth, the increased saliva and gastric juice was an unconditioned, or unlearned, response. When food was merely observed, however, the same response had to be learned; it thus was called a conditioned response.

In a series of studies, Pavlov placed a dog in an experimental situation and presented a light, followed shortly by a portion of meat. At first, the animal did not salivate when the light was turned on, but it did salivate when eating the meat. The study was repeated a number of times. The light was turned on, followed by the offering of meat, followed by an unconditioned stimulus, which was followed by a response (eating). This sequence was called reinforcement.

After enough trials, Pavlov noted an interesting result. The light could be turned on without the presence of food and the dog still would salivate. In this case, the stimulus (light) was followed by a conditioned response. This relationship between a stimulus and response is *classical conditioning.* The process can be illustrated as follows:

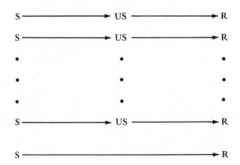

In classical conditioning, a stimulus (S) is presented as a signal that an unconditioned stimulus (US) will follow. When the unconditioned stimulus occurs, the response (R) results. Finally, after a series of trials, the response follows the conditioned stimulus *without* the presence of the unconditioned stimulus. Technically, the conditioned stimulus is substituted for the unconditioned stimulus; thus, the process is referred to as stimulus substitution. When the conditioned stimulus is *not* followed by the unconditioned stimulus, the animal or person soon "learns" again and ceases to respond. When reinforcement no longer occurs, extinction results, that is, the learned behavior no longer occurs. The stimulus precedes the response in classical conditioning.

Operant Conditioning   When we teach a dog a trick, like shaking hands, we do not do it with unconditioned and conditioned stimuli. Instead, we say, "Shake!" and when the animal responds properly, we reward it with a piece of meat or some other favor. The dog does not raise its paw and offer it for shaking because of some unconditioned stimulus; it does so because the reward is expected.

By the same token, we know it is time to attend class when a certain bell rings. This ring, unlike an unconditioned stimulus, is called a discriminating stimulus. It tells us that class is about to begin, but it does not require us to attend class in the same way that meat causes a dog to salivate.

The well-known psychologist B. F. Skinner is identified closely with this type of learning, which is known as *operant conditioning.* Skinner distinguishes carefully between respondent and operant behavior. The former is controlled by a stimulus, as in classical conditioning. In the latter case, the behavior precedes or occurs simultaneously with the stimulus.[13] When the response is related to a stimulus, the operant behavior is known as operant conditioning. The word *operant* is used because the behavior operates on the environment to cause some effect, such as a dog's "shaking hands" to get its treat. For this reason, operant behavior is sometimes called instrumental learning, since it is designed to produce some specific result. Figure 5.4 illustrates operant conditioning.

According to Skinner, the same principles used in teaching dogs to shake hands or pigeons to ring bells can be used in shaping human behavior through properly designed reinforcement.[14] The problem as Skinner sees it is that we fail to use the knowledge available. We will see how the principles of operant conditioning can be applied to practical affairs in Chapter 6, which deals with motivation. First, however, we must examine learning in some detail and the controversies associated with operant and respondent conditioning.

As shown in Figure 5.4, a stimulus is perceived and meaning is assigned on the basis of past experiences and future expectations. A response then is selected. Once a response is made, one or more consequences result. This is where the *law of effect* takes place. This law states that a response will be repeated when the results are

Figure 5.4 The General Process of Instrumental Learning

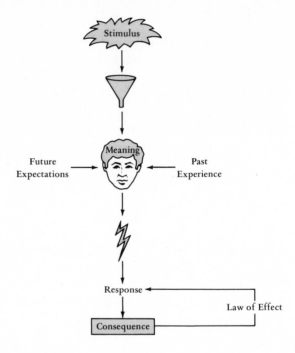

favorable; when results are unfavorable, however, some other response will be chosen in the future.

The supporters of operant conditioning emphasize the value of
using the law of effect in a positive way. For example, Henri Cartier's
past supervisors tried to get him to improve his unsatisfactory performance by threats of unpleasant consequences, but Benjamin Lyon
got better results from Henri by rewarding his good performance. In
both cases, the law of effect is operating; however, the reward
worked better than threats of punishment.

*Proposition
5.4*

Human beings learn by means of classical conditioning, as in our
customary eating schedules. We also learn through operant conditioning; for instance, we learn to produce at higher levels when rewards are presented for outstanding performance.

Figure 5.5 Selected Learning Patterns

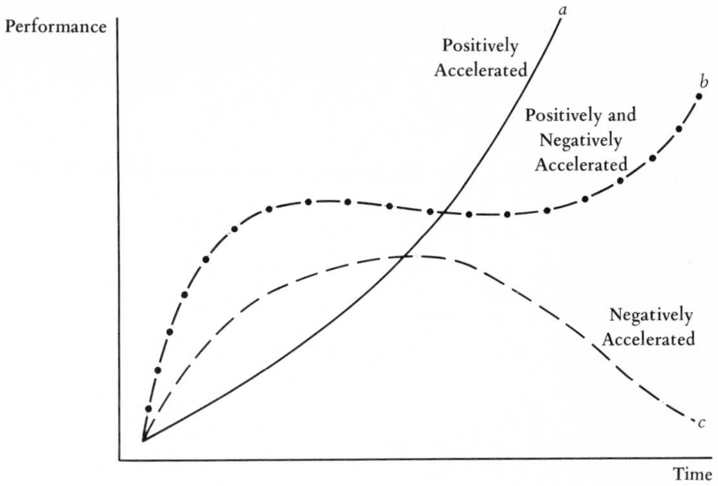

Measuring Learning

Learning is measured by means of a learning curve. Figure 5.5 illustrates several learning patterns. For example, curve *a* is said to be positively accelerated; curve *c* is negatively accelerated. Curve *b* is S-shaped and is a combination of a negatively accelerated curve and a positively accelerated one.

A positively accelerated curve traces the learning effects of a difficult task such as solving a mathematical problem. At first the task is difficult, and progress is slow. Once the principles are mastered, however, the task becomes much easier. A negatively accelerated curve, on the other hand, is characteristic of a simple task such as a routine movement or an assembly job. Here the job is learned quickly, and performance increases. However, the task soon loses its excitement, and performance levels out. The S-shaped, combined curve describes a task that is learned quickly so that a level of performance is reached. However, a new aspect is introduced (for example, the job may be redesigned) so that the task becomes more difficult and challenging, and performance again increases.

The practical applications of learning curves are easy to find. For example, a company that manufactures airliners may keep records

Figure 5.6   Learning and Forgetting

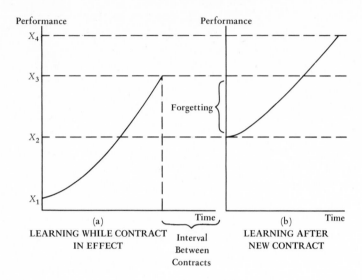

on learning effects. It may note that considerable time is required to put the first models of an aircraft into operation. As more units are produced, however, the work takes less time, because managers and workers are more experienced and more efficient.

Consider the effects on learning experienced by producers, who are subject to the ups and downs of government contracts. What would happen if a number of aircraft were produced, and then the contract was lost? It may be necessary to lay off experienced workers while efforts are made to secure another contract. Obviously, the benefits of experience would be lost to some extent, but not completely. This is shown in Figure 5.6.

In Figure 5.6, we see that learning before the expiration of the contract reaches level X_3. Then the contract expires, and employees must be temporarily laid off, with some loss of skills. When the new contract is awarded, employees come to work and begin to perform at level X_2. Thus the factor of forgetting, or a reduction in performance, is equal to $X_3 - X_2$. After a period, however, performance reaches a new level of X_4. This gives us some idea of the inefficiencies involved when production is interrupted.

Implications of Learning for Management

Several implications can be drawn from the research on learning for management and organizational behavior. The most obvious area affected is training. Most organizations develop a training department, and every supervisor must provide daily training to employees. Therefore, managers need information about learning if their training programs are to be an effective motivational tool. The arguments of operant conditioning, for example, suggest anew the importance of rapid and frequent reinforcement of exceptionally good performance. Research supports the observation that feedback, or a knowledge of one's performance, can increase performance levels. When three groups of workers were observed, a direct relationship was found between the level of performance and the group's knowledge of their performance.[15]

To illustrate, think of your own experience as a college student. What happens when you repeatedly are given assignments but your grades are not reported to you? Can you remain enthusiastic about completing the assignments? Probably not! The old saying that "no news is good news" simply does not apply. If you get feedback, however, good marks will excite you and encourage your continued high performance. Bad grades also will let you know where you stand and (ideally) will encourage greater effort. In either case, feedback is helpful.

Problem Solving

Perception and learning lead to the third cognitive process: the necessity of making choices, or problem solving. Perception provides information and lets us know when we have problems; learning helps us to relate the newly perceived information to past experience. Next, choices must be made.

Consider a real and important problem facing university administrators with regard to women's athletics. Title IX of the educational amendments of 1972 requires colleges and universities to provide equal athletic opportunities for women. There are several ways that the requirements of the law can be satisfied, and each solution has its unique advantages and disadvantages.

For example, all sports might be made coeducational so that everyone, regardless of sex, would have an opportunity to seek scholarships and positions. Or identical programs for each sport could be developed for men and women. Another possibility would be to provide a mixture of some male, some female, and some coeducational sports. In all three possibilities, questions arise concerning type and independence of various sports programs, the scholarships available to males and females, the budgetary aspects of athletic events, and the desire for nationally competitive teams. How do administrators make this decision? We will explore this question by looking at human problem solving.

In speaking of problem solving, we usually refer to a series of acts such as searching for information, choosing, and so on. The actual choice of a solution is a decision. To understand problem solving, we will look at the various steps involved.

Acquiring Information

The amount of searching a person does to solve a problem is related to several factors. The first, and perhaps most obvious, is the information from which one begins. Research has shown that the amount of confidence a manager seeks in the information is related to the desirability of an outcome or result.[16] For example, decision makers frequently require less information to select a favorable course of action than to choose an unfavorable one. That is, managers will select a favorable action—such as making an investment with a high likelihood of increasing profits—on the basis of less information than they might require to do something unpopular—such as closing down a plant in a small town.

The extent of an information search also is related to the uncertainty in a situation. As a general rule, the greater the uncertainty, the greater the search. Uncertainty can arise in several ways. For example, when a person perceives a stimulus that is unfamiliar, unique, or surprising, uncertainty increases.[17] When a manager confronts a genuinely unique employee who reacts in a completely unusual way, uncertainty may result. Should the employee be fired because he or she cannot conform to expected behavior patterns? Or is this person valuable because of the new insights and diversity he or she provides? Considerable thought and evaluation will go into the decision. In contrast, a manager spends little time or effort working with people who behave in the expected manner, for there is nothing unique about the situation. We can relate this information to our example of university administrators and equality in athletics. Since administrators rarely have much experience with such a decision and are probably uncertain about handling it, we would expect their information search to be extensive.

Finally, the personality and background of the problem solver are likely to influence the search for information. If a manager has a boss who gives little freedom of action, there is little incentive for an extensive search. Problem solvers have an idea of how much freedom they have in decision making. Thus they form a concrete conceptual structure and view only selected aspects of the problem.[18] The aspects they select are related to past experience. Perhaps a manager has been restricted in implementing programs. If so, problem solving will revolve around considerations about the ease of implementation; only brief attention will be given to other aspects of the situation.

Another decision maker may have had considerable freedom of action in early childhood and in his or her career. This individual develops an abstract conceptual structure and evaluates more aspects of a problem. This approach requires a greater search for information.

Proposition 5.5

> The extent of an information search is related to a variety of factors, including the uncertainty of available responses, the importance of the choice, and a person's past experience in problem solving. The greater the uncertainty, the more important the choice, and the more abstract the problem solver's conceptual structure, the greater the likelihood of an extensive information search.

The implications of this research for organizational behavior are substantial. Since usually better-informed decisions are preferred, decision makers should have as much flexibility of action as possible. Then, and only then, can decision makers be assured of arriving at the best-informed decisions.

Action in Decision Making

Human choice is an element common to all behavior. When we awake each morning, we are faced with choices. Should we shower first or brush our teeth? Should we eat breakfast before deciding which clothes to wear? In organizations, the choices are often more complex, but they are just as frequent. Should we answer our mail or prepare for our meeting? Should we return our calls or talk with an employee who has a problem? Should we decide to purchase a new piece of equipment or delay for another day?

Behavioral scientists have examined human choice. One study showed that decision makers usually behave in unexpected ways. For example, it has been illustrated that when executives were faced with a choice between an action that had a certain outcome and an action that had two possible outcomes (each with a probability of .5) the managers preferred the former choice—even when the less certain outcome promised greater gains for the organization.[19]

In another study, researchers asked a sample of students to choose among a set of men's neckties on the basis of attractiveness, durability, and so on. Surprisingly, the students made their choices faster when presented with four equally desirable ties than when the choice was between two attractive and two unattractive ties. The researchers speculated that this resulted from the reinforcing effects and confidence that built up through the rejection of the two undesirable ties.[20] In a practical classroom setting, students, taking a multiple-choice test—once they have been successful in rejecting half the possible alternatives—may develop confidence in their ability to examine additional choices. They may thus think longer about the remaining choices.

Strange as it may seem, some managers make a decision *not* to decide. With clean air legislation, for example, some first decided not to meet the deadlines established for 1975. The firms were betting that the energy crisis would worsen and thus take pressure off of them. They were right. By 1975, legislators were more concerned about the shortage of energy than about the quality of air.

Cognitive Dissonance

A choice, once made, is not the end of the problem solving. Psychological implications continue. The most common post-decision phenomenon experienced by problem solvers is called *cognitive dissonance.*

Leon Festinger is primarily associated with the description and examination of cognitive dissonance. According to Festinger, all people have expectations and experiences about themselves, others, and their environments.[21] Dissonance occurs when a person is forced to choose one course of action over others, even though certain aspects of the rejected alternatives may appear favorable. For example, executives who choose the certain outcome over the uncertain one probably feel some regret over the rejected alternatives that promised higher profits. As a result, decision makers develop some anxiety.[22]

Fortunately, a great deal is known about cognitive dissonance. The more important the decision and the more attractive the alternatives not selected, the greater the resulting dissonance.[23] For example, a manager will feel more anxiety about relocating a multimillion-dollar plant when there are several equally desirable locations than when one location is clearly preferable.

Dissonance increases when a person must choose among equally attractive alternatives regardless of the importance of the decision.[24] This finding is interesting when related to our previous analysis of choice. Choices are made faster when a problem solver is faced with four equally attractive alternatives, as compared with two attractive and two unattractive ones. Based on this, it seems accurate to say that the faster a choice is made, the greater the resulting dissonance becomes.

Proposition 5.6

> Problem solving involves information search, the choice among alternative courses of action, and postdecision consequences. Each stage in problem solving is characterized by events that influence the degree of search, the speed of choice, and the extent of dissonance.

This conclusion raises a practical issue. What does a decision maker do when faced with cognitive dissonance? Some response is required. Perhaps the most frequent response is defensive behavior such as rationalization. The problem solver usually focuses on the positive aspects of the decision and psychologically minimizes the virtues of rejected alternatives. Such behavior is documented by research on betting at a horse race. Researchers showed that bettors who were confused before they placed a bet displayed greater confidence after the bet was made. The purpose of this behavior was to reduce their anxiety or dissonance.[25]

Modern Trends in Decision Theory

The most immediate application of problem solving to management is in decision making. Each time a manager makes a decision, he or she solves a problem. A unique course of action is selected from a larger set of alternatives. Research reveals two views of decision making. Each view is based on assumptions and seeks to accomplish a specific goal. Because both views are important for organizational behavior, we must look briefly at decision theory.

Normative Decision Making

Normative decision theory is designed to provide a set of procedures that, if followed, will maximize the long-run profitability or minimize the costs of the organization. For this reason, normative theory is often called prescriptive theory: it specifies a norm or goal to be obtained.

Normative decision theory is based on three assumptions. First, it assumes that people are economic beings who attempt to maximize something, such as profits, revenues, or satisfaction. Next it views the decision makers as possessing perfect knowledge and knowing not only the choices available but also their consequences. Finally, normative decision theory assumes that decision makers have an order of preference that allows them to rank the relative desirability of the consequences.[26]

These assumptions result in the process shown in Figure 5.7. The process begins with a maximizing goal. The problem solver then defines and analyzes the situation. Theoretically, all possible courses of action and their consequences are then compared, and the course of action promising the best outcome is selected. The decision is

Figure 5.7 Normative Decision Theory

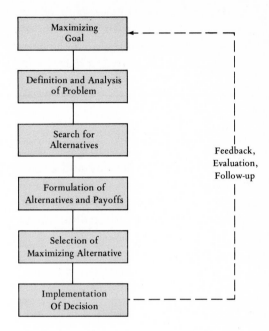

then implemented and evaluated on the basis of the original goal. In this view, decision makers are viewed as rational, maximizing human beings.

Behavioral Decision Theory

Behavioral, or descriptive, *decision theory* analyzes decision making without reference to a specific norm or goal. As is true of normative theory, behavioral theory is founded on several assumptions.

1. The decision maker is an administrative person who attempts to "satisfice" rather than to maximize.
2. Human beings are unable to acquire perfect knowledge of alternatives, outcomes, and payoffs. Thus, they operate under conditions of bounded rationality.
3. The search process is sequential, so that the order in which alternatives are evaluated may, and often does, influence the process of choice.[27]

The idea of satisficing, or compromising, is presented in two places. First, the organization is viewed as subgroups made up of owners, managers, employees, and customers. The decision maker, rather than maximizing the interests of a single group, attempts to compromise the values of all groups. In this way, a satisfactory compromise, rather than a maximizing outcome, is pursued.

To illustrate the nature of satisficing, consider how you select a job. You may have several offers. One is from a chemical company that wants an industrial sales representative; the position pays a high salary but requires a great deal of traveling. Another offer comes from a national company in the computer hardware industry. This job offers less money and requires little travel, although the company expects you to relocate every two or three years. Your third offer is from the local heart association, which wants a line manager. The salary is low, but there are almost no travel demands or relocation requirements.

You can maximize your money with the chemical company and maximize your security with the heart association. Unfortunately, you cannot live comfortably on the heart association's salary, and your family strongly objects to excessive travel. Therefore, you accept the job with the computer company and satisfice the desire for money and security. You are not able to maximize either value.

As Figure 5.8 illustrates, decision makers first identify the satisfactory goal and then define and analyze the problem. Then they evaluate alternatives. However, rather than comparing *all* alternatives, they randomly select and evaluate one choice. It is recognized that even well-informed decision makers know only some of the choices available to them. Thus there are bounds to their rationality, or knowledge.

The sequence described by behavioral decision theorists is that the decision maker generates one alternative at a time and evaluates it with respect to the satisfactory goal. If the first alternative is equal to or greater than the satisficing goal, it is selected. If not, the decision maker generates and evaluates additional alternatives until a satisfactory outcome is encountered. The decision then is implemented, and the follow-up begins.

In this manner, behavioral theory attempts to describe human problem solving. Normative theory, on the other hand, provides a procedure for maximizing revenues or minimizing costs.

Figure 5.8   Behavioral Decision Theory

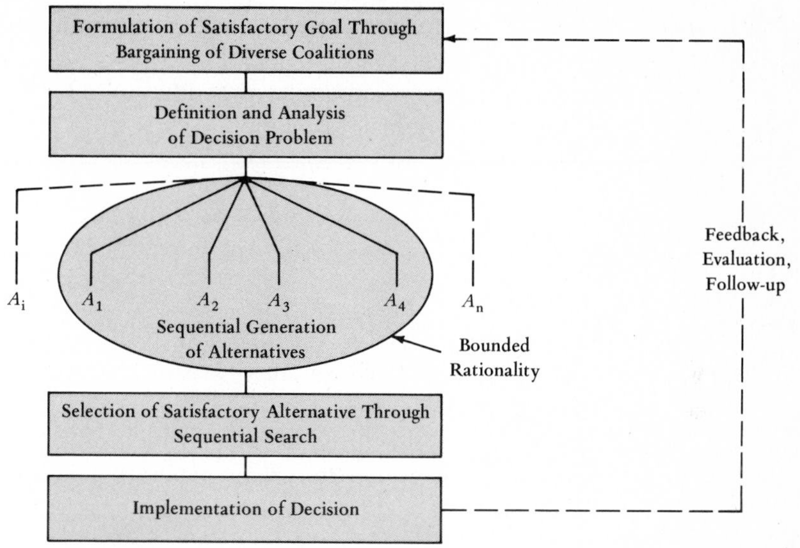

A Critique of Decision Theory

Normative theory is more familiar to students of organizational behavior than is behavioral theory. It requires that decision makers generate all relevant alternatives, estimate the probabilities of uncertainties, and evaluate precise outcomes of various courses of action.[28] In reality, however, numerous important factors—especially behavioral elements—cannot be precisely measured for practical purposes. Normative techniques are limited to large, fairly sophisticated organizations. Even in such organizations, however, subjective methods are frequently used.

Behavioral theory may be more suitable for short-term, recurring problems than for strategic decisions.[29] Cyert and March, however, have shown impressive results, based on the assumptions of descriptive theory, in simulating decisions concerning sales estimates, output levels, and pricing decisions in a large retail store.[30] Other studies also have confirmed the validity of the assumption on which the descriptive argument is based.[31]

Proposition *5.7*	Normative theory and behavioral decision theory are relevant to an understanding of organizational behavior. The former theory does not provide an accurate description of human problem solving, but it prescribes procedures leading to maximizing behavior. The latter theory does not prescribe procedures; rather, it provides insights into human decision making.

What Managers Need to Know About Cognitive Processes

Perception is the filter through which employees sense the world around them. When the manager does something as familiar as investigating an accident he or she must be sure not to overlook important facts. Or, when evaluating an employee's performance, managers must consider only those issues relevant to performance. It is equally important that we do not needlessly close our evaluation because we think we know all the facts.

Since so much attention is given to operant conditioning and behavior modification, it is essential that managers familiarize themselves with learning theory so that they can use modern motivational approaches. Learning, for example, is a key concept in understanding motivation.

And what about problem solving? Almost every minute of every working day managers are solving problems. Much time is spent collecting information, analyzing data, and choosing among alternative courses of action.

Managers must also learn to cope with stress. A great deal of tension is caused by cognitive dissonance resulting from the choices they make. When a decision is made to fire an employee, the anxiety may continue for weeks or months. To the extent that this anxiety encourages managers to seriously calculate such decisions, the dissonance is good. To the extent it needlessly increases tension, it is not good. When we recognize the reality of dissonance, we can deal with it more effectively.

Summary

This chapter has examined three basic cognitive processes—perception, learning, and problem solving—and has illustrated their importance in organizational behavior. We began by looking at perception, which has three main characteristics. First, it is a selective activity. People cannot perceive all the stimuli confronting them in the environment. Thus managerial actions usually occur on the basis of imperfect or incomplete information. The stimuli selected are those that reinforce the existing attitudes of the perceiver. Second, perception is characterized by closure. Even though people selectively screen environmental stimuli, they fill in gaps and complete the perceptual picture as though they had complete information. Third, perception takes place within a context. The context helps people to orient themselves to reality. In practical terms, perception is important to management because it determines the quantity and quality of information on which decisions are made.

Learning was discussed as a cognitive process. A distinction was made between classical and operant conditioning. In classical conditioning, a stimulus is presented prior to or simultaneously with a response. In operant, or instrumental, conditioning a response occurs in anticipation of some consequence. Some of the most important recent implications of learning theory for management are in the area of motivation.

We also looked at problem solving. Few situations present individuals with one, and only one, course of action. Usually, we must choose among alternatives to solve problems. Two approaches to decision making were analyzed. Normative decision theory tells us how decisions ought to be made if we want to maximize behavior. Behavioral decision theory describes how decisions are actually made and does not prescribe normative guidelines.

Questions for Discussion

1. What is meant by *stereotyping?* How does perception influence this process? Give some examples of how stereotyping can lead to results that are dysfunctional from the managerial perspective.

2. Compare and contrast normative and behavioral decision theory with regard to their goals and assumptions. Which do you think is more important for practicing managers? Why?

3. What is the law of effect? Is it associated with classical or operant conditioning? Give at least one example of the law as it can be observed in organizations.

4. What is your personal reaction to ESP? Assuming that someone could acquire such abilities, what type of ESP do you think would be most useful to managers? Explain your response.

5. Briefly explain what is meant by satisficing behavior, bounded rationality, and sequential search. Are these concepts found in normative or behavioral decision theory? How are they related to one another?

Exercise: Academic Stereotypes

At some time during academic study, every student must make decisions. One of the most familiar decisions is the choice of a major field of study. Some students research job opportunities, salary levels, and so on extensively. Others engage in very little information search and simply gravitate to a certain major.

Regardless of the specific approach, a student often considers several fields of study and, in one way or another, evaluates the advantages and disadvantages of each. Most students conduct this evaluation on the basis of their impressions of the fields.

Below are listed ten career options. Look over the list carefully.

1. Accounting
2. Business administration
3. Education
4. Engineering
5. Forestry
6. Geology
7. Law
8. Medicine
9. Political science
10. Psychology

After you have read the list, write a few ideas that come to mind about each area. Use adjectives such as *hard, easy, rewarding, unrewarding.* When your list of initial impressions (evaluations) is complete, try to state seriously and objectively why you have the ideas you do about each field.

Do you have stereotyped images of the areas? What aspects of each do you selectively perceive? Have you made the decision not to pursue certain fields on the basis of substantial knowledge, or have you decided on the basis of emotion and limited information?

Finally, rank ten areas of study according to how prestigious you consider them to be. What is the basis of your ranking? What problems can academic stereotypes create within a college or university?

Case: Management Practice and Management Theory

Students who study management and organizations often are surprised to find that much of the theory they learned in college is not used in business. Business people are equally amazed to discover that little of the art they practice can be found in a management program.

The fact is that managers and management researchers rarely talk to one another or read the same literature. Managers seem to stereotype researchers as being too theoretical, and researchers view managers as hopelessly practical.

Attempts have been made to improve communication between managers and researchers, but few have proved successful. Perhaps the greatest problem is an inability to understand how these two important groups can completely misunderstand each other.

Think carefully about our discussion of perception. Think also about the current problems that exist between managers and researchers. Then answer the following questions.

1. List several of the selectively perceived characteristics you think each group perceives with regard to the other. How do you think selective perception contributes to this problem?
2. What factors do you think encourage closure between managers and researchers, making effective interaction difficult?
3. How does context contribute to this problem? Be as specific as possible.

Suggested Readings

"At Emery Air Freight: Positive Reinforcement Boosts Performance." *Organizational Dynamics* (Winter 1973): 41–50.

Deci, E. L. "Paying People Doesn't Always Work the Way You Expect It To." *Human Resource Management* 12 (1973): 28–32.

Dermer, J. D. "Cognitive Characteristics and the Perceived Importance of Information." *Accounting Review* 48 (1973): 511–519.

Duncan, W. J. *Decision Making and Social Issues.* Hinsdale, Ill.: Dryden Press, 1972.

Everett, D. B., S. C. Hayward, and A. W. Meyers. "The Effects of a Token Reinforcement Procedure on Bus Ridership." *Journal of Applied Behavior Analysis* 7 (1974): 1–9.

Goodall, K. A. "Shapers at Work." *Psychology Today* 6 (November 1972): 53–62, 132–138.

Gray, F., P. Graubard, and H. Rosenberg. "Little Brother Is Changing You." *Psychology Today* 7 (1974): 42–46.

Luthans, F., and R. Kreitner. *Organizational Behavior Modification.* Glenview, Ill.: Scott, Foresman, 1975.

Manis, M. *An Introduction to Cognitive Psychology.* Belmont, Calif.: Wadsworth, 1971.

Ritchie, J. R. "An Exploratory Analysis of the Nature and Extent of Individual Differences in Perception." *Journal of Marketing Research* 11 (1974): 41–49.

Motivating Human Performance

> Motivation concerns the mainspring by which people are activated to do what they do. It is the key to understanding and directing others.
>
> Dalton E. McFarland,
> *Managerial Achievement*

The story is told that Thomas Watson of IBM once asked a woman on one of his assembly lines what she disliked most about her job. "Doing the same thing over and over again," she replied. Her comment led to many changes at IBM. Specifically, IBM began to look seriously at how jobs could be made less routine.

Routine and repetition have become a serious problem in modern manufacturing plants. Although repeated procedures can lead to efficiency and lower production costs, they are also boring and tiresome.

In the 1960s, Volvo, the Swedish car and truck producer, recognized the problems of workers on its automobile assembly lines and tried to do something about them. The company's goal was to improve the image of the auto industry, thereby attracting employees and keeping them. Too often, workers grew tired of their jobs and left them. To end this pattern, Volvo redesigned its jobs. Instead of assigning workers to a standard assembly line, the company set up teams of fifteen to twenty-nine workers to complete all the work on a particular function, such as the electrical system or wheels and brakes. Under this plan, up to six cars would be kept in the work area at one time, and workers could decide how and when to do their various tasks.

Volvo also made other changes to reduce boredom and to increase workers' control over production. As a result, employee morale and job satisfaction improved. Even production efficiency improved. Volvo took an unusual approach to motivate employees. This chapter examines some of the factors that the company had to consider and control.

Before we begin this discussion, think of your own needs and desires concerning a career. Perhaps you have resisted a career as an accountant or a researcher because the work seems too routine. Or maybe you dislike the idea of selling because you want to use tangible skills. Every employee is unique and requires individual treatment. This basic principle of motivation is the focus of our discussion. We will begin by defining and analyzing motivation and the relationship between job satisfaction and performance. Then we will explore some important theories of motivation.

A Definition of Motivation

To understand motivation, we must understand human behavior in general. This is why we have examined attitudes, needs, perception, learning, and problem solving. Everyone seems to agree that all these factors influence motivation. In general, *motivation* is concerned with how behavior is activated, maintained, directed, and stopped.[1] From a managerial perspective, motivation refers to any conscious attempt to influence behavior toward the accomplishment of organizational goals.

The process of motivation is illustrated in Figure 6.1. It begins with the stimuli initiated by a manager or by anyone wishing to activate behavior. The stimuli then are perceived by an individual. As we saw in Chapter 5, perception is affected by many factors, such as attitudes, personality, past experiences, and future expectations. Once the stimuli are perceived, they are interpreted according to the unique needs of the individual, and an information search is initiated. A series of possible actions is generated and evaluated, and finally a choice is made through problem solving. The individual then evaluates this choice on the basis of intended results.

Figure 6.1 A General View of Motivation

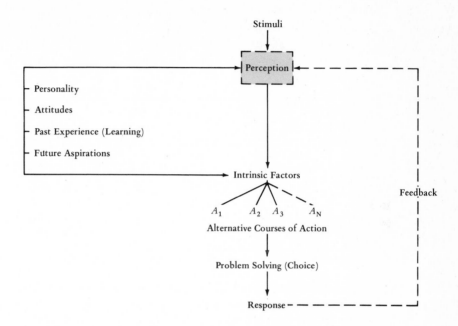

The personal nature of motivation should be clear. Throughout the process, the individual's uniqueness is important. Some people, because of past experiences and future hopes, want money. Others seek fame, security, or countless other objectives. For example, a young person from a disadvantaged background may wish to earn a high enough salary on the first job to be free from financial worry—a luxury never before available. Someone who comes from a wealthy family may not understand what financial stress is all about. This person might seek an opportunity for self-expression and freedom, regardless of the pay. Obviously, these two people have different needs, and they will be motivated differently.

Job Satisfaction and Motivation

Much early research on motivation focused on the relationship between job satisfaction and performance. In fact, this concern was so widespread that early human relations theory and practice can be seen as an attempt to increase output through the satisfaction of human needs.[2] Because of this interest in the relationship between job satisfaction and performance, much research sought to answer the question: Are the happiest workers the most productive workers? In other words, does job satisfaction lead to higher performance?

In a technical sense, the research does not firmly answer this question. Some studies found a weak relationship between job satisfaction and performance, whereas others showed little relationship at all.[3] There simply is no solid evidence to prove or disprove the relationship. We can illustrate the problems involved in such research with some examples.

Three Cases

The Happy Jogger Tony Visconti jogs about twenty-five miles a week. He really dislikes leaving work, dressing for the run, taking a shower, and returning to work. Nevertheless, some almost magical force keeps Tony on his running schedule. When his workout is over, he feels wonderful. He notices that there is little relationship between how well he runs and how he feels on any given day. Sometimes, when he is satisfied with his progress, he lets up and his time drops. But when Tony gets dissatisfied, he tries harder and improves his performance.

The Bitter Recruit Roger Peters joined the army but is not happy. Basic training is everything he was told—and more. Early wake-up, exercise, field maneuvers, kitchen duty, and numerous tasks are the order of the day. In spite of his dissatisfaction, Roger is an honor recruit and is at the top of his unit. Why? He is scared. The penalty for not working hard is to be "sent back"—having to spend extra weeks in basic training. Right now Private Peters wants only to get out, and so he works hard. In fact, he works so hard that he is almost exhausted. Even so, Roger is far from being happy or satisfied.

The Uncertain Installer Sarah Stein works for the telephone company as an installer. Sometimes she is highly satisfied with her job. The pay is good, and so are the benefits. Some days Sarah works hard. On other days she thinks about her supervisor and how demanding and unfair he is. She also thinks about the "crazy" company policies, which, she feels, stack the deck against female employees. On these days, Sarah does not produce very much. In fact, she hardly works at all.

What a strange series of cases! Tony Visconti, the jogger, seems to be satisfied because he is a good runner, but he does not run better when he is satisfied. Private Peters works hard, but only because he wants to end his basic training. Sarah Stein, as many would expect, does seem to work better when she is satisfied and to work less when she is not. But there certainly is no steady relationship between her job satisfaction and performance.

No wonder people are confused about whether or not satisfaction motivates performance. We certainly cannot dismiss the issue.[4] We will keep it in mind as we examine the main theories of motivation.

Selected Theories of Motivation

A number of motivation theories are supported by managers and researchers. Because there are so many theories, we will review only the more popular ones. Our discussion will divide motivation theories into two groups: instrumental theories focus on a person's goals; content theories focus on a person's needs.

Instrumental Theories of Motivation

We have already discussed instrumental learning in Chapter 5. As summarized in Figure 5.4, this learning occurs when a person acts because he or she thinks the act will assist in achieving a certain outcome. For example, you take a course in organizational behavior because, among other things, the course is a means to a degree. It is "instrumental" in your receiving a degree.

We will discuss three motivation theories that are based on *instrumentality*, the idea that a person behaves in a certain way to

Figure 6.2 An Illustration of Exchange Theory

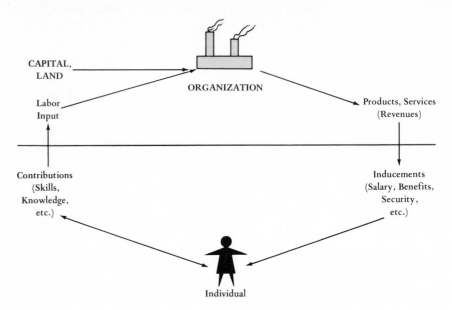

acquire some desired outcome. The theories we will examine are exchange theory, expectancy theory, and operant conditioning.

Exchange Theory   This theory is very simple in some ways, yet it can be used to describe much of our behavior. The basic ideas of exchange theory are often referred to as the Barnard-Simon model of organizational equilibrium.[5]

In many ways, exchange theory is like an economic exchange. People make contributions to an organization with their skills and knowledge. These contributions are combined with other resources (such as land and capital) to produce the goods and services that result in revenues. The revenues are used to provide the inducements (such as salary, paid vacations, and pensions) needed to convince us to make contributions.

According to exchange theory, we contribute to an organization as long as we value its inducements more than we value our leisure and freedom. Indeed, our contributions provide the revenue that, in turn, determines the organization's ability to offer inducements. As shown in Figure 6.2, exchange theory views motivation as an economic exchange. We contribute as long as the inducements are great enough to provide an incentive. But the inducements can be sufficient only if our contributions help generate revenues and other resources.

A brief example will illustrate this economic exchange. Ray Chung is looking for a job and has applied to Fremont Industries for a position as consumer sales representative. The company is examining Ray's skills and past record in sales. At the same time, Ray is looking at the salary and benefits offered by Fremont. Skills and knowledge are the contributions Ray can make to the organization. Fremont will take these contributions (in the form of sales) and convert them into revenues and profits that will be used to pay for the inducements needed to acquire Ray's contributions to the Fremont organization.

Theoretically, Ray Chung will make his contributions as long as he values Fremont's inducements more than he values the contributions he must make. In the same way, Fremont will offer inducements as long as it values Ray's contributions more than the benefits it must offer. Exchange theory thus emerges as a very general description of human motivation. Unfortunately, the description is too general to be of much practical value. It describes behavior, but it provides almost no guidelines for managers to use in improving performance.

Expectancy Theory   Like exchange theory, expectancy theory is considered instrumental because it argues that people choose a course of action based on expected outcomes. Expectancy theory, however, cannot be explained adequately without first defining the following terms.

1. *Expectancy.* This involves a person's perception of the probability that a specific act will result in a specific outcome. Like any probability, it can assume a value of from 0 to 1 ($0 \leq P \leq 1$). For example, how certain can you be that studying for an examination will result in a higher grade?
2. *Valence.* This involves the strength of an individual's desire for a

Figure 6.3 Basic Logic of Expectancy Theory

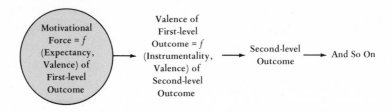

specific outcome. In other words, how important to you is the higher grade?

3. *Instrumentality.* A valence has a value because a certain outcome is considered instrumental in obtaining one or more other outcomes. A student's desire for a high grade may have great importance (valence) because the grade is seen as instrumental in obtaining a desired job.

4. *Outcomes.* Outcomes are the results of particular actions. A first-order outcome such as a high grade may encourage higher performance levels because the grade can be used to acquire a second-order outcome such as a desirable job.[6]

Figure 6.3 illustrates how expectancy theory views the motivational process. The circle at the left of the figure may be viewed as the motivational force, such as a salesperson's motivation to close an important deal. The strength of this force is a function of both expectancy and valence. The salesperson's motivation, therefore, is related to the individual's perception of the likelihood that closing the deal will result in a high commission. If the salesperson knows that he or she will receive a commission, the expectancy of a return from the sale is 1 ($P = 1.0$). The valence, on the other hand, is related to how important the return (money, or the first-order outcome) is to the salesperson. This return, in turn, is a function of how instrumental the first-order outcome (money) is in acquiring the second-order outcome (perhaps membership in an exclusive sales club) and the importance of that outcome. The same process can be applied to additional outcomes.[7]

Figure 6.4   An Expanded View of Expectancy Theory

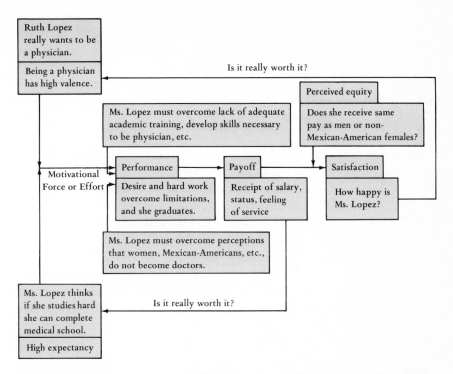

Source: Adapted from Lyman Porter and Edward Lawler III, *Managerial Attitudes and Performance* (Homewood, Ill.: Richard D. Irwin, 1968), p. 17. © 1968 by Richard D. Irwin, Inc.

The basic expectancy model shown in Figure 6.3 has been expanded to provide more information. For example, some have expanded the theory to suggest an unusual view of the relationship between satisfaction and performance. Porter and Lawler use the argument illustrated in Figure 6.4 to conclude that, in reality, it is performance that leads to job satisfaction (rather than the other way around).

In Figure 6.4, we begin again at the left, where we see that Ruth Lopez wants to become a doctor. This desire is very important; it has a high valence. Ruth has a high expectancy or belief that if she works hard she can complete her medical degree. Therefore, she has a strong motivation. However, Ruth must face certain realities that could influence her performance. First, she is a woman and has felt many pressures of discrimination and stereotyping that make her wonder whether women really can become doctors. Second, she is a Mexican-American and has a somewhat disadvantaged background especially in education. Her basic skills and abilities are less well developed than those of many individuals from better backgrounds.

Regardless of these limitations, Ruth does become a doctor and begins to receive the status and pay of her new position. Whether or not she is satisfied will depend on whether she finds the rewards are fair, relative to the rewards of other physicians.[8] If Ruth is not given the rewards other doctors receive (because of her sex, national origin, or any other reason), her satisfaction will be low. If she is rewarded fairly she will be satisfied and will value the additional outcomes resulting from her work. In this way, some expectancy theorists argue, it is performance that leads to satisfaction through the perception of fair rewards. Notice that this is different from exchange theory, in which satisfaction leads to performance.

The applications of this distinction are significant. Most important is the emphasis placed on rewards and on the manager's responsibility for developing and implementing incentive programs that employees will perceive as fair. In this manner, expectancy theory and the equity formulation provide a unique dimension to motivation theory.

Operant Conditioning   In recent years, a new interest has developed in learning theories as applied to motivation. By far the most popular is the theory of operant conditioning popularized by B. F. Skinner (see Chapter 5).[9] Again, we must introduce some basic terms. Environmental consequences, the effects of environmental consequences, and reinforcement schedules are illustrated in Figure 6.5.[10]

Environmental consequences are the results of behavior. Positive reinforcers increase the frequency of a response. (For example, a wage incentive given for increased performance falls into this category.) Negative reinforcers, when absent, increase the frequency of a response. (Punishment is an example of a negative reinforcer.) Fi-

Figure 6.5 Elements of Operant Conditioning

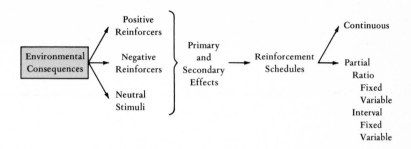

nally, to cover all possible cases, neutral stimuli have no effect on the frequency of response.

Positive and negative reinforcers may have primary or secondary effects. Primary effects do not depend on past experience. For example, a person receives a burned finger (primary effect) when he or she touches a hot stove regardless of whether that person touched a stove before. Secondary effects do depend on past experience. Thus the total effects of a new retirement program are likely to be associated with one's previous experience with such plans. In other words, secondary effects are learned.

Perhaps the most important element from a motivational viewpoint is the *schedule of reinforcement:* how often and how regular the reinforcement is. Reinforcement may be continuous, as when certain behavior is always followed by a specific result. For example, an automobile salesperson who works on a commission receives $125 each and every time he or she sells an automobile. Schematically, continuous reinforcement appears as follows:

$$B{-}C, B{-}C, B{-}C, B{-}C$$

B signifies the behavior (a sale), and *C* represents the consequence ($125 commission).

Reinforcement also may be partial, in that the consequence may not follow every time one behaves in a certain way. Partial reinforcement may be applied on a ratio or interval basis, and these may be broken down further into categories of fixed and variable. A fixed-ratio partial-reinforcement schedule appears as follows:

$$B, B, B{-}C, B, B, B{-}C, B, B, B{-}C$$

In this case, the consequence is experienced every third time the behavior is repeated. Such reinforcement, for example, would be experienced by a freelance editor who is paid after editing is completed on every three chapters of a book. A fixed-interval schedule is basically the same, except that reinforcement is received at predictable intervals of time. For example, a wage earner may become eligible for a merit wage increase at three-month intervals.

The variable-ratio partial-reinforcement schedule appears as follows:

$$B-C, B, B, B-C, B, B, B, B, B-C, B, B-C$$

In this case, the consequence comes randomly after a series of behaviors; it cannot be predicted. The payoff of a slot machine follows this pattern. A person may spend a lot of money or only a quarter before a "hit" occurs. The variable interval once again relates to time, with reinforcement coming randomly over time. In this case, one cannot predict the intervals between behavior and a reward.

One can, however, predict the type of performance most likely to occur under these various reinforcement schedules. Continuous reinforcement most likely results in slow, steady performance. The goal is to make it through the week, or to the next pay period, so that wages will be received. The fixed-ratio partial-reinforcement schedule probably encourages increased performance rates, since the objective is to get to the critical or last aspect of the job, after which rewards are received as soon as possible. Variable-ratio and interval schedules probably have similar results, since no one knows exactly when a reward will be received. The fixed-interval pattern most likely results in performance similar to that resulting from continuous reinforcement.

One organization that has made use of operant conditioning in a practical sense is Emery Air Freight, which developed a system of positive reinforcement. In its customer service department, performance increased from 30 to 95 percent of standard in a single day, and it retained this level for several years.[11]

Proposition 6.1

> Operant conditioning offers a simple and potentially powerful theory of motivation. It does not, however, provide the perfect answer, in that it tends to view human behavior as simply as it views the behavior of experimental animals.

Operant Conditioning and Behavior Modification. Much of to-day's emphasis on operant conditioning and motivation revolves around behavior modification. Although this topic is complex, we can deal with the most important issues by answering three questions: What is behavior modification? What does it do? Why are many people concerned about it?

First, behavior modification is an element of learning theory because of the importance it places on the relationship between changes in the environment and changes in behavior. Second, it is behavioristic in that it focuses on changes in observable behavior.

To use a given program of behavior modification, a manager must determine certain things. First, the behavior to be changed must be identified. (The frequency of what response is to be decreased or increased?) Next, the current environmental factors supporting the response must be specified. Finally, the environmental changes that must be made to alter behavior must be identified.[12]

We can answer the question "What can behavior modification do?" by illustrating some practical management situations. Some writers in psychology and management are beginning to view operant learning as an effective means of motivation, rather than relying on unproven assumptions about human needs and hopes.[13]

Let us assume that a worker produces at a very high rate in a high-performing group. Common sense tells us that the employee has strong affiliation needs and is seeking acceptance by fellow workers. This may be true. However, the same response could be explained by environmental factors without considering all possible explanations. If an employee is not working at a satisfactory rate, the poor performance is the object of change. The managerial task is to identify both the environmental factors that reinforce the poor performance and the substitution of factors that will change behavior. Then the environment must be changed systematically so that the desired behavior is reinforced positively. In this way, behavior modification is accomplished.

Why the present-day concern about the subject? Managers are obviously interested in behavior modification because it promises to provide a less mystical way of dealing with performance problems. They can devote more time to observable behavior and do not have to guess about need structures, motivating factors, and so on.

Some behavioral and management scientists, although recognizing the potential of this approach, have certain fears about its widespread use. The fears relate to questions about whether or not behavior modification violates people's rights. This is an important philosophical question, but not within the scope of this book. However, we can raise other questions that we can attempt to answer here.

First: Who is going to specify the behavior that should be changed? For example, what if a company decides that its managers should spend more time at home working on organizational problems, and it develops a behavior modification program to accomplish this end?

Second: When behavior is changed, is the person the same, or has the human being been altered in the process? By defining human behavior in such a way as to eliminate the individuality of needs, do we make the person appear less unique? How is it possible to violate an individual who possesses no individuality?[14]

These questions, of course, are not raised only by operant conditioning. All approaches to motivation attempt to influence and alter behavior. But behavior modification is directed so clearly toward observable results that many people fear that the individuality of human behavior will be violated, ignored, or simply assumed away in the quest to accomplish goals.

Implications of Instrumental Theories   The instrumental theories discussed in this section relate to the logical (and at times illogical) nature of human choice. To people who insist on observable proof, various aspects of these theories—such as valences and expectancies—are difficult to measure and accept.[15] In spite of these problems, some ambitious attempts have been made to use expectancy concepts in predicting such things as occupational choice.[16] Generally, expectancy theory seems to be a good predictor of satisfaction and performance.

The implications for areas such as salary administration seem significant. If managers are to increase performance (the basic motivational problem), they must increase the perceived relationships between effort and the satisfaction of needs. They may bring salaries into a direct relationship with performance and make it obvious, through some appropriate means like publishing salary scales, that effort does lead to a reward.[17] Moreover, these concepts suggest more strongly than other popular motivational theories that monetary rewards may be very important as a motivating factor.

Finally, expectancy theory puts forth an interesting causal relationship between job satisfaction and performance. The supporters of expectancy theory often propose that instead of satisfaction leading to improved performance, the reverse is true. Performance leads to satisfaction through the operation of fair rewards.

<table>
<tr><td>Proposition 6.2</td><td>Instrumental theories of motivation are general and describe behavior in terms of rational choice. These theories, though based on acceptable assumptions, are difficult to test. They are valuable, however, because they raise questions about the link between job satisfaction and performance.</td></tr>
</table>

Content Theories of Motivation

Content theories focus primarily on the motives or needs that are important in motivating someone. We will examine two content theories: Frederick Herzberg's two-factor theory and David McClelland's theory of achievement motivation. Another important content theory, proposed by Maslow, was discussed in Chapter 4.

Herzberg's Two-Factor Theory Herzberg began his work by surveying motivational research as it existed in the mid-1950s. His main conclusions were that motivation theory was in a state of confusion and that attempts to resolve the problems were, at best, incomplete. According to Herzberg, some research dealt with the factors influencing job attitudes: What factors cause employees' attitudes about their jobs to be favorable or unfavorable? Other research looked at the effects of attitudes on performance: Are satisfied employees more productive than dissatisfied ones? Herzberg found that an approach was needed to deal with the entire cycle of factors, attitudes, and effects.[18]

To examine the potential of this new approach, Herzberg selected a small sample of accountants and engineers for analysis. These research subjects were asked to describe incidents in which they felt extremely satisfied or dissatisfied with their jobs and also to describe how long these feelings lasted.

From this information, Herzberg concluded that the factors leading to job satisfaction when present were not the same factors that, when absent, led to dissatisfaction. The reverse is also true. Simply stated, this means that job satisfaction and dissatisfaction are not opposite attitudes. Instead, the opposite of job satisfaction is *no* job satisfaction, and the opposite of job dissatisfaction is *no* dissatisfaction.

If this limited study had ended the research, we would question the validity of the theory. Fortunately, other studies have been conducted in a variety of environments and through the participation of a number of work groups ranging from unskilled to highly professional employees. Such studies have generally supported Herzberg's findings.

The two-factor theory proposes that there are certain factors in the job environment known as *hygiene factors.* When these are not present, they cause a person to be dissatisfied. These same factors, however, will not result in satisfaction and thus do not increase performance when they are present. Such hygiene factors are listed on the left in Table 6.1. They include such things as company policy and administration, supervision, relationships with supervisors and peers, and working conditions.[19]

Other factors, known as *motivators,* do not cause dissatisfaction when they are absent, but they are capable of providing satisfaction when they are present. Such factors include opportunities for achievement and recognition, the work itself, responsibility, advancement, and personal growth (see Table 6.1).

To illustrate these ideas, consider John Bentley, a railroad inspector. He works in a clean, cool shop that is comfortable year round. The job is not hard, but it is not very exciting. John's salary is good, and his benefits are far better than most of his neighbors'. John Bentley is not *un*happy with his job or his life. Nor is he very excited about them.

Have you ever felt like John? Just because you are not happy does not mean you are sad! According to Herzberg, you may be at a point of no satisfaction. You do your job, but no better than the task requires. In other words, you are not motivated to do your best.

Frame 6.1 shows how numerous factors can affect satisfaction. In this case, participation is a critical factor in ensuring satisfaction.

The basic argument of two-factor theory is that a worker doing a routine job in pleasant working conditions will be neither dissatisfied nor motivated to higher levels of performance. The same worker doing a routine job in unpleasant surroundings may be dissatisfied.

Table 6.1 The Two-Factor Theory of Motivation

Hygiene Factors		Motivation Factors	
Factor	*Example*	*Factor*	*Example*
Company policy and administration	Decisions to promote outsiders to high-level executive positions, reserved parking spaces for selected employees, and vacation pay rules.	Achievement	An opportunity to feel something important is being accomplished.
Supervision	Relative freedom allowed for participation by rank and file employees.	Recognition	Combat medals in the armed services, a pat on the back from a supervisor, one's name on bulletin board indicating outstanding performance.
Relationship with supervisor	Degree of respect a particular person has for his/her supervisor. May be a personal relationship.	Work itself	How enjoyable and rewarding is the actual task?
Working conditions	Piped in music, air-conditioned office, lighting, and noise.	Responsibility	Delegation of authority to allow employees control over and accountability for their jobs.
		Advancement	Promotion up the ladder of success.
		Growth	Professional development and maturity.

Note: Salary and relationship with peers were noted both as hygiene factors and as motivators.

Source: Adapted from Frederick Herzberg, "One More Time: How Do You Motivate Employees?" *Harvard Business Review,* January–February 1968.

Frame 6.1

Codetermination: Europe's Answer to Participation

Do employees really need control over their own destiny? Apparently, many desire some control over their job—if what is happening in Europe is any indication.

Codetermination is designed to provide workers a right to sit on the board of directors. Austria, France, Germany, Norway, Sweden, and other countries have highly developed codetermination arrangements.

In some countries—such as Sweden, France, and Germany—laws require worker participation. The workers are given special rights to be involved in decisions centering on hiring and promotion, use of company facilities, and organizational changes such as plant closings.

West Germany in many ways has the most advanced codetermination laws. It is also the country most likely to influence American corporations, because of the many United States business investments in Germany. However, Thomas Murphy of General Motors has been quoted as having little concern over the growth of codetermination.

Even though the American Chamber of Commerce has attempted to gain exemptions for American corporations, it seems that firms doing business in Germany will have to live with codetermination laws. German workers seem determined to get and keep participation in decisions influencing their economic well-being. Codetermination is a legal response to employee needs. Who knows what other systems will develop in the future as the needs and hopes of employees, managers, and owners continue to change?

The hygiene factors are the necessary conditions for motivation. If they are not present, dissatisfaction will result. But if they are present, employees are not necessarily motivated. Only when the hygiene factors are present with motivators will high levels of performance result.

In examining this research, one thing becomes clear: the elements classified as hygiene factors are all external to, or extrinsic to, the job. In other words, they relate to the environment within which work takes place. In contrast, all the motivators are intrinsic to the work being done. The secret, therefore, is to design and develop meaningful jobs, or to enrich jobs.

Implications of the Two-Factor Theory   Job enrichment, including feedback about performance, is a practical means of providing employees with independence in accomplishing a complete task. It is an attempt to design tasks in a way that ensures the presence of motivators.[20] Job enrichment attempts to remove controls while still making individuals accountable, to provide each person with a logical work unit, and to provide frequent feedback on performance directly to the person responsible for the job.

Although several well-known and successful companies such as AT&T, Maytag, and Motorola have enthusiastically adopted job enrichment, problems have been observed. At least one study has questioned the basic foundation of the two-factor theory by showing that intrinsic job factors predict both satisfaction and dissatisfaction. In other words, some data suggest that these elements may, indeed, be opposite attitudes rather than separate factors.[21]

The two-factor theory has been criticized on other grounds as well. Some have suggested that it may depend on specific applications and people, and that it cannot be proved outside these instances. There are questions about whether the theory can be applied in every case. Job enrichment programs may be satisfying only to certain types of workers, such as managerial personnel. In fact, they may alienate specific classes of workers, such as urban blue-collar employees, who may not accept the middle-class values on which the programs are based (for instance, the idea that work should be satisfying).[22]

Another issue has to do with the questions asked in job enrichment studies. Herzberg and other researchers used open-ended questions that asked workers to relate job incidents or situations describing states of extreme satisfaction and dissatisfaction. This type of question may lend itself to a bias introduced by defensive behavior. For example, respondents with low esteem tend to ascribe satisfying experiences to themselves and their jobs. On the other hand, they tend to blame dissatisfying experiences on external, uncontrollable factors. Thus it can be argued that job enrichment programs are founded on defensive behavior. Satisfying experiences are thought

to result from intrinsic factors, whereas dissatisfying ones originate
—at least in the minds of respondents—in extrinsic factors.[23]

Proposition
6.3

> Research supports the argument that the factors leading to job
> satisfaction are distinct from those leading to job dissatisfaction.
> Some researchers, however, recommend caution in accepting this
> conclusion, since the same results could illustrate nothing more
> than defensive behavior on the part of respondents.

McClelland's Achievement Motivation   Work on achievement
motivation is closely identified with David McClelland, who refers to
the need for achievement with the symbol *n Ach* (see Chapter 4). In
this theory, all motives, such as the desire for achievement, are
learned. For this reason, a person's childhood is a critical time
in the development of motives. Numerous experiences during
childhood—such as the presence of demanding yet understanding
parents—can establish a person's pattern of expectations throughout
life.[24] A youngster who is encouraged to experiment with toys, for
example, can devise expectations about what a toy can do. The more
the child expects, the more expectations are increased, and the
greater the potential achievement.

We can relate some arguments of job enrichment to achievement
motivation. Perhaps the reason why Volvo had success with the
group assembly plan is that the job was made less routine. For employees with higher achievement motives, the increase in uncertainty
when the assembly line was dismantled could have provided an opportunity for achievement and increased motivation. Perhaps, too,
the problems of validating job enrichment experiments can be explained in terms of achievement motivation. We noted that white-
collar workers and blue-collar workers from rural backgrounds seem
to desire job enrichment more than do blue-collar workers from
urban backgrounds. This was explained by a middle-class value system that promotes the idea that work should be challenging. However, this value system itself is learned and could be the basis of a
need to achieve.

Achievement motivation is interesting to managers because organizations value decision makers who have high achievement needs.

McClelland even has developed courses to increase the decision-making abilities of managers.[25] Even so, achievement motivation has not received the attention that Herzberg's or Skinner's theories have. Perhaps the most obvious reason for this is that the achievement needs of an individual can be traced, to a great extent, to early childhood. Nevertheless, McClelland convincingly illustrates how the need to achieve can be increased even among adults.

Proposition 6.4

> Achievement motivation illustrates an attempt to explain behavior by focusing on a primary need. To the extent that achievement can be learned, this theory has potential for improving managerial performance.

What Managers Need to Know About Motivation

Asking what managers should know about motivation is like asking what a chef should know about cooking. Much of a manager's job from becoming a first-line supervisor until acquiring the top executive position involves motivation.

Because motivation is so important, almost every publication directed toward managers regularly carries discussions of motivation. Therefore, administrative personnel have to know how to evaluate all the theories and speculations evident in the subject.

Managers who only superficially understand motivation may become victims of fads and invalid theories. They may redesign jobs, for example, without creating the necessary environment or preconditions.

It is important that managers no longer chase intuitively logical but unproven relationships like the one between job satisfaction and performance. Just think how much time, energy, and resources have been devoted to improving job satisfaction on the premise that to do so will increase productivity. No such cause-and-effect relationship has been shown to exist.

For this reason, some managers and organizations have recently directed less attention to traditional motivation approaches and have experimented more with revised learning theory. Of particular contemporary importance are positive reinforcement programs based on instrumental learning theories.

Summary

Volvo experiments with group assembly of automobiles; IBM and AT&T enrich jobs in a variety of ways. Emery Air Freight applies the principles of positive reinforcement, and western Europe enacts codetermination laws. What is all this activity saying to managers?

More than anything else, these events underscore the fact that motivation remains an important issue in organizational behavior. Many questions remain unanswered, but the search for the best explanations continue. Given the present state of motivation theory, the best strategy for a manager is to become as familiar as possible with all theories available. There is something new and something true in all of them. The manager's problem is to choose carefully which new things are true and to decide which true things are really new. This, of course, is not an easy puzzle to solve. Even behavioral scientists who devote most of their time to studying motivational problems find the issue complex and frustrating.

Once the foundations of motivation theory and practice are understood, we can confront the more philosophical questions of how behavioral science should be used in a management context. We must deal immediately with questions concerning the ethics of behavior modification. Thoughtful people cannot avoid the issue—nor should they. Social pressures and legal issues will make these questions even more important as we seek ways to protect and enhance individual rights on and off the job.

Questions for Discussion

1. Do all forms of motivation involve manipulating human behavior toward predetermined ends? Explain.

2. If you answered yes to question 1, why do you think behavior modification has been singled out for ethical criticism? If you answered no, do you think only some approaches involve manipulation? What is the critical difference between manipulation and motivation?
3. Of what importance are reinforcement schedules in operant conditioning? Can negative reinforcement (punishment) be used as effectively as rewards? Explain.
4. Explain in everyday language what exchange theory says about motivation. Give some real-world examples.
5. Why do you think the theory of achievement motivation is important to managers? What do you think organizations value in a person who has a high need for achievement?

Case: Two Approaches to Motivation

Nancy Carlsberg and Harry Simpson are neighbors, and both are employed as supervisors in local organizations. Nancy is the tax assessor for the municipal government; Harry is a production manager at Grayville Foundry. Both are considered successful managers and display considerable pride in their jobs. The primary difference between the two jobs is that Nancy's employees are white-collar workers, whereas Harry's are blue-collar workers. The employees, however, possess similar skill levels.

During the past few years, Nancy has attended several management training and development programs. Recently, at an informal neighborhood party, Nancy was describing the success her office had experienced with a new motivational program. The story she told went as follows.

Work in the tax assessor's office, like most jobs, consists of elements people enjoy and of unrewarding, yet necessary, work. For example, the office employees generally dislike posting records and filing. On the other hand, they like the relatively less frequent opportunities to talk with people who come in to ask questions about taxes or to report a sale of property.

In the past, the person who talked with the public was selected by accident—whoever occupied the desk closest to the counter, whoever happened to be walking past the reception desk, and so forth. One night, in a class she was taking at the local university, Nancy heard the professor discuss the Premack principle. According to this idea, a more desirable task may reinforce less desirable tasks, provided the former depends on performance of the latter.

Nancy decided to give this principle a try. Over the next several weeks, she made it clear that only those employees who had performed best in posting and filing would interact with the public. Records would be kept, and each Friday an announcement would be made as to who would perform the receptionist's job for the following week.

Nancy was quick to admit that the system was not perfect, since, for example, a person could not perform the task for two consecutive weeks. However, there were fewer complaints and performance increased. And performance, after all, was her concern.

At this point, Harry interrupted the story with complete disbelief at what he was hearing. He has also attended classes at the university. To him, the real problem in the assessor's office was that the jobs, as he pictured them, were degrading. Why not redesign and enrich all the jobs so that everyone would be happy, rather than just the lucky person who happened to file and post faster than anyone else. Besides, Nancy is manipulating employees, not motivating them. As for himself, he would not treat his children or his employees in such a manipulative manner.

As with most arguments at neighborhood parties, sides were chosen and the debate continued. Nancy and Harry remained good friends, but they never again discussed motivational philosophy.

1. If you had been at the party, with whom would you have agreed? Why?
2. Could Nancy's approach really be based on principles of operant conditioning? Explain.
3. What do you think about Harry's job enrichment idea?

Case: Cork Manufacturing Company

Frank Harrison is the personnel assistant at Cork Manufacturing Company. He has been reading about work motivation and job satisfaction. Although he agrees with the basic arguments of job enrichment, he is confused by the fact that some people apparently do not desire more satisfying jobs. Since Frank believes that jobs become more enriched as a person moves up the ladder of success, he decided to conduct a survey to test his idea.

Frank constructed a questionnaire on which a score of 90 represented the highest possible level of satisfaction. A score of 18 indicated the least satisfaction and 54 was neutral, the midpoint between the two extremes. He gave the questionnaire to a sample of top, middle, and supervisory managers. The results are shown in Exhibit 6.1.

Frank is particularly interested in examining what effect organizational level has on job satisfaction. With this in mind, he started his analysis.

Exhibit 6.1 Responses to Survey Questionnaires

Top Management Scores	Middle Management Scores	Supervisory Management Scores
80	81	79
78	79	77
75	78	76
74	77	71
68	76	71
67	70	70
	64	69
	62	68
	61	66
	58	63
		61
		56
		51
		45

1. Was Frank's belief about job enrichment and success confirmed?
2. What do you think about the overall level of job satisfaction at Cork Manufacturing?
3. How would you explain the results of this survey? What general conclusions might you draw from these data?

Suggested Readings

Bjork, L. E. "An Experiment in Work Satisfaction." *Scientific American.* 232 (March 1975): 17–23.

Clary, T. C. "Motivation Through Positive Stroking." *Public Personnel Management 2* (1973): 113–117.

Green, C. N., and D. W. Organ. "An Evaluation of Causal Models Linking the Perceived Role with Job Satisfaction." *Administrative Science Quarterly* 18 (1973): 95–103.

Luthans, Fred, and Robert Ottemann. "Motivation vs. Learning Approaches to Organizational Behavior." *Business Horizons* 16 (December 1973): 53–62.

Mills, Ted. "Human Resources—Why the New Concern." *Harvard Business Review* 53 (March/April 1975): 120–134.

Moore, Lewis. "Motivation Through Positive Reinforcement." *Supervisory Management* 21 (October 1976): 2–3.

Reinharth, Leon, and M. A. Wahba. "Expectancy Theory as a Prime Factor of Work Motivation, Effort Expenditure, and Job Performance." *Academy of Management Journal* 18 (1975): 535–537.

Rosen, J., and J. L. Livingston. "An Expectancy Theory Approach to the Motivational Impacts of Budgets." *Accounting Review* 50 (1975): 677–685.

Schappe, R. H. "Twenty-two Arguments Against Job Enrichment." *Personnel Journal* 53 (1974): 116–123.

Staehle, J. C. "How to Motivate Others." *Administrative Management* 35 (May 1974): 57–58.

Groups in Organizations

INDIVIDUALS MOST OFTEN perform in groups. Culture, society, the family all contribute to what an individual is, yet behavior is directed toward and related to other people. For this reason, a great deal of organizational behavior is *interpersonal*; it occurs in the small group.

Interpersonal behavior can be of various kinds. Sometimes our interaction takes place to satisfy social needs. And since the work of an organization is broken down into smaller work groups, interpersonal behavior is also, at times, task oriented, or directed toward accomplishing organizational goals. Finally, interpersonal behavior is also political and is directed toward influencing others' behavior through bargaining and negotiation.

Part III examines individual interaction in groups from the social, task, and political perspectives. Of course, behavior can rarely be separated neatly into these three categories. On the other hand, for practical reasons we can look at elements of behavior that are chiefly social, task oriented, and political, thereby illustrating how they are important to organizational behavior as a whole. Overlapping circles are one good way to show the interrelated nature of these three types of small-group behavior. The figure at the top of the next page makes it clear that small-group behavior is interrelated yet essential in accomplishing our numerous individual and organizational goals.

Chapter 7 deals with selected aspects of social behavior. After defining the small group, we examine interpersonal communication in detail because of its importance in providing social links between and among group members. Other important social processes, including status structures, also are examined.

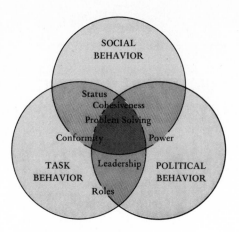

Work groups and task-oriented behavior are the subjects of Chapter 8. Group norms are examined because they are important in explaining normative (standard) behavior. Conformity and group problem solving also are discussed. Then we analyze role relationships and consider how ambiguity and conflict affect job satisfaction and stress.

Chapter 9, the final chapter in this part, deals with power and leadership in groups. The sources of power are reviewed, and examples of political behavior in organizations are presented. We will discuss leadership sources and styles. The chapter concludes by examining leadership effectiveness and modern developments in leadership theory and practice.

Another diagram, which appears complex but need not be, shows how interrelated social, task, and political behavior are in reality. Social factors like communication and status structures have great impact on work groups and political behavior. Similarly, task behavior is partly social, and it certainly influences performance and satisfaction—both directly and through political bargaining. Finally, political influences such as leadership also affect performance and satisfaction, which again relate to social and task behavior. In this way, the three kinds of interpersonal behavior that usually occur in small groups also influence each other within an organization.

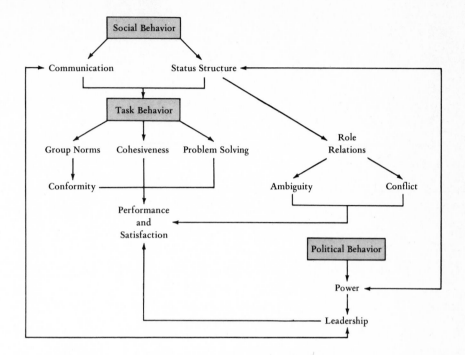

chapter 7

Social Behavior in Groups

Groups promote conformity as well as unwise foreign-policy decisions, riots, panics, and even create a tendency to leave waiters small tips in restaurants.

Christian J. Buys,
reported in *Psychology Today*

Imagine what you would have thought if, almost two centuries ago, you walked through a textile mill in Scotland and saw yellow, green, and red ribbons hanging on the machinery. Who would dream that the ribbons represented an effort by Robert Owen, the mill's owner, to increase production? Owen's approach revealed that he had a keen understanding of groups and the pressure they can exert on an individual employee's performance. In a deceptively simple plan, Owen tied yellow ribbons on the machines of workers who produced less than the factory average and green ribbons on the machines of workers who produced the average amount. Red ribbons were reserved for above-average producers. Within two months, everyone in the factory had a red ribbon.[1]

What can account for the effect of such a simple incentive? As this chapter will suggest, it was the social pressure of the group: each individual desired positive recognition from fellow workers. The employees were not trying to impress Mr. Owen, for the ribbon itself was worth little.

Groups obviously can influence the behavior of individuals. Have you ever received the highest grade on a test and covered your score so that classmates would not learn it was you who "set the curve"? This chapter will help explain why you acted as you did. We will examine the ways in which groups exert social influences on an individual's behavior. First, we will define the term *group*, and we will identify several types of groups. Then we will discuss some social processes that affect behavior, such as status relationships. As you read, relate these ideas to your own experiences in class, at work, and in social activities.

Groups in Organizations

Groups are found in all organizations. Committees, surgical teams, and school classes are examples of common, everyday groups. In general, a *group* is defined as two or more people who interact to accomplish a common goal(s); the interaction is lasting and displays at least some structure. More specifically, a group possesses the following four characteristics:

1. *Common motive(s) leading to group interaction.* Individual members of the group have at least one common goal. For example, a baseball team shares the goal of defeating the opposing team. An emergency medical squad works together to save an accident victim's life.
2. *Members who are affected differently by their interaction.* The interaction that occurs in a group affects its members in different ways. Thus a skilled surgeon may become calm during an operation, whereas an intern may become nervous.
3. *Group structure with different degrees of status.* Leaders and followers emerge in a group, although who is a leader and who a follower may change from one situation to another. Under routine conditions, the highest-ranking police officer is in charge of operations. However, under unusual circumstances, such as when a terrorist holds hostages, a lower-ranking head of a tactical squad may be given control.
4. *Standard norms and values.* Because a group has shared goals, certain expected patterns of behavior develop. In a college fraternity or sorority, for example, all members are expected to display friendship and concern for one another.[2]

In summary, members of a group are bound together by a common motive or goal. Each is influenced differently by the group's interaction, and a structure emerges that defines authority and status relationships. Finally, the group is bound together by common values and norms.

Types of Groups

We can classify organizational groups in many ways. For example, groups have been classified as formal or informal, as membership or reference, and by size.

Formal and Informal Groups   A *formal group* is created deliberately to accomplish specific goals. A work group in a foundry, a departmental faculty, and a group of switchboard operators are examples of formal groups. These groups are characterized by specialized roles, rigid norms, and sanctions designed to ensure conformity.[3]

An *informal group*, on the other hand, is more spontaneous, emotional, and flexible. It may arise within a formal structure and may be held together by such things as friendship, longevity, or some similar factors. Unlike formal groups, informal ones are ends in themselves; they exist only to satisfy the needs of their members. The members of a city council make up one formal group, but they may form social or informal subgroups within it.

Membership and Reference Groups   A *membership group* is one to which a person belongs but has no more than a minor relationship. All of us, for example, belong to the student body or faculty of a college or university. Thus the college or university is a membership group. We identify with it, but not always closely. Religious denominations and nations are other examples of membership groups.

Reference groups are more intimate. These are groups that we belong to, or hope to belong to; we allow them to influence our behavior. A high school sophomore may aspire to make a varsity team, for example, and will do whatever is needed to achieve that goal. For this reason, he or she may be greatly influenced by individuals who have already made the team.

Whether or not any particular group is a membership or a reference group to a specific person is highly personal. One person may feel that the nation to which he or she belongs is a membership group, because the association is not intense and the citizenship has little influence on the person's behavior. Another person may be influenced considerably by his or her citizenship. Therefore, we cannot classify groups without referring specifically to the individual involved.

Groups Classified by Size Another way to classify groups is according to size. The size of a group influences both how its members behave internally and how the group relates to other groups.

Dyads, or two-person groups, involve the simplest form of interpersonal behavior. In a dyad, such as a husband and wife with no children, we find an interdependence seldom found in other settings. Both members are equally responsible for the continuation of the relationship. Hence there is an emphasis on feelings and sentiments directed toward reducing conflict.[4]

From a managerial viewpoint, the dyad is unique because it has no identity apart from the two members it includes. It is not a true "organization," as are larger groupings.[5] When one member is replaced, a new dyad is created, not an extension of the old one.

Since a dyad is not an organization that maintains an identity greater than the individuals within it, dyads have not received much attention in the literature of management. One study, however, attempted to examine managerial dyads.[6] In this study, Greene examined 142 dyads in four industrial settings. He did this by asking a supervisor to select the highest-performing subordinate and another one whose performance was different. The researcher found that the accuracy of the subordinates' perceptions of the supervisor's expectations and the degree to which these expectations were met were related to the subordinates' degree of satisfaction and the supervisor's evaluation of the employees. From this study, we can infer that when supervisors communicate their evaluations to employees, the relationship between leader and follower is likely to improve. When employees are satisfied and receive frequent feedback about their performance, they better understand a supervisor's expectations. The result is improved group performance.

Another type of group is the *triad*, or three-person group. In a triad, each member can serve two functions—to bring the group to-

Figure 7.1 A Possible Structure of a Triad

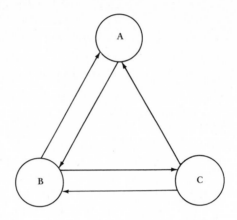

Note: In this variation of a triad, A relates directly to B, who relates directly to A and C. C relates directly to B and A. A does not relate to C.

gether or to push it apart. Usually, triads are less unified than two-person groups. In fact, two members of triads often are directly related, as are *A* and *B* in Figure 7.1, and only indirectly related to the third individual, *C*.[7] Because of this imbalance, jealousy can develop easily.

One kind of behavior is particularly characteristic of a three-person group. This is the development of *coalitions*, or associations of two against one. Coalitions are common within families, as when a father and son "gang up" against the mother when the son wants to, say, ride a motorcycle. Or the mother and son might form a coalition against the father, who wants his son to go to law school and take over the family law practice.

Familiar examples of coalitions can be seen in third-party politics involving two major parties and one minor, less powerful group. If neither major party can obtain a majority without the support of the weaker group, that third party often becomes disproportionately powerful and may receive competitive favors for its support. The same thing can occur in small groups such as triads.[8]

In triads, the way in which coalitions form and their durability are related to such factors as the relative power of the members and their objectives. We will look at three types of triads: the continuous, the episodic, and the terminal. We then can relate these to the coalitions that are likely to emerge in three-person groups.

A continuous triad is made up of permanently related members within a larger organization. A three-person work group is an example of a continuous triad, if the group is clearly subordinate to the larger organization. Because it is subordinate, the group is expected to be unified in pursuit of organizational goals—despite any other internal aims.

An episodic triad is also found in a larger organization, where coalitions are formed to secure power through interactions governed by formal rules. Legislative coalitions, for example, engage in political maneuvering. Usually, such episodic coalitions cease to exist after the goal is accomplished.

Terminal triads exist unwillingly. Each participant would prefer to be independent but agrees to an association to accomplish a goal. For example, three executives—none of whom has enough resources for a certain venture—may choose to pool their money, when each would prefer to remain independent. Such coalitions may arise for many practical reasons, but they cease to exist at the first opportunity.[9]

This discussion of group size has aimed to specify the importance of defining *group*. From the examples given, it is clear that dyads and triads are important for practical as well as theoretical reasons. This is especially true of triads, which are likely to involve coalitions. We will note the impact of coalitions at several points throughout our study.

Proposition 7.1

> Groups may be classified according to various characteristics. Formal groups are different from informal ones in their structure and durability. Membership groups and reference groups differ in their influence on members' behavior. Dyads and triads are important subgroups based on size.

Dyads and triads deserve our attention for another, perhaps equally important, reason. Dyads and triads behave differently than do groups of four or more persons. In fact, social psychologists have described the unique characteristics of dyads and triads extensively. Thus we must recognize the importance of these groups while clearly stating that most theories about small groups do not describe the behavior of dyads and triads.

In whatever type of group, individuals usually communicate with one another. Such interpersonal, or person-to-person, communication is one of the links that holds a group together. Communication may be a memorandum from the plant safety officer or written rules about absenteeism from the personnel department. Usually, however, most communication in a group is social. John talks with Allison about the local election for mayor; Jane and Pete discuss finding a parking place at work. Interpersonal communication is basic to social behavior in groups.

Person-to-Person Communication

Interpersonal communication has received much attention in organizational behavior. This is not surprising, since communication is a basic aspect of group behavior. We communicate all the time—but not always successfully. Consider the following incidents:

But Larry, I thought you were criticizing me when you said I was as tough as a union steward.

Excuse me, professor, but I didn't understand the word *ecosystem*. If you had said something like "environment," I could have answered the question.

I'm sorry, but I don't have a CB in my car. That's why I didn't hear your emergency call.

I can't hear over all that shop noise!

Such communication problems take place every day. We will examine them with the aid of Figure 7.2, which illustrates interpersonal communication.

In examining Figure 7.2, consider Bill Cosper's problem. Bill is trying to get his neighbor, Nancy Marshal, to keep her dog in her own yard. Bill decides to visit Nancy for a talk. He thus becomes the *source* of the message and Nancy is the *receiver*. To communi-

Figure 7.2   The Interpersonal Communication Process

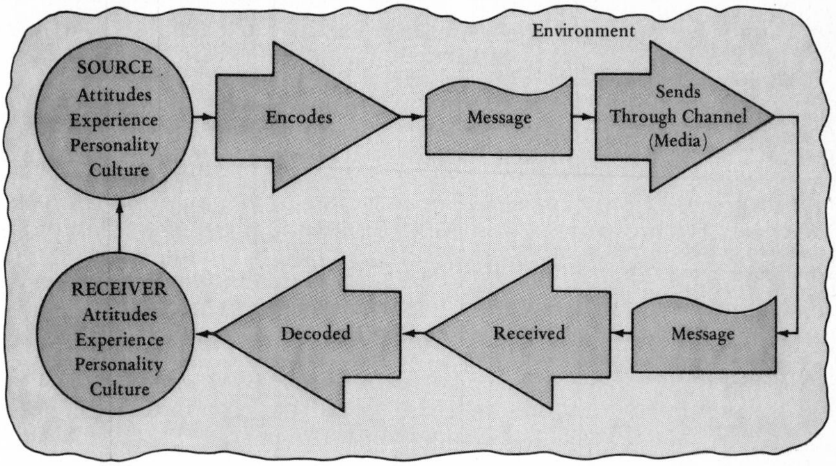

cate his problem, Bill must encode, or formulate, his message in a way that Nancy can receive it. That is, he must state his complaint in a way that Nancy can understand. Once Bill's message is encoded, he can send it through the channel, or medium—in this case, the spoken word.

Next Nancy must decode, or convert, the message (spoken words) into a thought that she can analyze mentally. She then tells Bill to mind his own business, or she agrees to keep the dog tied up. With either response, Nancy provides feedback; she then becomes the source of the message, and Bill becomes the receiver.

Now their communication is complete, and they have forged a vital social link. Unfortunately, however, we can never really be sure that a message has been sent and received accurately. Let's examine some barriers that might arise during communication.

Barriers to Communication

Communication barriers reduce the accuracy of information transfer.[10] Some examples of communication problems were given at the start of this section. Now let us look briefly at some common barriers that might have caused them.

Experience Bypass   The statement "But Larry, I thought you were criticizing me when you said I was as tough as a union steward" suggests that the source and the receiver have had different experiences with union stewards. What seemed to be a criticism was meant as a compliment. The source perhaps pictured union stewards as being tough fighters for workers' interests. Unfortunately, the receiver thought of stewards as troublemakers. The message was misunderstood because the source did not consider the experience of the receiver. In ignoring or bypassing a receiver's experience, the source runs the risk of miscommunication. The message will not be received as sent.

Use of Technical Terms   "Excuse me, professor, but I didn't understand the word *ecosystem*." All of us are guilty at times of using technical terms when it would be just as easy to use familiar language. When we assume that the receiver knows what we mean by special terms, we present a barrier to communication. The more simply a message is encoded, the more likely it is a receiver will decode it correctly.

Even more serious is the problem that arises when a familiar word can be used in special ways. One construction supervisor in a manufacturing firm tells how he misled a summer employee by asking for a "dog." In this construction setting, a *dog* is a coupling used to connect two steel beams. It is not the gentle creature that the summer employee found and presented to the supervisor.

Media Selection   "I'm sorry, but I don't have a CB in my car. That's why I didn't hear your emergency call." A person who does not have a citizens' band radio obviously cannot receive a message over one. A source must select the proper medium or channel by which to send a message. Sometimes a written memo is better than a spoken word. For example, if you want to be sure that an employee understands an instruction and you also need to show that you gave the instruction, you should write the message as well as speak it.

Environmental Distortion   "I can't hear over all that shop noise!" A message may be distorted because of interference from noise or other factors in the environment. For example, the presence of other people may distract the receiver and lead to miscommunication. This distortion can have serious consequences. In a hospital emergency room, for instance, noise and confusion can disrupt the routine and make it difficult to transfer messages. Or time pressures may make it impossible to give complete instructions about how to handle an emergency. Environmental factors often affect communication.

Abstract Nature of Words   Our language is made up of symbols that represent things and ideas. Words are abstractions; they represent other things. Unless we recognize the abstract nature of words, the exact meanings of messages can be distorted or lost. Thus when employees say they can drive a truck, we may be surprised to learn that they cannot. The employees thought we meant a pick-up truck, not an eighteen-wheeler. But how are they to know what we mean by an abstract word like *truck*? A message must be encoded carefully and fully.

Notice how easy it is for communication barriers to arise. Our best defense is to be aware of and to think about possible problems. With a little thought and planning, the barriers to communication can be reduced if not avoided.

Proposition 7.2

> Interpersonal communication can be distorted and messages can be weakened by a variety of barriers.

Nonverbal Communication

Not all communication is spoken or written. Many messages are *nonverbal*; they take the form of a smile, an approving glance, or even the clothes we wear. Some experts suggest that only 30 to 35 percent of our communication is verbal. "The remainder consists of expressions, body movements and other 'nonverbal cues'."[11]

The following nonverbal behaviors have been identified:

1. *Kinesics.* This behavior involves body movements, facial expressions, hand motions, and so on. Kinesics give clues about how a

message is being received. For example, if you are talking with a friend who leans back in a chair, with folded arms and appears to be thinking, you can infer that your friend is becoming defensive. You can expect a defensive response.

2. *Proxemics.* This category refers to how people place themselves physically in relation to one another during communication. For example, during collective bargaining, the representatives of the union and management may move toward the table and become physically closer as they reach agreement. When they disagree, however, they will tend to move away from one another and the table. Proxemics thus may indicate how well the message transfer is going.

3. *Chronemics.* This behavior includes the pauses and silences that fall between verbal statements. Long periods of silence indicate uncertainty, whereas short pauses imply excitement.

4. *Oculesics.* As you might guess, oculesics refers to eye movements. Some eye movements are voluntary, but others cannot be controlled. It is no accident that poker dealers often wear visors. The pupils of a receiver's eyes dilate, or enlarge, as interest increases. Just think what your pupils would look like if you were dealt a royal flush!

5. *Physical appearance.* Do people judge us by our clothes? Sometimes the answer is an emphatic *yes.* Job recruiters frequently are more impressed by dress suits than by sport coats or slack suits. One study noted that college presidents consistently wore conservative suits with few fad styles. Lower-level administrators on the other hand, tended to dress less formally and even followed a few fads.[12,13]

This discussion of nonverbal behavior is not meant to suggest that every movement or article of clothing has a hidden meaning. However, nonverbal communication is extremely important. It can ease our understanding of a message, and it can help us send one. Often a quick but obvious glance at the clock can get the same results from a friend who has stayed too long—and without causing the hard feelings that would arise if we asked the friend to leave.

Eventually, communication between two people extends to others, forming a network. In fact, communication networks are so characteristic of small groups that we can identify various patterns. Let us now analyze the basic patterns of group communication.

Patterns of Group Communication

Information flows through groups in a variety of ways. Sometimes group communication centers on a single person. At other times, it travels freely throughout the group.

Researchers have tried, under controlled conditions, to determine the characteristics of message transfer in various communication networks. Several networks are presented in Figure 7.3. For example, in studies by Leavitt, five group members were positioned around a table that was divided by partitions.[14] They were asked to solve a problem by passing information cards to one another according to the patterns shown in Figure 7.3. The wheel was the fastest and most accurate network; the circle was the slowest and least accurate. However, the circle brought higher levels of satisfaction to members, probably because in such a network each person is equally important.

Figure 7.3 Common Group Communication Networks

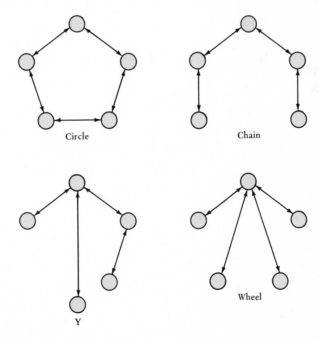

More generally, group communication networks can be classified into two main types: centralized and decentralized. The wheel, the chain, and the Y are highly centralized, because information passes through and from a single (central) source. The circle, on the other hand, is decentralized, since no one is responsible for all messages.

We should note the following things in comparing the speed and accuracy of centralized and decentralized communication patterns:[15]

1. Centralized networks tend to be more accurate in solving problems.
2. Accuracy increases with problem familiarity and authoritarian leadership.
3. More messages are transferred in decentralized networks.
4. Group satisfaction increases when centralization and authoritarian leadership decrease.
5. Leadership emerges more rapidly in centralized patterns.
6. Centralized patterns are more efficient at solving simple problems, whereas decentralized networks handle more complex problems better.

Of what help can these principles be in managing an organization? Suppose, for example, we were designing a work space such as an office layout. If job tasks were routine and most problems that arose were simple, we would do well to devise a highly centralized communication network, routing work through one person. If most tasks and problems were complex and unique, however, a decentralized design would work better. Thus a word-processing group would function well with a centralized pattern whereas a group of engineers or researchers would communicate better with a decentralized pattern.

Proposition
7.3

> Communication is a vital link among individuals in small groups. Different centralized and decentralized communication networks have different effects on the speed and accuracy of problem solving in groups.

Status Structures and Group Behavior

When individuals come together in a group, status-seeking behavior inevitably results. *Status* involves the social ordering within a group, or the relative position each person holds. Thus status seeking occurs when one group member relates to others and organizes social relationships.[16]

Status Relationships

Status systems, or social orderings, develop in groups and large organizations for many reasons. Usually, the position an individual holds in a group is related to how much he or she is perceived to contribute to the accomplishment of group goals.

For example, all organizations have at least two status structures. The first is a formal system; this matches the hierarchical structure of the organization. In a hospital, a physician has more formal status than a technician, and the chief of staff has more status than a staff physician (who, in turn, occupies a higher level than a resident or an intern). In a public school system, the principal commands more status than a teacher, and a science teacher has more status than a food-service worker. In a formal system, then, one's status is closely related to the chain of command.

In a social system, things are different. A public school coach often has more status in the community than the principal does. With social status, the organizational hierarchy is not the important factor. Instead, the values of the group determine an individual's status.

Although the formal and social systems are different, status is based on one or more of the following factors:

1. *Different physical, mental, and social abilities.* These abilities are usually related to education, training, or experience.
2. *Differences in the ease with which various tasks are performed.* The more difficult the task, the fewer the individuals who can perform it and, consequently, the higher the status of those who do the job. For example, surgeons have more status than bricklayers, but

the salt maker in a tropical tribe may have more status than the witch doctor. In both cases, the individual receives status because few others can perform the valued task.

3. *The importance of the task being performed.* The pilot of a commercial airliner has more status than the steward because the pilot's job is considered more important.[17]

Status develops in a group because someone possesses or contributes things to the organization that are regarded highly by the members. William Whyte, in a famous study of a street-corner gang, observed that the status of gang members was associated with their bowling scores.[18] In the bank-wiring group examined in the Hawthorne Studies (see Chapter 2), the people who adhered most closely to group norms acquired the highest status. The connector wiremen valued high levels of output and perceived their jobs as most important. Consequently, they tried to improve the performance of the selector wiremen, who possessed a low productivity norm. The latter group, however, gave status to low producers, and they maintained the low productivity norm because they knew it irritated the connector wiremen. The most productive connector wiremen held the highest status in their group, whereas the least productive selector wiremen were most esteemed in theirs.[19] Status is indeed a tricky issue. Imagine the headaches these problems cause managers!

Some Research Findings

Status structures have an important influence on an individual's behavior and performance. For example, studies in experimental groups have shown that there is a relationship between a person's status in a group and the value he or she places on membership. We might assume, if this is true, that status will be closely related to a person's compliance with group rules. That is, the higher one's status, the more one values membership; and the more one values membership, the more one conforms to group norms. This, however, is only partially true, as illustrated in Figure 7.4.

This figure reveals that group members with low status usually reject group influences because they see nothing to lose through deviation. Average-status members usually display high levels of conformity because they enjoy membership and desire higher status.

Figure 7.4   Relationship Between Status and Compliance

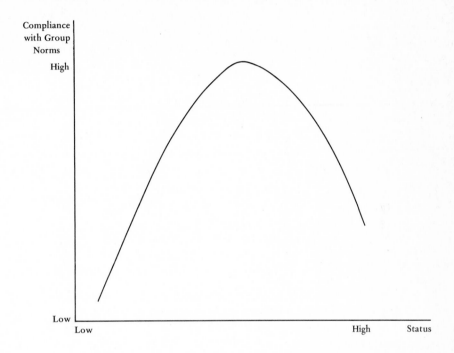

Yet it is interesting that members with high status often do *not* comply with group expectations, for they enjoy a group-given freedom to deviate and are secure in their positions. This conclusion requires some clarification. Let us look at it from the standpoint of a person's tendency to assume risk. A person with high status who agrees with group judgments stands to gain more when the judgments prove to be correct than when they are incorrect. Therefore, the high-status person can gain more through disagreement or noncompliance, since status will be enhanced greatly if the group is wrong and the individual is correct.

Hollander, for example, argues that competence in performing "focal activities" favors a person's emergence as a group leader.[20] These focal activities are the primary tasks of the group. The competence and compliance that help a person become a leader, however, accumulate over time in the form of "positively disposed impressions known as idiosyncrasy credits, which eventually allow him (or her) to deviate with greater impunity."[21] In other words, to gain status, one must comply and be competent. Once status has been attained, noncompliance is important in maintaining it.

Consider how these status relationships apply in the real world. An executive who rises in an organization does so by being a competent and capable manager of various departments. Such management is expected to follow the organization's existing philosophy and policies. When the executive gets to the top, however, he or she no longer is expected merely to manage in the same old way. Now creativity and change are demanded. The executive who merely manages things as they are and have always been is not likely to maintain the position of leadership.

In contrast, the best approach for people of average status is compliance. If such people agree with a group judgment, they gain or lose little—regardless of how the judgment turns out. However, if they disagree with a course of action that proves correct, their status may suffer. On the other hand, low-status people gain little if they agree with a group judgment that proves to be correct. And if they disagree with an action that is wrong, their status may be improved. Thus the logical strategy for low-status members is noncompliance.

A situation at Unity College illustrates these points. The college decided to place student representatives on the board of trustees to assist members in understanding the students' views regarding policies. Unintentionally, they gave student representatives a lower status than regular members, even though the students could vote and were invited to participate. When questions about how to handle parking problems on campus arose, the student representatives were asked for a recommendation. Basically, they had two alternatives:

1. They could recommend that parking problems continue to be handled as in the past. With this approach, their status would remain the same. If the problems should correct themselves, the students would be given no credit for resolving the issue. Nor, however, would they be criticized (and lose status) if the problems did not disappear.

2. The students could recommend a radical solution. If the board rejected the plan, the students' status would not change. However, if the board tried the radical plan and it worked, the stu-

dents' status would be increased greatly. If the plan failed, no serious damage would come to the students' status, since it was already low and could not be reduced much.

A low-status group can gain little from maintaining the status quo. The only hope for improvement is to recommend change. Members with extremely high status, on the other hand, are actually expected to deviate from the status quo at times.

Status and Patterns of Interaction

The manner in which groups interact often provides insights into status structures. It has been shown in experimental groups that people who receive more interaction from others than they initiate are likely to evolve as leaders. In other words, when members direct or originate contact with a central figure in a group, they bestow on that individual a higher status than they do on rank-and-file members.[22]

As we have noted, status in a formal sense may follow established organizational relationships. Consider a symphony orchestra. Westby noted that the positions with the most status are called "principal chairs" and that members try to "move toward the front." Several musicians in "back" positions found it threatening to appear in these positions before audiences.[23]

More generally, the patterns of interaction have implications for status congruency. Status congruency is said to exist when each member of a group ranks all status attributes equally. For example, all members give the same value to such things as competency, compliance, and so on. People usually desire status congruency because it ensures consistent behavior.[24]

In an organization, rewards are distributed according to the perceived value of the skills required by the task. Thus the status system is kept consistent with the reward system. It follows that the lower a person's status, the fewer that person's rewards, whereas high-status persons should receive more of the total rewards available to the group. Studies have shown, for example, that a group member is not dissatisfied with another's rate of pay as long as he or she feels that everyone's rewards are consistent with their training and experience.[25]

We can summarize much of what has been said by relating status structures to behavior. Consider the following points:

1. Behavior is directed toward preserving status—especially by people in high-status positions.
2. Behavior is directed toward improving one's status—especially by people in lower positions.
3. Any change perceived as disruptive to the status structure is considered threatening—especially by people in higher positions.
4. Any change perceived as potentially blocking an equilibrium in the status structure is perceived as threatening.[26]

Status structures also can be dysfunctional, although they perform many valuable functions, such as defining relationships and providing for consistent behavior. They also may create too much social distance between such personnel as physicians and nurses, who could benefit from closer interaction. Finally, they may restrict free and open communication between such groups as political scientists and economists, because of the status perception each group possesses.

Proposition *7.4*	When people come together in groups, status structures develop. An individual's position in the structure is determined by such things as education, experience, or how that person reflects the primary values of the group. The outcome of status structures can be functional, as when they provide for consistent behavior. They also may restrict communication and encourage emotional stress.

What Managers Should Know About Social Behavior in Groups

Social factors can influence human performance in groups. Much group behavior is facilitated through interpersonal communication. Managers who effectively communicate recognize that they must "put themselves in the other person's place." By using familiar terms and relating to the experiences of employees, they can transfer messages effectively. Managers also need to understand that not all communication is verbal. The clothes we wear, the way we sit at a table, and our facial expressions may send important messages to those sensitive enough to recognize them.

Status is also an important social phenomenon. Managers should appreciate the fact that the status of group members is determined by many factors. The union steward may have very high status in groups with high levels of satisfaction. Or the person who works in the freezer department of a food warehouse may have high status among other group members because the job is hard to perform. The manager who does not recognize the reality of this status structure may have difficulty understanding why the group behaves as it does.

Also think of how important it may be to recognize why an employee who once followed orders and did his or her best when working at a relatively simple job may become less dependable when promoted to a more important job. Perhaps the fact that employees must behave differently before and after receiving high status explains the behavior. All these insights will help managers do a better job motivating social behavior in directions that support the accomplishment of group goals.

Summary

Groups are found everywhere because we need them so much. When an individual fails to accomplish a difficult task, he or she seeks the assistance of other people.

Groups often form for social reasons—people simply like to be with other people. This chapter defined and analyzed group interaction and illustrated why it is so important to managers. We also classified groups in several ways. One useful classification differentiates between formal and informal groups. Having emphasized informal groups in this chapter, we will turn our attention to formal groups in Chapter 8.

We will not, however, put social groups aside, for they will remain important throughout the book. We will continue to emphasize the extremely important role of interpersonal communication in holding groups together. Although most group behavior centers on verbal communication, we can understand few situations completely without an awareness of nonverbal cues. As noted in this chapter, such cues range from an individual's general appearance to body movements and even to enlargement of the pupils in one's eyes.

Finally, we examined status. Status structures develop whenever groups form. Often status structures and status-seeking behavior result in positive outcomes. Competition and consistency in a group are developed by status-oriented behavior. At the same time, status structures can be dysfunctional if they result in too much distance among group members.

In Chapter 8, we will move to more formal, task-oriented behavior in small groups. This perspective will allow us to investigate how group behavior functions in an organizational setting.

Questions for Discussion

1. What is a coalition? Why do you think coalitions are especially important in a triad?
2. In your view, what are the most important favorable and unfavorable aspects of status structures? Do you think status structures should be eliminated? Why or why not?
3. What do you think are the most important barriers to communication? Give examples to defend your answer.
4. What effect does centralization have on communication patterns in small groups? Give examples to support your answer.
5. Specify the difference between a membership group and a reference group. List four membership and four reference groups to which you belong.

Exercise: Sizing Up Those Around You

What messages can people send you with their nonverbal behavior? Briefly record what you would think in each of the following cases. Be prepared to say what really "tipped you off" to how you should respond in each situation. Also, do you really think nonverbal communication is an important part of the total message in each case? Why or why not?

1. You are shown into an examination room at your doctor's office. As you enter, you notice that the doctor is wearing a T-shirt and blue jeans.

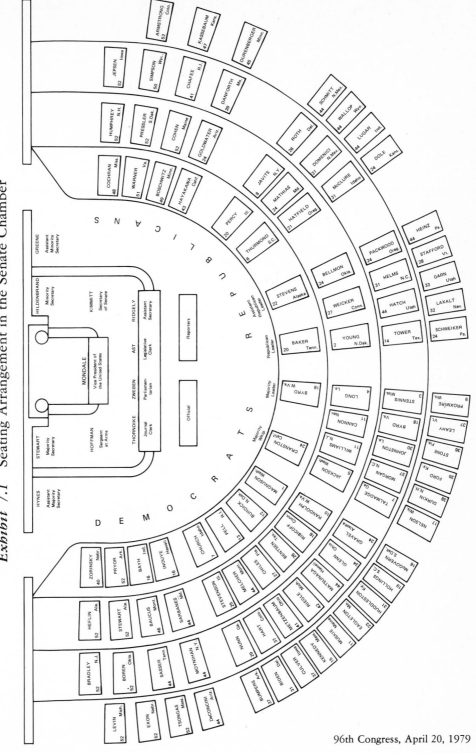

Exhibit 7.1 Seating Arrangement in the Senate Chamber

96th Congress, April 20, 1979

2. You are waiting outside the terminal at a major airport for a taxi. Although you see no cabs, a well-dressed man in a business suit asks whether he can drive you to town for a reduced rate.

3. Your boss is telling you that your performance has been unsatisfactory for the past month. However, you note that your boss is unwilling to look directly into your eyes and seems uncertain and insecure.

4. You have joined a neighborhood discussion group that always seems to form its interactions around a small circle in the middle of a room.

Case: Status in the Senate

That rank has its privileges is certainly true in the United States Senate. Did you ever wonder how senators choose their seats? Not surprisingly, seating is based on rank. And with few exceptions, rank is determined by how much time a person has been in the Senate.

Exhibit 7.1 shows the seating arrangement for the Ninety-sixth Congress as of April 1979. Notice that Republicans sit on one side and Democrats sit on the other. Senators may select their seats on the basis of time in office. The number that appears in each name box shows that person's rank or seniority. The majority leader and whip as well as the minority leader and assistant leader sit in the front row.

Examine the seating arrangement to see whether you can discover the status system that applies in the Senate. Specifically, respond to the following:

1. Where do newly elected senators (with low ranks) tend to sit? Why do you think senior members do not desire this area?

2. How would you describe the movement of senators in the Senate? Based on your analysis, why do you think senators want to move in specific ways?

3. List some potential advantages and disadvantages of this seniority system.

Suggested Readings

Brown, D. S. "Barriers to Successful Communication." *Management Review* 64 (December 1975): 24–29.

Caplow, Theodore. *How to Run Any Organization.* Hinsdale, Ill.: Dryden Press, 1976.

Freese, Lee. "Conditions for Status Equality in Informal Task Groups." *Sociometry* 37 (1974): 174–188.

Gallagher, James, and P. J. Borke. "Scapegoating and Leader Behavior." *Social Forces* 52 (1974): 481–487.

Gibbons, C. C. "Marks of a Mature Manager." *Business Horizons* 19 (October 1975): 54–56.

Ivancevich, J. M., and J. H. Donnelly. "A Study of Role Clarity and the Need for Clarity in Three Occupational Groups," *Academy of Management Journal* 17 (1974): 28–36.

Ritti, R. R., and C. R. Funkhouser. *The Ropes to Skip and the Ropes to Know.* Columbus, Ohio: Grid, 1977.

Taylor, Gary. "Joking in a Bush Camp." *Human Relations* 26 (1973): 479–484.

Weick, K. E. *The Social Psychology of Organizing,* 2nd ed. Reading, Mass.: Addison-Wesley, 1979.

Wolosin, R. J. "Group Structure and Role Behavior." *Annals of the American Academy of Political and Social Science* 413 (1974): 158–172.

chapter 8

Work Groups in Organizations

The nature of the group determines the character of its impact upon the development of its members. The values of the group, the stability of these values, the group atmosphere, and the nature of the conformity demanded by the group determine whether a group is likely to have a positive or negative impact upon the growth and behavior of its members.

Rensis Likert,
New Patterns of Management

How many atomic bombs would an aggressor need to reduce the heavy industrial production of the United States to 25 percent after the outbreak of a war? This is an important question in defense planning, but one person cannot answer it. At least, Rand Corporation thought no individual had all the expertise needed to answer such a question. Therefore, it developed a group problem-solving technique to acquire the best available information from a panel of experts. The goal was a method of group problem solving for issues too complex for one individual to handle. The emphasis was on diversity of thought, stimulation of discussion, and better decision making. This technique will be discussed later in the chapter.

This chapter will examine work- or task-oriented groups. Such groups sometimes are like the social groups discussed in Chapter 7. In fact, such characteristics as size and group make-up are always similar. The difference is that a task-oriented group is deliberately formed to achieve a goal sought by the larger organization. A sales department in a retail store, a production department in a factory, and an emergency room in a hospital are all examples of work groups. Although such social behaviors as status seeking and communication do occur in work groups, our focus here is on the more formal aspects of group behavior in organizations. We especially are interested in how groups function to accomplish organizational goals.

Specifically, this chapter examines four related issues that directly affect the performance of groups in organizations. First, we will examine the nature of group norms, or standards of performance, and their impact on individual behavior. Second, we will relate group norms to cohesiveness, or the amount of "in-groupishness" that any collection of individuals has. The influence of cohesiveness seems to depend on the norms that prevail among group members. Third, we will discuss the important and practical matter of group problem solving. Some comparisons will be made with our previous discussion of individual decision making. Fourth, we will conclude by investigating the role relationships that help determine a person's position within a group.

Normative Behavior in Groups

Group norms are rules or guidelines of accepted behavior that are established by the group and used to control the behavior of its members. In a very structured, formal group, the norms are stated as operating rules. The legal system of a nation, for example, is a set of rules by which all members of the society must conduct their behavior. Similarly, an industry may have certain norms. In most states, for example, physicians do not advertise their services, because doing so is considered unprofessional and violates an accepted norm. For the same reasons, college professors usually do not openly criticize colleagues to students.

Even in smaller groups, norms guide behavior. Some unions have accepted rates of performance that govern members' work. Even when the union contract does not specify the number of bricks that can be laid in a day, or the number of miles that a crew may drive a train, social limits often develop. Thus from the group perspective in a credit reporting agency, it may be "illegal" to read more than fifty reports during a given day. Such norms often influence behavior more than official procedures do. They certainly demand a certain behavior, for a standard is clearly understood by the group.

Norms and Conformity

Norms provide standards of behavior. Because of this, behavioral scientists are interested in determining the extent to which people adhere to or deviate from accepted norms.

Conformity, Compliance, and Acceptance

Conformity can be defined as a modification of behavior in the direction of a stated or implied norm. Hollander, however, provides a different definition. He states that conformity results when a person is aware of a norm and behaves in accordance with it.[1] Perhaps the most effective definition is given by Kiesler and Kiesler, who say that conformity is a change in behavior or belief toward a group as a result of real or imagined group pressures.[2]

Consider your friends and classmates. Although there probably are some exceptions, most people wear their hair similarly and dress in similar clothing. Why is this so? More than likely, we dress, talk, and act like others because if we are different we might be teased or insulted. Such real or imagined group pressures are sufficient to keep most of us conforming.

To understand normative behavior, we must distinguish between two types of conformity. The more familiar is compliance, which has been the topic of interest in most studies of conformity. Compliance results when outward behavior is directed in line with group norms. Personal acceptance, on the other hand, is a change in attitude. Acceptance alters not only outward behavior but inner value systems as well.[3] We would expect acceptance to be more influential on long-range behavior. No doubt it is. Unfortunately, long-range behavior is difficult to measure because it is not often observable. However, we can illustrate compliance and personal acceptance through the following example.

Suppose a group of factory workers listens to speeches and attends seminars about the penalties for stealing company property. The employees may comply with (outwardly accept) management's point of view and may not steal when anyone is around. However, acceptance is not achieved so easily. Thus the employees may steal tools or supplies when the supervisor is away. Covert, or hidden, behavior has not been influenced by either threats or supervision. The employees are not completely convinced that stealing company property is wrong, and their hidden behavior shows that personal acceptance has not been achieved.

In discussing certain economic principles, Dow and Duncan looked closely at the problems decision makers have in a corporate society.[4] They viewed decision makers as being members of many groups, each of which has different norms. For example, a decision maker is a member of society and belongs to a membership group held together by social values. As noted in Chapter 7, a membership group has a general influence on a person's behavior, but the person is not highly aware of it. A reference group, on the other hand, is one the member identifies with and allows to influence his or her behavior. As members of society, decision makers may dislike a nuisance such as pollution and may deplore it in discussions with neighbors. However, the decision makers' reference group may be the owners or fellow managers of a polluting firm. If the managers are employed by the polluting firm, they are likely to choose in favor of the organization (reference group) when its values and those of society (membership group) conflict. This, of course, does not mean that the organization's values are privately accepted, but that the reference group influences behavior more than the broader social system does. Through indoctrination and experience, many decision makers may come to look on pollution as a lesser evil than unemployment. They thus accept the idea that pollution is the expected and necessary result of a productive industrial system.

Proposition 8.1

All people affiliate with membership and reference groups. When conflicts develop, behavior is directed more toward the perceived norms of the reference groups and less toward the norms of membership groups.

Studies of Conformity

Conformity has been studied through a variety of techniques. To grasp this research, we will examine two of the more familiar approaches and their implications.

Sherif's Technique[5]   In Sherif's experiments, a subject was placed in a dark room, and a fixed beam of light was shown on the wall. The light was turned off, and after a short time it was turned on again. The experimenter then asked the subject how far the beam had moved. In reality, the light had not moved. However, the phrasing of the question implied that it had, and so the subject felt pressure to make a guess about the distance moved. The implication of the question, along with the illusion that the light had moved, usually resulted in some estimate of movement and the distance covered.

The effect of groups became evident when several other subjects were placed in the room and were asked one by one to estimate how far the beam of light had moved. Sherif observed that the estimates of one or more subjects influenced the estimates of others. If the first subject guessed 2 inches, the second might say 3 inches. The third, having heard the guesses of the other two subjects, would likely estimate some distance such as $2\frac{1}{2}$ inches, whereas the fourth might say $2\frac{3}{4}$ inches. If the first subject began with an unrealistic estimate, such as 3 feet, the second subject might temper this guess and say the distance was something like 10 inches. Such an estimate, being more realistic, then became the norm, and other subjects might suggest movements of 8 to 11 inches. In this example, we see the formation of a norm within the small group of subjects and the clustering of their behavior around the norm. The experiments thus demonstrate how group norms influence individual behavior.

If you are a golfer, these experiments may suggest an answer to why you "shoot a better round" when you join a foursome whose average player is better than you are. Or if you jog for health or for fun, why do you have a better time in a race than during your solitary run? To some extent, you probably do better because of the group pressure to do well.

Unfortunately, the reverse also can occur. Consider what often happens to conscientious workers in an organization. The low performance of other workers may pressure them to slow down lest everyone be expected to work at a higher rate. There is little question that the presence of a group can influence an individual to behave in line with established group norms.

Asch's Studies   Perhaps the most widely referenced technique in the analysis of conformity is that used by S. E. Asch.[6] A subject was asked in the presence of other subjects to match the length of a given line with one of three uneven lines.

In these studies, Asch used college students in groups of eight. Seven students were "confederate" subjects who had been instructed to make wrong guesses about the lengths of the lines at specified points. The eighth, or "naive" subject, was thus presented with a conflict between what he or she saw and what apparently was being perceived by others. Would the naive subjects go along with the confederates or voice their convictions? In Asch's studies, a little more than 30 percent yielded to the group judgment, and those who voiced their own perceptions did so with considerable discomfort. When the number of confederates was varied from zero to fifteen, interesting results were obtained. There were almost no errors when no confederates were present. The full group effect seemed to be achieved with three confederates. If only one dissenter emerged in a group of fifteen confederates, the group effect on the naive subject was reduced greatly. Once again, group norms affected individual behavior.

Proposition 8.2

> The existence of group norms, pressures, and the tendency toward conformity make the interpersonal aspects of human behavior important. Normative behavior greatly influences individual responses to motivation stimuli.

Historically, managers have emphasized teamwork and the virtues of pulling together. As Frame 8.1 shows, however, teamwork is not necessarily more productive. In a related study, students were asked to cheer and clap individually and in groups.[7] The researchers observed that as the number in the group increased, the gap between a person's individual performance and his or her performance in the group became larger. Individual performance was greater in all cases.

Frame 8.1

> ## Group Influences: The Ringlemann Effect
>
> In the 1920s, a German student named Ringlemann tested how individuals worked in a group. The study was relatively simple. Ringlemann devised a rope-pulling task that was not specialized in any way. By putting a stress gauge on a rope, he could measure how much each individual could pull.
>
> We would assume that if person A pulled X amount alone and person B pulled Y amount, when they both pulled together the total stress would be $X + Y$. Let's say that person A applied 125 pounds of pressure and person B registered 130 pounds. With both pulling the same rope, the result should be 255 pounds of pressure. Not so, according to Ringlemann. Even more puzzling was that three people pulling together measured only 2½ times the sum of their individual pulls. And a group of eight men were able to register only four times their average individual rate.
>
> What a strange discovery. What can it mean? For one thing, it seems to show conclusively that groups do not always perform better than individuals would. Indeed, if this case is representative, groups may not perform even to the combined level of individual efforts.
>
> There are many reasons why this result could have occurred. The task was simple and structured in such a way that groups of individuals could organize and achieve improvements. Moreover, the task was not designed to ensure positive group pressure, nor were incentives provided. The Ringlemann effect suggests how complex even small-group phenomena can be. Clearly, managers must not become dependent on any single explanation of group action.
>
> For a detailed description see A. G. Ingham et al., "The Ringlemann Effect," *Journal of Experimental Social Psychology* 10 (1974): 371–384.

This outcome does not conflict directly with Sherif's or Asch's studies, although we might have expected group members to goad each other toward higher performance levels. We must recognize that a single force seldom causes a specific outcome in complex, or even simple, social situations. It has been suggested that individuals develop an idea of what would be a fair and just contribution; as the group becomes larger, individuals adjust their performance to that level. It is also likely that reasonably intelligent members of a group will recognize that it is difficult to hold them individually accountable for a group's failure to perform at the highest level.

Conformity and Cohesiveness

If conforming behavior is an expected result of interpersonal relations, what is the effect of this behavior? As we might suspect, there are many possible effects. We are particularly interested in the effects of conformity on cohesiveness.

Cohesiveness is the power of a group to think and act as a single unit in pursuit of a common objective(s). The literature on small-group cohesiveness has been directed toward two major questions. The first question relates to the factors that produce or reduce cohesiveness. The second relates to the effects of greater or lesser degrees of cohesiveness.[8] Increased cohesiveness leads to greater frequency of interaction among group members. The greater the cohesiveness, the greater the changes that members can produce in the behavior of individuals.[9]

For example, consider the evening shift of firefighters in a municipal fire department. This is a very cohesive group. The members work well together and enjoy each other's company. They pursue every opportunity to be together. They entertain one another with family parties, and they have a softball team. They even compete with other shifts and other fire departments in exercises demonstrating their efficiency as a team.

This cohesive firefighting team and social group greatly influences the behavior of each individual. In fact, since members are so close, the group influence on individual behavior is even greater than it would be under less cohesive circumstances. Everyone works hard because the group expects it. Thus the greater the cohesiveness, the greater the tendency to conform.

Questions remain, however, concerning how cohesiveness influences the performance of groups and the individuals in them. Since highly cohesive groups are capable of influencing individual behavior, if the group norm is a high level of performance, the more cohesive group is likely to influence each member toward higher productivity. On the other hand, if the norm is low productivity, the

Figure 8.1 Hypothetical Relationship Between Cohesiveness and Performance

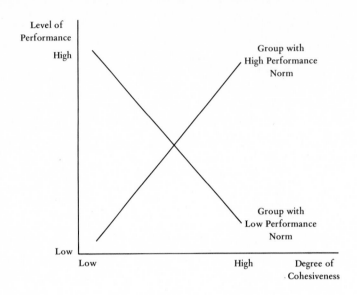

highly cohesive group is likely to restrict the performance of individuals.[10] This hypothetical relationship is diagrammed in Figure 8.1. For example, consider a team of mechanics that maintains a successful racing automobile. Because the team is on the road much of the time, its members socialize and work together with precision. Their goal is always to win the race. The group is cohesive and highly productive. Low performance is not tolerated because it would undermine the group goal of winning the race. Thus cohesiveness increases performance.

This group is quite different from a group of production workers who all dislike their supervisor. Members of the group socialize (except for the supervisor) and work closely with one another. Their mutual dislike for the boss makes the group cohesive, but the norm is low productivity. In fact, there is an effort to restrict production. Anyone who produces too much is suspected of being too friendly with the boss and is pressured to slow the pace. In this case, cohesiveness leads to low productivity.

Proposition
8.3

> Cohesive groups influence individual behavior and encourage conformity. The effect on performance is directly related to the group norm. If the norm favors high performance, highly cohesive groups are more productive than less cohesive ones. If the norm does not support performance, cohesive groups are less productive.

Our discussion so far has answered several important questions about small groups. We have defined group norms and have seen how they influence individual behavior through cohesiveness. Let us now see how groups solve problems.

Group Problem Solving

What factors influence a group's effectiveness in solving problems? Until the early 1960s, there was much skepticism among researchers regarding the superiority of groups in problem solving. One writer, after reviewing numerous studies, stated that "results of experiments comparing the quality of group and individual problem solving are, taken as a whole, inconclusive."[11]

Are Groups Superior?

When we discuss group problem solving, definitions become critical, for there are many types of groups. Most important to us are *interacting* and *nominal* (or noninteracting) *groups*. An interacting group is a conventional discussion forum, such as a committee.[12] In an interacting group, members assemble and interact openly with one another to find a solution. A nominal group, on the other hand, is a group in name only. Its members may be and often are geographically close (perhaps in the same room), but they do not interact freely.

Further examples will clarify the distinction between interacting and nominal groups. The advisory board for a school of business administration is an interacting group. It typically includes business leaders from the community as well as state and perhaps even national leaders. Group members meet in a central place once or twice a year and advise the school's administration about important policy decisions. In contrast, the process used by Rand Corporation (see the beginning of the chapter) involved a special type of nominal group called a "Delphi panel." In this group, experts from throughout the world may provide input by means of a mail questionnaire. At each stage, all panel members are given the feedback of other members, as well as an opportunity to alter their own responses. In this way, at least some indirect interaction results.

In general, research literature focuses on various overall aspects of group decision making. It has been shown, for example, that individuals in a group generate about twice as many ideas as when they work alone.[13] Attention also has been given to the make-up of groups. Heterogeneous groups, in which members' background and experience differ, usually produce decisions of higher quality that have greater acceptance than homogeneous groups do. Homogeneous groups, in which individuals have similar backgrounds and experience, offer the advantages of facilitating satisfaction, reducing conflict, and ensuring that the proceedings are not dominated by a single person.[14]

A familiar heterogeneous group is an executive committee designed to advise the president of a company. The committee might include officers from finance, production, marketing, personnel, and other departments, thus providing the greatest amount of input from as many different perspectives as possible. In contrast, a homogeneous group includes representatives who share the same general perspective. For example, a family physician who discovers an unusual problem with a patient may consult with a group of specialists. Although the problem may involve only the patient's ear, specialists familiar with ear, nose, and throat problems may work together to provide the greatest possible knowledge.

Recently, much interest has been directed toward the advantages and disadvantages of group problem solving. Researchers have examined various problem-solving patterns and conclude that nominal groups seem superior to interacting groups in all phases of problem solving except the synthesizing phase, in which ideas are brought together, discussed, and combined with other ideas. Based on these findings, Van de Ven and Delbecq suggest the following sequence for effective group decision making:

1. Use of nominal grouping for fact finding and generating ideas
2. Use of structured group interaction and informal discussion for clarifying and evaluating the ideas generated
3. Use of nominal grouping for voting and for final independent judgment[15]

An example illustrates this sequence. James Nelson is the general manager of Exchange Industries. He is extremely supportive of continuing education activities for employees, particularly management personnel. Nelson is convinced that most supervisors would benefit from greater knowledge of management theory. Unfortunately, he does not know exactly which problems concern supervisors most. Therefore, he decides to bring the supervisors together to identify the topics to be included in a training course.

Note, first of all, that this involves a homogeneous group. Since the training program will relate to supervisory problems, Nelson decides to use the group most directly involved in management. Furthermore, he noticed in previous planning sessions that several strong personalities dominated the discussion. Apparently, many supervisors are hesitant to voice their opinions in the presence of the few strong personalities. Therefore, Nelson chooses a nominal format to generate ideas. Rather than asking supervisors to state their problems aloud, he gives each supervisor three notecards on which to identify the three most important problems in descending order. After the cards are collected, all problems are written on the blackboard. In this way, supervisors are not inhibited by group pressure, since no one is identified with a particular problem.

Once all problems are identified, the group as a whole interacts by discussing and evaluating the ideas generated. Interaction is important at this stage because of its stimulating effect. All members are encouraged to participate. After the discussion session, choices must be made concerning which topics to include in the supervisory training course. Since group pressures again may emerge, Nelson asks group members to vote privately, again ranking the three most important topics on notecards. The nominal format is adopted at this stage to ensure that everyone has an opportunity to vote freely. The highest-ranked items then will be included in the program.

This example uses both interacting and nominal groups so that all members will participate. As a result, adverse pressures from the group can be kept to a minimum. Individuals are encouraged to express themselves freely, and yet the benefits of group interaction are attained.

The combined nominal and interacting formats yield higher-quality group decisions. The goal is to use whichever group pattern is most effective for each stage of problem solving. Contrary to the opinion of many people, committees (in other words, groups) are not bad in themselves; they simply have been used improperly.

Groups and Risk

When discussing group problem solving, it is important to examine other outputs besides quality. One output relates to the risk that a group is willing to assume. There are two basic schools of thought.

Some researchers argue that groups make riskier decisions than individuals do because in a group no one is really responsible for the outcome. Since no individual can be held fully responsible, groups tend to assume risks that individuals acting alone would not assume. This view is called the *risky-shift hypothesis,* because it hypothesizes a tendency to share risk with others and to increase the risk acceptable in decision making.[16] Thus decision makers are likely to assume more risk when a group is substituted for lone individuals.

Proposition 8.4

> Groups stimulate individuals in generating ideas and can improve the quality, as well as the acceptance, of decisions. Because nominal and interacting groups offer unique advantages at various stages of problem solving, the manager's challenge is to use both formats effectively. The advantages of group interaction thus can be achieved without risking the dysfunctional effects that group pressures can create.

Another point of view argues that, because of the dynamics of group interaction, collective decision making has the opposite effect.

In short, when individuals come together for the purpose of problem solving, the situation favors compromise. Thus extreme or risky points of view are offset immediately, so that solutions tend to be averages or compromises. The result is a solution that is less risky than one an individual might suggest.[17] More recently, some have argued that people who support the risky-shift hypothesis do so because of certain flaws in research design.[18] Although the evidence for both views is impressive, research literature does suggest that groups are more likely to have a leveling effect on individual judgments than they are to encourage risky behavior.

We have examined how normative behavior and pressures to conform relate to group problem solving. Now let us turn our attention to individuals within groups. In the rest of the chapter, we will examine how roles and role relationships influence group members.

Role Relationships and Behavior in Groups

Role relationships may seem to be a topic of concern only to behavioral scientists. However, this topic has important implications for managers in their daily operations. If administrators are to manage others effectively, they must recognize what is expected of them by the organization and by the many groups within it.

A *role* is a behavior pattern that others expect of a person when he or she interacts with them. It is important not to oversimplify this complex topic. Thibaut and Kelley state that the role is undoubtedly the "most complex organized response pattern" the human being is capable of making.[19] Job descriptions, for example, specify formal roles. Such job requirements appear absolute, but people's perception of them vary.

In Figure 8.2, the manager is pictured at the center of a network of role perceptions. The manager has a perception of his or her own responsibilities. This perception may or may not agree with higher management's. Similarly, managers' expectations and employees' expectations may diverge. When incongruities develop among all these expectations, role ambiguity results. We need to examine this important behavioral phenomenon.

Figure 8.2 Network of Role Expectations

Role Ambiguity

When a person is sure about his or her role, role clarity is said to exist. In reality, few people achieve perfect clarity about any expected behavior pattern; some ambiguity almost always exists. *Role ambiguity* is the extent to which a person is uncertain about the behavior expected.[20] Often, as research suggests, this lack of clarity results in reduced job performance.[21]

Although role ambiguity is not easy to measure, attempts have been made. Kahn and others have developed a type of Likert scale for constructing an index of ambiguity.[22] Using this index, respondents are asked to react to four questions such as: Are you always as clear as you would like to be about what is expected on your job? Subjects respond on a five-point scale ranging from 1 (not clear) to 5 (very clear). Results of these questions then are related to other aspects of organizational behavior.

Effects of Ambiguity

We would expect a person experiencing role ambiguity to show a reduction in job satisfaction and an increase in job stress. Research suggests that role clarity is, in fact, positively related to job satisfaction and inversely related to job stress.[23] A person with little ambiguity will be more satisfied and less tense about the job. This relationship is important, for it suggests that our understanding of what is expected of us is closely related to the quality and meaningfulness of our working lives. However, it says little about how clarity and ambiguity influence productivity because, as we noted in Chapter 6, nothing conclusive can be said about how satisfaction influences performance.

Proposition 8.5

> The degree of role clarity can influence the quality of organizational life and the emotional well-being of each individual. However, no hard evidence is available to show how clarity and ambiguity influence job performance.

From Ambiguity to Conflict

We have defined role ambiguity as a lack of clarity concerning what type of behavior is expected of a person in an organization. *Role conflict* is a related but different concept. Conflict may result from ambiguity; however, it can exist even when role clarity has been achieved. For example, a manager may know what top management expects and what subordinates expect. A problem arises, however, when the expectations are in conflict.

In Figure 8.3, the manager is shown as being pulled in two directions by such conflicting expectations. Given a fixed amount of revenues, owners want as much profit as possible. Employees, on the other hand, want higher wages. Higher profits can be obtained by keeping wages constant; wages can be increased by reducing profits. The manager's problem is to decide which course of action to rec-

Figure 8.3   A Hypothetical Role Conflict

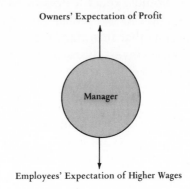

Owners' Expectation of Profit

Manager

Employees' Expectation of Higher Wages

ommend. When such demands are opposing, should the manager side with the owners or employees?

Some Examples of Role Conflict

Managers do not operate in a vacuum; rather they play many roles, such as those of specialist, member of the management team, friend, head of a family, and so on.[24] The pressing problem is for managers to evaluate priorities and responsibilities constantly and to ensure that they are using their energies efficiently and effectively.

For example, all jobs have more exciting and less exciting aspects. One person may find supervising challenging but may be bored by completing reports. Someone else may be insecure in supervising but may feel a great responsibility for completing records accurately. Since both managerial functions are essential, all aspects of the task must be completed.

A more complicated role conflict has been observed in organizations recently. This conflict has to do with working women who are expected to be homemakers, mothers, and full- or part-time employees.[25] Such role conflicts appear especially threatening when more highly trained women are confronted with choices among competing roles.[26]

Examples of role conflict also are seen in international management. One writer has examined the conflicts faced by managers sent to foreign countries. When an American manager, for example, is placed in charge of a Latin American operation, he or she is likely to experience problems in relating both to the home culture and to the foreign culture. One explanation for this lies in the special role conflict such a job involves.[27]

A More General Framework

In more general terms, Rosen has itemized three aspects of role conflict.[28] The first is intrasender conflict. For example, the supervisor of a work group may be confused because upper management has asked that the style of supervision be altered to accommodate untrained or unskilled employees; yet management has not relieved the supervisor of responsibility for high performance. The supervisor has difficulty deciding how these roles should be balanced. College professors also may face such problems when their institution adopts an open-admissions program and at the same time insists on high academic standards. In both cases, the managers are faced with orders to help the disadvantaged as well as with demands for high performance.

Intersender conflicts, as Rosen points out, also can confront the same supervisor. When management expects the supervisor to assist new employees, old employees expect the supervisor to protect their rights and to treat everyone consistently.

Interrole conflicts may also develop. When the supervisor's formal role is ambiguous, he or she may assume a class or race role. This role de-emphasizes the supervisor's responsibilities for primary tasks.

An organizational member can make many responses to role conflicts. Some responses are highly personal, such as withdrawal from contact with others, emotional stress, lower morale and satisfaction, and a reduction of confidence in the organization. Tensions and frustrations can affect job attitudes, and the resulting ambiguity can lead to insecurity.[29]

From this discussion we can develop certain inferences about role clarity and conflict. First, conflict results from a variety of factors within organizations. Second, intense conflict may have adverse effects on performance. These can be minimized only when people with organizational responsibility recognize the conflict and develop communications systems and policies and procedures to combat ambiguity and conflict.

Proposition 8.6

> Role conflict, although different from ambiguity, is a closely related concept. Ambiguity occurs when a person is not sure about the role to be played. Conflict results when a person is clear about expectations but must choose among conflicting demands.

What Managers Should Know About Work Groups

Group norms influence behavior. When possible, managers need to influence the norms toward high productivity. Periodic performance evaluations provide an excellent opportunity to influence norms because future goals are always discussed. To the extent that commitment can be established, formal goals may become closely related to group norms.

Managers learn quickly to recognize the difference between compliance and acceptance of goals. An employee may comply with a future goal but will only pursue it with enthusiasm when he or she personally accepts the values on which the goal is based.

The extent to which a particular employee is influenced by a group norm is related to how "closely knit" or cohesive the group is. If the group is very cohesive, each person will allow the group to influence him or her to a great extent. However, unless managers are confident that a high performance norm can be maintained, cohesiveness might not actually be desirable. Although cohesiveness can increase productivity in the presence of a high-performance norm, it also can reduce productivity when low performance is the goal of the group.

Managers also will benefit from understanding how interacting and nominal groups can assist in solving problems. It is hoped that future managers will overcome the temptation simply to appoint interacting committees to help in decision making. Instead, a more productive route will be to explore new ways of achieving the advantages of both interacting and nominal procedures.

Finally, role relationships can highlight potential areas of increasing stress for managers and employees. It is essential that the conditions which contribute to role ambiguity and conflict be removed.

Summary

In many ways, work groups are like social groupings. However, work groups are designed to accomplish specific goals and to contribute to the attainment of organizational objectives. Such groups are familiar parts of all organizations.

Many topics in this chapter involve social phenomena. For example, the pressure that a group places on individual members is often social. Yet regardless of how it develops, the pressure has important effects on organizational performance. By the same token, the basis for a group's cohesiveness may be friendship, but the cohesiveness will still influence how individuals respond to group pressures. Similarly, role relationships influence a person's satisfaction and stress levels and thus may seriously affect productivity. Finally, group problem solving can extend the potential of an individual. All these aspects of group behavior strongly influence how groups perform their assigned tasks and the methods they use to accomplish goals.

We discussed how groups perform in organizations. First, normative behavior was divided into two categories: compliance and personal acceptance. The latter is a more pervasive influence on behavior. Next cohesiveness was presented as a key force intervening among conforming behavior, group goals, and performance. Cohesiveness does *not,* however, ensure group productivity. Yet the more cohesive the group, the more each member will allow group norms to influence his or her behavior. If the group has a high performance norm, a cohesive group will be more productive. If, on the other hand, the group has a low performance norm, a cohesive group will be less productive.

We questioned and perhaps dispelled certain myths about group problem solving. Not all group problem solving is better than the problem solving of individuals. The effectiveness of groups is related to how well various nominal and interacting formats are followed at various stages during the problem solving.

A discussion of role relationships concluded the chapter. We paid careful attention to how role ambiguity and role conflict influence the performance of task-oriented groups. Only the political nature of interaction in small groups remains to be examined. Thus power and politics are the subjects of Chapter 9.

Questions for Discussion

1. What relationship exists between role ambiguity and stress? Illustrate this relationship with an example of your own experience in a group.
2. What is the difference between an interacting group and a nominal group? Do you think groups make riskier decisions than individuals do? Give examples.
3. What is role ambiguity? Why is it important to an understanding of group behavior? What are the primary effects of role ambiguity? How is ambiguity different from conflict?
4. Define a group norm. What relationship exists between group norms and conforming behavior? What is the difference between compliance and private acceptance?
5. How is cohesiveness related to performance? What implications does this relationship have for improving performance in organizations?

Case: Janice Yeager, R.N.

Janice Yeager is a registered nurse who received her B.S. and M.S. degrees from a well-known school of nursing located in a renowned medical center. When she received her B.S. degree, she began working in a modern six hundred–bed hospital. She found her job very rewarding and was particularly happy working closely with patients.

Two years after Janice began work, her husband received his medical degree and three years later completed his residency in internal medicine. During this time, they had a daughter who is now eighteen months old.

For financial and professional reasons, Janice continued to work and even completed her M.S. degree. Her primary motivation for pursuing graduate work was to acquire a staff position as director of in-service nursing training and thus have regular working hours, enabling her to handle her family responsibilities as well.

Throughout recent months, even though she has received several promotions and salary increases, Janice has grown more frustrated. In her new job, she never has contact with patients but instead teaches classes and designs short courses.

To add to her problems, Janice has had great difficulty finding day care for her daughter, who has been ill for some time with ear problems. Janice's husband now has a successful practice and a good income. He has mentioned several times that there is really no need for her to work and that perhaps she would be better off at home with the child—especially because of the little girl's illness.

As director of in-service training, Janice often must attend seminars in other cities and must offer night classes for working nurses. Her mother, who lives in the same city, is always willing to keep her granddaughter when Janice's husband is on call. The mother, however, is much less diplomatic about voicing her opinions about Janice's responsibilities as a mother—which, in the mother's view, are clearly being neglected.

Thus Janice is under great stress. She prefers to work directly with patients, but continues in a staff capacity to make her hours as predictable as possible. She prefers to work, but is constantly being told that she is neglecting her responsibilities as a mother. She is quite confused, and is tempted to resign her position and reconcile herself to the roles of wife and mother.

1. Is Janice experiencing role ambiguity? If so, specifically explain how it has come into being.
2. Is Janice experiencing role conflict? Explain in detail.
3. What can Janice do to regain a sense of satisfaction?

Case: Role Relations in Bravo Platoon

Bravo Platoon is a unit in the U.S. Army. Its chain of command can be traced from the company commander to the platoon leader to leaders of individual squads. The platoon was recognized as a high-performing unit and has received many commendations for readiness and efficiency.

In an effort to analyze the group's organizational characteristics, the company commander decided to examine the role relationships in the platoon. Thirty-five members of Bravo filled out a questionnaire that asked

Exhibit 8.1   Most and Least Preferred Members of Bravo Platoon

Most Desired	**Individuals Selected**
Friends	Sgt. Lopez, Lt. Washington
Leaders	Sgt. Hatfield, Sgt. Chung, Sgt. Baker
Best performers	Lt. Washington, Pvt. Berg, Pvt. Kae, Pvt. Megs
Counselors	Sgt. Hatfield, Sgt. Chung, Sgt. Baker
Trainers of new recruits	Lt. Washington, Pvt. Berg
Least Desired	**Individuals Selected**
Friends	Sgt. Lopez, Pvt. Megs, Pvt. Harris
Leaders	Pvt. Halsey, Pvt. Amost, Pvt. Perkins
Best performers	Pvt. Mintz, Pvt. Halsey, Pvt. Kerr
Counselors	Sgt. Lopez, Pvt. Halsey, Pvt. Harris
Trainers of new recruits	Pvt. Langley

which group members were the best friends, leaders, performers, people with whom to discuss problems, and trainers of new recruits. Platoon members also were asked to identify which members were worst in each category. Results are given in Exhibit 8.1.

Next the commander carefully reviewed the data to determine the role relationships that existed. He was particularly interested in the following questions:

1. Are those platoon leaders who are liked as friends the same ones who are accepted as leaders?
2. Are the best performers in the platoon selected as leaders?
3. Are individuals who are selected under a given category ever rejected under the same category?

Assume you are the commander and analyze the role relationships in Bravo Platoon. Take the approach suggested above. As the commander, what conclusions do you draw about the role relationships and organization of Bravo Platoon?

Suggested Readings

Cooper, C. L., and D. Torrington. "Identifying and Coping with Stress in Organizations." In *Behavioral Problems in Organizations,* edited by C. L. Cooper. Englewood Cliffs, N.J.: Prentice-Hall, 1979.

Cummings, L. L., G. P. Huber, and E. Arendt. "Effects of Size and Spatial Arrangements on Group Decision Making." *Academy of Management Journal* 17 (1974): 460–475.

de la Porte, P. C. A. "Group Norms: Key to Building a Winning Team." *Personnel* 51 (September/October 1974): 60–67.

Delbecq, A. L., A. Van de Ven, and D. H. Gustafson. *Group Techniques for Program Planning.* Glenview, Ill.: Scott, Foresman, 1975.

Duncan W. J. "An Analysis of a Sociometrically Generated Measure of Group Cohesiveness in Four Diversified Health Care Settings." *Allied Health and Behavioral Science* 1 (1978): 71–80.

Fleming, J. J., Jr. "Social Position and Decision Making Involving Risk." *Human Relations* 26 (1973): 67–76.

Ivancevich, J. M., and J. H. Donnelly, Jr. "A Study of Role Clarity and Need for Clarity for Three Occupational Groups." *Academy of Management Journal* 17 (1974): 28–36.

Johnson, T. W., and G. Graeri. "Organizational Assimilation and Role Rejection." *Organizational Behavior and Human Performance* 10 (1973): 72–87.

Leavitt, H. J., W. R. Dill, and H. B. Eyring. *The Organizational World.* New York: Harcourt, Brace, Jovanovich, 1973.

Manners, G. E., Jr. "Another Look at Group Size, Group Problem Solving, and Member Consensus." *Academy of Management Journal* 18 (1975): 715–724.

chapter 9

Power and Leadership in Groups

Jazz is not the only native American contribution to world culture. Leadership as a body of theory and research is distinctly an American creation.

Ralph M. Stogdill,
Journal of Contemporary Business

In his book *Crosswinds*, Najeeb E. Halaby of Pan American Airlines stated that his corporate epitaph probably would read, "A man who did his best at the worst time." Halaby clearly stated that he was not a ruthless enough decision maker to change an entire company. He suggested that his style of leadership did not fit the situation he faced at Pan Am in 1970.

Professional football coaches, like business executives, can operate in different ways to obtain positive results. One survey of professional coaches included such greats as Chuck Fairbanks, Bart Starr, Hank Stram, and Tom Landry. Although it was not shown conclusively, the survey suggested that successful coaches are probably more fluid and adaptive in their leadership styles than are less successful leaders. This research supports the widespread view that leaders must adapt to situations and that "a business manager is still a business manager, even when a playbook takes the place of a briefcase and the job at hand is actually a game."[1]

In Chapters 7 and 8, we examined social and task-oriented behavior in small groups. Now we will conclude Part III with a look at power and leadership. We have seen that social behavior simply evolves whenever people interact and that managers take great care in designing the most efficient work groups possible. However, when people work or play together, some individuals emerge as leaders. Leaders obtain their ability to influence through their power. Such power may result from superior physical strength, as with the pecking orders of barnyard hens and colonies of monkeys and seals. Or power may result from superior intellect, as might happen when a Nobel Prize–winning scientist joins a university faculty.

Regardless of the source, power and leadership are complex. They also are basic processes in all human interaction. This chapter first will look at power and how a person acquires it. We will examine some actual examples of political processes within organizations, drawing on our discussion of coalitions in Chapter 7. Then we will turn to leadership, emphasizing leadership styles and the situational theory of leadership effectiveness.

Power

Our daily newspapers offer countless examples of how the quest for power has built and destroyed nations, brought lovers together (and torn them apart), and provided the mold around which great empires have grown, prospered, and declined.

In this section, we will study several aspects of power relations in organizations. First, we will define power and review its origins. Next we will present an outline for analyzing power structures. We then will look at group power within complex organizations, using the theory of coalitions as our guide. Finally, we will present a political theory of how organizational goals are formed. This will show how power relates to organizational behavior.

Power is best defined as potential social influence. It is the ability to influence others through some personal or situational characteristic. From this perspective, we can see power for what it is—a political phenomenon.

Unlike authority, which arises from the formal organizational structure, power springs from less obvious sources. Thus secretaries influence their bosses, students influence professors, and salespeople influence marketing managers. The influential party has no official authority over the party being influenced. Yet each of these persons does have power. How do they obtain their ability to influence others? What, indeed, are the sources of power?

Sources of Power

Questions about how one person can influence another have been pondered by political scientists, business executives—probably by all of us at one time or another. Obviously, there are many reasons for a person's acquiring social influence. Sometimes this influence is related to what a person knows, or who a person knows, or the position a person holds. French and Raven have provided an efficient framework for classifying the sources of power.[2] They identified five types of power: coercive, reward, legitimate, referent, and expert. To this list we will add a sixth category—charisma.

Coercive Power   This type of influence "stems from the ability to mediate punishment for the influence."[3] In past centuries, the nobility had the power to influence the behavior of serfs, because nobles could punish any refusal to obey. Today parents similarly produce certain behavior patterns in their children through threats of punishment. A person who can punish another can influence that individual's behavior.

Reward Power   Closely related to coercion is reward power. This influence exists when one person determines the rewards another person receives. For example, the supervisor in an industrial work group periodically evaluates the performance of employees and can determine what rewards the workers will receive. Employees know how important a satisfactory evaluation is, and so they follow the supervisor's instructions.

Legitimate Power   Institutionalized values often dictate that a person has a legitimate right to influence others. Power is institutionalized when those who are influenced accept the legitimacy of the person's right to influence. Sociological literature has paid much attention to this influence. Max Weber, in particular, was concerned with it.[4] Legitimate power is exemplified by the influence the clergy have over the congregation. Much of the world's population willingly submits to the behavioral guidelines presented by religious leaders, whether by the Pope or the Ayatollah Khomeini.

Referent Power   Everyone has observed the psychological process known as identification, whereby one engages in behavior adopted from another person or group. Often we imitate those with whom we wish to identify. Thus both college students and aspiring executives adopt the hair styles or clothing fashions of their groups. In fact, as shown by our discussion of reference groups in Chapter 7, we all allow the individuals and groups we respect to influence our behavior in countless ways.

Expert Power   When we perceive someone as possessing special expertise, we often allow that person to influence our behavior. If we have a broken arm we do what our physician prescribes. If we are in a court of law, we need the advice of a lawyer. Our behavior is influenced because we assume that physicians and lawyers have expert knowledge about the situations.

Charismatic Power   Since less has been said about charisma as a source of social influence, we must look more closely at this basis of power. Weber stated that charisma is a "gift of grace" which is composed of some magical power or heroism.[5] Some behavioral scientists argue that charisma is less influential today because of growing sophistication and higher levels of education among the general public.[6] But looking at the almost supernatural influence of such leaders as Mao Tse-tung, Fidel Castro, and Charles Manson, we can conclude only that charisma remains a potent factor.

More recently, charismatic power has received serious analysis designed to illustrate its potential usefulness in building organizational commitment and meaning in people's working lives.[7] Whether or not behavioral and management scientists will come to understand this phenomenon remains to be seen. There seems little doubt, however, that charisma is an important basis of political power.

Power and the Source of Leadership

Power and leadership are closely related, for leadership always implies some influence. More precisely, Stogdill notes that leadership is the "process of influencing group activities toward goal accomplishment."[8]

Power probably is related most closely to the *source-of-leadership controversy*. This argument deals with how a person becomes a leader. There are two basic answers, and both can be illustrated by referring to the sources of power. In brief, do leaders emerge because of their traits or because of the situation at hand? Are leaders born or made?

Trait Theory   *Trait theory* proposes that leaders emerge because of superior physical or psychological characteristics. Compared with the past, today there is less emphasis on traits as predictors of leadership. In fact, most researchers probably would agree that a person does not become a leader by some combination of traits but by personal characteristics that have some relationship to the characteristics, activities, and goals of followers.

Some writers have attempted to predict leadership through personality typing.[9] Yet there is little to suggest conclusively that any personality pattern predicts leadership ability and managerial success. This conclusion should be no surprise, for the human personality includes a staggering number of traits that might be related to leadership ability. On the other hand, if we consider this traitist view in terms of the sources of power, as described above, some sources do appear as individual traits.

For example, we can think of referent, expert, and charismatic power as being unique individual traits that originate biologically or socially. Celebrities like the Beatles or Diana Ross or Henry Winkler may cause countless people to imitate their dress, speaking style, or even political preferences because the "average" person admires their personal traits. Aspiring scientists may let their hair fly free like Albert Einstein's or may name a child after him because they respect his scientific expertise.

Although there may be many ways to explain the influence of famous people and experts on others, we will see later that charismatic power is related more directly to personal traits. In fact, charisma itself is often seen as a unique trait of certain personalities. Much has been written about the charisma of John F. Kennedy, for example. People often are willing to yield to the leadership of such a person. The influence is not always beneficial. The tragic mass suicide of Peoples' Temple members in 1979 is a vivid example of the power of charisma.

But is there another way to explain the influence exerted by teen idols, national heroes, and power-hungry maniacs? Perhaps there is. Let us examine another view of the source of leadership.

Situational Theories The second popular explanation for the emergence of leadership is known as the *situational view.* This view suggests that it is the situation, not a person's traits, that makes the leader. In other words, the leader is the person most likely to respond to a given set of circumstances.

The situation giving rise to leadership is not predictable. A college professor who takes students to visit a factory may find one of the students leading the group. Similarly, the safety officer of a factory is likely to have much influence on the company president if complying with some standard of the Occupational Safety and Health Act is at issue.

One of the most common cases supporting the situational argument is seen when an organization hires an outside consultant to solve a certain problem. The consultant enters the organization with no formal authority and no right to influence operations. On the consultant's advice, however, management may take significant actions, such as redesigning the organizational structure, diversifying the company's product line, or otherwise altering its operations. The only source of power is the consultant's perceived expertise.

Other cases illustrate situational influence more specifically. For example, the physical position that a person occupies in group interaction can result in social power. One study illustrated how an individual's position in the flow of communication among a bomber crew influenced the number of leadership choices involved.[10] Another study showed that a person's visibility, as determined by how much he or she talks, often can influence the group's perception of that person's leadership capabilities.[11]

The study of group dynamics has reinforced much of the situational argument by showing that a person's control over information flow in a small group can result in leadership status.[12] Figure 9.1 illustrates this point. In the X and Y communication patterns, individuals like C tend to emerge as the leaders because they occupy a position central to information flow. Because of this control of information, these people can influence the behavior of group members in several ways. For one thing, individual C can act as a censor of information, passing on only what he or she considers desirable.

Figure 9.1   Leadership and Small-Group Communication Patterns

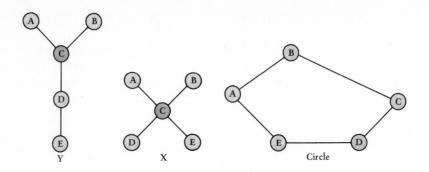

Thus person C can greatly influence the informed behavior of others. Moreover, since the possession of information is often considered important, individual C can "reward" or "punish" other group members by selectively sharing or withholding desired information.

In the circle, there is no such central control over information. As a result, information is more difficult to control and maintain. Thus it is more difficult to become a leader by controlling information.

The situation also can be said to determine who receives legitimate or reward power through promotion. Yet in many cases it is difficult to conclude whether the traits of a person created a particular situation or whether the situation called forth a person with specific traits. The issue is a bit like the argument over whether the chicken or the egg came first. A lot depends on one's perspective.

A General View   Fortunately, there are some ways to put the traitist-situationalist argument into perspective. We can, for example, venture the following generalizations based on existing research:

1. No specific traits are necessary for the emergence of leadership in all situations. However, the more similar two situations are, the more likely the transfer of traits will be.[13] For example, a retired army officer is more likely to be successful as chief of police than as director of a research laboratory. (There are, of course, exceptions.)

2. One does not become a leader by possessing particular traits, although the traits possessed must have some relevance to the

situation.[14] Thus the captain of a football team is usually competitive by nature.

These generalizations lead to a proposition concerning leadership.

Proposition 9.1

> Since there are similarities among all organizations, we can speculate about types of people who are likely to lead. At the same time, all organizations are unique. The more unique the organization is, the less likely the transfer of traits will be, because of situational factors.

Styles of Leadership

Another controversy that has received much attention in management literature concerns the way in which influence is exercised. Some leaders allow a great deal of participation from the group. Others are autocratic and make decisions with little consultation. From an administrative standpoint, we must ask which leadership style is most useful in accomplishing individual and group goals.

A Leadership Classification

When we talk about the way a person leads, we really are looking at the power of influence the leader has in comparison with group members. Because of this, there is an almost infinite range of leadership styles. For simplicity, we discuss three common styles: the autocratic, the democratic, and the laissez-faire. (See Figure 9.2.)

The autocratic style may be exercised when the leader has a high level of influence over followers. The main concern of an autocratic leader is to accomplish a task, although the results may vary according to the situation. An autocratic leader typically determines unilaterally what tasks will be performed and how they will be accomplished. However, it is not true that autocrats, in all cases, have no concern for the members of the group. For example, one may encounter the benevolent autocrat, usually a high-status, powerful

Figure 9.2   Selected Leadership Styles

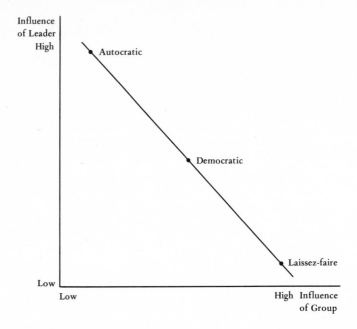

individual who unilaterally makes decisions. The distinguishing characteristic is that this person is benevolent; he or she is genuinely concerned with employee welfare as well as task accomplishment.[15]

The democratic style is characterized by power sharing and participation. We usually think of the leader and the followers as exhibiting equal amounts of power. The democratic style allows for the consideration of group members' views in forming and accomplishing goals. It is hoped that meaningful participation will promote the individual's sense of accomplishment and personal development.

At the lower right corner of Figure 9.2 is the laissez-faire style. This style can be viewed as the opposite of autocracy. Followers are the dominant influence. For practical purposes, leadership is meaningless, since no individual has substantial influence.

We can illustrate the three leadership styles by considering a typical class. Professor Jane Rigors realizes it is time for the midterm examination in her management course. Since the schedule is tight, she decides to behave like an autocrat. Without consulting the class, she announces that the midterm will be given during the next class meeting. The matter is closed.

Professor Rigors might have approached the problem another way. She realizes that her students have several exams during the middle of the term, yet she knows she must stay on schedule even if it causes some hardships. She explains this dilemma to the class, presenting her problem and stating her concern about the inconvenience. Then she announces that the test will be given during the next class period. This solution is no less autocratic than the earlier one, but Professor Rigors is more benevolent and is concerned about resulting hardships.

Rather than setting the date for the test herself, Professor Rigors also could select two or three choices for the class to consider. Members then could select an examination date by the largest number of votes. In such a case, the professor would be adopting a democratic style of leadership.

Finally, Professor Rigors might simply allow the class to suggest a date on which everyone can agree. She sets no guidelines and conducts no voting. The date is set in a purely laissez-faire manner. Frame 9.1 provides another illustration of the different approaches to leadership.

Frame 9.1

Consider Your Assumptions: Theory X and Theory Y

Psychologist Douglas McGregor wrote many influential books, including *The Human Side of Enterprise.* In this book, McGregor noted how the assumptions we make about other people can influence the way we behave toward them. He labeled the two ends of the assumption continuum theory X and theory Y.

Theory X managers assume that workers are lazy, indolent, and maybe even a bit dishonest. Workers are viewed as lacking ambition and as actually wanting to be directed. In this view, employees are resistant to change, self-centered, and gullible. Theory Y managers take a different view. They see employees as mature adults who want to contribute their talents toward organizational goals. This view sees workers as being somewhat creative and as having substantial undeveloped potential.

McGregor argues that theory X managers develop a group leadership climate based on the authority of the boss. They design the work place accordingly. Employees must punch in and out to protect against dishonesty and cheating; they must follow instructions exactly, lest the group degenerate into an uncoordinated mob; and authority must be exercised constantly, because employees want a leader. The result is dependency. Employees may give a reasonable day's work, but they remain undeveloped and dependent.

Theory Y managers are not afraid to give employees freedom. They encourage employees to exercise creativity and to pursue responsibility. Theoretically, these employees respond by being creative, mature, and responsible.

Of course, no manager strictly follows theory X or theory Y. McGregor states that managers must "selectively adapt" to situations. When employees are immature, more control is needed. When they are responsible and mature, freedom is desirable.

As we would expect, the question that has preoccupied writers on management is: What leadership pattern results in the highest level of group performance? Fortunately, there has been much research in this area.

Selected Research Findings

Perhaps the most important early research on leadership styles was conducted in the 1940s by a group of individuals at Ohio State University. These studies are frequently referred to as the two-dimensional theory of leadership. Through the use of a questionnaire, Fleishman, Harris, and Burtt isolated two categories of leadership behavior.[16] The first, initiating structure, concerns how much structure a leader imposes on the group in accomplishing its task. This is related to task orientation, because it is assumed that the person imposing structure is more concerned with the task than with group relationships.

The second factor was labeled interpersonal effectiveness, or consideration. This factor relates to the leader's concern with interpersonal relations within the group. The researchers found a direct association between the leader's consideration and a low incidence of grievances. The reverse was also true. In follow-up studies, it was noted that the lowest grievance rates were obtained when there was simultaneous concern for both initiating structure and consideration.[17]

Equally important are the results of related investigations. For example, in one case, the proficiency of production supervisors positively correlated with their scores on initiating structure. A negative association with consideration was also observed. Interestingly, the reverse was true for nonproduction supervisors.[18] The prevailing thought today, however, is that both consideration and initiating structure are important determinants of the effectiveness of leader behavior.[19]

In another series of leadership studies, Kahn and Katz conducted a survey to study influence patterns in various organizational settings. The organizations selected included an insurance company, a tractor factory, and section gangs on a railroad. The key result of these studies was that employee-oriented leaders (those who emphasized interpersonal relations) tended to have high-performing groups. By contrast, the low-performing units more often were supervised by task-oriented leaders. It also was noted that the closeness of supervision was related inversely to group performance. That is, leaders who closely supervised group members had lower-performing units.[20]

In a more formal sense, Kahn and Katz noted that three important factors relate to leadership in work groups. First, leaders of high-performing groups do not supervise as closely as do leaders of low-performing units. Second, leaders of high-performing groups are more employee-oriented and encourage participation. Third, leaders of high-performing groups spend relatively more time on supervisory functions (for example, planning work) and less time duplicating the jobs of employees.

The final group of studies we will review are those of Rensis Likert, which classified leaders under two headings: job centered and employee centered.[21] The job-centered leader, like the task-oriented leader, relies on structure and is preoccupied with task accomplishment. The employee-centered leader is more concerned with group relations. Likert's basic finding after extensive research, was that employee-centered leaders achieve more favorable results.

Measuring Leadership Styles

Although we frequently talk about various leadership styles, it is difficult to verify them within an organizational setting. A supervisor may really be autocratic, but perceived by the group to be demo-

Figure 9.3   A Hypothetical Control Graph

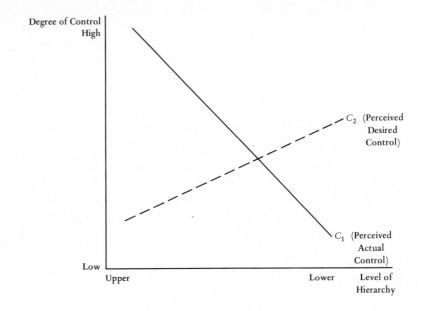

cratic. From a behavioral perspective, it is probably safe to say that what a person is perceived to be is the important factor.

Arnold Tannenbaum has developed and popularized a technique for measuring how employees perceive the leadership environment in an organization.[22] The technique also illustrates how employees think the environment ought to be. This perceived and desired environment is called the control structure of an organization, and it can be analyzed by means of a control graph.[23]

As shown in Figure 9.3, a control graph reveals two important aspects of the perceived control structure within an organization. First, the slope of the curve (solid line) shows the manner in which participants perceive the control to be distributed from upper to lower levels of the hierarchy. The average height of the curve shows how much total control is perceived to be present in the organization.

To illustrate, consider a case in which rank-and-file employees are asked to indicate, on a five-point Likert scale, the amount of control they think each level in the hierarchy, including employees, has. The members also are asked to evaluate how much control they think each level should have.

The hierarchical levels are plotted on the horizontal axis, and the degree of control is placed on the vertical axis. The vertical scale ranges from 1 (very little control) to 5 (a great deal of control). The central tendency of the group members' responses then is calculated and plotted to acquire the control graph. Although there is some question about which measure of central tendency should be used, for simplicity we have plotted the mean (midpoint).

The solid line in the diagram (curve C_1) illustrates that the group members perceive the control structure to be autocratic. This perception is shown by the high amount of control ascribed to top management and the low amount ascribed to employees and lower management. The curve slopes downward to the right. The broken line C_2 shows that group members desire a more democratic structure (slope of curve) and a lower level of total control, as shown by the overall lower level of the C_2 curve and by its upward slope to the right.

Supporters of the participative approach to management argue that a curve sloping upward to the right is desirable, because it illustrates a democratic organizational environment. Some studies have been advanced that suggest the existence of an association between participative control structures and organizational effectiveness.[24] Tannenbaum, in related research, argues that an association exists between the average height of the curve and the effectiveness of the organization.[25]

Proposition 9.2	The way power is exercised relates to the styles of leadership. Leaders exercise their power in a variety of ways ranging from the extremes of autocratic to laissez-faire.

The potential usefulness of the control graph as a means of analyzing organizational power and control structure is significant. The technique is easy to use, and the data generated are relatively simple to analyze. However, various methodological problems require additional research before control graphs can be used properly and effectively to examine organizational processes.[26]

Contingency Theory

Much contemporary research in leadership is related to the controversy about leadership styles. One particular tradition, pioneered by Fred E. Fiedler, has become known as *contingency theory*.

The contingency model argues that the effectiveness of a group depends on two things: the personality of the leader and the degree to which he or she receives power (influence) from the situation (or, more precisely, the degree to which the situation presents the leader with uncertainty).[27] In other words, the contingency view is situational. Because of this, it is difficult to trace the evolution of the theory. There is evidence, however, that the formalized contingency model was relatively well developed by the early 1960s.

Elements of the Theory

Fiedler defines *leadership* as a personal relationship in which one person directs, coordinates, and supervises others in the performance of a common task. *Leadership style* refers to the underlying needs that motivate the leader's behavior.[28]

Classifying the Leader In analyzing leadership effectiveness, the most pressing research problem is to classify leaders. To do this, Fiedler developed an interesting procedure. The first step was to ask subjects to think of all the people with whom they had worked and to concentrate on the person they had worked with least successfully. Respondents then were asked to describe this individual using a semantic-differential questionnaire.[29] This type of questionnaire usually consists of a list of opposing adjectives with possible choices between them. The questionnaire might appear as follows:

Least-Preferred Coworker

Good __ __ __ __ __ __ __ __ Bad
Friendly __ __ __ __ __ __ __ __ Unfriendly

Usually about twenty adjectives are used to describe the least-preferred coworker (LPC). The scales are summed to provide an LPC score. According to Fiedler, the person who receives a high score (one who describes the least-preferred coworker favorably) is classified as a group- or relations-oriented leader. The person who scores low (describes the least-preferred coworker unfavorably) is said to be task oriented.

The logic of this classification is that an individual who ranks the least-preferred coworker with a high score is concerned with interpersonal relations even though the situation may be tense.[30] The person who rates the least-preferred coworker with a low score has task accomplishment as the major goal. Thus he or she is said to be task oriented.

Using this classification technique we now can compare two basic types of leaders. However, we must consider some other factors to complete the analysis.

Classifying the Situation   In contingency theory, the situation is classified according to three variables: position power, task structure, and leader-member relations.[31] The interaction among these determines the favorableness or unfavorableness of the leadership situation. Let us look more closely at each of these variables.

Position power involves the extent to which the leader's position compels group members to accept commands. A leader has considerable position power when operating in a formal organizational role that allows for the granting or withholding of rewards. In this sense, the supervisor of a work group or the principal of a public school has more position power than does a member of the group or a well-liked teacher.

Task structure refers to the job being performed. If the task is repetitive, or if its procedures are predictable, it is easier to control than if it is unstructured. Thus the leader of a group of bricklayers has an easier job with task structure than does a professor in a school of business. The professor's job does not follow a step-by-step sequence, as the brick mason's does.

Finally, the favorableness of the leader's job is related to leader-follower relations. When the followers trust the leader and the leader trusts the followers—when a generally cordial relationship exists—the situation is more favorable than when hostility prevails.

We have, then, a three-dimensional view of leadership. Depending on how these three factors come together, the leadership situation can range from favorable to unfavorable. The combinations are set forth in Table 9.1.

Fiedler's extensive research shows an interesting relationship between the favorableness of the situation and the most appropriate

Table 9.1   The Leadership Situation

Situation	Position Power	Task Structure	Leader-Follower Relations
1	Strong	Structured	Good
2	Weak	Structured	Good
3	Strong	Unstructured	Good
4	Weak	Unstructured	Good
5	Strong	Structured	Poor
6	Weak	Structured	Poor
7	Strong	Unstructured	Poor
8	Weak	Unstructured	Poor

Adapted from *A Theory of Leadership Effectiveness* by Fred E. Fiedler, p. 34. Copyright © 1967 by McGraw-Hill, Inc. Used with permission of McGraw-Hill Book Company.

leadership style. A general summary is found in Figure 9.4. We find something surprising from an intuitive perspective. The diagram clearly shows that in situations where the leadership situation tends to be reasonably favorable, a task-oriented leader is more effective. The same is true when the situation is unfavorable. Only in intermediate stages—where we would classify the situations as moderately favorable or unfavorable—does a relations-oriented style seem to be more effective.

Implications   Before listing some of the implications of contingency theory for management, we should note that contingency arguments are basically descriptive. That is, Fiedler is not saying theoretically that this is how it should be. Instead, he is saying that, based on extensive research, this is how it is! Contrary to much past leadership theory, an employee orientation does not appear to be the most effective leadership style in all situations. Rather, there is no one best way to lead. To a considerable extent, style depends on the situation. Thus the contingency theory rests on a situation's relativity.

The argument proposed by contingency theory is not an easy one to understand intuitively, because the theory is based on data, not

Figure 9.4   Leadership Situations and Styles

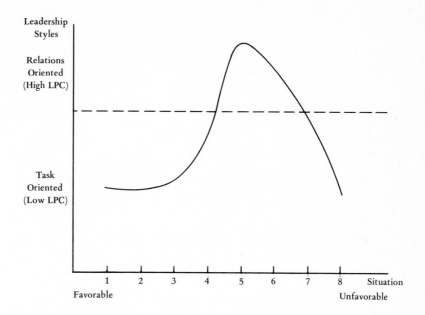

Source: Reprinted by permission of the Harvard Business Review. Exhibit adapted from "Engineer the Job to Fit the Manager," by Fred E. Fiedler (September-October 1965). Copyright © 1965 by the President and Fellows of Harvard College; all rights reserved.

theoretical prescriptions. Therefore, it seems advisable to examine the relationships in greater detail and to provide some examples of what is being said, along with some theoretical speculations about the main points. Table 9.2 presents a familiar real-world situation for each of the eight combinations of situational characteristics and to propose a possible explanation for the data collected.

Although the situations presented are hypothetical, and numerous similar examples could be developed, the point of the table is simple. Unlike the prescription of traditional leadership theory, contingency theory argues that there is no one best way to lead that transcends all situations. The appropriate leadership style is determined by the interaction of at least three situational factors—position power, task structure, and leader-follower relations. Thus a successful leader in

Table 9.2 Some Hypothetical Cases Illustrating the Logic of Situational Leadership

Situation	Case Example	Position Power	Task Structure	Leader-Follower Relations	Effective Leadership Style	Possible Explanation for Effectiveness
1	Popular squad leader in army	Strong	Structured	Good	Task-oriented	Members respect task expertise, recognize possible risk, and willingly submit to autocratic style.
2	Tallyman or straw boss in a production group	Weak	Structured	Good	Task-oriented	Person usually selected for this position because he or she is recognized by group as exhibiting its values while also being acceptable to management. Since this person is so much one of the "old gang," he or she displays task orientation to get things done, and group allows it.
3	Popular sergeant of detectives in law enforcement agency	Strong	Unstructured	Good	Task-oriented	The sergeant has formal position power but must supervise an unstructured task. Here the orientation is still task oriented but less so, because some freedom must be given for dealing with unprogrammed situations.
4	Popular department head in university	Weak	Unstructured	Good	Almost equal balance between task and relations orientation	Because of the professionalization of the faculty, the department head has little real position power and the task is unstructured. If liked and respected, the department head can be task-oriented in routine administrative affairs such

relations-oriented in issues such as policies, curriculum, and so on.

5	Unpopular foreman of a machine shop	Strong	Structured	Poor	Relations-oriented	In this case the job is predictable and can be controlled by authority if necessary. However, effective performance depends on how well a basically unpopular supervisor can motivate people to better-than-minimum performance. This is best accomplished through interpersonal skills.
6	Unpopular captain of athletic team	Weak	Structured	Poor	Relations-oriented	The task each member is to perform is clear. The coach has major authority, but captain must motivate. If captain is unpopular, the most effective strategy is to use relations-oriented approach.
7	Unpopular chief of medical staff in hospital	Strong	Unstructured	Poor	Almost equal balance between task and relations orientation	Although authority may be exercised, unprogrammed activities are difficult to directly control. Since leader-follower relations are poor, most effective approach is to use task orientation only when essential and to concentrate on relations.
8	Unpopular project leader of group of professional certified accountants	Weak	Unstructured	Poor	Task-oriented	The task to be accomplished is not easily programmed, and the project leader has little real authority and is disliked. Best hope for effectiveness is to concentrate on task and exercise available authority.

one situation may or may not be successful in another. A person who wants to be a successful leader in many settings probably will have to change leadership styles as the situation demands.

Managers in organizations thus are told to be careful in generalizing about the way leaders *should* behave—unless they take into account the importance of varying situations. This approach requires managers to know the strengths and weaknesses of subordinate leaders and to place them in jobs with the likelihood of success. Perhaps more time should be spent on learning how to alter leadership situations and less time on the typical human relations approach of remaking leaders to fit situations.[32]

One should not, of course, blindly accept the contingency argument as a final answer to the leadership question. Objections and cautions have been raised. Interestingly, most objections have related to methodology. For example, the stability of the LPC score has been questioned. What would happen to the theory if it could be shown that someone who receives a high score on the LPC questionnaire at one time receives a low score on a later questionnaire?[33] Certainly, this would challenge the wisdom of fitting jobs to people who could not be classified accurately.

Finally, contingency theory itself presents another methodological problem. Since environmental complexities are involved, control problems are more serious, and the requirements for testing such theories are more severe.[34]

Proposition 9.3

> Early leadership research supports the idea that employee-oriented leadership leads to increased levels of group performance. More recent research, however, supports the idea that there is no one best way to lead. The most effective leadership style is contingent on the situation.

From this discussion of contingency theory, we move to one final theme in leadership research. This has to do with path-goal formulations—a topic we briefly discussed in connection with motivation (Chapter 6).

Path-Goal Theory

A relatively new development in leadership theory and research is the *path-goal theory*. House and Mitchell state that this theory is concerned primarily with how the leader influences the followers' perceptions of their work goals, personal goals, and paths to goal accomplishment.[35]

The path-goal model is part of the more general expectancy theory discussed in Chapter 6. We noted there that expectancy theory is based primarily on instrumentality. That is, we behave in a certain way because we perceive that the action will contribute to, or be instrumental in, achieving some desired end. Thus a person's behavior is related both to the perceived probability (expectancy) that a certain action will lead to a certain outcome and to the desirability (valence) of the outcome. This idea is important in leadership, because it generally is assumed that leaders can influence which goals followers pursue and the extent to which the goals are valued.

Research has shown that two important functions of leaders are (1) to clarify goals, that is, communicate to followers what behavior will be rewarded, and (2) to increase the rewards for goal attainment by supporting followers in their quests for desired behavior.[36]

Thus two important propositions are advanced by path-goal theory. First, leadership behavior is acceptable to the extent that followers perceive the behavior to be immediately satisfying or instrumental in achieving future satisfaction. Second, leader behavior is motivational to the extent that it relates need satisfaction to successful task performance and supports the behavior necessary for successful performance.

A simple path-goal model appears in Figure 9.5. Of course, we could examine additional considerations. However, since we dis-

Figure 9.5   A Simple Path-Goal Model

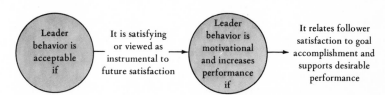

cussed expectancy previously, we will summarize with an example. Assume that a supervisor is attempting to motivate high levels of performance within a work group. One of the first things the supervisor must do is assist the group in clarifying its goal—the task to be performed. If the task is repetitive, little effort is necessary. If the goal or task is less specific, attention must be given to defining it.

It is important for the supervisor to show how the desired goal will be instrumental in accomplishing members' personal goals. This helps to increase the importance (valence) of the goal. It is also essential for the supervisor to make it evident that personal goal accomplishment and need satisfaction will occur in proportion to the successful completion of the task. Instrumentality is thus established.

Proposition 9.4

> The leader's behavior is viewed as acceptable by followers when it is perceived to be immediately satisfying or instrumental in future satisfaction. It is motivational if it relates satisfaction to goal accomplishment and supports goal-oriented behavior.

What Managers Should Know About Power and Leadership

Managers must be leaders, but they must understand that not all leaders are managers. Power is important to a manager because power is the ability to influence. Managers clearly must be able to influence employee behavior if they are to accomplish organizational goals. The exercise of power does not in itself mean that a manager is autocratic or too demanding.

In a group setting all managers also should be aware that group members themselves possess power, for they can influence the action or nonaction of others. Thus it often may be possible for managerial personnel to exert influence indirectly by creating the proper work environment. When the group is behind goal accomplishment, individuals will work hard in the interest of group membership.

Managers can gain the ability to influence by providing a good example and by using rewards fairly as an incentive for high performance. Few supervisory personnel today can be successful if they use only legitimate and coercive power.

The notions of power that a manager entertains will influence his or her leadership style. Therefore, successful administrators become sensitive to the situation and are able to adapt to environmental demands. The myth of "one best" leadership style has been destroyed. Future managers must recognize the need to respond to the realities of the situation. There is no reason to believe that democratic styles will be accepted universally or that autocratic methods will be rejected immediately. Rather, there is evidence to suggest that managers will be required to size up the situation continually and then decide how to lead in the most effective manner.

Summary

Sometimes power is easy to identify, and sometimes it is difficult to understand why we allow certain people to influence our behavior. Yet the ability of a person to influence another is at the heart of leadership in groups. This chapter aimed at illustrating how closely individuals and the situations they face interact to produce unique influences on the particular group. Specifically, we examined how individual personalities and situational factors contribute to a person's power in an organization.

Once leadership is attained, questions about how to use power most effectively become relevant. Some leaders are autocrats and feel little need to encourage the participation of others. Others like to exercise their power as little as possible, allowing the group free rein. Both approaches have advantages and disadvantages. Autocratic leaders maintain control but do not allow individual group members to develop their own abilites of leadership. Laissez-faire leaders emphasize individual growth and responsibility but may allow control and efficiency to diminish.

Contemporary leadership research has provided valuable insights into the use of power by illustrating that there is no single most desirable leadership style. The key to effective leadership seems to involve an ability to adapt one's style to the situation.

Questions for Discussion

1. What is the main difference between situational and traitist views of leadership? Which view do you consider to be more accurate? Why?
2. Why do we say that the path-goal theory of leadership is part of the more general expectancy theory of motivation? Explain in detail.
3. What is the basic argument of the contingency theory of leadership? How is it different from earlier leadership theory and research?
4. Do you think the idea of the least-preferred coworker score is sound? Explain.
5. Why do you think leadership has received so much attention by behavioral scientists? What practical implications does leadership research have for management?
6. Do you consider charisma to be an important source of social influence? In your opinion, are people becoming too sophisticated to accept charismatic influences? Give examples.

Exercise: Classifying the Sources of Power

Power can be obtained from many sources. Unfortunately, it is not always easy to determine exactly how or why a person has the ability to influence others. Consider the five people described below and identify the source(s) of each person's power. Then answer the following questions:

1. What type(s) of power does each person possess?
2. What is the basis for each response you make?
3. Why is it difficult to identify exactly what type of power a person has?

Professor Lelia Scott Professor Scott is the chairperson of the Department of Behavioral Medicine in an outstanding American medical school. She received an M.D. from Johns Hopkins University and holds a Ph.D. in psychology from the University of Chicago. She is a fellow of the American Society of Behavioral Medicine and is a well-known author and lecturer.

Janice Baylor Janice Baylor is the chief executive officer of Advanced Systems Corporation (ASC), one of the largest producers of microcomputers. She has moved to the top of the organization because of outstanding mathematical and administrative skills. She is responsible for overall policy making and is accountable only to the board of directors. Baylor currently serves on the board of directors of four companies in the Fortune 500. Recently, she was appointed to the president's task force on technology utilization.

Barnard Cole Barnard Cole is chief of police in a large eastern city. He is the first black officer to come through the ranks and be appointed head of a major urban law enforcement department. Cole began as a rookie officer twelve years ago and has advanced rapidly. During this time, he successfully completed a doctoral degree in criminal justice. At present, he is directing a national study on the reform of the criminal justice system.

Becky Blye Becky Blye is the lead singer of a successful rock group known as Becky and the Bows. She has one of the strongest voices in the business but is most noted for her unconventional performance methods. Besides singing, she plays six different musical instruments during every show. She wears her hair differently and dresses uniquely for each performance. Young adults throughout the nation have begun to copy her style.

Sir Jerry Sir Jerry is the director of the Institute for Self-Control and Stress Reduction. He has developed a new form of meditation and biofeedback that has helped many people control high blood pressure and depression. More than sixty thousand people subscribe to his magazine *Coping*. The institute's new office building and headquarters is estimated to have cost $25 million; it was financed completely by voluntary contributions.

Case: Good Leader in Hard Times

On September 9, 1976, Mao Tse-tung died at the age of eighty-two. To many people the news of Mao's passing was not sad, but few would argue that a significant era of modern history had not come to an end. For anyone interested in leadership, Mao's life is indeed an unusual case study.

Mao Tse-tung was born to hard times, the son of a peasant. Although Mao's life became a little better as time passed, his father remained a rigid man with great devotion to hard work and little appreciation for formal education. In spite of this Mao managed to obtain a relatively good education through his own determination.

His revolutionary tendencies and ability to survive in hard times were clear throughout his youth. During much of the early growth of the Communist movement in China, Mao and other revolutionaries lived in caves. It was probably this existence that made the future leader of China so accepting of hardships and that led to his advocacy of labor-intense methods. In fact, Mao often remarked that during the years of Communist revolutionary struggles, he and his fellow warriors were always at their best when times were hard.

Looking back, one thing becomes clear about China under Mao. Many social reforms were accomplished, and the methods by which they were realized always had certain similarities. Thought control was an essential element, and force and terrorism were the tactics employed. Reforms of thought were evident before 1955, but the most dramatic changes occurred as part of the Cultural Revolution and the Red Guard activities that accompanied it between 1966 and 1969. In fact, Mao was convinced that continuous revolution was necessary to ensure China's place of world leadership, which he so greatly desired. One can document numerous cases in which bad planning and management were overcome only through revolution, thought control, and force. Yet this individual who led so well in hard times managed to survive even when conditions improved. Thus some key questions about leadership need investigation:

1. How can the ability to lead best in hard times be explained by leadership theory and research?
2. Is it possible to classify the situation faced by China's leadership using contingency theory? If so, how would you classify it?
3. Do you think that leadership theory can be applied to larger political entities, such as national governments? Why or why not?

Suggested Readings

Bartol, K. M., and M. S. Wortman. "Sex Effects in Leader Behavior, Self-Descriptions and Job Satisfaction." *Journal of Psychology* 94 (1976): 177–183.

Chapman, J. B., and F. Luthans. "Female Leadership Dilemma." *Public Personnel Management* 4 (May/June 1975): 173–176.

Csoka, L. S. "Relationship between Organizational Climate and the Situational Favorableness Dimension of Fiedler's Contingency Model." *Journal of Applied Psychology* 60 (1975): 273–277.

Fodor, E. M. "Disparagement by a Subordinate as an Influence on the Use of Power." *Journal of Applied Psychology* 59 (1974): 652—655.

Michaelsen, L. K. "Leader Orientation, Leader Behavior, Group Effectiveness and Situational Favorability." *Organizational Behavior and Human Performance* 9 (1973): 226–246.

Mitchell, T. R., ed. "Current Perspectives in Leadership," *Journal of Contemporary Business* 3 (1974). Entire issue devoted to leadership research and theory.

Nebeker, D. M., and T. R. Mitchell. "Leader Behavior: An Expectancy Theory Approach." *Organizational Behavior and Human Performance* 11 (1974): 355–367.

Pfeffer, Jeffrey, and G. R. Salancik. "Organizational Decision Making as a Political Process." *Administrative Science Quarterly* 19 (1974): 135–151.

Starke, F. A., and Orlando Behling. "A Test of Two Postulates Underlying Expectancy Theory." *Academy of Management Journal* 18 (1975): 703–714.

Stogdill, R. M. *Handbook of Leadership: A Survey of Theory and Research.* New York: Free Press, 1974.

Vroom, V. H. and A. G. Jago. "Decision Making as a Social Process: Normative and Descriptive Models of Leader Behavior." *Decision Sciences* 5 (1974): 743–769.

part IV

Foundations of Organizational Design

IN PARTS I THROUGH III, we have examined how individuals and groups behave in organizations. Now we will analyze organizational design, or structure, and relate it to selected behavioral issues.

Chapter 10 begins with intergroup relations. A basic management problem is to coordinate groups within an organization such as production and sales staffs in a business firm, surgery and radiology personnel in a hospital, public safety and community development agencies in a city government, and business and humanities departments in a university. In analyzing the relationships between groups in an organization, we will deal specifically with such key issues as coordination, competition, conflict, and conflict resolution. A manager in any organization frequently must handle situations involving conflict. When line units like production conflict with staff units like data processing, the manager must know the strategies of conflict resolution. Even more serious is arbitrating a settlement between management and union representatives.

Classical management theory views conflict within an organization as dysfunctional. However, modern behavioral theories suggest that conflict can be useful. Chapter 11 presents some general theories of organizational design and the relationships between individuals and organizations. It also reviews some basic principles of classical organization theory and introduces the contingency theory of management. In brief, classical theory is based on a prescriptive approach that seeks the one best way to organize. Contingency theory, on the other hand, is situational. It emphasizes adapting to different conditions. Its only prescription is that managers remain responsive to changing circumstances within the organization.

Chapter 12 concludes Part IV by examining how organizations interact with their environment. We will pay special attention to organizational designs that respond readily to change. Specifically, we will compare the project and matrix structures of organization. Then we will explore some newer, increasingly important design options such as professional hierarchies and organic-adaptive structures.

Coordinating Intergroup Relations

What could be more important in management development than learning to deal skillfully with intergroup conflict and friction in order to resolve it?

Robert Blake and Jane Mouton,
Group Dynamics: Key to Decision Making

For years General Electric Company used a unique approach in labor negotiations. The approach was called "Boulwarism" after the executive who devised it, Lemuel Boulware. Although the traditional interpretation of Boulwarism has been questioned in recent years, it is generally considered to be a hard-line bargaining stance. General Electric, after deliberation and study, would make its best offer to the union. After that, the company would refuse to "horse trade" with union officials further.

Negotiation between labor and management is a classic example of intergroup conflict. Indeed, collective bargaining or negotiating behavior is one important approach to conflict resolution. Boulwarism was an unusually rigid labor relations philosophy, because collective bargaining is generally based on good conscience and free bargaining between two parties of relatively equal power. In fact, in 1964, the National Labor Relations Board ruled that Boulwarism constituted bad-faith bargaining. Further appeals by General Electric were overruled.

This chapter examines intergroup relations—an important topic for many reasons. First, conflict between such key groups as pro-

245

duction and marketing or between data processing and finance can greatly reduce the efficiency of an organization. Second, some proposed solutions to conflict are clearly more effective than others. The various strategies to resolve conflict must be analyzed carefully to evaluate their advantages and disadvantages.

In examining intergroup relations, we have three main goals. Initially, we want to explore the unique nature of intergroup behavior. Then we will investigate its political aspects. Finally, we will present a detailed look at conflict between groups and how it can be resolved.

Intergroup Behavior

Management literature rarely analyzes intergroup behavior, although such topics as interdepartmental relations and line-and-staff conflict clearly deal with how groups interact. Thus we must be specific in defining our subject at the outset if we are to understand it. An important place to begin is with the environment, or *relevant set,* within which intergroup behavior takes place.

Uniqueness of Intergroup Analysis

Researchers often speak of the *organizational set* when conducting management studies. In other words, when analyzing organizations, we must look at all the interactions involving the subject of the research.[1] When we study intrapersonal behavior, we look at an individual. When we study small groups, we concentrate on a collection of individuals, or the interpersonal dimension. However, when we study the interaction of groups, we must expand our analysis to a more complex level.

Consider Figure 10.1. Although this diagram is simplified, it illustrates the complexity of group interaction. First, we see that intergroup relations in organizations may be horizontal, as with groups one and two. Such horizontal interaction takes place when two groups on the same organizational level interact. Examples include the production and sales divisions of a manufacturing firm or the various departments in a hospital such as surgery, internal medicine, radiology.

Relations between groups may also be vertical, as with groups one and three. In this case, two groups from different organizational

Figure 10.1 Relevant Set in Intergroup Analysis

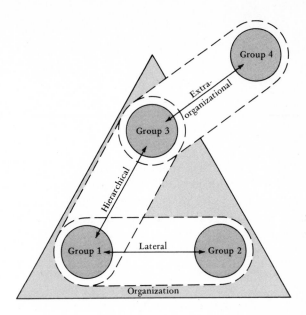

levels interact. Examples include a group of deans interacting with a group of department heads in a university, supervisors interacting with employees, or city council members interacting with various department heads in some municipal governments.

It is also common for a group in an organization to interact with one or more groups outside the organization. This relationship occurs, for example, when a management group bargains with representatives of the local union or when a Senate committee works with outside consultants.

The brief overview of intergroup analysis presented in Figure 10.1 makes it clear that we must look at a variety of possible interactions between groups in an organization. Only in this way can we adequately understand intergroup behavior.

Conflict and Control

When we move to the level of intergroup analysis, we confront certain problems. First, although conflict certainly develops within individuals and among individuals in the same group, most people in

Figure 10.2   Hierarchy of goals

a group will eventually, through effective management, direct their behavior toward attaining the group's objectives. However, when we deal with more than one group, one set of goals must be related to another. For example, the sales department has one goal and knows what it is. The same is true of the production department. At the same time, there is a higher-level goal toward which both sales and production are directed.

To illustrate, consider Figure 10.2. In this case, sales and production may go their merry way unless action is taken to emphasize that their goals are interdependent. It makes little sense for one group to produce unless another group is selling the output. By the same logic, no one can sell items that are not produced. Thus a structure, or hierarchy, develops in the organization. Units are created to ensure that the efforts of different groups with different interests are coordinated toward the overall organizational goal. Coordinating groups rather than individuals is one unique problem of intergroup behavior.

Ensuring coordination between groups is often made more difficult because the values and interests of individual group members can lead to conflict. Conflict occurs when the accepted rules of constructive competition are violated and groups with different goals engage in actions that harm one another. We shall say more in a later section about the methods of reducing such dysfunctional conflict.

One of the most troublesome problems of intergroup behavior is coordinating overall activities.[2] In Figure 10.1, for example, groups three and four, though related, are not in the same organization. When conflicts develop, no commonly recognized authority exists who can step in and resolve them.

Such a situation is common within organizations. What would happen, for example, if General Electric, using the collective bargaining approach of Boulwarism, made its best offer to the electrical workers' union but the union found it unsatisfactory? Who could resolve the disagreement? If two departments *within* General Electric had such a problem, a higher-level executive responsible for coordinating the two departments could force a resolution. But no such higher-level official exists to handle labor-management disputes. In an extreme case—and after much legal activity—a third party such as the government might step in and resolve the conflict. Even this, however, would be difficult, given the question of final authority.

Or consider the complexity of intergroup problems when extended to the international setting. Take, for example, the case of the Iranian student takeover of the American embassy with hostages in 1979. The students and the U.S. government were in conflict, but there was no recognized authority to which the case could be appealed. It was suggested that the Swedes or the Palestine Liberation Organization or the United Nations might negotiate a resolution, yet none of these groups had any real authority to enforce a solution. No outside group could require that the United States return the shah for trial or that the students release the hostages. The complexity of such intergroup conflict leads us to advance our first proposition.

Proposition 10.1

> Intergroup behavior is unique in several ways. Among the most important considerations are (1) that conflict arises more frequently when two or more groups are involved and (2) that authority hierarchies often do not exist to resolve conflicts among groups that do not belong to the same organization. Thus intergroup analysis becomes complicated.

Coordination in Historical Perspective

Coordination is a virtue in classical organization theory. Conflict, or anything reducing effective coordination, is clearly undesirable.[3] The emphasis in management literature has been not so much on understanding what causes conflict and reduces coordination as on how to resolve conflict. In other words, conflict has generally been assumed to be a problem that management is obliged to resolve.

In more recent times, a different view has developed concerning the necessity for complete coordination among precisely functioning groups. Coordination is important because it leads to efficiency. Equally obvious is the prescription that good management eases coordination. Modern behavioral scientists, however, have pointed out that conflict is not always dysfunctional. To the contrary, under certain circumstances, it can stimulate change.[4] When an organization is precisely functioning and efficient, it often becomes resistant to change. Limited conflict, however, encourages change.[5]

Consider the following example. The municipal government of Lakeville has been stable for the past ten years. The mayor is enjoying a fifth term, and the city council has been re-elected, with few exceptions, during the past eight years. The heads of the departments work well together, and they experience little friction with the elected legislative officials.

From all indications, Lakeville is a well-managed and efficiently operated government. Its only problems relate to matters that receive too little attention. For example, the fire department has outdated equipment, as does the department of public works. The school system is stable but has changed little in philosophy or technique during the past ten years. The sanitation department does a good job collecting garbage and keeping the streets clean.

Unfortunately, Lakeville's public schools are in danger of losing their accreditation because of an outdated library and inferior teacher qualifications. The city is also under order from the federal government to do something about its "sanitary" land fill, which fails to meet environmental standards. Lakeville's government is reasonably efficient, and its employees work well with one another. However, given the pressures for innovation, the city might have avoided its present problems by anticipating change.

The Traditional Argument

The traditional, or classical, view of intergroup relations sees groups as machines that operate automatically and consistently to achieve some end. Both bureaucratic theory and the more functional orien-

Figure 10.3   Structure of Bureaucracy

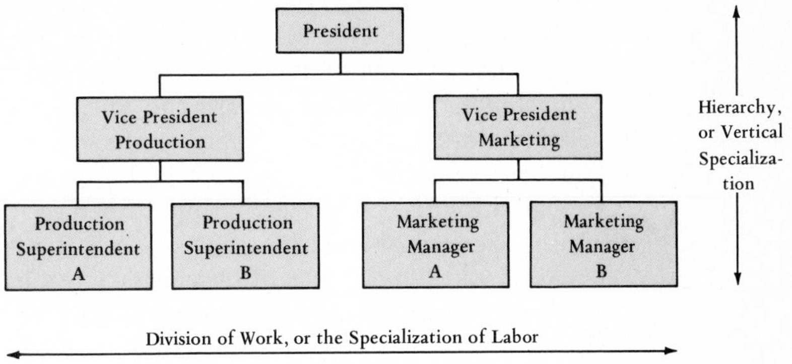

President

Vice President Production

Vice President Marketing

Production Superintendent A

Production Superintendent B

Marketing Manager A

Marketing Manager B

Hierarchy, or Vertical Specializa- tion

Division of Work, or the Specialization of Labor

tation of writers like Henri Fayol see coordination from this perspective.

The Bureaucratic Perspective   The *bureaucratic perspective* is usually identified with Max Weber. Because of his concern for order, efficiency, and rationality, Weber considers effective coordination to be the natural state of affairs.

Weber's theoretical, or ideal, bureaucracy is an organizational form that possesses certain characteristics.[6] Figure 10.3 illustrates some of its elements. The first characteristic is the specialization of labor, or the division of work. This idea is similar to the economic principle of comparative advantage, which states that an individual, group, or country should specialize in doing the work for which he, she, or it is best qualified. In this manner, the greatest output is obtained. In Figure 10.3, this specialization is illustrated by the horizontal dimension of the organization. Production specializes in manufacturing, marketing specializes in sales, and so on.

The second characteristic of a bureaucracy is its hierarchy, or vertical specialization. Through this structure, top management supervises the coordination efforts of middle management, which in turn coordinates the actions of supervisory levels.

In bureaucratic theory, each level passes relevant information up through the organization. Experts at lower levels determine what is relevant information and pass it upward. Top management thus becomes knowledgeable, but it is not overburdened with information.

Other important characteristics of bureaucracies are not so evident on the organization chart. For example, bureaucracies establish a complex system of procedures and rules to deal with most situations. Interpersonal relationships are based on impersonality. That is, rules and regulations are applied without emotional involvement. Punishment is directed toward the infringement of the rules, not toward individuals. Finally, recruitment and promotions are made on the basis of competence, not on the basis of loyalty to an individual organization. Nepotism and arbitrary behavior are avoided, at least in the theoretical ideal.[7]

Many of the problems of bureaucracy result from practical rather than theoretical limitations. In spite of the structure and the controls it introduces, it is people who actually manage bureaucracies. Thus nepotism and arbitrary behavior do at times result.

The very nature of the ordered, logical structure also has certain behavioral and managerial implications. Individuals at times feel insignificant in complex organizations and work loses its value to employees. Administratively, the structure that provides for order and the procedures that are designed to improve efficiency make bureaucracies resistant to change.[8] They are efficient in the short run, but they often fail to innovate and adapt to change in the long run.

Functional Arguments Functional writers in classical organization theory are less concerned with structure and direct most of their attention toward developing principles of effective administration. As might be expected, however, little can be said about effective administration without giving some attention to how organizations should be structured.

As with the views of bureaucratic writers, the first principle of organization from the *functional perspective* is the division of work. Functional writers also direct a great deal of attention toward the unity of command. This principle states that no individual in an organization should be accountable to more than one supervisor. Functional writers also emphasize a workable span of management. That is, how many people can a supervisor manage effectively?

Other topics that are analyzed by this school of classical thought relate to departmentalization, or how an organization can be divided effectively into operating and supportive units. Business executives, including Alfred P. Sloan of General Motors, contributed greatly to the success of individual firms by forming manageable structures around products and geographical areas, and by creating other similar divisions.

Functional writers continue to influence modern managers in organizations, probably because such authors are generally practical and provide specific guidelines for administrative action. Behavioral scientists, on the other hand, criticize this functional orientation for two reasons. First, they argue that functional writers are far too normative and promanagement in specifying what should be done in a given circumstance. They say that functional writers place less emphasis on understanding organizations than on providing a manual for managerial behavior. Second, behavioral scientists assert that management guidelines lack scientific validity. As one writer notes, classical principles are "little more than ambiguous and mutually contradictory proverbs."[9] These observations by behavioral scientists lead us to a proposition and to a final stage in our examination of the historical perspective of intergroup behavior.

Proposition 10.2

> Bureaucratic and functional management theories view conflict as dysfunctional because it reduces efficiency. Modern behavioral scientists, however, view conflict as a stimulant to organizational innovation and change.

Behavioral Alterations

One of the earliest behavioral contributions to administrative thinking about intergroup behavior came from Mary Parker Follett during the early twentieth century. As a political scientist, Follett was interested in the politics of group interaction. As an administrative theorist, she was interested in coordination of organizational units, which was a major problem of that time. Follett also recognized some potential benefits that could result from conflict, thus anticipating the arguments advanced later by modern behavioral scientists.[10]

As time progressed, behavioral scientists recognized that the precise coordination of diverse groups is not always the desired state of organizational affairs. Bennis and others have argued that conflict can be eliminated only if differences among individuals can be eliminated. Such a situation, according to these writers, is not desirable. Therefore, conflict management should not aim to eliminate differences completely. Rather, it should aim at easing coordination by accepting and reconciling group and individual differences.[11] The existence of conflict has thus taken a significant shift in the behavioral science and management literature. No longer is it viewed as organizationally and socially dysfunctional. Instead, it actually possesses a real and practical value, as long as it is not excessive and does not significantly hinder the accomplishment of organizational and individual goals. This shift in perspective can be referred to as the behavioral alteration with regard to conflict resolution.

Robbins takes the behavioral view even further. In his "interactionalist" views, he sees conflict as necessary and as something that should be encouraged as a stimulus for organizational members. He places on managers a major responsibility for successful conflict management.[12]

A Closer Look at Conflict and Conflict Resolution

A discussion of intergroup conflict at once raises problems of definitions and meanings. The three terms we must clarify are *conflict, competition,* and *coordination.* Let us look briefly at each concept to specify their relationships to one another.

Conflict

Conflict has been defined as all kinds of opposition or antagonistic interactions in or among individuals, groups, and/or organizations.[13] Opposition and antagonistic interactions may be tangible or intangible; they may be covert (hidden) or overt (apparent). Covert conflict may be little more than a refusal to cooperate because of personal dislikes, competing goals, or other aspects of group interaction. Overt conflict may be obvious hostility as in a labor-management dispute, a war, or some similar observable event. As a general rule, hostility is an implied part of conflict. In a war, the parties involved try to do harm to one another. The same is true of many labor-management and line-staff conflicts.

Conflict in organizations occurs for various reasons. It sometimes results from basic differences in the values of the involved parties.[14] Consider conflict between the administrative and medical staffs in a hospital. The administrative staff is judged on how efficiently the organization operates. It thus is likely to stress accurate records, accountability, and so on. The medical staff is not evaluated on administrative accountability and may place importance on other values. In fact, one group even may attempt to undermine the other's programs.

Conflict also can result when tasks are interdependent and when there are imbalances in task dependence. The fact that conflict may result from interdependence among groups is significant because it is precisely this interdependence that makes complex organization essential. Indeed, coordination is necessary because various organizational units are interdependent.

For example, sales and production functions are usually performed by separate groups in an organization. At the same time, the areas are clearly interdependent and must be coordinated to make the organization as effective as possible. In a completely rational and nonemotional (also unrealistic) world, we would expect that everyone involved would recognize each unit's interdependence and would cooperate. In reality, the situation is more complicated.

When some factor enters the picture and two interdependent units cease to cooperate, their interdependence may intensify the conflict. The sales unit may recognize as never before that its efforts are of little value unless it has a product to put on the market. The production staff also may become aware that things are produced to be sold, and that without an active marketing unit they may face layoffs. Thus sales becomes hostile toward production, because the latter will not or cannot produce at a rate that satisfies demand. At another time, production may be hostile toward sales, as inventories build and layoffs are threatened. When one unit has little or no effect on another unit, both groups can be unemotional and objective. However, interdependence brings with it not only the logic of cooperation but also the potential of intense conflict.

The problem of dependency imbalance is somewhat different. This situation develops when group A is more or less dependent on group B than B is on A. Although the amount of dependence is perceived subjectively, for the sake of illustration consider the following case.

Work group A is located on the first position of a high-speed production line. This group receives raw materials from a large warehouse, performs certain operations on them, and passes on partially finished goods to work group B, which assembles a finished product. The plant has an incentive plan that emphasizes speed of production. The work pace of group A determines the speed of B's work, and so B's earnings are related to the speed with which A passes on partially finished goods. No such dependence exists in A's relationship to B. Thus dependency imbalance results. It is not difficult to imagine the intergroup problems that could develop if group A worked at a pace too slow for B. Group B would be likely to feel resentful and helpless, and conflict would result.

When variations, and especially incompatibilities, exist in the criteria by which different units are evaluated, conflict is also likely to result. If a faculty member's reputation is judged by peers and professional colleagues on the quality and quantity of research he or she publishes, and the administration's effectiveness is evaluated in terms of costs, the potential problems are evident. Faculty members will want to reduce teaching loads and increase research activities. Administrators will insist on heavier teaching loads to reduce costs. The outcome will be conflict.

Finally, when groups must draw on the same base of fixed resources, the stage is set for conflict. In a full-service hospital, for example, the laboratory facilities may have fixed resources. All units therefore may become hostile toward one another in attempting to obtain a larger share of the fixed laboratory services.[15]

Competition

Competition is not conflict but may, in extreme cases, lead to hostility. *Competition* is viewed most accurately as the striving of two or more groups for the favors of an outside entity. For example, Figure 10.4 illustrates the competitive situation facing American automobile producers. The diagram relates only to the market shares of these four domestic producers; it does not include foreign competitors. Thus we can view the total sales by all four major producers as

Figure 10.4 Market Share of Four Major Competitors in the American Automobile Market

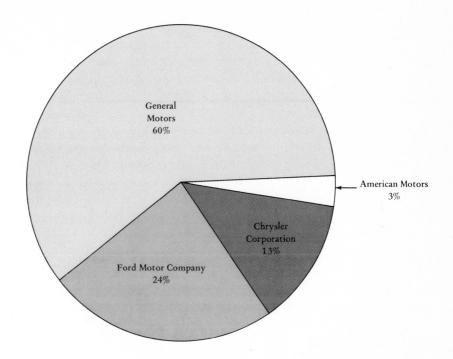

the total market for American automobiles. Through design innovations and marketing programs, each firm attempts to capture the largest market share possible. In other words, competition develops because each company attempts to gain the favors of consumers (the outside entity).

Frame 10.1 illustrates how competition affects both the automobile producers and their market (consumers). In an economic setting where cooperation is probably illegal and conflict is not encouraged, competition may result in the destruction of a single firm—even though it may work toward the overall efficiency of the larger system.

The competition described in Frame 10.1 is not really conflict, however, because each company's goal is not to harm the others but rather to increase its own gain. Also the manner in which the favors are pursued is subject to certain understood rules. One does not

Frame 10.1

Chrysler and Competition

By the end of 1979, the American automobile industry was experiencing trouble. Chrysler Corporation faced more problems than any of its major competitors. General Motors, in fact, had increased its share of the domestic market to 60 percent, whereas Chrysler was fighting to hold 12 percent. Chrysler even hired Lee A. Iacocca, a former president of Ford Motor Company, to turn things around.

In a competitive marketplace, some companies prosper while others try hard to stay afloat. Even in a market like automobiles—where competition is often seen as being less than it should be—the various effects of cooperation, competition, and conflict can be observed. For example, cooperation is discouraged and may even be illegal. Automobile makers cannot legally set cooperative prices and then divide up the market.

At the same time, General Motors' fight for 60 percent of the market and Ford's bid for its share is not done with the intent of putting Chrysler out of business. Instead, all three companies as well as American Motors compete for the favors of consumers. Apparently, Chrysler missed the market through misguided sales programs and production problems.

Even though General Motors, Ford, and American Motors are not trying to bankrupt Chrysler, they seem to be winning under the present rules of the competitive game. Chrysler lost over $1 billion in 1979, and 1980 losses were expected to be nearly as large. Unless it can turn the tide with its approved federal loan and again compete effectively, this country soon may have only three major producers of automobiles. Competition is not intended to be hostile, but it may be deadly just the same.

"cheat" by fixing prices or performing similar illegal acts. To be sure, harm may come to the party that loses, but inflicting harm is not the goal.[16]

It is possible that too much competition can lead to hostility and conflict. A baseball team, for example, may compete in a close game until the pressure grows too great. Then a questionable call by an umpire may result in a free-for-all or other open conflict. In moderation, competition can be, and probably is, one of the most important factors leading to departmental and industrial efficiency. The administrative task is to maintain constructive competition without encouraging destructive conflict.

Consider the case of a land developer who proposed to build a new airport on the outskirts of a large southeastern city to service private airplanes. It became clear at once that local residents opposed the idea. As a result, the county commission decided to hold a public hearing so that the developer could present the plan to the residents. This hearing would also allow the residents to voice their complaints to the developer. The date was set, and three hundred community members assembled to debate the plan and "solve" the problem.

Unfortunately, collective problem solving did not resolve the conflict. Both groups left the meeting with a renewed commitment to fight each other to the end. Problem solving and face-to-face interaction are not always the solution.

Coordination

Coordination is the effective direction of individual and group actions toward some desirable goal. The coordination of sales, production, and supporting units toward the attainment of profitability has historically been a key problem of management.

Although task dependence can cause conflict, it probably also is the key to effective coordination. Rational behavior demands that groups such as sales and production, public works and public safety, or surgery and nursing work together to accomplish organizational goals. This is the only way the goals can be attained.

For example, let us take a common-sense, intuitive view of how organizations operate. We can do this by referring again to Figure 10.2. The overall production goal of manufacturing five hundred units per week is accomplished only when the production unit's efforts (of producing five hundred units per week) are coordinated with the marketing goal (of selling five hundred units per week). The overall organizational goal is achieved only when the efforts of sales and production are coordinated effectively.

It should be obvious that the coordination of diverse organizational units is one of management's primary tasks and responsibilities. As we have noted, coordination is neither desirable in all cases nor inevitable. Therefore, we must examine how conflict may be resolved and coordination may be restored once hostility has developed.

Managing Intergroup Relations

It has been said that the only known methods of *conflict resolution* are force, arbitration, and integration.[17] This, perhaps, is too simple. In fact, some other rather well-defined techniques of managing conflict deserve our attention.

Problem Solving This technique of conflict resolution involves bringing the hostile parties together in an effort to define the problem, examine causes for the disagreement, propose alternatives, and select a course of action that is agreeable to both parties.[18] The logic of this technique is that people can sit together, communicate, and derive satisfactory solutions when they understand problems and analyze them objectively.

The assumption on which this method of conflict resolution is based is that communication and face-to-face contact can ease understanding.

Superordinate Goals Sherif and Sherif conducted several experiments designed to identify effective ways of resolving conflict.[19] The solution suggested by the Sherifs was the introduction of superordinate goals. A superordinate goal is one that is compelling and appealing to all conflicting groups and can be obtained only through their mutual cooperation.

For example, suppose that two racial groups in a country are in conflict and the nation is attacked suddenly by a third country. Because cooperation is required to defeat the common enemy, the conflicting groups get together and pursue the superordinate goal of victory. Thus conflict is resolved, but only for a while. After the superordinate goal has been achieved, conflict will return unless new goals are introduced. Administrative art is required in using superordinate goals, for new and mutually appealing objectives must be introduced constantly.

Expansion and Contraction When two or more groups are in conflict, they may react in various ways. One usual approach is for each group to tighten its boundaries and isolate itself from the others. Thus two departments in a business school may simply cease to communicate and may refuse to interact. Such a strategy, however, fails to deal seriously with the sources of conflict. Another possibility is to expand the group's boundaries until the conflicting parties become one.[20] The idea is to develop an intragroup alliance rather than to preserve the intergroup conflict.

The Follett View As might be expected, Follett, because of her interest in the politics of organizations, dealt extensively with conflict resolution. She proposed three basic methods to reduce hostilities.[21]

Domination or force is the most obvious way to resolve a disagreement. One group (the winner) is satisfied, whereas the loser is dissatisfied. An alternative technique, compromise, is probably the most commonly employed. The problem with compromise is that neither party is completely satisfied.

Recognizing the limitations of domination and compromise, Follett suggested *integration* as the most promising method of conflict resolution. The important advantage of integration is that innovation is encouraged so that a new solution to the problem is developed to satisfy both parties.

Proposition 10.3

A variety of methods is available for resolving intergroup conflict. The exact technique used depends on the situation, the personality of the manager, and the hostile parties. It generally is agreed that force and compromise are not productive, since they result in dissatisfaction for one or both parties. Methods that seek new and creative alternatives are the most promising means of conflict resolution.

For example, consider a union-management dispute. The union wants a 10 percent increase in wages. Management, on the other hand, wants to give only 6 percent. The two groups could compromise and settle on 8 percent, but neither would be happy. Instead, they work together to develop a package of wage and nonwage benefits that satisfies both groups. Integration has been accomplished, both parties are happy, and better union-management relations probably will develop. Most important, two hostile parties have used their resources to devise a creative solution, and innovation has been encouraged.

Coalitions of Groups

Sometimes groups voluntarily coordinate their activities by forming power-oriented coalitions. A coalition is an extremely important group phenomenon. Chapter 7 introduced power groups and political coalitions. Now we will extend that discussion to intergroup relations.

Political alliances among groups are formed to direct the joint resources of the groups toward the accomplishment of a collectively desirable goal.[22] That goal is to increase the coalition's power in a bargaining process.

Assume that you are the manager of operations for Frontier Manufacturing Company. The firm makes specialized containers to transport manufacturing equipment by ship to countries abroad. The containers must be assembled, sealed, and painted carefully to ensure they do not leak when exposed to saltwater. The operations department includes eighteen employees, all of whom are qualified to perform any of the tasks demanded by the department.

The social structure of the operations department is illustrated in Figure 10.5. Each individual is represented by a triangle with an enclosed number. It is relatively easy to identify a series of coalitions in three-person subdivisions, or triads. For example, in the triad 1-2-3, individuals 1 and 3 form a coalition against 2. Coalitions are highlighted in the diagram by oval shapes numbered 1 through 8.

We also can identify three major groups in this organization. Group 1 is a "newcomers" group composed of individuals who were hired recently. Group 2 is an "upwardly mobile" group that includes people who have been employed for three years or more and who are striving for promotion to first-line supervisor. Group 3 is an "oldtimers" group made up of employees who have worked in the department for ten years or longer.

Figure 10.5   Coalition Formation in the Operations Department

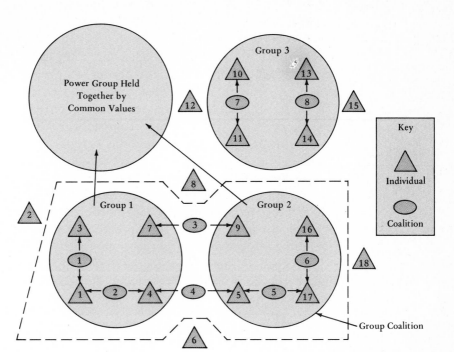

Coalition Formation   Coalitions form because of an interesting mixture of rational and emotional factors. In terms of rational motivation, coalitions can be seen as being based on practical concerns. In 1961, Gamson proposed a theory of coalition formation based on the minimum-size principle.[23] Since the assumption is that resources—and therefore power—are fixed in the short run, and since the spoils of victory are divided according to the resources committed by each group, the logic is to keep the coalition's resources as small as possible while ensuring a winning outcome. In this manner, each coalition member receives the greatest portion of the payoff relative to inputs.[24]

The minimum-size principle is associated with the cohesiveness of the coalition. Cohesiveness, in turn, is related to the heterogeneity (diversity) or homogeneity (similarity) among group members. Heterogeneous groups have difficulty maintaining a common goal because of their diverse interests. Homogeneous groups have an easier task maintaining cohesion, but they have less potential power in a large organization because their values are so limited.[25] In other words, they do not appeal to a large portion of the organizational membership because of the group's narrowly defined self-interest.

To illustrate, consider a management department in a large business school. The faculty is attempting to develop a new curriculum that will include more behavioral sciences. This curriculum will involve dropping some courses that are presently required. As a result, resistance is being met from several other departments.

The management department has several choices. It may attempt to raise as much support among its members as possible in an effort to present a powerful unified front and deal with the other departments in a direct manner. To be successful, the management department must be sure that all faculty members support its proposed change. In other words, the department must obtain the greatest cohesiveness possible within its homogeneous group.

Another option is for the department to become less homogeneous by devising a different strategy. For example, an attempt could be made to require additional research methods courses, which might gain the support of the department of statistics. This gives the management department a larger power base, but it is sure to upset some of its own members. Thus this strategy would risk the loss of some cohesiveness to obtain the support of another group. Heterogeneity is increased (at the cost of some in-group cohesiveness) to expand support.

The final factor in coalition formation is perhaps the most obvious. It relates to ideological differences that are as apparent in small groups and departments of large organizations as in political parties. Ideologies can assume many forms, including socioeconomic groupings, regional alliances, and ethnic associations. From the standpoint of socioeconomic groupings, occupational and educational levels are important. Doctors and nurses may form a useful coalition against the administration of a hospital, just as bricklayers and carpenters may align themselves against contractors in an industrial dispute. In both cases, the coalition groups possess similar values compared with those of the third parties (administrators and contractors).

Regional groupings are evident in almost every national political election. Within an organization, regional alliances are equally evident. Workers in one plant of a large company may be extremely competitive toward workers in other plants. Similarly, anyone who has had experience in a multicampus university system is probably aware of the extreme regional loyalties that develop.

Proposition 10.4	Coalitions are practical associations that form for the specific purpose of increasing the group's power in relation to other groups. Coalitions are formed on a variety of bases. Some important factors are the minimum-size principle and regional and ideological differences.

Coalitions and Organizations

A business firm provides an interesting case study of how coalitions form and affect organizational interests. Power is acquired through political bargaining. Consider Figure 10.6. The various coalitions, or interest groups, maintain a power base founded on such factors as dependence and cohesiveness. The outcome of the process depends on how the various parties interact, bargain, and compromise.

George England, in a frequently cited study, surveyed over one thousand decision makers to gain some insight into the relative power of various coalitions.[26] This study found that managers consider the

Figure 10.6   The Organization as a Set of Coalitions

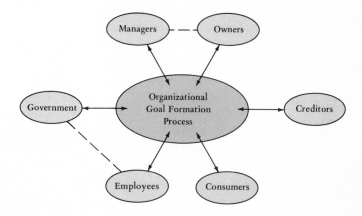

interest of owners to be the main determinant of managerial actions, followed by the values of employees and the community.

This view of an organization as a set of political coalitions is helpful in understanding how decisions actually are made and how some groups are allowed more input than others. How might one actually go about managing the horizontal dimension of an organization? That is, how can managers coordinate groups when formal departmental structures provide the boundaries of various groups? Before addressing that question, we must summarize with a proposition.

Proposition 10.5

> The view of organizations as a series of political coalitions is only one means of visualizing the organizational process. It provides the advantages, however, of describing the reality of group-bargaining processes and assisting in the identification of relevant groups within the larger organizational context.

Managing Horizontal Relationships in Organizations

One reason intergroup behavior is so important from a managerial viewpoint is that the relationships among departments or functional units form the basis of complex organizations. As was pointed out earlier, management has been viewed historically as the act of coordinating such diverse units.

Now that we have looked at coordination and conflict, we can conclude our discussion by examining some of the stereotyped relationships among units in an organization. Walton, Dutton, and Fitch have proposed a method of classifying horizontal relationships. According to them, such relationships can be grouped on the basis of three criteria of interaction. These are (1) the freedom with which information is shared among the units, (2) the flexibility and informality of communication, and (3) the trust and friendliness evidenced among the units.

An *integrative* relationship is said to exist when information exchange is free, communication is flexible and informal, and friendliness and mutual trust exist among units. The relationship is called *distributive* when information is distorted and protected, communication is formal and structured, and distrust prevails.[27]

Perhaps integrative and distributive relationships can be understood best by looking at some examples. First, consider a university hospital in a large midwestern urban center. Numerous departments within this medical complex are required to interact. The two of particular concern to us are the Department of Grant Acquisition and Administration and the Department of Medicine. The first department's responsibility is to remain in constant contact with the sources of funds for medical research, to provide assistance in making grant proposals, and to administer the grants obtained. The other department is responsible for conducting research and supplying personnel for approved grants.

Over the years, the university hospital, along with its teaching and research units, has ranked in the country's top fifty hospitals in terms of federal grant funding. Much of this success has resulted from the integrative relationship between the two departments named. The Department of Grant Acquisition and Administration has kept the Department of Medicine aware of funding priorities, which have been carefully considered in all recruiting and staffing activities. Medicine, on the other hand, has kept Acquisition and Administration aware of its own strengths, weaknesses, and planning priorities. Both departments are completely informed about what the other is doing and wants to do in the future.

To ease interaction, a very informal relationship has developed. Communication is exchanged with little formality. Periodic meetings are held so that departmental personnel can discuss, informally, exactly what is happening from the viewpoint of each group. Finally, the closeness of this relationship has been fostered by fair and open dealings over administrative budgets and related issues. Each group trusts the other and is convinced of the other's honesty. The result speaks for itself. The departments are closely integrated and highly successful in accomplishing their joint mission.

Contrast this situation with the case of the city of Valleyridge. Until four years ago, the city operated under a mayor-council form of government, in which the mayor served as the chief administrative

officer, supervising all city departments. The council functioned as
the legislative body. In an election the voters decided—against the
wishes of the mayor—to hire a city manager, who would become the
chief administrative officer. The city would retain the mayor, but
only as chairperson of the council. The mayor, having few choices,
was re-elected in spite of the change in the form of municipal government.

Ever since the city manager was hired, the mayor has done everything possible to make the manager's job difficult. The manager has
responded with less than complete cooperation with the council. The
council's policy statements are vague and provide little administrative guidance. The manager reports only what is required. When
reports are made by either group, they are formal, well documented,
and released carefully to the press. Neither side trusts the other, and
each publicly has questioned the other's integrity. The relationship is
clearly distributive, and the citizens of the city have put up with
inefficiency and ineffectiveness because of it.

Proposition
10.6

Managing intergroup relations often means reaching a balance
between integrative and distributive relationships. The most effective relationship is situational and thus requires the administrator's
judgment and an accurate evaluation of the task, the individuals,
and the environment.

In reality, most interrelated groups display tendencies toward both
integrative and distributive relationships. Few would be as extreme
as is illustrated by our examples. In fact, it is not even possible to say
whether either extreme would be better or worse in real-life situations. The manager's task in administering relationships between
groups is to encourage free information flow, communicative flexibility, and friendliness to the point that goal accomplishment is
maximized (subject, of course, to the need for order, documentation,
and procedural efficiency). Once again, the artistic ability of the manager to identify and evaluate a unique situation determines organizational effectiveness.

What Managers Need to Know About Coordinating Groups

Most new managers move quickly from the supervisory level, where the emphasis is on coordinating individuals, to the ranks of middle managers. At the middle management level, coordinating individuals is still a problem and a new one is added. This is the problem of coordinating two or more groups.

Unfortunately, as we have shown already, groups sometimes have their own norms and values. Hostile relations thus may develop between groups. The sales department may like to sell products even when the production unit cannot supply the demand. Relations may be strained, and the manager will need to be skillful in resolving conflict. But how can a manager be effective unless he or she knows something about superordinate goals and has developed some negotiating skills?

Successful managers in modern organizations cannot be naive. Although conflict reduces efficiency, it can provide desirable outcomes. A reasonable amount of conflict can be innovative. Only the most idealistic person would expect or strive for complete tranquillity in intergroup relations. Even if such harmony could be achieved, it is unlikely that the groups would then adapt to change very well. Therefore, conflict must be managed, not eliminated.

A manager also needs to recognize that competition is not conflict. When groups compete for limited organizational resources according to acceptable rules and without hostility, performance can be significantly improved. Only when the rules break down and the parties involved try to hurt one another does competition become dysfunctional.

Summary

Intergroup behavior is an essential, though seldom discussed, aspect of managing complex organizations. We can say accurately that complex organizational design rests on coordinating diverse yet interrelated groups.

Our analysis began with the relevant set, or environment, of intergroup behavior. We noted that group relations may be vertical, as in a hierarchy; horizontal, as when two units at the same level interact; or extraorganizational, as when groups within and outside an organization relate to one another. Each interaction is unique. However, because hierarchical and extraorganizational relations are discussed elsewhere in the text, this chapter has emphasized horizontal relations.

Although the relevant set is a primary distinguishing characteristic of intergroup behavior, other factors deserve attention. Conflict, for example, takes on special significance when it occurs between groups, because frequently there is no higher-level arbitrator.

Three basic relationships can exist among groups. They may coordinate their activities, compete, or be in conflict. Historically, conflict was viewed as dysfunctional, in that it reduces the efficiency of organizational goal accomplishment. More recently, however, conflict has been recognized as a force that stimulates change.

Stimulating as it may be, conflict always undermines efficiency. Therefore, it is important for the manager of intergroup behavior to recognize excessive conflict. The manager's task is to resolve the conflict and restore operational efficiency. Many strategies are available, including bargaining or problem solving, introducing superordinate goals, expanding and tightening organizational boundaries, and developing innovative solutions that require neither force nor compromise.

Groups sometimes coordinate their actions voluntarily when they perceive it advantageous to do so. This occurs in power groups or coalitions of groups. Thus two or more groups with a common interest may align themselves to overpower another group with different interests. This voluntary coordination is practical and power oriented. However, careful attention must be paid to the minimum size of the coalition, to the make-up of the groups, and to the cohesiveness that can be achieved.

The final section of the chapter dealt with the management of horizontal relationships in organizations. We illustrated the advantages and disadvantages of integrative and distributive relationships. This aspect of organizational behavior is obviously important, as evidenced by labor disputes, wars, line-and-staff conflicts, and so on.

Questions for Discussion

1. Compare the contrast coordination, competition, and conflict among groups. In what sense is each functional and dysfunctional in accomplishing goals?
2. After looking carefully at the factors determining whether or not intergroup relationships are integrative or distributive, give one example of each. Use a situation with which you are familiar. Describe the effects, as you see them, of the different relationships between the groups.
3. Of the various strategies of conflict resolution discussed, which do you think is the most useful? Explain your response by giving examples of organizations with which you are familiar.
4. Why is it accurate to state that the management of intergroup relations provides the basis for complex organizational design? Explain in detail.
5. Explain intergroup power coalitions. Why is it important to understand such coalitions to understand organizational behavior?

Case: Maryville Hospital

Maryville Hospital is a 250-bed health care facility located in a municipal area with a population of about twelve thousand people. Recently, the medical staff has become increasingly concerned about its general working conditions. Last week, Dr. John Door, spokesperson for the medical staff, wrote the memorandum shown in Exhibit 10.1 to Dr. Janice Keys, chief of medical staff, outlining several concerns.

Dr. Keys, as a physician, can understand the staff's concerns. She also knows from informal discussions with colleagues that the staff is prepared to initiate a "sick-in" or some other work slowdown if their requests are not accepted and if immediate action is not taken.

With this information, Dr. Keys went to David Belk, the hospital administrator. Belk was prepared for her visit, since he had received a copy of Dr. Door's memorandum. In response, he immediately presented Dr. Keys with similar demands, which he had received from a representative of the sanitary worker's union. He also revealed some financial data illustrating the funding problems of the hospital. At present and for the past two years, the facility has barely broken even financially.

Belk then reminded Dr. Keys of her administrative responsibilities as chief of staff, as well as her obligations as a physician. Dr. Keys left the

Exhibit 10.1

Memorandum

To: Janice Keys, M.D., Chief of Medical Staff
From: John Door, M.D., Staff Physician
Subject: Concerns of the Medical Staff

As you know, there have been frequent meetings of the medical staff relating to the general working conditions of staff physicians at Maryville Hospital. A few of the most pressing issues are:

1. Length of Duty Assignments. Because of the limited number of physicians, existing staff are required to work unrealistically long hours. The typical physician, for example, works approximately fifty hours in the facility and is on call an average of twenty-four additional hours per week. This will ultimately result in reduction in the quality of patient care and the development of personal and emotional problems on the part of physicians.
2. Outdated Equipment and Lack of In-service Training. Because Maryville is not proximate to a large urban area, there are few facilities for keeping medical skills updated, and the equipment available provides only the minimum level of recommended support. Even the medical library is grossly lacking. There are, for example, no journal subscriptions in three of the seven areas of medical specialities represented on the staff.
3. Lack of Protection of Malpractice Cases. Although the hospital has policies to protect itself against malpractice cases, physicians are solely responsible for their own protection. With the rates of such policies continuing to increase, the real income of each physician is correspondingly reduced.

Although there are other concerns I would like to discuss with you personally, the three itemized above are the most pressing. We the staff, therefore, request that you immediately discuss these matters with the hospital administrator and insist on the following:

1. An increase in the medical staff to the point where no physician is asked to work on-site more than forty hours per week and be on call no more than an additional fifteen hours per week.
2. A relationship with the Southwest Medical Center that would make continuing education courses available via television to the Maryville Hospital medical staff.
3. An immediate increase of $50,000 per year for equipment acquisition to provide minimally adequate patient care. In addition, the technical

library funds must be immediately increased to provide resources for all medical specialities.

4. An immediate insurance sharing program whereby the hospital will assume responsibility for 25 percent of each physician's malpractice premium. This amount should be increased by 25 percent over the forthcoming years until the hospital pays 75 percent and the physician 25 percent of the premiums.

---

administrator's office without any commitments from him, and still facing the responsibility of answering her colleagues' request.

1. Does anything in this example suggest whether an integrative or a distributive relationship exists between the administration and the medical staff? If so, what are they?
2. If you were in Dr. Keys's position, how would you approach the medical staff after meeting with Belk?
3. How do you think Belk can handle the problem with the medical staff and the sanitary workers, given the financial constraints? What are some strategies he might use?

Case: Subscribers' Services

Subscribers' Services is a periodical subscription agency that places orders for libraries and other large periodical users. To keep up with all the correspondence, the company has organized an orders department that is responsible for all subscriptions, renewals, cancellations, billing, and so on. The department also publishes an information booklet that is widely circulated.

In processing orders, preprinted forms often are used so that computer techniques can be applied. Other orders are processed through the data processing department. Unfortunately, things have not been going well in Subscribers' Services. The orders department and the data processing department have been fighting bitterly over the manner in which order forms are to be printed and who will process them.

Management of Subscribers' Services does not think conflict is all bad. In fact, the president often calls interdepartmental hostility "controlled conflict." However, the conflict between the two departments is so serious that it has become dysfunctional. There has been a great deal of dissatisfaction throughout the organization with the behavior and performance of the data processing unit. In an effort to resolve the conflict, top management has decided to move the data processing function into the orders department. It will have equal status with other groups such as new orders and billing.

The members of the former data processing department are unhappy because of their reduced prestige. Even so, many of the employees think the new arrangement is useful because now they can work directly with the orders department.

1. What type of strategy did top management use to resolve this conflict?
2. How successful do you think this strategy will be in the long run? Why?
3. Can you think of a different strategy that management could have used to resolve this conflict? Explain.

Suggested Readings

Biller, A. D., and E. S. Shancey. "Understanding the Conflicts between Research and Development and Other Groups." *Research Management* 18 (September 1975): 16–21.

Brooker, W. M. "Eliminating Intergroup Conflicts through Interdepartmental Problem Solving." *Management Review* 64 (June 1975): 39–44.

Hinings, C. R., *et al.* "Structural Conditions of Interorganizational Power." *Administrative Science Quarterly* 19 (1974): 22–44.

Laboritz, Sanford, and Robert Magedorn. "A Structural-Behavior Theory of Intergroup Antagonism." *Social Forces* 53 (1975): 444–448.

Okum, M. A., and F. J. DiVesta. "Cooperation and Competition in Coacting Groups." *Journal of Personality and Social Psychology* 31 (1975): 615–620.

Pfeffer, Jeffrey, and Juseyin Leblebici. "The Effects of Competition on Some Dimensions of Organizational Structure." *Social Forces* 52 (1973): 268–279.

Rabbie, J. M., Fritts Benoist, Hans Oosterbaan, and Lieowe Uisser. "Differential Power and Effects of Expected Competitive and Cooperative Intergroup Interaction on Intergroup and Outgroup Attitudes." *Journal of Personality and Social Psychology* 30 (1974): 45–56.

Workie, Abaineh. "The Relative Productivity of Cooperation and Competition." *Journal of Social Psychology* 92 (1974): 225–230.

Zechmeister, Kathleen, and Daniel Druckman, "Determinants of Resolving a Conflict of Interest." *Journal of Conflict Resolution* 17 (1975): 63–89.

Perspectives on Organizational Design

Most ambitious young men and women ultimately succumb to
the historically aristocratic view of finding one's position and
filling it, rather than accomplishing something more than good
acting.

David Moment and Dalmar Fisher,
Autonomy in Organizational Life

Our discussion of intergroup relations in Chapter 10 provides the
foundation for analyzing the design of organizations. *Organizational
design* is structuring organizations so as to direct human behavior
toward goal accomplishment. Effective designs relate human and
nonhuman resources to group goals

Historically, major corporations have been organized around such
functional tasks as manufacturing, sales, finance, and personnel.
Alfred P. Sloan, Jr., of General Motors is recognized as a major
contributor to management for his idea of reorganizing GM around
industrial divisions such as Oldsmobile, Buick, AC Spark Plugs, and
so on. Under this plan, control was maintained at the top, but in most
cases the divisions operated as separate companies. The functional
tasks (sales, manufacturing, and so on) were managed independently
under each division. This organizational design has apparently been
successful for General Motors.

Other organizations also have restructured operations to meet
new competitive or economic realities and challenges. General Elec-

275

tric, for example, has engaged in at least three major reorganizations since 1950.

Some organizations seem quite responsive to changing conditions and show little hesitation in restructuring operations. Others are more reluctant to change. Yet all organizations operate on assumptions concerning the value of different structures and the way in which individuals relate to various designs.

This chapter describes three basic perspectives on organizational design. We will begin with a brief look at structural design theory to illustrate the importance of absolute organizational principles. Then we will examine the behavioral design perspective and show how it, too, is based on absolute principles. Finally, we will investigate the situational, or contingency, perspective. The chapter concludes with a comparison and summary of these perspectives to set the stage for Chapter 12, which will explore some ways to make organizational design more responsive to the environment.

Structural Design Theory

Regularity and predictability have been recognized as essential elements in the efficient pursuit of organizational goals. Jobs must be standardized, work must be coordinated, and authority relationships must be defined clearly.[1] Structural writers thus place more importance on the roles to be played in organizations than on the individuals playing the roles.[2] To illustrate this *structural view,* we will examine two examples.

Rationality Versus Irrationality: Weberian Logic Applied

Max Weber, as we noted in Chapter 10, is known primarily for his formulation and refinement of the theory of bureaucracy. The structural characteristics of a bureaucracy promise efficiency by replacing the irrationality of human emotions with rational, well-informed behavior.

Weber's concept of bureaucracy was theoretical and abstract. He described a model that was useful for theoretical purposes, rather than attempting to describe organizations as they exist in the real world. To appreciate Weber's bureaucracy, we must look at it in much the same way as we view the perfectly competitive market in economics. It is a model against which we can compare reality.

The idea of bureaucracy is built on the principle of legal authority. In traditional forms of organizations, behavior and decisions are judged against past experience, precedent, and ceremonial customs. Some government bureaucracies, for example, yield status to the positions of people such as kings, queens, and ministers because historically they have done so, regardless of whether present conditions necessitate such respect.

At the same time, even the most modern organizations use ceremonies and traditions to accomplish their goals. For example, ceremonies often are used to produce desired values, norms, and expectations among all employees. They also are used to ensure that values are consistent among all group members, in an attempt to reduce anxieties about role expectations.[3] In some organizations, employee orientation programs and periodic staff meetings are little more than ceremonies. In other organizations, however, such activities are planned, organized, and evaluated carefully to keep them relevant to organizational needs. In other cases, orientation programs are conducted only because they always have been conducted, and staff meetings take place whether or not they are needed. Thus they become as ceremonial as a fourth of July parade.

Ceremonies have their value. In some cases, new employees are made to feel part of the organization. Anxieties about behavioral expectations are reduced, and middle management may even be convinced that it is communicating effectively with top management. Ceremonial traditions develop because they are satisfying to members and make impersonal organizations more rewarding. But ceremonies also tend to oversimplify complex problems and may result in resistance to constructive changes.

In a bureaucracy based on legal authority, operations differ greatly from those in other organizational forms. First, legal norms or standards of behavior are established on the basis of expediency or rational values. Obedience is required from group members. Second, the norms of behavior are established intentionally and are applied consistently. These norms are administered impersonally. As a result, the group members' obedience or loyalty is directed toward the office, not toward the individual occupying the position.[4]

Besides the structural properties that develop in real bureaucracies, a bureaucratic mentality emerges from the legality and impersonality often found in large complex organizations. In other words, there is a ceremonial commitment to do the things "by the book."

Thomas Burns, reflecting on his experiences at International Telephone and Telegraph Corporation (ITT), reported how the internal audit staffs operated in that organization.[5] According to Burns, staff controllers manipulated power in a detached and almost academic manner without being committed to the overall responsibility for profit and loss. They handled internal coordination well, but their concern for overall goals was not evident.

An organization's procedural operations soon become policies designed to ensure specific results. At ITT, the abundance of staff members with "tunnel vision" was an important means of achieving efficiency. Similarly, it is well known that the British Foreign Office rotated embassy staffs frequently to prevent any foreign civil servant from staying too long in a single country. This procedure ensured that any good feelings generated in foreign governments was directed toward the government in London, not toward a particular person who was its representative. Frame 11.1 illustrates some possible problems arising from the bureaucratic structure.

Frame 11.1

Bureaucratic Waste

Max Weber supported bureaucracy as a way to organize efficiency. Sometimes this approach works, but sometimes complications and even waste develop. Consider the following examples from the area of government.

In 1975, the Federal Metal and Nonmetallic Mine Safety Board of Review was abolished after costing American taxpayers a quarter-million dollars. In the beginning, the board was established to hear owners' complaints when mines were closed for safety reasons. During the first year of its operations, there were no appeals, so the executive secretary of the board tried to return over $100,000 of unexpended funds. The only real function the executive secretary had performed during the year was to arrange board meetings and to process expense vouchers associated with the get-togethers. The rest of the time was spent drinking coffee and listening to the stereo that had been installed in the office.

> Another publicized bureaucratic blunder concerns a foreign service officer who roamed around the State Department for three years trying to get a reassignment—all the while making $36,000 per year. Although this officer checked with the personnel office frequently, attended a seminar, and rewrote a manual, most of his time was spent reading in the Library of Congress.
>
> As one final example of bureaucracy gone bad, consider the man from Milwaukee who was pronounced dead by his local social security office. When he called in to check after his wife had been informed she qualified for widow's benefits, a clerk said his file was clearly marked "D" for deceased, and so he must be dead. Finally, he was told "someone hit the wrong button." Maybe in fifteen to twenty days the problem could be corrected.
>
> For all the humorous yet tragic details see E. H. Methvin, "Tale of Two Bureaucrats," *Reader's Digest,* December 1975, pp. 211–214; and "Man Won't Take Death Lying Down," *Birmingham News,* Aug. 21, 1975, p. 51.

Roles, Not Personalities: Perrow's Sociology

Charles Perrow, a well-known sociologist, shares many of Weber's views about the value of bureaucratic structures. In fact, he clearly states that "bureaucracy is a form of organization superior to all others we know or can hope to afford in the near or middle range future."[6] This does not mean, of course, that Perrow—or Weber, for that matter—denies the disadvantages that can result from bureaucratic structure. The writings of both men show an appreciation for the problems that can arise. Their defense is of the design itself, not of the manner in which the bureaucracy is used.

Recall the Watergate scandal and the widespread lack of confidence in government bureaucracy that arose among the public. Structuralists acknowledge such problems but accurately note that cover-ups, espionage, and hidden activities of the type involved in Watergate do not result from basic weaknesses in bureaucratic design. Rather, such problems are laid to the individuals who improperly use the bureaucracy for personal reasons. Perrow does admit to some fear about how complex structures—although using resources toward desirable ends—have the effect of placing power in the hands of a few people.

Perrow begins by stating that his structural view "considers the roles people play rather than the personalities in the roles."[7] It focuses on relations among groups, structural characteristics, and organizational goals and expectations.

This structural view challenges two accepted assumptions of management. The first assumption states that organizations are merely people and that the solutions to organizational problems must be found by changing people. The counterview, however, is that a distinct organizational effect occurs whereby organizations influence individual attitudes and values at least as much as do other influential factors such as culture, peer groups, and related social phenomena.

Another assumption Perrow attacks is that organizational success is a function of leadership. This implies that organizational effectiveness depends on effective leadership. Sociologists, however, call on the growing body of research suggesting that leadership is a dependent variable determined by structural and environmental factors.

To clarify this, consider our previous discussion of leadership (Chapter 9). There was a time when leadership was seen as personalized, with the individual leader determining the effectiveness of group behavior. The contingency theory, however, views leadership effectiveness in a more situational context. According to this approach, effective leadership is related to the leader's position power, task complexity, and leader-follower relations. The last factor is indeed a personal one. However, position power and task complexity are clearly structural and environmental variables.

The result is that someone who is an effective leader in one situation may not be effective when the structure and environment are altered significantly. A general of the army who retires and becomes president of a university may, and probably will, find it necessary to alter the style of leadership to achieve effectiveness. Thus, as Perrow would argue, it is not leadership determining the effectiveness of the organization, but the organization and the environment determining the leadership style that is most likely to result in organizational goal accomplishment.

The arguments of structural sociologists make some distinct assumptions about the factors leading to organizational effectiveness. The structure of the organization and general environmental conditions increase the importance of design factors in influencing organizational behavior. Therefore, we can offer the following proposition.

Proposition 11.1	Structural theories of organization take a view that is oriented toward design characteristics. They emphasize the positions, tasks, and roles contained within the structure, rather than the personalities of individuals occupying the positions or playing the roles.

Behavioral Theories of Organizational Design

Not everyone involved in the theory and practice of management agrees with the structuralists. And, of course, not all sociologists entertain structural views. Therefore, we must look at another side of the controversy—*behavioral design theories*, which emphasize human factors in organizational design.

Structure and Personality: Argyris's Hypothesis

Chris Argyris, a psychologist, confronts the problem of organizational design from a different direction. His argument is that a basic conflict exists between the demands of the organization and the mature human personality.[8] The structure, process, and procedures of complex organizations cause individuals to become, in a psychological sense, dependent children rather than independent adults.

One essential element of Argyris's point of view is his model of the "total personality" (see Figure 11.1). Argyris begins with a description of the human personality. The picture of the developing personality, or self, moves from a state of infancy to adulthood. The changes that occur include self-determination and a movement from a passive to an active state. The individual also moves from dependence to independence. He or she acquires skills or improves expertise in the skills and becomes oriented toward the future rather than

Figure 11.1   The Argyris View of the Total Personality

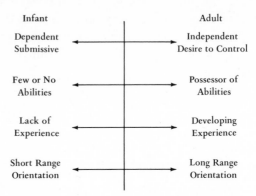

Infant		Adult
Dependent Submissive	⟷	Independent Desire to Control
Few or No Abilities	⟷	Possessor of Abilities
Lack of Experience	⟷	Developing Experience
Short Range Orientation	⟷	Long Range Orientation

Source: Adapted from Chris Argyris, "Personality and Organization," *Organizational Dynamics,* Fall 1974 (New York: AMACOM, a division of American Management Association, 1974), pp. 2–5.

the present, which is the infant's focus.[9] The result is a profile of a mature personality that is independent, autonomous, and future oriented.[10]

To illustrate, think about human development. Small children rely on their parents for all the necessities of life. They are dependent on and, for a time, submissive to them. Children also have few abilities to provide for themselves, and because of youth they have limited real-life experiences. Their primary concern is for short-run need satisfaction. Few children have any meaningful concern for the long run. Allowances are spent quickly, and saving is a chore.

Mature adults, however, are pictured as individuals desiring independence and control over their destiny. Adults also have the ability to sustain life and, in some cases, to earn a comfortable living. Experiences develop with time, enriching and expanding the acquired abilities. Also experience emphasizes the need for a long-range orientation. Adults recognize, at least conceptually, the need to provide for the future.

Next Argyris gives a view of organizations. He sees organizations as rational entities ruled by logical order. This logical order employs procedural planning, task specialization, hierarchy, chain of command, and so on (that is, Weberian logic). The manner in which

Table 11.1   Individuals Versus Organizations

Needs of the Mature Personality		Demands of the Organization
1. Freedom and self-determination	→ Conflict ←	1. Rationality, order, and control
2. Self-realization and achievement	→ Conflict ←	2. Contribution to collective goals
3. Development of expertise	→ Conflict ←	3. Specialization in a limited task role
4. Future orientation	→ Conflict ←	4. Emphasis on short-range efficiency

organizations form goals shows little concern for individual objectives, needs, and hopes. Restricted spans of control encourage dependence. So do hierarchy and specialization.[11]

By placing the characteristics of the mature personality and the organization side by side, Argyris concludes that there is a basic conflict between the needs of the mature individual and the demands of the formal organization. The idea is that individuals demand freedom, whereas organizations seek to control behavior. Organizations encourage passivity rather than activism, and they require a short-term orientation in their quests for efficiency. Organizations also demand only infrequent use of an individual's talents. Table 11.1 summarizes the conflict between individuals and organizations.

In this view, the adult's desire for freedom and independence is countered by the organization's wish to standardize behavior through procedures, rules, and operational controls. The need for achievement through the use of one's individual abilities is forced to conform to the normative standards of the group's collective goal(s). The quest for the acquisition of additional experiences and personal development is met with the demand to perform a specialized task. The individual, instead of having twenty years' experience on a job, begins to feel as though he or she has had one year of experience twenty times. Finally, the desire to look toward the future is constrained by the need to maximize performance during the one-year budget or performance evaluation period.

The result of this conflict, according to Argyris, is psychological frustration, which can cause a variety of outcomes. A few of the more obvious results are apathy, resignation from the organization, and unionism. Thus we have a picture of complex organizations that is quite different from the view proposed by structuralists.

Democracy and Change: Bennis on Bureaucracy

One of the most outspoken critics of bureaucracy is Warren Bennis. For years he has argued against the claims of bureaucratic superiority. Although Bennis voices many of the same concerns as Argyris about the effects of structure on individuals, his primary fear relates to the inability of bureaucracies to change and, consequently, to respond to alterations that constantly occur around us.[12]

Bennis cites four major threats to the continued superiority of bureaucracy.[13] First, all areas of society are subject to rapid and unexpected change. Values are changing, revolutionary legislation is becoming commonplace, and economic circumstances present new challenges to established theory. The significant shift in the values of young people from the revolutionary liberalism of the mid-1960s to the conservatism of the late 1970s is an example of such change.

Second, increases in organizational size and complexity present threats to bureaucracy. Eventually, structure fails to provide the necessary controls, and diseconomies of scale result. The suggestion is that we are reaching this point in advanced societies. For example, it is interesting to note that some large corporations in the United States now acquire larger revenues each year than some states do.

Third, modern technology—the basis of bureacracy—presents its own dangers. Advancing technology requires trained specialists. The solution of complex and interrelated problems, however, requires coordinated efforts and interaction among all kinds of specialists. The rigidity of bureaucracy reduces and even discourages cooperation among such trained experts.[14] Difficulties in establishing interdisciplinary problem-solving teams for such fields as education, mental health, and other areas where such efforts are needed have received much attention in recent years.

Finally, Bennis notes that changes in managerial behavior are needed to meet the demands of the future. This will require managers of organizations to develop new concepts of human beings, power, and organizational values in line with democratic ideas.[15]

This managerial philosophy obviously requires a significant break with the traditional view of bureaucracy. When all these criticisms are seen together, a pessimistic picture of bureaucracy emerges. We see an organizational system hopelessly out of touch with today's realities. The alternative is a new era of management systems that will replace models of complex structures with temporary, problem-oriented, democratic designs.

In contrast to the structural perspective, behavioral theorists focus on people. Standardization and specialization are viewed skeptically. Although recognizing the economic advantages of structure, behavioral theorists are concerned about the routine tasks and boring jobs that often result from overspecialization. To offset this, they recommend that management enrich jobs and make work more meaningful—even if costs must be increased.

Standardization also bothers behaviorists. A basic principle of behavioral management is that every human being is unique. This individuality is denied when everyone is forced to follow exact rules about work. The recent trend toward "flex time" work scheduling illustrates the point. Many firms are asking, "Is it reasonable to assume that everyone should work from 8:00 A.M. to 5:00 P.M.?" As a result, the U.S. Social Security Administration, Firestone Tire and Rubber, Sun Oil, Samsonite, and other organizations have changed their traditional work schedules to allow employees more flexibility.[16]

Proposition 11.2

Behavioral theorists reject the unqualified superiority of bureaucratic structures. Some view the demands of organizations and the needs of the mature adult personality as being in basic conflict, leading to anxieties and frustrations. Others see the primary failing of bureaucratic designs as an inability to respond to the changes constantly taking place in contemporary society.

Perhaps as much as anything, behavioral theorists have questioned the legal and rational arguments of bureaucracy concerning the sole right of managers to make decisions. Many theorists advocate power-equalized systems in which employees participate in decision making. They argue that participation improves satisfaction and increases an individual's commitment to support decisions.[17]

Thus behavioral and structural theorists disagree about the importance of individuals in organizations. They do, however, agree that there is one best way to organize. Only the "way" is argued.

Situational Design Theory

Structural and behavioral theories are different in the objects studied and in the emphasis placed on human and nonhuman resources. Yet both viewpoints imply that their principles can be applied to managerial processes in different organizations and at different times. The third perspective on organizational design questions whether any theory can be applied absolutely. It tries instead to relate management knowledge to situational differences. This general approach to organizational design is known as *contingency theory.* Although relatively new, it already has many supporters and an impressive body of research to back up its claims.

Contingency theory "seeks to understand the interrelationships within and among subsystems as well as between the organization and its environment . . . [it] is ultimately directed toward suggesting organizational designs and managerial practices most appropriate for specific situations."[18] At the level of organizational behavior, this definition raises a variety of questions. For example, is democracy always better than autocracy in organizations? Is conflict always dysfunctional? Is job enrichment equally applicable to all workers? In asking such questions, we move from the absolute realm of classical theory to the level of organizational relativism.

The basic proposition of contingency theory is that organizations must adapt their tasks and social structures to environmental realities. Survival and effectiveness depend on the way in which these factors relate to one another.[19] To see how this concept has been developed, we will review some selected studies.

Joan Woodward's South Essex Studies

The studies of Joan Woodward, an industrial sociologist, were begun in the 1950s by a group of researchers at the South Essex College of Technology. The studies involved one hundred manufacturing firms in the area that had one hundred or more employees. The original aim was to test the "one best way" assumption of classical management theory. The basic hypothesis that eventually developed was that different manufacturing technologies require different organizational designs and patterns. Thus there should be no single best organizational pattern but rather a series, or set, corresponding to technological alternatives.

It seems apparent that Woodward agreed with other researchers who consider technology one of the most important determinants of work behavior. She also adopted a twofold definition of technology. Technology was defined as the tools and machines needed to perform the required tasks, as well as the ideas expressing the goals of the work and the rationale of the methods used.[20]

Initially, the South Essex researchers could not correlate organizational characteristics with the successful operation of the sample firms. Their attention then shifted to an analysis of various technologies or production systems. At this point, the primary thesis of the study emerged. The researchers identified three systems for purposes of analysis:

1. *Unit, or small batch.* In this system, goods such as tailored suits were produced to individual specifications.
2. *Mass, or large batch.* This type of production involved large-scale production in which units were produced according to uniform specifications. An example of such a technology is automobile engines.
3. *Process, or continuous production.* As the label implies, this production involves a process. Chemical or oil refining is an example.[21]

These studies revealed that organizational characteristics are closely related to the type of technology the firm employs.[22] Units and process firms differed most from one another in such things as median levels in the hierarchy, span of control of first-line supervisors, and the ratio of supervisors to line personnel. Mass-production firms were located between the two extremes. Significant variations were noted in the organizational (structural) characteristics of the firms using these three technologies.

The details are less important than the major point being made. In the Woodward studies, evidence was presented that questioned the idea that there is one best way to organize. Different structures are required for different technological demands.[23]

The Woodward studies also suggested several important points about interpersonal relations in organizations. For example, the "flat" organization pictured in the unit (small-batch) processing firms says a great deal about the work and the specialists performing it. Because of the craftsmanship involved, less direct supervision is required, and spans of supervision thus can be larger. In process, or continuous, production, less specialized skills are required. One gets the picture of a "tall" centralized structure with closer supervision over individual tasks. Finally, the mass-production industries revealed a curious combination of large span of control and an intermediate ratio of supervisors to line employees.

The Lawrence and Lorsch Studies

Paul R. Lawrence and Jay W. Lorsch also began by examining the inadequacies of classical organization theory and the normative prescriptions of the "one best way" to organize. To obtain the necessary environmental variations, these researchers first accomplished a detailed study of selected firms in the plastics industry, where a dynamic, rapidly changing environment existed. Next they studied successful and less successful firms in the slowly changing standardized container industry. Finally, they observed the packaged foods industry, which had an intermediate degree of environmental change.[24]

Basic Variables In conducting their research, Lawrence and Lorsch examined three aspects of the behavior and thinking of managers in the manufacturing, sales, and research units of the organizations included in the sample. A fourth factor relating to structure was also included. These four variables were:

1. *Goal orientation.* This factor related to the objectives toward which production, sales, and research managers were oriented.

Sales managers, for example, may be oriented more toward sales volume, whereas production managers are more attuned to manufacturing costs.

2. *Time orientation.* This variable related to the long- or short-run orientation of the different functional managers. Are research managers oriented more to the long run, and sales executives more concerned with the present time period?

3. *Interpersonal orientation.* Questions dealing with this factor examined the leadership styles of various managers and attempted to determine whether some functional units are more or less democratic than others.

4. *Formality of structure.* This dimension related to the degree of structure as evidenced by such traditional measures as span of control, levels in the hierarchy, and so on.

Differentiation and Integration After defining their terms, Lawrence and Lorsch used the idea of *differentiation* to refer to the extent to which managers of functional units exhibited different orientations toward the first three factors and the degree to which the units differed in formality of structure.

In other words, when managers of production, sales, and research and development possessed different orientations toward goals, time, and interpersonal relations—and when their units exhibited differences in formality of structure—they were said to be "differentiated." *Integration* was the term used to describe the state of collaboration existing among the managers in the three units that was necessary to achieve coordination, or unity of effort. Together, differentiation and integration provided the core concepts of the contingency theory proposed by Lawrence and Lorsch.

After an extensive examination, the researchers observed that the more dynamic the environment, the more differentiated were the production, research, and sales units. In this environment the structure was less formal, but integration (coordination) was more difficult to achieve. More complicated integrating devices thus were required to prevent conflict, or to resolve it once it emerged. The main finding was that the internal states (managerial orientations and structure) of more successful firms were consistent with the external environmental demands placed on them. Thus internal practices and structures of successful firms differed among varying organizations.

Successful firms in the plastics industry organized and operated differently from their counterparts in the standardized container industry. The same was true in the packaged foods industry.

The implications of this study for organizational behavior are clear. The managerial behavior required in one organization may be different from that required in another. Where differentiation is great, considerable skill at conflict resolution is required. Also in different functional subunits, varying interpersonal orientations probably lead to more effective organizational performance.

Proposition
11.3

> The Woodward studies and those by Lawrence and Lorsch provide clear implications not only for the design of organizations but also for behavior in organizations. The most important inference is that managers of high-performing units must behave in different ways when facing various environmental demands. Knowledge of management concepts alone—important as they may be—are not sufficient conditions for success. Adaptability and the ability to respond properly to change are also important to ensure organizational success. The theory must be mastered, and the ability to adapt the theory to changing conditions must be developed.

What Managers Need to Know About Principles of Organizational Design

Why would any manager today need to know what Alfred P. Sloan did for General Motors or why almost every organization today is structured in a hierarchical fashion? Managers need to know such things because design principles reveal the logic of how organizations are built and maintained.

All managers assume certain things about what is really important in achieving organizational goals. Are people really important, or is the system the determining factor? How many managers really feel people are important (despite the bulletin board memoranda emphasizing human relations)?

Not many managers ever have the opportunity to design an organization. Every manager, however, influences the environment of his or her work group. For this reason, managers must understand the differences between traditional design and situational variations.

Very often a manager has the opportunity to relax the atmosphere in a way that encourages employees to offer ideas and suggest new ways of doing things. Moreover, current research seems to confirm that different situations demand different structures and methods of operation. An understanding of different perspectives on organizational design will provide managers with the knowledge needed to adapt to different situations and to respond in ways that can ensure the greatest benefits to the organization.

Summary: The Three Perspectives Compared

Organizational design theories have evolved significantly since the early days of administrative thought. In some ways, the evolution is similar to other changes in modern society. Like ethics, organizational design has moved from the absolute "one best way" of structural and behavioral theory to the situational or relative orientation of contingency theory. Table 11.2 compares the important features of the three design traditions discussed in this chapter.

In examining the table, we should note that early structural and behavioral theories first were formulated to provide practical guidelines for managers. It has been argued convincingly that these early theories have remained popular for so long mostly because of their promanagement bias. Managers often can justify actions and reduce uncertainty by applying the principles derived from structural and behavioral theories.[25]

Modern contingency theory is more descriptive, although practical inferences certainly can be drawn from its findings. Its aim has been more to describe situational variations in the application of organizational theory than to offer practical guidelines for managers to follow.

Table 11.2 Comparison of Structural, Behavioral, and Contingency Design Theories

Elements	Design Theories		
	Structural	*Behavioral*	*Contingency*
1. Objective	Development of principles on which managerial practice could be based	Development of practical principles and the efficient use of human resources	Description of organizational processes and elimination of situational conflicts in structural and behavioral theories
2. Methodology	Primarily deductive or based on universal assumptions and logically derived conclusions	Empirical with little attempt to stratify samples according to significant criteria	Controlled empiricism whereby situational variables are isolated and examined for explanatory differences
3. Time	Evolved in the environment of nineteenth-century science with resulting emphasis on deterministic relationships	Product of some reactionary movements from the objectivity of deterministic science; emphasizes probabilistic causes and effects	Clearly a partner of twentieth-century relativism and the distrust of universal principles

Structural theories are unique in that they are abstract. Weber and Fayol devised theories through deduction rather than making inferences from data. Argyris and Bennis also used the deductive approach, even though behavioral theory in general tends to be more empirical.[26] Contingency theory, on the other hand, evolved almost completely from data collected in actual organizations. In fact, it was probably the sampling process in different settings that suggested the original situational argument.

The deductive orientation of structural theory probably was influenced by the nineteenth-century view of science, within which it evolved. The abstract scientific approach was dominant, and it certainly influenced such thinkers as Weber and Taylor.[27] Behavioral theory evolved later and was more open to statistical descriptions. Contingency theory, as a twentieth-century concept, was even more receptive to probabilities and relativistic arguments.

We now have examined various organizational design theories, as illustrated in the writings of six people. Obviously, not all contributors nor all their contributions could be presented. However, these writers represent the origin, evolution, and current thinking about organizational design. Chapter 12 will look more closely at applications of modern contingency theory.

Questions for Discussion

1. Define contingency theory. How is contingency theory unlike the traditional view of management and organization? How is it similar?
2. What similarities do you note between the Woodward studies and those by Lawrence and Lorsch? In what ways are they different?
3. In analyzing organizational behavior, why do we emphasize the interface between individuals and the organization? What cautions should be observed in analyzing this topic?
4. In what ways is Weber's structural view different from Perrow's arguments? How are the views similar?
5. Why do we refer to Argyris's view of the relationship between individuals and organizations as humanistic? Explain.

Exercise: What Goes Wrong in Organizations?

Think seriously about your experiences in organizations. On the basis of your experiences, write down your thoughts about each of the following statements.

1. Top managers are usually well informed because they surround themselves with well-informed and capable staff.
2. People are the most important resource available to the organization.
3. Running a "tight ship" is the most important task performed by most supervisors.
4. Procedures must be established to ensure that everyone will be dealt with fairly and consistently.
5. Managers should delegate authority to responsible subordinates and should focus only on the few unique and demanding problems that develop.
6. In this organization, there is a place for everything and everything is in its place.
7. Our economy is too complex to think we can make decisions in a vacuum. We must stay informed about the actions of those around us.

After you have written down your reactions to each of these statements, exchange your responses with a classmate who has also done this exercise. Using each others' responses, classify each organization by basic design theory. Do your classmate's responses suggest that each organization is based on structural, behavioral, or situational theory? List the items in each response that caused you to arrive at your decisions.

Case: Clarkville University

Clarkville College was established in 1883 as a four-year liberal arts institution. During the early years of its development, it attracted a small but highly qualified faculty and student body. It also was supported generously by a religious group that considered the main goal of the college to be the training of ministers. The list of past presidents includes several distinguished leaders in higher education. Classes were held to intentionally small sizes, and everyone recognized Clarkville as an excellent institution of undergraduate education.

In the late 1950s and throughout the 1960s, the increase in demand for higher education was evidenced at the college. The supporting agency, sensing the change, decided to open the college's doors to more students and appointed a president who was "more able to deal with the contemporary realities and had the businesslike approach necessary to meet the demands."

By 1964, enrollment had increased to 7500 students, four schools of specialized study had been incorporated into the structure, graduate education had been added in eight fields, and the name had been changed to Clarkville University to reflect the changes.

Today, the university has almost 11,000 students, classes are large and somewhat impersonal, the faculty is divided into disciplinary specialties and ideological camps, and most people concede that Clarkville is an institution of just average quality. The sponsoring agency is even negotiating with state educational authorities about the feasibility of transferring ownership of the school. The reason, according to one spokesperson, is that there is "really nothing distinctive about Clarkville anymore. Perhaps the state should take it over."

Many older faculty members sadly remember the time when educational quality was more important than instructional costs and everyone on the faculty was on a first-name basis with everyone else. Graduates returning to the campus for infrequent visits feel little identity with the complex structure they observe. Their only real contact is with an alumni office that sends out periodic, computer-coded information bulletins and requests for contributions.

Most people, when talking about these changes, complain about impersonality, the size of the school, and related matters. However, one cannot deny the growth that has taken place, the diverse needs now being served, and the "new era" evident on campus.

1. Would you classify the organizational design strategy of the new administration as being structural, behavioral, or situational? Explain.
2. What do you think are the strengths and weaknesses of the design strategy now governing Clarkville University?
3. Do you believe the current strategy will be successful in the long run? Why or why not?

Suggested Readings

Anderson, J. P., and Duncan, W. J. "The Scientific Significance of the Paradox in Administrative Theory." *Management International Review* 17, (1977): 99–106.

Deegan, M. J., and L. E. Nutt. "The Hospital Volunteer: Lay Person in a Bureaucratic Setting." *Sociology of Work and Occupations* 2 (1975): 338–353.

Dowling, John, and Jeffrey Pfeffer. "Organizational Legitimacy: Social Values and Organizational Behavior." *Pacific Sociological Review* 18 (1975): 122–136.

Hummel, R. P. *The Bureaucratic Experience.* New York: St. Martin's Press, 1977.

Leavitt, H. J., W. R. Dill, and H. B. Eyring. *The Organizational World.* New York: Harcourt Brace Jovanovich, 1973.

Perrow, Charles. "The Short and Glorious History of Organization Theory." *Organizational Dynamics* 2 (Summer 1973): 2–15.

Ritti, R. P., and C. R. Funkhouser, *The Ropes to Skip and the Ropes to Know.* Columbus, Ohio: Grid, 1977.

Scott, W. G., and D. K. Hart. *Organizational America.* Boston: Houghton Mifflin, 1979.

Simon, H. A. *Administrative Behavior,* 3rd ed. New York: Free Press, 1976.

Weinstein, A. K. "Management Issues for the Coming Decade." *University of Michigan Business Review* 31 (September 1979): 29–32.

Designing Modern Organizations: Environment, Structure, and Behavior

Each age produces a form or organization appropriate to its own tempo. During the long epoch of agricultural civilization . . . the pace of individual life was comparatively slow. And organizations were seldom called upon to make what we would regard as high speed decisions.

Alvin Toffler,
Future Shock

Bulova Watch Company has been around a long time. In fact, at one time Bulova watches were as "American" as Coca Cola and Chevrolet. But even old standbys can make costly mistakes. Bulova learned this the hard way when digital watches entered the marketplace. Although the market appeared shaky at first, Seiko, Texas Instruments, and Timex turned digital watches into high-profit items. By 1975, when Bulova finally decided to make its own digital models, the competition had captured much of the market. Within five years, Bulova saw its 15 percent hold on the watch market in this country shrink to about 10 percent.

There doubtless are many reasons why Bulova did not respond quickly enough to the demand for digital watches. Many organizations have made similar errors—and will continue to do so. However, a major goal of the current trend in organizational design is to devise structures that will sense such environmental change and respond to it rapidly.

This chapter introduces open and closed organizational systems and shows how important this concept is in understanding an organization's interaction with its environment. We also will examine several organizational designs that have been recommended for their ease in responding to changes both inside and outside the organization.

Open and Closed Organizational Systems

Much current concern in organizational behavior and design is directed toward the relationship between an organization's environment and its structure. In turn, the structure can be related to both individual and group behavior in organizations.

Environment and Organizational Design

The structure of an organization is often influenced by outside forces such as the technology employed in the industry, the competitiveness of the market, and the degree of governmental control. The Woodward studies (see Chapter 11) noted that firms in custom-built or small-batch industries had different organizational characteristics from firms in mass-production or continuous-process industries. It should not surprise us, then, that companies like Standard Oil, Uniroyal, and Rolls Royce are different with regard to such things as the number of organizational levels and the span of management.

If an industry is highly competitive, a firm's organizational structure may reflect certain properties. For example, small businesses often have difficulty surviving competitive pressures and usually are quite centralized in their decision making.[1] Since an ill-advised decision may make the difference between prosperity and bankruptcy, a few top managers are likely to maintain close control.

In fact, research done at Boeing Aircraft Company and in other settings indicates that when managers face an uncertain environment, they tend to develop organizational designs that can respond to situations as they occur.[2] More recently, we can see the potential for outside control and influence that is created when an organization goes to a governmental agency to seek financial support. When Chrysler Corporation asked the federal government for assistance in 1979, a congressional committee suggested that support be granted only if Chrysler agreed to a five-year wage freeze. Such a condition would significantly influence the corporation's internal administration and operation.

Proposition 12.1

> Environmental forces such as competition, dependence, and uncertainty can influence the design of organizations.

Any comparison of models of organizational behavior requires generalization. Generalization is dangerous because convenient categories often lead to oversimplification. Taking that risk, however, we will examine two stereotyped views of organizations. Keep in mind that we are generalizing for the sake of simplicity. The end, however, justifies the risk, for we will be able to analyze two major views of behavior as they relate to human action in organizations.

The Closed System

A *closed system* emphasizes the precision of internal structure. This model views organizations as predictable, rational entities.[3] Perhaps the best example of this orientation is the typical bureaucracy.

In more contemporary terms, this model sees organizations as being buffered and unaffected by forces outside the structure. As a general rule, this approach is taken because it allows managers to reduce uncertainty and to avoid dealing with the complexities of environmental factors. By looking only at the internal system, one can view individuals mainly as inputs. Uncontrollable and less measurable factors such as values and attitudes can be avoided. The manager can, as Bennis notes, look at "organizations without people."[4] The focus of analysis becomes similar to the illustration in Figure 12.1.

Figure 12.1   Closed-Systems View of Organizations

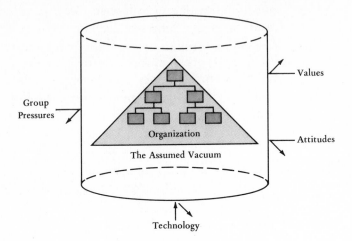

The diagram pictures the organization as existing within a vacuum. Scientific experimentation often observes the behavior of physical objects in a near-perfect vacuum to control the effects of real-world complications like friction. Experimenters do not deny the existence of friction. They simply observe the phenomenon in isolation to better understand what is taking place.

In organizational behavior, the closed-systems view does not deny the reality of group pressures, attitudes, values, and technology. Instead, it attempts to isolate structure and understand its properties while controlling as many complications as possible. However, no one would attempt to apply scientific principles to actual problems without introducing the influence of external factors. To anyone constructing a jetliner, what would be the good of an aeronautical design that was produced to perform in a near-perfect vacuum? Organization theorists, unfortunately, have not always been so practical in extending knowledge to reality and in anticipating potential complications.

Opening the System

The *open system,* in contrast, is distinguished by its interaction with the environment. In its most simple form, the open-systems model

Figure 12.2 Input-Process-Output View of the Organization as an Open System

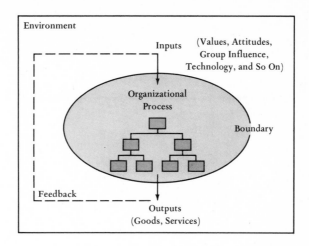

of organization is illustrated in Figure 12.2. Notice the input-process-output format. The organization is pictured as a process that takes inputs such as land, labor, capital, and information from its environment. Processes, or operations, are performed on these inputs, and goods and/or services are produced. The products then are sent back to the environment. Finally, the evaluation of the output is converted into information that becomes input for later operations by means of a feedback process.

The distinguishing characteristic of the open-systems model is that organizations are viewed as dynamic and changing rather than as machines. An open-systems view looks at the whole as well as the parts.

Proposition 12.2

Closed systems are distinguished from open systems because the latter actively interact with environmental forces. When adopting the open-systems view, one no longer sees the organization as being isolated. Instead, organizations are viewed as integral parts of an extensive environmental-organizational interface.

Even though there is a clear and useful interface between the organization and its environment, interaction is not totally open because of boundaries or limits presented by the organization's structure. At the boundaries, interaction is restricted. The degree of openness is determined by how permeable the boundaries are.

Framework for Viewing Behavior in Organizations

The major thrust of the modern systems view of organizational behavior is to emphasize the importance of the environment to organizational structure. In turn, the structural characteristics of the organization are then related to the behavior within the structure. This *holistic approach* (so called because of the importance it places on environmental factors) progresses in the manner illustrated in Figure 12.3. This diagram allows for the influences that behavior can, and frequently does, have on structure. Let us briefly examine the logic of the argument at this point.

First, we can recognize the importance of environmental forces in determining organizational structure. Although much emphasis has been placed on the importance of technology, other factors also must be included. Organizations are contained within an institutional framework and are subject to numerous economic, political, and cultural forces that can be reflected in the organizations' structures.

However, to look only at the environmental influences on design would be to consider only one part of the relationship. Internal factors, such as the occupational characteristics of employees and the

Figure 12.3 Holistic View of Organizational Behavior

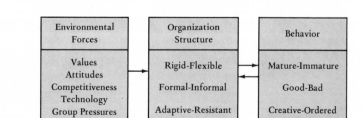

demands of the tasks, also influence structure. Thus we see a complex set of forces affecting organizational structure. These forces originate both outside and within the organization.[5] The implication is that an organizational design that influences group and individual behavior reflects more than arbitrary administrative action. It results from a combination of external and internal forces as well as from conscious managerial behavior.

Proposition 12.3

> Organizational structure influences organizational behavior. However, structure is primarily an intervening variable that reflects both external environmental forces and internal occupational and task characteristics.

To illustrate the complex relationships we are proposing among environment, organizational design, and behavior, consider the example of Research Associates (RA). This privately owned research and consulting firm specializes in solving financial and administrative problems in nonprofit organizations. Since its many projects are varied, RA does not have a formal structure. Any of its ten partners can negotiate a contract with a client, thereby obligating all ten associates. For legal purposes, one partner is designated as the firm's president, but the presidency rotates each year. At any given time, a partner may be the director of one project and thus responsible for coordinating all activities related to it. The same partner also is likely to be a secondary resource for two or three other projects directed by other partners. Thus RA needs a fluid, informal structure because of its business as well as the professionalism of the partners.

Within the organization, this structure, or lack of structure, has significant influence on the partners' behavior. Each partner freely reports to and leaves the office at will. No attempt is made to account for hours worked or to check expense items closely (as long as they remain within agreed-upon ranges). In effect, all the partners consider themselves to be self-employed and to be working within the framework of RA only for practical and legal purposes.

This is a clear case of how an organization's environment demands a loose and flexible structure. In turn, this flexibility leads to free and relatively autonomous behavior.

Responding to Contingencies

In stable environments, the mechanical, bureaucratic structure performs quite well. Classical organization theory, therefore, is generally adequate in such a situation. Problems with it develop in dynamic environments, because we have much less experience with the types of contingencies that arise. What is needed, according to some theorists, is a temporary, problem-oriented organizational form that can adapt constantly to changing environmental demands.

Task Force or Project Groups

The plea for temporary problem-solving groups has been reinforced by several writers who predict that such structures will be used increasingly in organizations that face rapid changes as well as by those existing in uncertain environments.[6] Bennis refers to these task forces as organic-adaptive structures, each composed of diverse specialists who have expertise relevant to the problem at hand. The leader in this type of group does not hold a hierarchical office but coordinates various task forces that operate simultaneously. The individual members are arranged according to their functional skills and talents. The groups are temporary because they exist only as long as there is a need—in other words, until the problem is solved or the project is completed.

In a sense, a group of physicians called in to deal with an especially complex case illustrates such a task force. Since the doctors may be uncertain about the cause of a specific problem, a team consisting of an internal medicine specialist, a radiologist, a surgeon, and a neurologist may be formed. Leadership is not a hierarchical matter. When the solution is found, the team is disbanded.

The team in a *project structure* is similar in that it is a problem-oriented group created to solve a specific issue.[7] As a general rule, this team is developed in a way that provides representation from various specialties relevant to the problem being solved. In functionally structured organizations, all necessary expertise rarely is available to solve a particularly troublesome issue. When this is the case, project teams provide distinct advantages.

Figure 12.4 illustrates the project structure used in the engineering division of Sigma Systems. The Engineering Division is headed

305

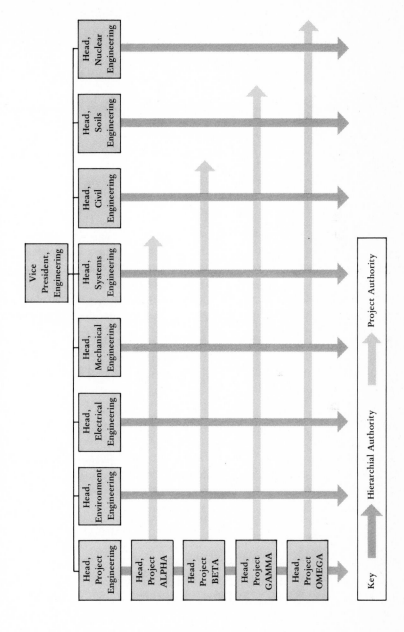

Figure 12.4   Engineering Project Structure at Sigma Systems

by a vice president. Under this vice president of engineering are eight department heads. Seven of the department heads are responsible for functional engineering areas such as electrical, mechanical, civil, and so on. The other department head is responsible for coordinating a series of projects.

The solid downward-pointing arrows illustrate the hierarchical authority of the organization. The head of systems engineering has authority over and is accountable for all activities relating to systems engineering. The same is true of soils, environmental, and nuclear engineering. However, few of Sigma's contracts relate only to one functional area of engineering. Most require the interaction of several functional areas. Therefore, the vice president of engineering has designated a head of project engineering and continuously sets up task forces or projects to deal with specific contracts as they are implemented. The head of project engineering is responsible for coordinating all the projects operating at any time. Each project, in turn, is led by a *project director* who is responsible for acquiring the specific resources needed from each functional area to complete the requirements of the project. The project director's authority relates to the specific project only (as is illustrated by the horizontal arrows).

For example, Project ALPHA is a contract with a municipal government to remodel and modernize a general-purpose office building. The project required an environmental impact study and a series of systems cost estimates. Also new heating and air-conditioning systems were required, along with completely new wiring. Therefore, the head of Project ALPHA had to negotiate with the heads of environmental, electrical, mechanical, and systems engineering to obtain the expertise needed to engineer all phases of the remodeling and renewal. No single department had all the expertise needed to complete the job.

Project OMEGA is the most comprehensive work under contract at Sigma Systems. This project involves the planning of a nuclear power generation facility and involves all engineering departments.

The project structure at Sigma Systems enables the firm to organize the engineering efforts around specific problems or projects. It allows the firm to rally the required resources where they are needed, and it provides an easy way of dismantling projects when contracts are complete. Frame 12.1 further illustrates project organization by looking at the American space program.

Frame 12.1

Managing a National Space Program

The tremendous scientific accomplishments of the U.S. space program over the past three decades are well known. The pioneering task of managing the massive National Aeronautical and Space Administration (NASA) has been no less impressive, but this achievement is generally not so well known. When James E. Webb was appointed administrator of the newly formed NASA, he faced a unique and challenging organizational task. His job was to search through existing management and behavioral science theory and judge what was and was not applicable to the space program.

The most immediate problem in organizing NASA was to develop an appropriate mix between the need for control and accountability and the flexibility necessary to ensure continuous innovation. This problem was especially complicated. As Mr. Webb noted in his book *Space Age Management,* the Marshall Space Flight Center generated twenty-two railroad boxcars of data each year, whereas the Apollo project was estimated to require 300,000 tons of data.

It was against this background of uncertainty and challenge that NASA developed its organization. Throughout NASA's history, the organization has been re-evaluated, adjusted, and even redesigned several times. In the end, however, most observers agree that NASA did well both organizationally and technically. Its experience with the administration of large-scale, complex systems has yielded major contributions to organizational design theory.

Advantages of Project Structure   The main advantage in using a project approach to problem solving is that teams can mobilize their diverse talents effectively to solve specific problems.[8] Few problems encountered in complex environments can be solved by the talents available in a single functional division.

Consider a problem such as designing automobiles for the 1990s. It might be tempting to turn an automotive engineer loose with a drawing board to develop an elegant design that would be pleasing to the public. However, given the changes taking place today, it would be wise to include such individuals as market researchers, environmental scientists, and a multitude of other specialists in attacking this problem.

When project teams of equally qualified specialists are brought together, one can expect certain other advantages. In the project approach, for example, participation in decision making increases, formal authority and control is minimized, and each member of the team enjoys a great deal of personal satisfaction with regard to the completed task.[9] Also the interaction of diverse experts in a task force environment is helpful in stimulating the creativity of each individual involved.

Project structure also provides practical advantages for the organization. The identification of a project team with specific responsibilities has the advantage of giving visibility to the problem and acknowledging that the organization has a commitment to deal with it.[10] At the same time, the existence of a task force provides a focal point for all dealings with regard to the specific mission being accomplished.

Disadvantages of Project Structure   Often the existence of a project team violates the unity-of-command principle, which is a basic concept of classical organization theory. For example, in most projects, a portion of each individual's time is assigned to the project. During the time that the individual works on the project, he or she is accountable to the project director. On the other hand, when the individual is working on regular departmental assignments, accountability is directed toward the appropriate department head. Unless clear policies are established to govern project work, frustrations can develop when the project director and the department head demand excessive amounts of time from the individual involved in project work.

Project teams also have been criticized because of their tendency to encourage the overspecialization of project personnel. Frequently there is no place in the regular organization for the highly specialized talent required for a specific project. Thus members of problem-oriented task forces can feel insecure and fear that they will be fired when the project is completed. They see no place for their talents within the functional divisions.[11] Morale and the quality of work suffer, and project members have been known to actually create work to avoid the possibility of being terminated.

Finally, members of project teams often feel that they are isolated from the regular line organization. Since promotions and recognition generally come from recognized line officials, task force participants frequently feel that they are forgotten or may be overlooked when the opportunity for advancement presents itself. At the same time, some project members become so attached to the task at hand that they actually reduce their loyalty to the larger organization.[12] In this case, the project, rather than the organization, is the object of the individual's loyalty.

Not all of the problems of the project structure can be identified directly with members of the project team. This temporary unit also creates problems for effective management.

Leadership Behavior in Temporary Groups

Imagine for a moment that you are project director of Project ALPHA at Sigma Systems. Think of the managerial problems that you immediately face. First, you have to become an effective leader of the project team or task force that is directly under your control. On the other hand, you must possess the ability to obtain the cooperation from necessary units in the larger line organization over which you have no formal authority.[13]

Practically speaking, as a project manager you have authority over the individual members of the team. However, project members usually are selected because of their unique expertise. They are likely to be highly trained, professional, and specialized. The project manager should be cautious in using the authority available for implementing decisions. You are even more disadvantaged with regard to the functional organization because you have no authority over the necessary support units and can require little if any cooperation. The combination of these two factors creates what is known as a *managerial authority gap*.[14] As a manager you have more accountability than you have authority. The issue, therefore, becomes how to get things done in the project environment.

A study of project structures in state governments and in the aerospace, construction, and chemical industries has provided us with some insights into the dynamics of leadership in the project-oriented setting. The most important finding relates to the strategies by which project managers overcome the authority gap in their own groups and at the same time coexist and deal successfully with relevant functional units. These strategies are:

1. Technical competence
2. Powers of persuasion and personality
3. Ability to negotiate
4. Reciprocal favors[15]

Let us look briefly at each of these strategies. In highly technical and professional settings, one effective strategy available to the project manager is to use his or her own proven technical competence in doing the job. The fact that the project director is recognized as being highly competent enables the individual not only to attain the support of his or her own work group, but also to gain the necessary cooperation of the functional departments within the line administrative structure.

At the same time, the project manager must develop a diplomatic expertise through persuasive powers and personality characteristics. These factors are instrumental in developing the friendships and associations that give the project director influence in the organization and allow him or her to become sufficiently influential over the actions of subordinates and fellow managers.

If one cannot obtain the necessary power to influence others, the alternative is to bargain or negotiate successfully with project employees and functional department heads. Also one can resort to the political approach of providing reciprocal favors and concessions for the performance of duties and cooperation of other departments.

This study suggests that the project manager must become not only a skillful politician but also an expert in exercising leadership without formal authority. This brings us to an additional proposition.

Proposition 12.4

> Temporary problem-solving units such as project structures and task forces provide advantages in mobilizing organizational resources toward the solution of problems and encouraging the participation of diverse specialists. They bring disadvantages, however, in terms of their isolating effects on project personnel and their creation of complex leadership roles.

Figure 12.5 Matrix Management at Steller International Corporation

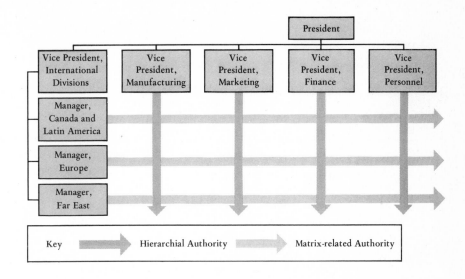

From Project Structure to Matrix Organization

A technical distinction sometimes is drawn between the project structure used by Sigma Systems and an organizational design known as *matrix structure.* As shown in Figure 12.5, the project and matrix designs are similar in principle. For example, the flow of authority is two-dimensional, with the traditional hierarchical authority flowing vertically and project authority flowing horizontally. This two-directional flow of authority results in a rectangular, or matrix, appearance.

Some writers view the project structure as being one stage in the evolution of a traditional bureaucracy to a more permanent form of matrix structure.[16] Although this is true in many cases, some organizations (like Sigma Systems) are not designed to evolve to a different form. Instead, they employ the project structure because of its usefulness in completing specific contracts.

Other organizations in different environments may evolve to a more permanent form of project structure that can be classified accurately as a matrix design. To illustrate, consider the case of Steller

International Corporation, which uses a permanent project or matrix design to manage its international operations. (See Figure 12.5.) Steller International manfactures and distributes worldwide a line of sports equipment for men and women. The firm is particularly well known for its ski clothing, hiking and camping equipment, and related lines.

As Figure 12.5 reveals, the company is organized around a functional arrangement. The vice presidents for manufacturing, marketing, finance, personnel, and international divisions report to the president. These vice presidents are responsible for the basic functions of the organization, and they directly administer domestic operations. At the same time, all international operations are overseen by three regional managers who report to the vice president for international divisions. The three regional managers are responsible for Canada and Latin America, Europe, and the Far East. Each of these regional divisions operates like an independent company because of the unique circumstances found in each region. Climates vary, and so must the product line. Language and cultural factors further require decentralized operations. In effect, each regional manager has authority over manufacturing, marketing, finance, and personnel matters in each region—even though the functions themselves physically remain in the headquarters operation. In this case, a matrix structure exists in the most accurate sense. Its distinction relative to the project structure seen in Sigma Systems is that the regional divisions are permanent. They do not disband when a project is completed or a problem solved.

Steller International believes this structure provides certain advantages. First, the regional divisions are "closer" to the actual operations in various areas and can respond faster to unique demands. Also the personnel can specialize in the various regional operations and sense more quickly when circumstances demand change. Because the regional offices operate like self-contained organizations, a team spirit can be generated, and better-quality information can be supplied to central management. Finally, better control can be maintained at the regional level.

There are, of course, certain potential problems that must be monitored constantly. For example, unless the top level of management is coordinated carefully, miscommunication and conflict can develop between regional managers and functional vice presidents. Questions may arise about who has authority over issues that do not "fit" neatly into regional and functional categories. Who, for example, would decide on financial policies relating to the terms of payment from customers that vary from one location to another? Moreover, the physical separation of the operations can, and often does, cause communication and coordination problems.[17]

In principle, project structure and matrix organization are similar. The main difference between the two lies in the planned longevity of the design. Project structure brings together teams that are designed to solve a problem and then dismantle. Matrix organization also operates in a two-dimensional manner, but it is conceived as a permanent arrangement.

Collegial Organizations

Project structure and matrix organization are extremely useful in overcoming some of the resistance to change that characterizes many bureaucracies. However, not only external, environmental forces require adaptation. Often changes are required by the people who make up today's organizations.

Workers now have more skills and are educated more highly than ever before. Many organizations and types of work have become so complex that workers' newly achieved skills are directed toward solving extremely complicated tasks. In fact, there seems to be emerging a "knowledge industry" that relies heavily on improved knowledge and education.[18] Such fields as health care, pharmaceuticals, and aerospace are particularly dependent on ever-increasing stores of knowledge and information.

Highly trained specialists frequently do not "fit" quite so well within hierarchical structures as do less skilled employees. The freedom and flexibility needed to take advantage of expertise and skill are rarely found in the typical bureaucracy. For this reason, a relatively new type of organizational design is being used in selected areas of high-technology organizations. This design approach aims at developing *collegial structure,* which is characterized by the following important distinctions:

1. *Emphasis on developing and using knowledge.* Collegial organizations are found most often in cases where structures have grown

around a core of highly trained and independent specialists (such as physicians, accountants, engineers, and other professionals).

2. *Governance by shared power and tradition.* The coordination of human activity in a collegial structure such as a hospital, university, or law firm is rarely achieved by authority or force. More often, tradition may dictate some authority (for example, only tenured professors decide on tenure decisions, or the family doctor maintains veto power when specialists are consulted about a treatment). Or the collegial organization may manage by means of a policy-making committee. Representatives of the core group of professionals will participate in deciding, for example, how profits will be distributed, what fringe benefits will be offered, and so on.

3. *Administration by nonprofessional staff.* Managers who are not experts in the work of the core specialists often are hired to look after the administration of the organization. In a group of doctors, a business manager may be hired to look after financial and personnel matters relating to all nonphysicians. Here the traditional hierarchy is reversed, for rank-and-file members are more powerful than the manager. This reversal is not uncommon in collegial structures.[19]

Therefore, the collegial model of organization emerges as an extremely unusual design. Its distinctive character is based on the high level of skills possessed by the average member, the power of the membership over management, and its use of committees and tradition or custom as the basis of decision making. This structure is so rare in most areas of business and commerce that it will be useful to examine two specific examples of its application.

The Professionalized Hierarchy

To illustrate a *professionalized hierarchy,* we will use the example of a hospital. This is not to say that all hospitals are professionalized hierarchies. It does mean, however, that many hospitals operate in this way.

In hospitals, there is a central core of medical personnel directed primarily by physicians and their representative—the chief of medical staff.[20] Within this structure, the ability of any given physician to influence another is based mainly on his or her perceived expertise.

A renowned heart surgeon, for example, is likely to be more powerful than a less well-known chief of staff and is almost sure to be
more powerful than the nonmedical administrator.

Hospitals also are decentralized with regard to decision making.
Like faculty members at a university, individual physicians in hospitals enjoy a great deal of freedom in the technical aspects of decision
making.[21] Few would dare question a physician's diagnosis or treatment program for a patient without substantial cause.

It is true that hospitals have a large group of nonmedical administrators. However, these individuals are responsible for such duties as
accounting, nonmedical staffing, general administrative planning, and
so on. Any decision that is clearly nonmedical can be made by this
group of administrators. The medical staff is often cautious about
delegating even administrative decisions to the professional managers lest the decisions affect medical care. For example, financial
decisions could influence medical equipment and facilities. For this
reason, an elaborate system of committees usually is employed to
ensure that the "primary" professional group maintains practical
control over important decision making.[22]

In a very real sense, there develops a "dual hierarchy" of authority
in a hospital. One is the medical hierarchy dominated by the physicians and headed by the chief of staff. This chain of authority has
absolute authority over all matters relating to medicine and patient
care. The second is an administrative hierarchy that appears to be
coequal but is, in reality, created and maintained to support the
medical functions. This chain of command has authority over housekeeping and general administrative decisions. Its authority, however,
is seldom complete and certainly not absolute.

Finally, it is important to note that the very top positions in the
administrative hierarchy are responsible for performing an important
boundary role. This behavior will be discussed in detail in Chapter
13. For our purposes here, it is enough to note that the top executives in the administrative hierarchy of a hospital or university are
expected to interact with important outside groups. A hospital administrator is expected to raise funds, to interact with patient-
protection groups and handle complaints, and to negotiate with representatives of the local nonprofessional employees' union to ensure
peace and productivity.[23]

Herein lies the great control dilemma faced by the "professional
core" of physicians in the hospital, professors in a university, or
research scientists in a laboratory. Such highly trained professionals

want to be free to use their skills and practice their arts, delegating all nontechnical administration to managers. Yet they remain free to "do their thing" only so long as the managers raise the funds and administer the resources successfully. If professionals are to remain free to practice their specialties, some control must be transferred to management so that administrators can complete their tasks. Otherwise, the specialists must assume administrative responsibility and engage in at least a limited amount of management.

Thus the professionalized hierarchy is a special type of collegial structure. It is extremely decentralized, may have a dual hierarchy of authority, and probably requires a relatively large number of committees to make and carry out decisions. Moreover, its top management level is expected to devote substantial energy to interacting with outside organizations and agencies.

Proposition 12.5

> The professionalized hierarchy displays a structure similar to the typical bureaucracy, but its mode of operation differs significantly. This is particularly true with regard to authority, whereby the legal authority of the bureaucracy is secondary to the power provided by technical expertise.

The Organic-Adaptive (Ad Hoc) Structure

The increasing sophistication of modern technology has shown that few fields of specialization have the expertise needed to solve real-world problems. Such goals as sending an astronaut to Mars or providing effective preventive medicine require the cooperation of many diverse specialists. Alvin Toffler, in his book *Future Shock* in 1970, discussed the necessity of ad hoc organizational arrangements in problem solving.

The main problem an ad hoc or *organic-adaptive design* attempts to overcome is innovation. This structure was conceived of as an extremely innovative organization. A secondary problem it addresses relates to coordinating the talents of diverse specialists. True innovation in a modern setting requires a multidisciplinary view. In this way—with maximum flexibility, minimum structure, and interre-

Figure 12.6 Aerodynamic Research Institute*

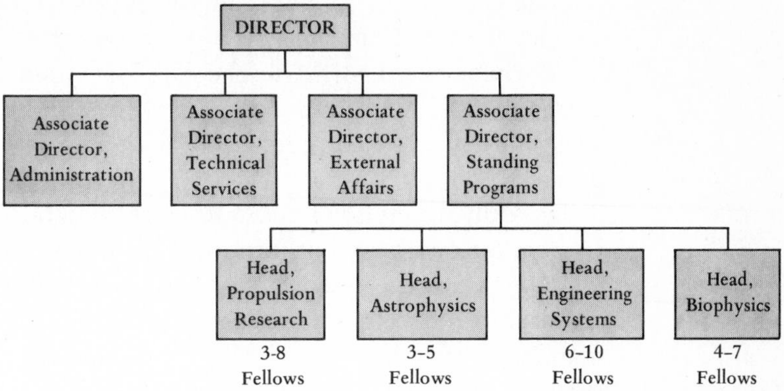

*All staff members are permanent except the fellows, each of whom works at the institute for one to three years.

lated specialists—the organic-adaptive design promises to be a useful structure for dealing with the complex problems of today and tomorrow.[24]

Some particularly good examples of organic-adaptive structures are the think tanks that have developed in and out of American universities. For example, the Center for the Study of Democratic Institutions in California and the Woodrow Wilson Center for International Scholars in Washington are designed to provide the highest degree of intellectual flexibility to encourage innovation.

We will discuss this design with the aid of Aerodynamic Research Institute (ARI). This laboratory is sponsored and operated by the government, and is charged with the responsibility of advanced research in aerodynamic systems to ensure that the United States remains on the frontier of manned flight. The institute has a small permanent staff, as illustrated in Figure 12.6. Being located on the campus of a major university in the northeast, the institute has a variety of formal ties and informal relationships with the university's departments of natural and physical sciences.

The organization of ARI is based on four programs: propulsion research, astrophysics, engineering systems, and biophysics. The programs are headed by a permanent staff member, and the major membership consists of a limited number of highly trained postdoctoral fellows. These fellows remain at the institute for one to three years. They are selected through national competition and are given complete freedom to work on any project they choose during the period of their visit. The only requirement is that they attempt to relate their own project to the work of other individuals and programs at ARI. As time has passed, a variety of multidisciplinary subprojects have emerged, along with a variety of subproject coordinators.

Typically, the fellows and staff work together in small, fluid groups that center on an area of interest, remain an unpredictable time, and dissolve when the need arises to diversify into different groups or research directions. In this design, there is no distinction between management and research. All permanent staff are qualified and recognized scientists. Thus administrative planning of projects, technical services, and outside linking activities are viewed as essential to all the institute's efforts.

In the organic-adaptive structure, as in the professionalized hierarchy, top management also performs an external role. In this case, the director interacts with the government agencies involved in science and technology and ensures useful relationships between ARI and its funding sources.

Proposition 12.6	The organic-adaptive design is the most flexible and innovative organizational structure. Because of its flexibility, however, it must be related to more structured organizations to implement the ideas it develops.

Aerodynamic Research Institute has an ad hoc or organic-adaptive structure in the most accurate sense. The emphasis is on innovation and multidisciplinary cooperation. To apply any of the ideas developed, ARI must be tied to more structured and specialized professional hierarchies in the university and the government. Because its mission is innovation and its structure reflects the need for flexibility, ARI has little or no means to achieve the implementation of ideas.

What Managers Need to Know About Designing Modern Organizations

What if a brilliant scientist developed a new product but could not manufacture or sell it because an appropriate organization could not be developed? What a paradox it would have been if this nation could develop the technology to put a person on the moon but could not organize the effort to achieve success.

People change, and so must organizations. More and more young employees are coming into organizations with high levels of education and training. Expertise is necessary if today's increasingly complex technology is to be used effectively. This new breed of employees do not fit easily into a rigid bureaucratic setting. They like to offer ideas, and they need some freedom if they are to contribute their best efforts.

Problems, like people, also change. Today it is becoming beneficial to organize around problems such as marketing a new concept or developing a new product. However, few concepts or products will support managers and organizations for many years. Success and survival depend more and more on the ability to introduce new ideas constantly. The key element in any organization is how rapidly the structure can respond to new demands and how effectively it can capitalize on new opportunities. Thus, if managers are to survive in a complex and competitive world, they must know more than the time-tested principles of organizations. They must know how to alter those principles when the situation demands.

As these structural changes evolve, their unique leadership challenges must be met and mastered. Very likely, managers will increasingly need to develop their negotiating and diplomacy skills as well as their managerial talents.

Summary

Bulova Watch Company missed an opportunity by not responding fast enough to the new demand for digital watches. Yet the watch industry is recognized as being oriented toward high technology.

In this chapter, we departed from traditional organizational design, which is primarily concerned with efficiency of operation. The precision of classical organization theory and closed-systems logic was acknowledged but discarded in an effort to look at a second dimension of organizational effectiveness—the ability to respond to change. We noted early in the discussion that an open-systems perspective is needed to ensure that important environmental factors are incorporated into decision making. However, an organization must do more than merely acknowledge the importance of external factors; the structure itself must be able to alter and change.

Throughout this chapter, we discussed two major types of adaptive organizations. The first was project structure and its extension to the permanent matrix organization. We investigated the advantages and disadvantages of project structure as well as the unique leadership problems that often arise for project directors. We then noted that longevity is the main distinction between project structure and matrix organization. Project structure is clearly temporary and is designed to be dismantled when the problem or project is over. Matrix organization, on the other hand, is designed to be permanent.

The collegial organization was the second major design discussed. This design centers most authority on core professionals rather than on managers. It makes extensive use of power-sharing arrangements such as committees, and it directs the energy of top management toward outside relations. The professionalized hierarchy was illustrated by the hospital and its unique dual-authority systems. The organic-adaptive (ad hoc) design was discussed with the example of a hypothetical think tank.

None of these designs is built around the bureaucratic notion of efficiency. Project, matrix, and collegial designs risk a loss of efficiency for the sake of adaptability to change.

Questions for Discussion

1. What is the basic difference between project structure and matrix organization? In what ways are they similar?
2. List and explain some unique leadership problems experienced by a project director. What are the causes of these problems?

3. What is a collegial organization? Why do you think it is called "collegial"?
4. What is the significance of an open organizational system? Is it possible for an organization to become too open? Explain.
5. What are the main differences, as you see them, between traditional bureaucratic structure and today's trends in organizational design?

Exercise: Recognizing Organizational Designs

Take a few minutes to draw your perception of your college's or university's organization chart. A campus telephone directory or student handbook will help identify the major academic and support units. React to the following questions on the basis of your perception.

1. *Objectives or mission.* What is the basic mission or objective of your institution?
   a. Are there any unique environmental factors that make your institution different? To illustrate, is it located in an urban area? Is it a private or state institution?
   b. What specific actions have been taken by the institution to reflect the uniqueness in its organization?
2. *Structure.* Is the college or university organized in a typical hierarchical form?
   a. If so, do any design factors imply that it is a professionalized hierarchy? For example, what is the core professional group? How does this group relate organizationally to other units?
   b. If not, what alternative designs are employed? Can you locate any temporary project groups or a permanent matrix structure?
3. *Alternative units.* Do any research, service, or teaching units fall outside the main organization?
   a. Look especially for multidisciplinary organic-adaptive units. How are they positioned relative to the professional hierarchy?
   b. Are there any other unusual variations that you consider important? Explain.
4. *Overall.* In general, how would you classify the organization of your institution? Justify.

Case: *Morningview Hospital*

Mr. Harry LaPlase is the administrator of Morningview Hospital. The hospital, located in a midwestern town of 37,500 people, is a privately owned, not-for-profit facility with 412 employees. There are 45 physicians on the active staff, as well as 30 courtesy staff physicians who are specialists in private practice. These specialists include urologists, obstetricians, emergency medical specialists, orthopedic surgeons, and so on.

There are eight support departments (maintenance, accounting, and so on), which report directly to LaPlase. The six medical departments report to the administrator through the chief of medical staff, Dr. Lois Hatcher.

At present, the hospital's policy making is done by an eleven-member board of directors. These directors serve one-year terms and can be re-elected as often as the board deems desirable. The board of directors is composed of eight prominent business people, two local physicians with courtesy staff appointments, and Dr. Hatcher.

LaPlase has worked hard selecting highly qualified business representatives. They include a certified public accountant, a self-employed lawyer, an insurance executive, and so on. All board members are involved in their own work and do not communicate regularly except at monthly board meetings.

For the first year or two, LaPlase was pleased with the activity of the board. Members appeared to study policy issues and to involve themselves in important problems. Recently, however, the board has become reluctant to discuss any issue relating to medical matters. The usual approach is simply to defer to the three physicians on the board, and other members support them. In principle this does not concern LaPlase, since he thinks medical decisions should be made by physicians.

The problem now seems to be that numerous proposals and projects are stated in medical terms though to the administrator they seem to be more economic or managerial in nature. LaPlase thinks the medical staff is, in effect, attempting to avoid the business board members and thus gain an advantage in the approval of their "pet" projects.

1. What are your thoughts about LaPlase's approach to board membership?
2. How do you think the present problem can be evaluated properly to determine whether or not an evasive strategy is being used?
3. What would you recommend that LaPlase do at this point?

Suggested Readings

Davis, S. M., and P. R. Lawrence. *Matrix.* Reading, Mass.: Addison-Wesley, 1977.

Downey, H. K., D. H. Hellriegel, and J. W. Slocum. "Environmental Uncertainty: The Construct and Its Application." *Administrative Science Quarterly* 20 (1975): 613–629.

Hackman, J. R., and J. L. Suttle, eds., *Improving Life at Work.* Santa Monica, Calif.: Goodyear, 1977.

Knight, Kenneth. "Matrix Organizations: A Review." *Journal of Management Studies* 13 (1976): 111–130.

Kologny, H. F. "Evolution to a Matrix Organization." *Academy of Management Review* 4 (1979): 543–553.

Lawrence, P. R., H. F. Kologny, and S. M. Davis. "The Human Side of the Matrix." *Organizational Dynamics* 6 (Fall 1977): 43–61.

McFarland, D. E. *Managerial Innovation in the Metropolitan Hospital.* New York: Praeger, 1979.

Perrow, Charles. "The Bureaucratic Paradox: The Efficient Organization Centralizes in Order to Decentralize." *Organizational Dynamics* 5 (Spring 1977): 3–14.

Sheldon, Ann. *Organizational Issues in Health Care Management.* New York: Spectrum, 1975.

Weist, J. D. "Project Network Models: Past, Present, and Future," *Project Management Quarterly* 7 (May 1977): 27–36.

part V

Changing Organizations

THROUGHOUT THIS BOOK, our plan has been to understand organizational behavior first by analyzing the individual and then by examining increasingly complex levels of behavior. In doing so, we have looked at individuals as they behave in groups and in larger organizational settings.

Now we are ready to examine the important but often neglected area of organizational outputs. After all, the real test of effective management is the results achieved. For this reason organizations try to be efficient at whatever they do. Ultimately, their survival depends on the outputs of performance and change.

Our goal in Part V is to examine organizational performance and change. To do so, we must broaden our view of organizational behavior to include the interorganizational level. We must understand why it is important for organizations to respond to external as well as to internal pressures for change.

Chapter 13 begins the discussion with a look at boundary-spanning behavior. How can managers deal with forces and groups outside their own organization? How well a manager deals with social pressures, competition, and numerous other factors can determine whether or not the organization will survive. As we will see, managers who are skillful at internal operations may or may not be adept at relations between and among organizations. Innovative behavior is a key topic examined in Chapter 13.

Chapter 14 looks at two important related issues: the review and measurement of individual performance and organizational effectiveness. We will emphasize the requirements for appraising performance accurately, and we will aim to develop a meaningful concept of organizational effectiveness.

Chapter 15 analyzes the issue of planned change and organizational development. Our primary goal will be to understand planned change. We will look at some reaons why employees may resist change, and we will explore several strategies that can be used to overcome resistance. Finally, we will illustrate selected techniques for organizational development. Our goal is not to build skill in using the techniques but to provide general information about some frequently used approaches.

Chapter 16 concludes our study of organizational behavior by reviewing our approach in this book and also looking toward the future. The hope is that this will put you on your way toward more effective management of organizational behavior.

Boundary-Spanning Behavior

The boundary is where the discretion of the organization to control an activity is less than the discretion of another organization or individual to control that activity.

Jeffrey Pfeffer and Gerald Salancik,
The External Control of Organizations

The office of grants and contracts at Hester Institute of Science and Technology was established to monitor the institute's sources of outside funding. When the office was created, it was given full authority over all matters relating to the external funding of research grants and contracts. The director of the office is a nationally known psychologist who reports directly to the president of the institute.

Although the office has been responsible for obtaining and administering millions of dollars of grants and contracts, it is the source of great controversy in the institute. The director is perceived by the faculty as a government bureaucrat who has forgotten how "the other half lives." According to them, he exercises too much control over grant and contract funds. The director, however, insists that he is only doing what the government requires. Recently, the director resigned, asking that he be allowed to return to the teaching and research faculty as soon as possible. He cited health reasons for his resignation, noting that he has been suffering from hypertension, headaches, and other assorted illnesses.

The director of the office of grants and contracts at Hester Institute occupies a boundary role. That is, the job was created to "ensure a continuous and efficient interface with external funding agencies."

As we will see, the director's problems are not unique or unknown. The need for boundary-spanning positions has created new challenges and problems in organizational behavior.

Managing Interorganizational Behavior

Chapter 10 examined the problems of managing intergroup relations. Our focus was on coordinating departments within the same organization, although we also looked at familiar forms of extraorganizational relations, such as labor-management conflict. Now we are ready to explore how managers handle relationships with outside organizations.

Specifically, we have several objectives. First, we want to look at organizational boundaries as part of organizational systems. Our discussion will deal with the practical problems of managing relations between organizations. Next we will present a detailed analysis of boundary-spanning behavior. The emphasis will be on the responsibility of managers to function effectively outside the limits of their own organization. Finally, we will discuss boundary-spanning behavior as it relates to innovation.

Organizational Systems and Boundaries

Organizations, as we noted in Chapter 12, can be viewed accurately as systems or collections of related parts that work toward a common goal. The individuals we discussed in Part I are the elements that make up the small groups or subsystems of the organization. In turn, these small groups are the elements of larger subsystems, such as the production and sales departments. Finally, the departments collectively make up the organization.

Each system or subsystem is defined by a *systems boundary*. For example, a production department's boundary relates to all activities involved in manufacturing a good.

Figure 13.1 illustrates this idea. Individuals are found at the center. A few individuals with a common purpose—such as a group of oldtimers in an organization—can form a small group. The boundary

Figure 13.1 Levels of Boundaries in Organizational Systems

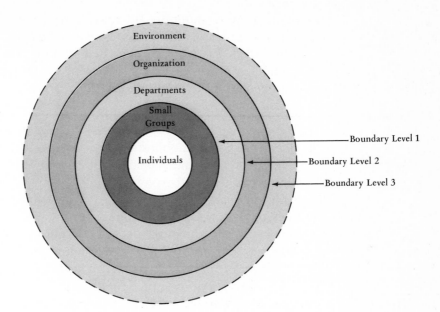

of the oldtimers' group is defined by its members' areas of interest and spheres of interaction. A newcomers' group also may exist with its own boundary to separate it from others. Such small groups make up level 1.

Both groups, however, exist within a larger subsystem, such as the production department. The activities of this larger group form its boundary and separate it from sales, finance, and personnel departments. Such groups make up boundary level 2.

The third boundary level in Figure 13.1 relates to the organization—say Fairway Materials Company. Boundary level 3 thus includes all functional departments, but it separates Fairway Materials from other foundries and organizations. This third boundary level is the focus of our attention now. Since a boundary can be discussed accurately only by taking a specific perspective, we will refer to boundary level 3 as the organizational boundary.

The organizational boundary is important because the ease with which it can be crossed determines how open or closed an organization is. If information flows easily across boundary level 3, the organization is open; if not, it is closed.

Interorganizational Issues

An important element in any organization's environment is the presence of other organizations. Universities must interact with accrediting agencies; hospitals must deal with health planning boards; and municipal governments must contend with state and federal governing agencies. This interaction among organizations is important for at least four reasons:

1. *Organizations depend on other organizations.* For example, manufacturers of automobiles depend on steel mills, rubber companies, and glass and plastic makers for the raw materials to make cars, trucks, and other vehicles.
2. *Strong dependencies influence survival and autonomy.* If a steel mill goes out on strike, automobile assembly lines can be shut down. If the state coordinating board of education decides to merge two colleges, they each may lose their autonomy.
3. *Organizations attempt to manage or control important aspects of the external environment.* If the United States Congress is considering legislation that will influence business or labor, corporations and unions try to influence the voting through lobbyists.
4. *Much organizational behavior cannot be explained by focusing only on internal factors.* Innovation, collective bargaining, and numerous other organizational phenomena cannot be explained adequately with an internal view. We also need to understand factors operating outside an organization.[1]

These four points make it clear that an organization must be viewed as only one element in a complex set of relationships. Almost no organization is self-contained, demanding nothing from and giving nothing to any other group. The more interrelated an organization is, the more external factors will influence its chances for survival. Therefore, the more important it is for managers to deal with outside factors.

We can illustrate these points by considering our country's energy crisis. Although the United States is far less dependent on imports and exports than many European nations—like England and Switzerland—at present we are highly dependent on foreign supplies of oil. So great is our dependence that the ability of foreign governments like Iran to control our oil supplies is a serious threat to our economic survival and national autonomy. We can be forced to do certain things (such as to support one country over another in the Middle East) or to restrict our economic development because other nations are "pulling the strings" on this critical resource. Even the problems of obtaining available oil are complicated, as Frame 13.1 illustrates.

Frame 13.1

> **Putting Gas in Our Tanks**
>
> The drawing on the next two pages, although illustrated in an interesting way, reveals a serious problem of oil supply. It also illustrates the complex interorganizational network that must be coordinated if the crude oil in the Middle East is to arrive in American automobiles. Half the world must be covered, and two months' time must be allowed. The logistics of this operation constitutes a series of serious problems for today's managers, even without the disruptions of war.
>
> Source: Drawing used with the permission of Exxon Company, U.S.A., from "Managing the World System of Oil Supply," Exxon, U.S.A., third quarter 1979, pp. 24–25.

What can a country like the United States or an organization like U.S. Steel do when it finds itself dependent on foreign countries or other companies for critical resources? The usual response is to manage the external relationship in a way that reduces the dependence. Thus the United States is launching a national program to become independent in meeting its energy needs. This is no simple matter. It involves technological innovation in discovering other energy sources as well as in developing domestic—and more expensive—oil supplies.

U.S. Steel responds in much the same way to critical outside influences. If it finds itself overdependent on others for coal and iron ore, it may negotiate long-term contracts to reduce uncertainty. Better still, it may "vertically integrate" by purchasing ore and coal mines outright, thereby ensuring that needed supplies are available. The desire to manage outside dependencies is a predictable response in organizational behavior, whether the organization be a country, a corporation, or a family. Such dependence and its resolution illustrates one of two general views about relationships between organizations.

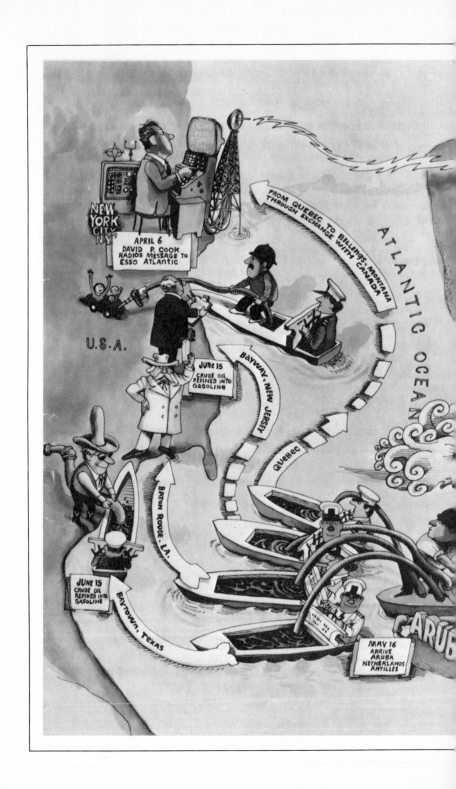

The Odyssey of the Esso Atlantic

Putting Middle East oil into America's fuel tanks requires about two months and employs a worldwide transportation system of extraordinary sophistication.

Two Views of Interorganizational Relations

The above examples have focused on the *power-dependency view* of interorganizational relations. This is contrasted with the exchange view, which some writers have adopted. Because we already have discussed dependence in some detail, we will look first at that approach to interorganizational relations.

Power Dependency   Consider the case of Fast Market Foods (FMF), a chain of convenience stores operating within a large metropolitan area. The firm recently opened a store in Brookhaven, a small incorporated city. Brookhaven's zoning laws prohibit the placement of advertising signs more than 50 feet from a business establishment. However, FMF needs to advertise by means of a sign 75 feet from its door, because its competitors have signs in similar locations on the busy street. The city council has refused FMF's petition, stating that the other stores were given the right by means of a "grandfather clause" when the zoning law was passed. In other words, the competitors already had signs located at the street when the law was passed, and so they were not asked to remove them. FMF has tried to appeal this decision, but the council has refused to reconsider its action.

The motivation for these two organizations to interact is asymmetrical, or out of balance, in terms of power dependency.[2] Whereas FMF depends on the city council, the council does not depend on FMF. This power-dependency relationship can be illustrated by four equations in which P equals power, D equals dependency, C equals the city council, and F equals Fast Market Foods. Here are the equations:[3]

1. $P_{CF} = D_{FC}$

2. $P_{FC} = D_{CF}$

3. $D_{FC} > D_{CF}$

4. $P_{CF} > P_{FC}$

In equation 1 the power of the city council (C) over Fast Market Foods (F) is equal to the dependency of F on C. Equation 2 is the reverse: the power of F over C equals the dependence of C on F. Since, as equation 3 illustrates, the dependence of F on C is greater than the dependence of C on F, then the power of the council exceeds the power of Fast Market Foods, as shown in equation 4. Thus the power-dependency relationship is asymmetrical.

In such an asymmetrical relationship, conflict often occurs. In this case, Fast Market Foods will be able to force continued interaction with the city council only if it can become as powerful as the government. The council, on the other hand, can interact with FMF at its pleasure, since the firm remains dependent on the government for permission to operate within its jurisdiction.

Exchange In contrast to the power-dependency view is the *exchange view,* which is illustrated by two or more organizations that perceive a mutual benefit to interaction.[4] For example, suppose a university and a privately owned research institute are located in the same area. The university is well equipped and is staffed to focus on pure scientific research, whereas the private institute specializes in applied problem solving. In this case, there is no reason for conflict. Instead, the two organizations may develop cooperative research ventures, with each party being responsible for its area of expertise. A cooperative relationship can be established because the resources of each organization can augment the other's, thus increasing the prospects for a better outcome.

Interdependence and Cooperation In the real world, it probably is not wise to separate power-dependency and exchange views. Most interorganizational relations are characterized by both types of interaction.[5] In any organizational setting, some outside organizations may have clearly superior powers, as when a business firm interacts with a government or regulatory agency. At other times, the interaction may be based on equal power and mutual dependency. Therefore, managers must understand both cooperative relationships and those in which conflict must be resolved because the parties have unequal power.

Proposition 13.1

> Organizations interact on the basis of equal or unequal power dependency. If the dependency is equal, the stage is set for cooperation; if not, the likely outcome is conflict.

Spanning Organizational Boundaries

When organizations have reasons to interact, they must overcome certain natural boundaries. For example, even though organizations may benefit from interaction, it does not follow that cooperation will be automatic. Often, special links, called *boundary-spanning roles,* are needed.[6] Figure 13-2 illustrates the point.

The relationship between business firms and government agencies is depicted in Figure 13.2 by the two overlapping circles. Obviously, it would be advantageous for businesses and government to cooperate with respect to regulations that directly affect business operations. For this reason, positions or roles might be established to make someone responsible for ensuring that the interaction takes place. In Figure 13.2, five key positions are shown at the points where the larger systems overlap. These are the boundary-spanning roles.

For example, a business firm might assign a lawyer the role of legislative liaison. This person would interact with key government officials both to communicate the firm's point of view about pending legislation and to obtain feedback for the company. In the same way, government agencies might establish an office of corporate affairs to obtain the views of business.

Figure 13.2   Boundary-Spanning Roles

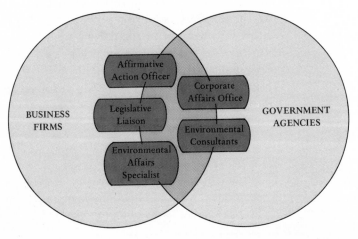

Environmental Influences on Boundary-Spanning Behavior

A particular organization's *boundary-spanning activities* include all those functions designed to improve its interaction with environmental forces including other organizations. The main influence on how much boundary-spanning activity occurs is the environment. A boundary spanner's responsibility is twofold. Spanners must transmit key information to selected aspects of the environment, and they must relay relevant information from the environment to the appropriate organizational officials.[7] Thus spanners become important "gate-keepers" of information flowing in and out of the organization. Obviously, the complexity of this task is related to the environment in which a given organization operates.

Consider some of the relevant factors. First, *perceived environmental uncertainties,* or the extent to which management perceives the environment to be uncertain, will influence the amount of boundary-spanning activity. In the late 1970s, for example, many industries that used great amounts of oil-produced energy faced high levels of uncertainty. The supply of Iranian oil was unpredictable, and the OPEC nations frequently increased their prices. It became necessary for energy-intense firms to span all types of boundaries in search of reasonably priced crude oil and alternative sources of energy. Thus boundary-spanning activities increased in the face of perceived environmental uncertainties. Moreover, management's need to ensure stable oil supplies increased both the complexity of its job and the potential dangers of failure.[8]

Such perceived environmental uncertainty can change even the structure or design of the organizations influenced by it. One study of work groups in a health and welfare organization found that flexible structures correlated highly with the degree of perceived uncertainty in the environment and with the amount of boundary-spanning activities taking place.[9]

Proposition 13.2	The extent of perceived environmental uncertainty influences the amount of boundary-spanning activity taking place and the degree of flexibility built into the organizational design.

Other aspects of the environment often influence the number and status of boundary spanning roles. It has been shown, for example, that organizations within diverse, rapidly changing, resource-scarce environments have a large proportion of boundary-spanning roles. Moreover, the power held by those who fill these boundary-spanning roles is related directly to the expertise needed to accomplish the task.[10] A hospital, for example, faces a diverse environment because its many clients are different (depending on whether they require emergency, long-term, ambulatory, surgical, or intensive care). It also faces a rapidly changing social and technological climate. We therefore would expect more boundary-spanning activity in a hospital than in a comparably sized firm that produces basic foods. And even more boundary-spanning activities would be expected in a poorly financed hospital than in one that is relatively prosperous.

Concerning the power held by various boundary spanners, it is safe to say that a legislative liaison usually has more power than does a director of public relations. The tasks of public relations are more routine and predictable, thus requiring less expertise than is needed by a highly trained legal specialist who must deal with the unpredictable behavior of legislatures and courts.

Finally, the technology of a particular industry can influence the amount of boundary-spanning behavior that takes place. Although there are many ways to classify technologies (such as the small-batch, mass-production, and continuous-process labels used by Woodward and discussed in Chapter 11), a particularly relevant framework has been developed by Thompson.[11] The following categories have been identified:

1. *Long-linked technology.* This is illustrated by the automobile assembly line, on which tasks are arranged sequentially. The frame must be constructed before the motor can be mounted, and the motor must be mounted before the drive assembly can be installed, and so on.
2. *Mediating technology.* In this variation the organization functions to bring together two parties who wish to interact. A real estate firm displays a mediating technology since it is designed to bring together home buyers and sellers.
3. *Intensive technology.* In this case, various techniques or groups must be brought together to achieve a change in some object. To build a school, for example, a construction company must bring

together engineers, carpenters, stone masons, plumbers, and electricians.

Aldrich and Herker have argued that organizations with mediating technologies have the highest proportion of boundary-spanning roles because they need to coordinate diverse techniques or groups. Organizations with long-linked and intensive technologies form internal departments that separate boundary-spanning roles from administrative units.[12]

Proposition 13.3

> The amount of boundary-spanning activity in an organization is related to such environmental characteristics as perceived environmental uncertainty and diversity, the speed of change, and the technology facing the organization.

Behavioral Demands on Boundary Spanners

In many ways the job of boundary spanner is not easy. Since they are responsible for bridging organizational boundaries, boundary spanners often are faced with a potential conflict of interest. Role ambiguity or role conflict may occur. This is one area where our intuitive feelings are not confirmed by research.

It has been suggested, for example, that boundary spanners are "torn between" the interests of their employer and those of the organization they are supposed to link. Thus a legislative liaison for the National Rifle Association might spend so much time in Washington that he or she could be influenced by legislators who believe that gun control is needed. That person's role as advocate for the National Rifle Association then would conflict with personal preferences, resulting in reduced job satisfaction and increased anxiety, stress, and tension. One study did, in fact, find such effects among a sample of first-line supervisors; but the same study showed no such influence over higher-level managers and engineers.[13]

A series of studies followed up on this theme and supported the nonintuitive view. That is, there was either no relationship or a negative relationship between the amount of boundary-spanning activity in a given job and the degree of role ambiguity and role conflict. Moreover, these studies found a positive relationship between boundary-spanning activities and the manager's satisfaction with work, coworkers, opportunity for promotion, and so on.[14]

There seems, then, to be no real proof that boundary spanning causes a manager to feel ambiguity, conflict, stress, or lower levels of satisfaction. In fact, the opposite appears to be the case. It seems possible that as boundary-spanning activities become more important, the manager's status and prestige are increased, making the boundary roles more rewarding and more satisfying.[15] In other words, the importance of boundary-spanning roles and the organizational emphasis on them are great enough to overshadow potential conflicts. Overall, boundary spanning is a satisfying task.

Proposition 13.4

> Boundary-spanning positions are no more subject to role ambiguity and role conflict than are other positions. Indeed, they offer the potential for high levels of job satisfaction.

Boundary Behavior and Systems Coupling

Not all organizations are linked to other groups in the environment to the same extent or in the same manner. Because of technology, social custom, or some other reason, the linkage among one set of organizations may be very close and almost automatic, whereas the linkage among another set may be insignificant or nonexistent. Systems theorists refer to the extent of linkage as *systems coupling*. The degree of coupling, therefore, relates to how responsive one system or subsystem is to changes in another.[16] Figure 13.3 illustrates coupling.

Systems or subsystems are said to be *tightly coupled* when they share many aspects so that a change in one quickly and directly causes changes in another. Tight coupling is illustrated in Figure 13.3a, which depicts the linkage between the American Assembly of Collegiate Schools of Business (AACSB) and the business schools accredited by this agency. In this case, the deans of the accredited schools are the policy makers of the AACSB, and the schools' faculty

Figure 13.3   The Degree of Systems Coupling

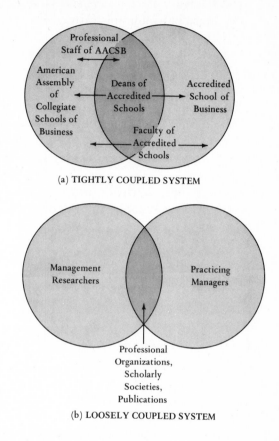

(a) TIGHTLY COUPLED SYSTEM

(b) LOOSELY COUPLED SYSTEM

members often participate on committees. The accrediting standards are incorporated rapidly into the operations of the schools of business, and since the deans are so closely involved in policy making, the accrediting agency is obliged to respond to the changes originating in the schools. Thus there exists a tightly coupled system.

If one system is not responsive to changes in another, it is loosely coupled. In extreme cases, this would result in total independence. The AACSB and the American Medical Association are examples that approach independence since, for all practical purposes, they are not involved in interaction.

Figure 13.3b illustrates a *loosely coupled* system such as the relationship among management researchers and practicing managers. In this case there is some linkage through joint memberships in professional and scholarly associations and subscriptions to publications. Yet, for the most part, administrative research and management practice is loosely coupled.[17]

In boundary-spanning activity, we can speculate that the greatest effort is expended in situations between the extremes of loose and tight coupling.[18] When systems are independent (extremely loose), there is little need for boundary spanning. For example, it would make little sense for the American Medical Association and the American Assembly of Collegiate Schools of Business to devote large amounts of resources to spanning their boundaries since the organizations are essentially independent. When systems are extremely tight, however, as is the case with the AACSB and accredited business schools, the relationship is so interlocked that boundary spanning is institutionalized by the governing process. In cases falling between these two extremes—such as the linkage between business and society or management and labor—boundary-spanning activity is more critical.

Innovation in Organizations

When behavioral scientists speak of *innovation,* they are talking about a specific process. An innovation is not simply an invention. Rather, innovation is a multistage process that includes inventing an idea as well as proposing it and eventually adopting it.[19]

One study of a research and development laboratory pointed out the importance of boundary-spanning behavior as it relates to an organization's ability to innovate.[20] Three levels of boundary spanning were found to be essential for innovation:

1. *Intraunit spanning.* Within a research and development laboratory, it is necessary to bridge the boundaries between departments (between, say, applied cancer research and biostatistics). This is similar to the managerial role of coordination.
2. *Intraorganizational spanning.* A research and development laboratory must be linked carefully with the systems that will use the research (such as marketing and production). This ensures that the research will establish and maintain a direction consistent with the organization's overall goals.[21]

3. *Extraorganizational spanning.* This level of linkage involves the boundary spanning we have been examining throughout the chapter. It stresses the importance of communicating with organizations outside the innovating firm. Such a linkage requires interaction with potential funding agencies, research laboratories, and university departments and resources.[22]

Innovation requires linkages at all these levels to ensure that the organization's individual units are coordinated among themselves as well as with higher-level departments. In addition, the entire organization must be in tune with environmental forces so that the opportunities for innovation are known and can be pursued efficiently.

Some organizations are more effective at innovation than others. An organization that is staffed with highly trained specialists is more likely to remain attuned to the environment because the specialists have many outside contacts. For example, researchers at American Telephone and Telegraph's Bell Laboratories are well aware of and in close contact with researchers throughout the world who are working on similar problems. Boundary spanning is critical when innovation is the goal.

Proposition 13.5

> Innovative behavior in organizations requires that boundaries be spanned to ensure the proper flow of relevant information from and to selected groups outside the organization.

What Managers Need to Know About Boundary Spanning

Historically, management and organizational behavior have concentrated on the efficient administration of activities within the organization. Individuals had to be motivated and groups had to be coordinated.

The organizational world today is more complex than ever before and the linkages among organizations are more critical to the survival of a single organization. Organizations in high technology industries must be linked to universities and research institutes to ensure that the latest knowledge is available. Public utilities, hospitals, and business firms must interact constantly with government regulatory agencies to ensure that their actions adhere to the latest rules and regulations.

Organizations are not automatically linked to the important environmental forces and external groups that will influence their performance and ultimate survival. Only conscious and continuous action by management will accomplish this task. This is where boundary spanning is important.

Because this interaction between the organization and external factors is receiving increased attention, future managers will likely be expected to understand more about it. We know, for example, that boundary-spanning activities increase with the perceived environmental uncertainty. But what factors and forces are really important in determining environmental uncertainty? This expectation requires that managers become increasingly sensitive to external realities such as the social and political climate, technology, and so on.

Moreover, as managers begin to actively span the boundaries of their own organization, they will be confronted with situations in which leadership rather than legitimate authority must be used to get goals accomplished. New and better skills of negotiation and diplomacy will be required. We might get away with being autocratic to an employee but not to a competitor, government regulator, or supplier.

Summary

This chapter has looked at interorganizational relations. The time and energy we have devoted to this subject points to the growing importance of outside forces in managerial decision making. We can safely say that today's managers must do more than simply "run a tight ship" to function successfully. The external environment has grown far too complex for such an approach.

Whether a manager is assigned specifically to a boundary-spanning role or merely is expected to develop outside relations from a traditional position in the organization, managerial success has come to depend on some expertise in boundary spanning. For some managers, this requires a change in behavior. Devoted managers who have pushed uncompromisingly toward organizational goals now must develop a sensitivity to the values of outside parties. Rigid managers must become more flexible and develop the skills of diplomacy and negotiation.[23]

The skills and personality characteristics of boundary-spanning managers are essential because these individuals have great influence on innovations. We have seen that the speed and efficiency with which new ideas and concepts are developed and adopted greatly affect an organization's survival. This is particularly true of technologically based and highly competitive industries.

Questions for Discussion

1. Why do you think the boundaries of an organization are important considerations for management?
2. Give a real-world example of a loosely coupled system and tightly coupled one. On what basis did you decide that the systems are loose or tight?
3. Explain the difference between the power-dependency view and the exchange view of interorganizational relations. Why does one tend to encourage conflict and the other cooperation?
4. Explain the difference between a mediating and a long-linked technology. Which technology is likely to have a larger proportion of boundary spanners and why?
5. Are boundary spanners more likely than other managers to experience role ambiguity and role conflict? Why or why not? Do boundary spanners experience less job satisfaction?

Exercise: Recognizing Organizational Roles

Assume that you are the director of personnel for a newly formed corporation, Checker Products. The president of the corporation has made you responsible for selecting key executives to fill the organization's immediate managerial needs. Following are the president's ideas about the positions and their responsibilities. You are to recommend which type of person can best fill each position and give reasons for your recommendations.

1. *Operations manager:* responsible for production and inventory control; involves supervision of production functions and ensuring the constant flow of operations
   Your Recommendation and Justification:

2. *Coordinator of environmental affairs:* responsible for working with community leaders and customers with regard to product quality and environment effects
   Your Recommendation and Justification:

3. *Director of safety:* responsible for coordinating corporate safety program; involves developing expertise in current trends relating to safety legislation
   Your Recommendation and Justification:

Case: A Managerial Debate

The annual awards banquet of Middle Eastern Steel Corporation has just ended. The food was good, and the speaker was unusually stimulating. Now the time has come for an informal discussion. It has become customary for employees to sit around after the banquet and socialize.

At the head table, Bill Mayer and Joan Gerber are especially talkative. They should be happy, for they have been named "Outstanding Managers of the Year." Besides being a great honor, this award brought each of them a bonus of $1,500.

As they sat around the table, they discussed the question: What makes a good manager? Joan, who is director of purchasing, responded by saying that a good manager should be understanding, flexible, and diplomatic in dealing with employees, customers, and representatives from other organizations. She pointed out that over the past year she had dealt with many sales representatives and that some long-time suppliers had experienced trouble in providing the materials needed for normal production levels. However, by working closely with the sales representatives, Gerber had kept Middle Eastern Steel well supplied. She also had maintained the good long-term relationships that had been developed.

Mayer, the manager of operations, did not like Joan's response at all. He quickly retorted that such a "soft" approach was one reason why the cost of materials was increasing. As Bill saw it, when suppliers have trouble supplying, "We ought to stick it to them and get all the price concessions we can. Don't worry about next year, when the situation may be different. Suppliers will always try to satisfy large purchasers like Middle Eastern!" Mayer's approach, then, was to look after the company's current interests first and always. He told Gerber to bargain hard with labor, to buy from the least costly supplier, to forget about forming lasting relationships with other companies, and to get on with the task of making good steel and big profits.

Steve Weng, a newly promoted middle manager, was amazed at this discussion. He had great respect for both Gerber and Mayer. After all, they had just been declared outstanding managers. How could they hold such different views about management?

1. How would you compare the requirements for Gerber's and Mayer's jobs?
2. How can these two managers' positions be reconciled? Can they be reconciled?
3. What would you say to Steve Weng about management and the roles filled by Gerber and Mayer?

Suggested Readings

Adams, J. S. "The Structure and Dynamics of Behavior in Organizational Boundary Roles." In *Handbook of Organizational and Industrial Psychology*. Ed. M. D. Dunnette. Chicago: Rand McNally, 1976, pp. 1175–1199.

Allen, T. J. *Managing the Flow of Technology*. Cambridge, Mass.: MIT Press, 1977.

Cummings, T. G., and M. L. Markus. "A Socio-Technical Systems View of Organizations." In *Behavioral Problems in Organizations*. Ed. C. L. Cooper. Englewood Cliffs, N.J.: Prentice-Hall, 1979, pp. 59–77.

Edstrom, Anders, and Jay Galbraith. "Management Transfer as a Coordination and Control Strategy." *Administrative Science Quarterly* 22 (1977): 248–263.

Katz, Ralph, and Michael Tushman. "Communication Patterns, Project Performance and Task Characteristics: An Empirical Evaluation and Integration in an R & D Setting." *Organizational Behavior and Human Performance* 2 (1979): 139–162.

Keen, P. G. W., and M. S. S. Morton. *Decision Support Systems.* Reading, Mass.: Addison-Wesley, 1978.

Perry, J. L., and H. L. Angle. "The Politics of Organizational Boundary Roles in Collective Bargaining," *Academy of Management Review* 4 (1979): 487–496.

Pfeffer, Jeffrey, and Gerald Salancik. *The External Control of Organizations.* New York: Harper & Row, 1978.

Scott, W. G., and D. K. Hart. *Organizational America.* Boston: Houghton Mifflin, 1979.

Tung, R. L. "Dimensions of Organizational Environments: An Exploratory Study of Their Impact on Organization Structure." *Academy of Management Journal* 22 (1979): 672–693.

Performance Evaluation and Organizational Effectiveness

> It is important to note that while efficiency and effectiveness tend to go hand in hand, they do not always. An efficient company might make no profits . . . and an inefficient one may return a high profit. . . . Moreover, overconcern with efficiency may limit the scope of activities of an organization, while effectiveness might require a large number of activities.
>
> Amitai Etzioni,
> *Modern Organizations*

The Air Defense Command of the United States Air Force is not recognized as an efficient operation. It has to keep aircraft and air crews ready to go twenty-four hours a day, seven days a week. This standby readiness is maintained despite the fact that year after year no foreign force has invaded U.S. air space. Indeed, supporters of the Air Defense Command see the absence of an invasion as evidence of the organization's effectiveness.

The Metropolitan Police Department, like the Air Defense Command, must be ready for action at all times. Compared with a typical business firm, the department is inefficient. After all, it costs a lot of money to maintain twenty-four–hour coverage of a metropolitan area. Unfortunately, the Metropolitan Police Department is not doing an outstanding job—even with all the resources at its disposal. The latest crime statistics from the Federal Bureau of Investigation show that violent crimes are up 12 percent in the metropolitan area, compared with only 7 percent for the nation.

Neither the Air Defense Command nor the Metropolitan Police Department is operating for profit. Yet the former organization seems to be doing an impressive job, whereas the latter appears to be doing a poor job. In considering these two examples, we can see how difficult it is to define and measure organizational effectiveness.

We are ready now to examine the outputs, or results, of organizational behavior. In previous chapters, we have looked at the inputs and at the processes within an organizational system. We will begin by analyzing essential aspects of control before moving to performance evaluation. Then we will introduce and examine organizational effectiveness.

Organizations accomplish their goals when individuals perform their tasks and managers coordinate activities at acceptable levels. Of course this is a simple view, since other factors are also important. However, the relationship between individual performance and organizational effectiveness seems promising enough to pursue. Therefore, we will begin by examining performance evaluation from a behavioral perspective.

Some Basics of Organizational Control

Feedback control is a multistage process of monitoring the outcomes of activities, reviewing results of performed tasks, and taking the required corrective action.[1] Accurate though this definition may be, it omits the important idea of *preventive control*, which seeks to keep deviations from the standard from developing. Both concepts of control are illustrated in Figure 14.1.

As shown in Figure 14.1a, control can be reactive; when variances develop, corrective action is initiated. In Figure 14-1b, however, the corrective action occurs *before* the activity is initiated. For example, much of the effort devoted to recruiting highly qualified applicants for a job is an attempt to avoid or reduce future problems. Thus such efforts are preventive control measures.

Consider the statistical quality control found in many manufacturing operations. In such a system, a sample of manufactured goods is collected and inspected closely. When a certain percentage of the

Figure 14.1 Control Processes

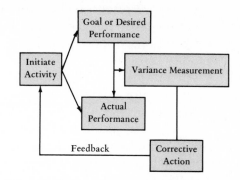

(a) FEEDBACK CONTROL (RELIES PRIMARILY ON
CORRECTING DEVIATIONS ONCE THEY DEVELOP)

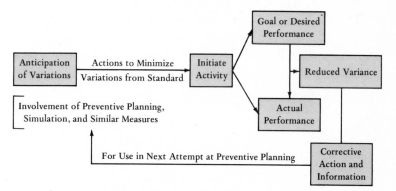

(b) PREVENTIVE CONTROL (RELIES ON PREVENTIVE
PLANNING TO MINIMIZE VARIANCE

sample is found to have defects, manufacturing operations are sus-
pended until the cause of the defects is corrected. This control is
reactive. The corrective action is taken after the deviation or abnor-
mality is discovered.

Another type of control takes place when we visit our dentist's
office twice a year—even though we perceive no problems. During
these visits our teeth are cleaned and examined to avoid problems.
This control is preventive. Corrective action is taken before problems arise.

The recent emphasis on simulating organizational processes illustrates a type of preventive control. Simulation methods aim to create

a simplified model of a real-world process. Decision makers then can manipulate critical variables in an effort to see what effects will occur even before resources are committed. The advantage is that some trial and error can take place before a single course of action is selected. Many options can be evaluated without risking the organization's resources.

Aircraft pilots, for example, are trained with simulation methods. The simulator is like an airplane in every way except that it never leaves the ground. Thus no lives or expensive aircraft are risked. The instructor can manipulate such things as weather conditions, wind speed, altitude, and fuel supply. Simulators also are used in *assessment centers* in organizational settings. Prospective managers can be trained by using fake telephones, closed-circuit television, and other equipment. In this way, the managers can be confronted with various situations that might occur, and the television tape can be used to review their performance. Simulation is often a useful way to train managers before they have to deal with risky, real-life situations.

Regardless of whether control is reactive or preventive, it must have several characteristics. First, controls must be understandable to the people who are contributing to goal accomplishment. Controls must register deviations quickly, and they must be flexible enough to respond to changing conditions. Finally, they must be economical: controls must save more than they cost to initiate and implement.[2]

With this background, we can look in greater detail at performance evaluation. In doing so, we will focus particularly on its behavioral aspects.

A Closer Look at Performance Evaluation

Performance evaluation is the climax of the managerial process. Its purpose is to evaluate the success of organizational behavior.

Some Behavioral Assumptions

Management literature suggests that performance appraisal is a threatening experience, both for the person doing the evaluating and for the person being evaluated. In other words, evaluators dislike evaluating others and are negatively inclined toward the task. Persons evaluated, on the other hand, are said to dislike being evaluated and to find the encounter threatening.

A study of two organizations—a small research organization and a farm supply company—was developed to examine these assumptions.[3] The conclusions indicated several things. First, it was observed that evaluators disliked the task only when they had to give negative evaluations. The appraisal was considered to be especially difficult when the person evaluated was extremely well liked or disliked by the evaluator. In general, however, the data did not support the assumption that managers inherently dislike the task of evaluating subordinates. Nor did the persons evaluated seem to object to the process itself, as long as the evaluators were perceived to be qualified for the task. Evaluations were considered distasteful only when they resulted in negative appraisals. In fact, many respondents preferred more frequent evaluations.

This study suggests that the samples analyzed did not dislike performance appraisals. Obviously, negative evaluations are more objectionable to both parties than positive ones. The effectiveness of the appraisal, however, is a different matter. It depends on a variety of factors that we will examine briefly.

Proposition 14.1

> The assumption is made that performance evaluation is threatening to the evaluator and evaluatee. Research suggests that this assumption is only partly accurate. Performance evaluation is feared only when it is negative and when it is done by individuals who are perceived to be unqualified.

The Criteria Issue: Setting Goals

Performance appraisal assumes that there is a standard against which actual behavior can be measured. Certainly, if an individual is to be motivated, some end or target must exist. Certain techniques, like management by objectives, place considerable emphasis on goal setting. Research supports the importance of establishing and communicating explicit criteria for performance evaluation.

Studies have revealed several things about goal setting. First, the existence of specific performance criteria results in higher motivational levels.[4] Important as criteria may be, however, they must be realistic. Impossible goals accomplish little. In fact, constant failure to achieve unrealistic goals can actually result in decreased performance.[5]

It is also important that performance criteria be relevant to the organizational values considered significant in a given setting. The criteria are not so important as the fact that organizational members know which things are valued by the organization.[6] These are the ends toward which performance must be motivated. This conclusion reinforces the idea that goal formation is an essential task of management.

Proposition 14.2

> Effective performance evaluation assumes the existence of relevant criteria or goals. These criteria must be clearly communicated to and understood by evaluatees if the appraisal system is to have a positive motivational impact.

Implementing and Using the System

Research shows that an effective appraisal system should allow for meaningful participation by members of the organization. It also should provide frequent feedback to the individuals who are being evaluated.

Participation generally results in two benefits. The first is that performance increases; the second is greater acceptance of performance criteria.

Using participation as the experimental variable, one study demonstrated that groups that were allowed to provide input in goal setting outperformed control groups in which participation was not allowed.[7] Participation also has been associated with higher levels of job satisfaction, although no causal relationship has been established between satisfaction and performance.

Behavioral scientists have also recognized the importance of participative techniques in gaining employee acceptance of new ideas.

The logic of this approach is straightforward. When individuals are allowed to participate in forming the guidelines for evaluation, they feel part of the system and are less resistant to proposed changes. There is also evidence that participation leads to higher-quality decisions.[8] This probably happens because the input gained through participation is more diverse.

Many of the management-by-objectives programs at companies like Black and Decker and Purex established participation as a basic part of the management system. Employees are allowed to assist in establishing the goals against which they eventually will be evaluated. It is believed that this opportunity to participate builds commitment to the goals and reduces resistance to improving performance.

Proposition 14.3

> The design and implementation of an effective performance appraisal system usually relies on a provision for participative inputs. Participation generally contributes to the motivation of employees, to a reduction in their resistance to change, and to an improvement in the quality of decisions used to formulate the standards of the appraisal system.

Some Specific Issues

In this section, we will look at three technical problems commonly encountered in appraisal: How accurate is the evaluation? What types of appraisals should be used? Who should complete the evaluation?

Validity of the Appraisal Instrument

Performance appraisal relies on the validity of the evaluation instrument. Although there are various types of validity, we are concerned primarily with *construct validity*. That is, we are interested in the constructs, or factors, accounting for individual variations in scores.[9] The important question is whether the appraisal instrument mea-

Figure 14.2 Various Degrees of Construct Validity

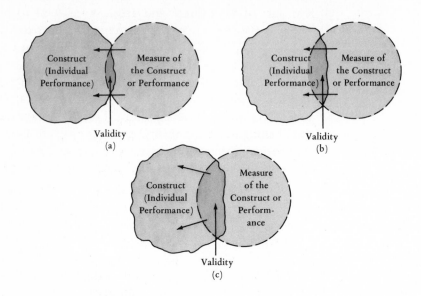

sures job performance or some other related construct(s) such as intelligence, achievement, and so on. For example, most appraisal forms ask questions that are closely associated with job performance. Sometimes a manager is asked to make a judgment about whether or not an employee is in good health. This may or may not relate to performance. Some employees work quite well even when they are ill. Moreover, few managers are qualified to make medical judgments except in extreme and obvious cases. Therefore, a question like this has little construct validity when measuring job performance.

Every manager has an idea of what constitutes high-performing individuals. How well the evaluation instrument measures the construct (performance) relates to validity. Figure 14.2 illustrates the point. The extent to which the measure perfectly overlaps the construct creates the validity of the measure.

Three conceptual situations are illustrated. For example, the measure shown in Figure 14.2a has little construct validity. Only a small portion of the actual performance is being measured. Instead, the measure includes many aspects of reality that have nothing to do with individual performance (as illustrated by the area of the circle not overlapping the construct). At the same time, it is not measuring a great deal of what is relevant to performance (indicated by the area of the construct not covered by the circle). In Figures 14.2b and 14.2c, higher levels of construct validity are attained, and the measurement errors are reduced.

Obviously, perfect construct validity is rarely, if ever, achieved. Errors may be caused by a variety of factors. Questions on an appraisal form may concern only part of an individual's performance. They may, for example, measure the quantity of output but not the individual's receptivity to change. Or the measure may be contaminated, because it includes such things as a halo effect or stereotyping on the part of the supervisor. For example, a manager who is prejudiced against women might stereotype a particular employee as irresponsible simply because she is a female. (Similar stereotypes exist for, say, Mexican-Americans, Baptists, and other groups.) Stereotyping takes place because all members of a particular sex, ethnic group, or religious denomination are assumed to be like one or more members of the class who have previously displayed a particular characteristic. Or, a halo effect can occur when a professor evaluates a student's essay examination as good because the student did well in another course. Both stereotyping and halo effects can distort the results of an evaluation.

Fortunately, there is much research concerning the factors that can contaminate measurements. Some factors relate to supervisory failures, such as a supervisor's inability to conduct a performance appraisal. In some cases, studies illustrate that the validity of performance ratings is associated closely with such factors as the supervisor's aptitude and achievement orientation.[10] Another study illustrates that more effective supervisors are more discriminating in their ratings than less effective supervisors, who tend to level the ratings by ranking all employees about the same.[11]

Highly motivated managers and those with high achievement needs may evaluate employees higher if they are perceived to possess similar needs—even if the employees are not high performers. Also managers who are not high performers may lack the confidence needed to rate employees as either high or low. When everyone gets an average rating, we can expect, over time, the performance will settle around average.

Finally, research suggests that the harshness with which the appraisal task is approached is influenced by certain characteristics of the supervisors. Tough raters are often young, inexperienced, skeptical toward others, and lacking in self-confidence. Lenient raters are often older, more experienced, and more self-confident, although they frequently lack ambition.[12]

Appraisal Methods

Ranking Techniques   Perhaps the most frequently used *appraisal method* is some type of ranking technique. Managers often are asked to rank the best (and worst) employees in relation to some broad dimension, such as job effectiveness. These techniques are easy to use, but they are usually unrealistic, since performance involves many factors.[13] One can restrict the number of factors included in each question, but it would be impossible to include all relevant aspects of performance.

To illustrate, consider the technique known as alternative ranking. A supervisor is given a list of employees arranged in alphabetical order and is asked to identify the best employee and the worst. These two names then are removed from the list and are recorded on another form. In this way, the manager can make selections from a successively smaller list, until all names are removed and all employees are ranked. Of course, this technique may be limited when intergroup rankings are being developed, since a superior performer in one group may be only average in another.[14]

Some of the limitations of ranking can be reduced through the use of forced distributions. In this case, supervisors are forced to consider several factors of performance and must place a specified number of employees in predetermined categories. For example, to assist in assigning term grades, a professor may require students to rank the value of classmates' participation. In a class of thirty, to avoid having everyone rank everyone else high, the guidelines may be formulated as follows. Participants are asked to place the five classmates who performed best in the top 10 percent category, the next five in the next 20 percent category, the next ten in the middle 40 percent, and the last ten in the lowest 30 percent category. Conceptually, the results appear as shown in Table 14.1.

Weighted Checklists   At times an organization may develop a weighted checklist for use in evaluating employees. First, a series of statements are developed that pertain to items representing aspects

Table 14.1 Forced Distribution Ratings

Percentage Category	Number of Class Members
Top 10%	5
Second 20%	5
Middle 40%	10
Lowest 30%	10
Total Class Members	30

of employee performance. Qualified judges then rate statements such as "He or she delegates authority to others" or "He or she is kind to customers" according to their importance. Each statement then is weighted in relation to the average scores obtained by group judgments.

The resulting form is a checklist with the statements displayed. Managers then check the appropriate statements that apply to each person evaluated. The values are computed, and relative ranking scores are developed. This technique allows an efficient breakdown of factors relating to job performance. It also overcomes many of the problems associated with broad criteria.

To illustrate the weighted checklist technique, consider the following example. The management faculty at City College has been searching for a way to obtain peer ratings for all members of the department. The department chairperson asked each faculty member to submit a list of "behaviors" describing the work of department members. The behaviors could be either favorable or unfavorable acts on the part of a faculty member. When all responses were gathered, a panel of ten experienced faculty members was asked to rank each statement on a scale from 1 to 7, depending on how each person perceived the favorableness or unfavorableness of the behavior. Statements that revealed a lack of agreement among faculty members were eliminated. In other words, if a particular behavior—such as "always attends class"—caused the ten panel members to give rankings of 7, 4, 3, 6, 1, 2, 4, 5, 3, 2, it was eliminated. Only behaviors for which there was substantial agreement were retained. For example, the first behavior listed in Figure

Figure 14.3

PEER EVALUATION FORM FOR MANAGEMENT DEPARTMENT

INSTRUCTIONS: Listed below are ten statements to be used in evaluating the performance of Professor _____. Read these statements and place an x in the corresponding space where you have observed the behavior on the part of the person being evaluated. If you have not observed the behavior, simply leave the space blank.

(6.0) 1. When discussing his/her subject of expertise the individual can communicate effectively with less informed colleagues and students. _____

(1.6) 2. Refuses to provide clearly stated criteria for evaluating class performance. _____

(5.5) 3. Demonstrates mastery of research literature and methods in area of expertise. _____

(2.5) 4. Fails to be available to colleagues and students. _____

(5.3) 5. Assists in "housekeeping" functions of department such as registration, committee assignments, etc. _____

(5.7) 6. Is actively involved in community service and available to local business firms. _____

(2.1) 7. Displays little interest in professional development as evidenced by participation in professional organizations. _____

(1.3) 8. Demonstrates little understanding of national trends and issues in management education. _____

(5.5) 9. Remains active in research as evidenced by publications in relevant scholarly literature. _____

(6.2)10. Shows interest in self-improvement. _____

14.3 was ranked 7, 6, 6, 5, 6, 6, 7, 6, 5, 6. This statement was retained, and it was given a value by adding all the rankings and dividing by 10 (the number on the panel). This gives the item a weight of 6.0.

The ten behaviors that survived the process are shown in Figure 14.3. In real situations, the weights are not shown of course; we have provided them in parentheses before each statement for illustrative purposes. To use this table in evaluating performance, all department members would rate their colleagues according to the ten behaviors. The weights of each statement marked for each person would be added, and the resulting scores would be compared to obtain relative rankings for each faculty member.

Although this technique is more complex than those discussed previously, it can be adapted to fit an organization's needs. For example, managers are asked to describe situations in which employees have been extremely good or extremely poor performers. The situations are then reduced under a relatively few general categories. Judges then assign values to the categories, and weighted rankings are developed.[15]

BARS One relatively new appraisal procedure that is receiving attention in the literature is known as *behaviorally anchored rating scales* (BARS).[16] Generally speaking, BARS are developed through five stages. These stages are:

1. *Identification of performance dimensions.* Usually, people who are experienced in the job to be evaluated are asked to identify several aspects or dimensions of the job that relate to performance. A group of research scientists, for example, may participate in defining what aspects of the job show high performance among research scientists.
2. *Determination of critical incidents.* The participants are asked to give specific incidents that illustrate high or low levels of performance.
3. *Repetitive classification.* To add consistency, another group of experienced participants is given the dimensions and incidents previously identified and is asked to place the incidents under the proper dimension as they evaluate it. Those incidents that "retranslate" (when the second group consistently places them under the same dimensions) are retained.
4. *Developing scales.* The second group is asked to rank the incidents according to how well they describe effective and ineffective behavior. Average ratings then are assigned to the incidents.
5. *Instrument construction.* The incidents with the highest rater agreement are used to anchor the instrument in relation to the various performance dimensions.[17]

BARS possess certain practical advantages. The participative element on which the concept is based ensures that job performance is defined by people who are knowledgeable about the job to be evaluated. It also makes the performance criteria less ambiguous.[18]

The superiority of BARS with regard to such factors as rater leniency and reliability has not been completely established.[19] However, the participative element and the relevancy of the dimensions generated are sufficient reasons to be encouraged about the potential of behaviorally anchored rating scales.

Conclusions and Evaluation This brief survey of appraisal and evaluation methods is by no means exhaustive. Our purpose was simply to represent the more familiar techniques and to show how they might be used. Issues relating to performance appraisal and evaluation are complex. The development and use of any appraisal instrument is a time-consuming and demanding undertaking. However, to use instruments that have little or questionable construct validity is seldom worthwhile—and almost always unjust. If job performance is evaluated by instruments that do not measure it with high degrees of accuracy, a serious administrative (and perhaps legal) risk is taken.

In a practical sense, the value of a particular appraisal method relates to how well it identifies desired behavior and provides feedback to the people being evaluated.[20] Such information is necessary, if performance is to be improved. This leads to the following proposition.

Proposition 14.4

> Performance evaluation techniques take a variety of forms. Critical questions relate to the content validity of the instrument, to how specifically the instrument identifies desired behavior, and to the quality of feedback concerning the relative importance of various categories in contributing to successful organizational behavior.

Who Should Evaluate?

The issue of performance evaluation and appraisal always raises questions about who should do the evaluating. This question underlies the current debate about evaluating teaching performance in higher education. For example, some people argue that administrators (supervisors) should evaluate; some say colleagues or peers should conduct the appraisals; others say appraisals should be accomplished by each teacher through self-reflection, by students, or by objective outside experts.

The most frequent form of evaluation is a supervisory review, in which an employee's supervisor completes the appraisal. The logic behind this approach is that the supervisor has legitimate authority to determine rewards. Also because the supervisor is close to the job being done and to the person doing it, it is assumed that the supervisor can present accurate rankings.

Closeness can also present problems, however. A supervisor may be viewed as a personal friend or enemy, and the appraisal may be questioned on that basis. This can put stress on the supervisor-subordinate relationship, particularly when the manager has worked up through the ranks and now holds the position of judge.

There seems to be a growing tendency to develop appraisal systems based on peer reviews. The logic of this approach is that individuals who do the same job are in a unique position to evaluate each other's work. This appears to have particular merit when supervisors may not be close to the work being done—for example, in a group of certified public accountants.

Although peer evaluation may reduce superior-subordinate stress, it also may lead to peer conflict. When employees who are in competition for the same promotion rate each other, the objectivity of the evaluations can justifiably be questioned.

Self-evaluation can be valuable for everyone. Few people have the opportunity to reflect on their own performances in a systematic manner. Unfortunately, it is extremely difficult to be objective about oneself. We all feel that the things we do are important. However, self-evaluation can be useful when the primary goal is to let a person know—without threat of loss of reward—how he or she perceives personal performance levels.

Another approach to evaluation is subordinate review; that is, employees appraise supervisors. Frame 14.1 presents an example. In general, subordinate evaluations create an atmosphere of power equality and participation. However, it is sometimes difficult for employees to understand all aspects of the supervisor's position. As a result, supervisors may be criticized for factors beyond their control.

Some documented research raises rather specific questions about subordinate reviews. Studies have shown, for example, that a person's formal position can influence ratings. In other words, there may be a tendency to give high performance ratings to individuals who hold high organizational ranks.[21] A vice president may receive a higher rating than a first-line supervisor—not because the former is a better worker, but because he or she is a vice president.

Frame 14.1

Turning the Table

Most discussions of performance appraisal revolve around the issue of managers evaluating subordinates. However, isn't it logical to suggest that if the best appraisals are learning experiences, then supervisors could benefit from knowing how employees rate their performances?

A study of nonacademic supervisors in a large university was designed to answer this question. The supervisors were responsible for areas such as laundry services, purchasing, accounting, and maintenance of the physical plant. Employees were semi-skilled, skilled, and clerical workers.

The results of the survey indicated that the supervisors thought they received positive benefits from the feedback received from employees. The results were particularly helpful in assisting supervisors to identify weaknesses and establish priorities for improvement.

After receiving the evaluations, supervisors were especially pleased with their ability to provide more information to subordinates and to assist in building employee confidence. Their tendency to consult with subordinates on relevant decisions also increased. The information received from the appraisals was less successful in influencing changes in long-standing supervisory styles.

Most of the managers involved in the survey believed that the feedback from employees helped them to become better supervisors. And, perhaps more important, almost all the supervisors said they would like more feedback in the future.

Adapted with permission of the publisher from W. H. Hegarly, "Supervisors' Reaction to Subordinates' Appraisals," *Personnel,* November–December 1973, pp. 31–35. ©1973 by AMACOM, a division of American Management Association.

Finally, an outsider may be asked to evaluate an individual's performance. This is especially true when factors such as a person's professional reputation are important aspects of performance. A research scientist, for example, may be considered a more valuable employee if he or she is known by other research scientists. As a result, outsiders who can be objective, at least theoretically, are asked to judge. The danger, of course, is that outsiders rarely have firsthand knowledge about the conditions under which the person being evaluated actually lives and works.

Ideally, evaluations involve a variety of inputs from different parties. Table 14.2 makes it clear that all types of evaluations provide important information that can be used in performance appraisal. At the same time, each type has its unique limitations. Thus performance appraisal involves a complex compromise of practical and theoretical considerations.

Table 14.2 Who Should Evaluate?

Evaluators	Advantages	Disadvantages	Appropriate Situations
Supervisor	Supervisor is the legitimate authority symbol who controls distribution of rewards.	Supervisors may not be qualified in evaluation techniques. Places stress on superior-subordinate relations.	When superiors influence the reward distribution.
Peers	Reduces stress in superior-subordinate relations. Reduces the social distance separating managers and employees. Useful when supervisors are not close to work being done.	May create an excessively competitive environment. May contribute to interpersonal conflict.	When rewards are not competitively determined and peer appraisals can be objectively considered.

Table 14.2 (cont.)

Evaluators	Advantages	Disadvantages	Appropriate Situations
Self	Eliminates defensive relationship between superiors and subordinates. May increase satisfaction.	Objectivity questionable. Probably results in a clear bias toward favorability.	When goal is to stimulate self-development and growth.
Subordinates	Creates atmosphere of power equalization. Useful as additional source of input with other appraisal forms.	May increase threats associated with managerial positions. Supervisors may be adversely evaluated for uncontrollable factors.	When additional input is needed to balance the overall appraisal system.
Outsiders	Usually contributes to objectivity. Also useful when specialized expertise is required.	Outsiders may not perceive the reality of intraorganizational conditions.	In highly professionalized environments.

Adapted from *Performance in Organizations* by L. L. Cummings and D. P. Schwab, chap. 8. Copyright © 1973 by Scott, Foresman and Company. Reprinted by permission.

Assessment Centers

Assessment centers have become increasingly popular as a method of identifying future leaders in organizations. They are relevant to performance appraisal because they are used to evaluate behavior under simulated conditions in an effort to predict leadership potential. A number of leading companies—including American Telephone and Telegraph, International Business Machines, General Electric, and Sears Roebuck—have used some variation of this technique.

Figure 14.4 Overview of AT&T Program Sequence

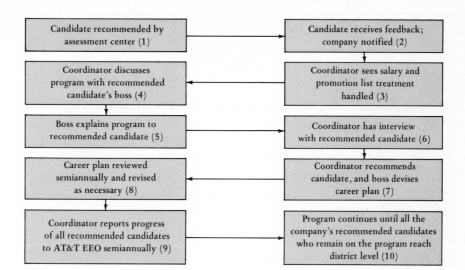

Source: Excerpted from "How Good Are Assessment Centers?" *Administrative Management* 36 (October 1975): 52, copyright © 1975 by Geyer-McAllister Publications, Inc., New York.

Essentially, in using the assessment center, an organization selects a group of participants who have shown some potential to participate in an assessment exercise.[22] Evaluators or assessors are also selected, usually from among established executives as well as outside consulting psychologists.

Participants spend from one to five days at the centers, during which time they are placed in simulated decision-making situations and their behavior is evaluated. The assumption is that one's performance in the exercise(s) is an accurate predictor of managerial potential.[23] Participants usually are given feedback, although the exact procedure may vary from organization to organization.

Evaluations of assessment centers show that they are most effective in predicting job potential, job progress, and job performance —in that order.[24] Obviously, the validity of this concept is not conclusive. Some people have proposed that assessment centers are far superior to traditional interviewing methods in determining executive promotions.[25] Whether or not this can be proved, assessment centers have been used to identify unusually promising candidates for promotion and rapid advancement. American Telephone and Telegraph uses a "fast-track career sequence" that is illustrated in Figure 14.4. After candidates are identified by means of an assessment center, they are put on a rapidly progressing career path.

Proposition 14.5

> Performance evaluation is an important topic in the applied behavioral sciences. As evidenced by the assessment center, practical interest has now expanded beyond performance review and appraisal to other areas of organizational life, such as the use of performance measures in evaluating managerial potential.

Examining Organizational Effectiveness

The objective of systematic performance appraisal is to ensure organizational effectiveness. In its broadest sense, this occurs when the organization's goals are accomplished. A precise understanding of organizational effectiveness, therefore, is necessary if we are to establish valid criteria for performance evaluation.

Evaluation of Effectiveness Models

Historically, the definition and measurement of organizational effectiveness has evolved from a relatively simple to an increasingly complex view. Traditional views of effectiveness typically selected some broad, overall performance measure and equate it with organizational effectiveness. The measure might be profits, or employee satisfaction, or something else, depending on the background and intention of the writer. As we noted previously, early bureaucratic theory equated effectiveness with efficiency.

More recently, attention has been given to developing multiple criteria for assessing organizational effectiveness. Structure is important to efficiency, but freedom of action also must be provided so that employees can respond to changing conditions within or outside the organization. One review of numerous studies conducted between 1957 and 1975 found that all used more than one criterion (such as profits, survival, flexibility, and so on) to evaluate organizational effectiveness. The most frequently used criteria were adaptability-flexibility, productivity, and satisfaction.[26] Thus we gain a new view of the organization. This concept depicts the group as striving for internal efficiency, while at the same time keeping its attention on developing environmental changes. Any definition of organizational effectiveness must consider its dual nature. In addition, efficiency and change must be related to the interpersonal dynamic of the system.

By looking at organizations from a more systems-oriented perspective, we are able to develop a comprehensive view of organizational effectiveness. Etzioni has noted the problems involved in simply equating effectiveness with the accomplishment of goals.[27] In reality, organizations are seldom able to proceed directly to their stated goals because the real world necessitates detours and diversions. Moreover, goals are reformulated constantly, so that the specific accomplishment of a particular goal is a rare occurrence.

A more defensible approach is offered by researchers who construct a measurement of effectiveness by using several elements in the successful organizational system. One study uses three basic elements: productivity (or efficiency in an economic sense), intraorganizational stress (evidenced by observed levels of tension and conflict), and flexibility (or the ability to adjust to external and internal change).[28]

In a similar vein, Steers has developed a process model of organizational effectiveness that includes three dimensions.[29] The first is known as *goal optimization,* whereby each of the several goals of an organization receive sufficient attention and resources. The second involves an open-systems perspective, which acknowledges the importance of interaction between the organization and the environment. Finally, there is the behavioral emphasis, which stresses the importance of human behavior in achieving organizational performance.

A comparison of recent trends reveals general agreement on the following points:

1. To define organizational effectiveness simply in terms of goal accomplishment is far too simplistic. Most organizations have diverse and competing objectives. The problem is how to best de-

velop the entire set of goals by applying an appropriate amount of attention and resources to each of them, rather than emphasizing any single objective.

2. No overall criterion of performance, such as profitability, can adequately describe an effective organization. An insistence on profit maximization in the short run, for example, may cause decision makers to overlook potential markets for the future, which may harm the organization's chances for survival. Or, an overemphasis on the future may neglect a reasonable level of current profits, also reducing the likelihood of survival.

3. Any meaningful measure of organizational effectiveness must include multiple criteria such as efficiency, adaptability, and the satisfaction of various behavioral factors. This concept is the general *multiple-factor model* of organizational effectiveness.

Together, these three factors (or similar ones) represent the formal task-oriented objectives of the organization, the interpersonal-humanistic social goals of the people who work in the organization, and the environmental changes that are taking place constantly and may influence the other elements because of their relationship to survival. No organization is really effective unless these elements are considered.

As an illustration, consider the following cases. Midwestern Research Center is a privately owned, scientific consulting and research organization. Over the years, the firm has established a tradition of high-quality services and has developed expertise in obtaining funds by attracting grants for research on contemporary issues. The personnel are highly trained professionals, are extremely happy with their jobs, and exhibit little evidence of conflict. The center, however, is experiencing tremendous financial problems because it has no expertise in managing current operations. Its accounting system is outdated, and internal control is nonexistent. As a result of the center's managerial inefficiency, the price of its services has risen significantly above competing prices. Employees are satisfied, and the organization is responsive to change. The problem confronting the center is its lack of operating efficiency.

The problem at Midwestern Research Center is different from the difficulty at Harris Drapery, Inc. This firm has been in business for half a century, but any year could be its last. Twenty years ago, the company entered into an agreement to manufacture a specialized drapery for a large producer of mobile homes. Since the order was large, and the plant's capacity was limited, almost all the company's resources were devoted to filling this large contract. The organization has continued to perfect its process and produces the draperies at a highly efficient level.

As the price of mobile homes has increased and the uncertainties of demand resulting from the energy shortage have developed, the mobile-home producer has attempted to cut costs by placing less expensive draperies in the standard equipment. Harris Drapery has resisted such efforts and is in serious danger of losing its only contract. Employees are satisfied, and the operations are efficient, but the organization is not adapting to inevitable changes in the competitive environment.

Finally, let us examine the case of the Lakeville City Police Department. The department is very efficient at law enforcement, has high employment standards, and uses the latest equipment. It is the only agency in city government that consistently operates within its budget.

The chief of police is impressed with modern management methods and uses them, along with available technological advances. If a technological change reduces the required manpower level, the chief simply terminates probationary employees and reassigns non-probationary employees as the situation demands. Because of this well-known mode of operation, it has become difficult to recruit new police officers, and the morale of career officers is very low. Efficiency and adaptability are present, but the social relations of the department are poor.

These three organizations clearly show the deficiency of the goal model of effectiveness. To appreciate the meaning of organizational efficiency, one must look at the condition of its three basic elements: productivity, flexibility, and intraorganizational stress.

A Descriptive Measure of Effectiveness

A satisfactory criterion of organizational effectiveness can be visualized in Figure 14.5. This illustration clearly presents the necessities of (1) organizing for efficient operation, (2) remaining flexible enough to adapt to change, and (3) maintaining an equilibrium in the social structure.

Neil Chamberlain has made a convincing case for the necessity of living in both the short and long runs.[30] In a given fiscal period,

Figure 14.5   Important Elements in Organizational Effectiveness

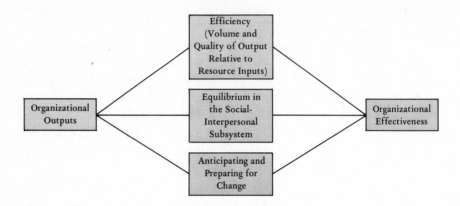

decision makers must use available resources in the most efficient manner possible. The goal is to develop an efficiency equilibrium in which organizational outputs are maximized in relation to inputs.

At the very time that managers are attempting to become maximally efficient, forces arise that require them to reallocate resources away from the short run to the long run. For example, some currently available resources may be directed into research and development. The result is less efficiency in the short run, with a hope of greater adaptability in the future. Effective organizations are willing to make such decisions and can do so without creating excessive tension and stress.

Proposition 14.6

Organizational effectiveness is more than efficiency. The effective firm is efficient; it is adaptive to change; and it maintains a satisfactory level of social equilibrium.

A Model of Organizational Effectiveness

The issue of organizational effectiveness forces us to examine all the factors influencing human behavior in organizations. Obviously, this

Figure 14.6 A Model of Organizational Effectiveness

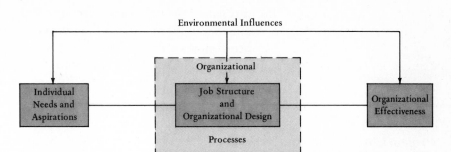

is a complex task. Therefore, for simplicity, we will look at the relationship among three primary variables: the individual, the organization, and the environment. Figure 14.6 provides a diagram of the model.

Individuals enter organizations with needs and hopes. Their needs, as we noted earlier, are a combination of lower-level desires (biological needs, security, and so on) and higher-level ones (social needs, self-esteem, autonomy, and self-actualization). Environmental factors may be instrumental in creating the intensity of the various needs. A person's hopes and expectations are equally important and are influenced by external factors. For example, one individual may have a tremendous need to excel because he or she comes from a family in which success is valued highly. That individual's expectations may be relatively high because the person has a history of success. Thus behavior that promises success is pursued enthusiastically.

The extent to which an individual can satisfy needs and pursue desires is related to the design of the job and the organizational processes involved. Supporters of job enrichment argue that need satisfaction and self-actualization are more likely to occur when individuals perform natural elements of work and maintain reasonable amounts of control over the task.[31]

The design of the job is part of the larger organizational structure. Excessively bureaucratic structures emphasize rationality and reliability. The means by which these elements are achieved include standardization and specialization. The quest for this type of order can lead to efficiency. At the same time, it can lead to the distortion of information, resistance to change, and organizational suboptimization.[32] This last condition occurs when one or more units within the organization become overconcerned with the performance of the units, without regard for overall goal accomplishment.

Finally, the environment also may influence organizational effectiveness. Contingency theory clearly illustrates that organizational structure must bear a relevant relationship to the environment if managerial behavior is to be successful.

Proposition 14.7

> Organizational effectiveness is influenced by a variety of interrelated factors. Goal accomplishment is determined, to a great extent, by the needs and desires of individuals and their relationships to job designs and organizational structure. In turn, individual needs and organizational structure are influenced by the environment.

What Managers Should Know About Performance Evaluation and Organizational Effectiveness

If we could sit in a room with experienced executives from business, government, education, and health care organizations and develop a list of important issues, we could bet performance appraisal and organizational effectiveness would be near the top. It is true that they may not use exactly the same terminology, but the idea would be there. Some might use words like *accountability* or *social responsiveness,* but in the end the questions are really what makes an organization effective and how do we know when effectiveness has been achieved?

Performance evaluation is important today because of the legal and moral concerns over equal opportunity employment and fairness in promotion. If managers are not aware of construct validity, they are not likely to recognize racial, sex, and age biases when they arise. It can be admitted that not all bias or prejudice is intentional; yet, the same results occur, regardless of intent. Therefore, a person in a managerial position needs to understand not only the mechanics but the theory of performance evaluation.

Relative to organizational effectiveness, the issues are equally confusing. We talk a great deal about successful management and effective organizations, but what does this really mean? Numerous tests can be applied, ranging from the financial success of a firm to the happiness of employees. In fact, effectiveness is related to both and more. Perhaps the issue of effectiveness—more than any other—underlines the complex responsibility faced by managers. Their real task is to acquire simultaneously the approval of owners, employees, customers, and numerous other parties.

Summary

This chapter has examined two of the most complex and controversial topics in organizational behavior: performance evaluation and organizational effectiveness. Both of these issues relate to the outputs of the organizational system.

In examining performance evaluation and appraisal, we illustrated how a properly conducted evaluation can both be preventive and provide feedback control. An evaluation can prevent problems from developing when it is motivational and inspires higher levels of performance. It provides feedback control when it effectively pinpoints deviations from the standard and assists in initiating corrective action.

For an evaluation to be effective, however, several conditions must exist. The evaluation instrument must have high construct validity; that is, it must accurately measure those aspects of performance that employees and the supervisor consider most important. An appropriate appraisal technique is also essential. Such techniques range in complexity from relatively simple forced distribution ratings to more systematic and time-consuming behaviorally anchored rating scales.

Finally, the manager responsible for the appraisal must decide who will evaluate. Various writers have stated the relative advantages and disadvantages of self-evaluations as well as appraisals by superiors, subordinates, peers, and knowledgeable outsiders. Ultimately, the manager must consider all the circumstances of a given situation and must decide who should provide input for the evaluation.

The second major topic of this chapter, organizational effectiveness, is extremely complex. What makes an organization effective?

Not all profitable firms or organizations with high levels of employee morale are effective. To define and measure effectiveness accurately, we must consider at least three factors: internal efficiency, responsiveness to external forces, and equilibrium within the social system. Such a measure is difficult to devise and use, but it is the best way to appraise organizational effectiveness.

Although we have viewed performance evaluation and organizational effectiveness from within an organizational system, we should not forget that both issues have social importance as well. Race, sex, and religious discrimination can be perpetuated through improperly designed and administered evaluations—intentionally or not. At the same time, a truly effective organization must respond to social aspects of the environment as well as to technological and legal factors.

Questions for Discussion

1. What does construct validity mean? Why is it an important consideration in the development of an instrument for appraising performance?
2. Why do you think the early bureaucratic writers equated organizational efficiency and effectiveness? Can you think of any case where an organization is efficient but not effective? Explain.
3. What are behaviorally anchored rating scales? Why are they particularly useful in evaluating performance?
4. What is the main difference between feedback control and preventive control? Give an example of each.
5. Explain why a useful model of organizational effectiveness must consider several criteria of performance.

Exercise: You, the Executive

Assume for a few moments that you are an unusually successful person. Two years after your graduation you have advanced to the position of personnel officer in a large corporation. After having completed several assignments, you have been given the responsibility of evaluating the performance of employees who are completing the company's one-year management training program.

The objectives of the program are well established and have been communicated to all participants. The primary goals are:

1. To orient new employees to the goals, philosophy, and policies of the organization
2. To provide exposure to various aspects of corporate involvement to assist in the placement of prospective managers in mutually agreeable career paths
3. To improve employees' knowledge of important management methods
4. To develop decision-making skills through on-the-job experience

To accomplish these goals, the company places each management trainee in the program. The training involves formal classroom sessions, simulated decision making, and actual on-the-job training under experienced managers.

Although the organization is reasonably satisfied with the training program, selected executives have become somewhat skeptical. Obviously, the company invests a great deal in each trainee throughout the first year of employment. No one is completely sure of the benefits received in return. Therefore, your specific assignment is rather complex. You have been charged with the responsibility of analyzing the following aspects of the program. What are your responses?

1. Are the objectives of the management training program satisfactory? That is, if the program accomplishes everything it proposes to do, is it adequate given the investment involved? If not, what should be added or deleted from the goals of the program?
2. What are the most effective means of accomplishing the revised or existing set of goals? In other words, are the methods presently employed the proper ones? What alterations would you suggest?
3. How can the output of the management training program be evaluated? What factors do you think should be measured as an index to future managerial success? How would you propose to measure each factor itemized?

Case: Employees Saving and Loan

Marion Schafer is president of Employees Saving and Loan, a financial institution in the northwestern United States. Except for two commercial banks and a government employees credit union, this is the only financial institution in the city of Conway.

Schafer assumed her position four years ago, after spending five years in a large business firm. At her former job she had devised and implemented an employee evaluation system as director of personnel. This was credited with greatly improving productivity and morale. As a result, Schafer came to the attention of Employees Saving and Loan.

When she took her present job, she again developed a comprehensive employee appraisal system. Moreover, she did something unheard of in Conway. Schafer actually requested that the board of directors evaluate the performance of the president—her own performance. Although the appraisal is open ended and can deal with any subject, several areas are specified. Here are a few examples:

What progress has been made this year in such key areas as

(1) establishing plans and accomplishing goals?

(2) providing leadership in the areas of control and efficiency?

What weaknesses do you perceive in the operations of the company?

You are asked to think about Schafer's unique evaluation program. Specifically:

1. Why do you think it is considered unusual for a president to ask the board of directors to evaluate his or her performance?
2. Do you think this appraisal is good or bad? Explain.
3. Can you see any dangers in this evaluation system? If so, what are they?

Suggested Readings

Bedeian, A. G. "Rater Characteristics Affecting the Validity of Performance Appraisals." *Journal of Management* 2 (1976): 37–45.

Field, H. S., G. A. Bayley, and S. M. Bayley. "Employment Test Validity for Minority and Nonminority Production Workers." *Personnel Psychology* 30 (1977): 37–46.

Ginsberg, S. G. "The 'I' Test—Evaluating Executive Talent and Potential." *Personnel Journal* 55 (1976): 168–169, 184.

Haynes, M. E. "Do Appraisal Reviews Improve Performance?" *Public Personnel Management* 2 (March/April 1973): 128–132.

Lefton, R. E., and Buzzota, Victor. *Effective Motivation Through Performance Appraisal.* New York: Wiley, 1977.

Newman, Jerry M. "Discrimination in Recruitment: An Empirical Analysis." *Industrial and Labor Relations Review* 31 (1978): 15–23.

Parrish, J. B. "Women and Minorities as a Professional Resource: A Study of Progress and Change." *Quarterly Review of Economics and Business* 18 (Autumn 1978): 58–66.

Patz, A. L. "Performance Appraisal: Useful but Still Resisted." *Harvard Business Review* 53 (May/June 1975): 74–80.

Sallery, R. A., Jr. "How to Hire an Executive." *Business Horizons* 19 (October 1976): 26–32.

Steers, R. M. *Organizational Effectiveness.* Santa Monica, Calif.: Goodyear, 1977.

Planned Change and Organization Development

> The ancient Celtic culture, in its spread from Ireland to Asia Minor . . . originated the word change. . . . For them the word change was rooted in the word exchange—the meeting place, the center for sharing. Perhaps buried in that word we use and misuse so often is the key to tomorrow.
>
> George T. Land,
> *The Internal Auditor*

The television industry is characterized by technological innovation and competitiveness. In 1966, Motorola introduced the solid state set, the first major technological innovation since the color tube. Because solid state sets were produced only in expensive console models, however, few sold. Consumers wanted smaller, less expensive, and even portable sets.

Anticipating the development of a brighter picture tube, Magnavox decided not to switch immediately to solid state sets. When the company finally did adopt the new technology, it introduced only a 25-inch console model—again missing the major market.

Zenith, on the other hand, entered the solid state market aggressively, a decision that brought substantial profits. Against all industry trends, Zenith used the opportunity to mechanize operations and move much of its production back to the United States from the Far East. Automation made labor costs less critical during the mid-1970s, and Zenith had the lowest manufacturing costs in the industry.

By planning its change to solid state technology, Zenith removed high-cost (and unprofitable) military-oriented electronics from its product line. It focused, instead, on its primary product and, by 1975, had almost one-fourth of the domestic television market.

Here we have three interesting cases of how firms responded to important changes. Motorola had the technology first, but it made the wrong decisions about the market. Magnavox delayed too long and missed the market when it finally made its move. Zenith took a chance, made a commitment, and enjoyed the rewards. Thus we see the uncertainty facing modern organizations—and the importance of dealing with change.

Chapter 14 examined performance appraisal mainly from a short-term perspective to introduce the general issue of organizational effectiveness. We noted that effectiveness is measured partly by an organization's ability to adapt. Now we will look at performance over a longer period of time to introduce the issues of planned change and organizational development.

First, change will be viewed as an ever-present social phenomenon. Even in technological change, people are involved. Our emphasis will be on the dynamics of planned change. Then this process will be related to the theory and practice of organization development. Finally, we will explore several popular development techniques used by organizations.

Change as a Social Phenomenon

A useful way to look at change is to determine whether it is imposed on an organization or initiated by it. In either case, the pressure for change begins as a social process. For example, people's values change, and this forces organizations to respond in some way. If employees demand more meaningful and more rewarding work, an organization may respond by redesigning tasks to enrich jobs. Thus a change is forced on the organization.

At the other extreme, the management of an organization may not be satisfied with a group's performance. Therefore, it may initiate a program to redesign jobs to improve productivity. In this case, the organization is initiating change, not responding to it.

Types of Change

A variety of elaborate and systematic ways of classifying change has been proposed.[1] For our purposes, we will differentiate between haphazard, or random, change and planned change. Change takes place whether or not one plans or initiates it. When we simply allow change to happen and make no attempt to plan for it or to influence its direction, it is said to be random or *haphazard change.*

In contrast, *planned change* is a conscious and deliberate attempt on the part of some agent (individual or group) to bring about alterations in a system.[2] Planned change, therefore, is goal directed. It is initiated to obtain a specific outcome.

Agents of Planned Change

A *change agent* is any individual or group that initiates or facilitates planned change. Thus a manager often functions as an agent of change. More specifically, change agents have been classified under four broad categories.

The first type of change agent is the external pressure group, for example, a conservation or consumer organization. Numerous groups have been organized to fight companies that are involved in pollution-generating manufacturing, that produce unsafe products, and that have misleading advertisements. This type of group usually emphasizes the need for an organization to recognize its responsibility to the larger social system.

Another important change agent is the internal pressure group. This may be a coalition, as mentioned earlier, or a more formal group like a labor union. The distinguishing characteristic of an internal pressure group is that its main goal in initiating change is to further its own interests.

The organization development (OD) consultant is discussed a great deal in management literature. This type of agent is an individual who can aid a group in solving relevant problems by applying behavioral science knowledge. Thus an OD consultant, being an outside change agent, needs to have skills in interpersonal relations. He or she also must have expert knowledge of the behavioral sciences. The role can be complicated, since consultants not only must be experts but must fit into organizations without projecting the expert role.

Consultants, if they assume the role of an expert, may increase organizational dependence on them, thus making it more difficult for the organization to mobilize resources toward solving problems.[3] One writer has noted that an OD consultant should be an expert on how to help an organization learn, not an expert on the actual managerial problems.[4]

Finally, there is the internal change agent or consultant. More and more organizations are employing individuals in a staff capacity to deal with organizational development problems. Usually these are highly trained people who are familiar with consulting. Such individuals have the advantage of knowing more about specific organizational problems, but they may find it difficult to maintain objectivity.

To illustrate, consider the case of Universal Industries. This large corporation often found it necessary to hire outside consultants to assist in behavioral matters ranging from performance appraisals to supervisory training courses. Noting that Universal Industries was spending almost $100,000 a year on outside consultants, the vice president for operations recommended that the company hire a behavioral scientist in a staff position.

Universal Industries decided to employ a psychologist who specialized in organizational change—for considerably less than the $100,000 paid to consultants. This staff psychologist was given a great deal of independence in functioning as an in-house consultant. Of particular importance was the psychologist's responsibility to conduct internal surveys and to design programs that would ease organizational change.

Proposition
15.1

> Since pressures for change come from a variety of sources, the agents of change vary. Change agents include external and internal pressure groups as well as individuals such as outside consultants or staff experts.

Planned Change

Attempts have been made to identify and describe planned change. In general, it occurs in three stages: (1) unfreezing the system, or preparing it for change; (2) initiating the change; and (3) refreezing, or stabilizing, the system after the change is implemented.[5]

Unfreezing the System

The first stage in the unfreezing phase involves search activities. The organization suspects that it needs change and is searching for a solution to some problem. The change agent also sees the need for alteration.

Stage two is the point of contact. The organization has identified an agent who can effect the change, and the agent has located the client. Diagnosis follows, in which the problem is identified, the goals of the organization are made explicit, and the resources of the organization and talents of the agent are identified. The diagnosis is followed by a planning stage. An action plan is developed, and possible outcomes are projected. Typically, the client organization and the change agent cooperate closely.

The various stages in unfreezing can be illustrated by the experiences of Hartsfield General Hospital's maintenance department. This group is responsible for all building and grounds maintenance at the hospital. Specialized medical equipment has not been part of the department's responsibility.

For several years, the maintenance department has had serious turnover and safety problems. Ruby Burkovitch, the assistant administrator for operations to whom the department reports, has speculated about the causes of the problems. She has known about the problems and has searched for answers by interviewing department members, talking with other administrative personnel, and reading all she could about turnover and safety.

At first, Burkovitch thought the boring nature of the work might be the source of the problems. She almost committed the hospital to the expensive course of redesigning and enriching jobs. However, before this decision was made, she happened to talk informally with Professor Charlotte McKinney, who taught management at the local university. Professor McKinney suggested that the problems might or might not be solved by redesigning jobs. She agreed to visit the hospital and study the problems firsthand.

On her promised visit, Professor McKinney soon concluded that she could help solve the problems, and the hospital agreed to hire her as an outside consultant. The contact was now complete. At this time the professor decided to survey the members of the department, observe their behavior at work, and generally become familiar both with the hospital's goals and with those of the department. Diagnosis of the problems was underway.

Through all these activities, McKinney and Burkovitch were able to develop several theories about the cause of the problems—only one of which was boredom. They began to project possible courses of action. Members of the maintenance department were completely informed about the plans to create an attitude and environment that would help in unfreezing traditional ways of doing things and would encourage acceptance of change. Now it was possible to form a final plan of action.

For example, Professor McKinney was convinced that the routine and rigidity of the work schedule in the maintenance department was a more serious problem than boredom. Therefore, she proposed that the department work on a flex-time basis. This plan was arranged to cover the staffing needs on all three shifts during a twenty-four–hour period while still allowing individual employees some flexibility in scheduling work hours. Burkovitch agreed that this flex-time might relieve employees' anxieties about such things as child care, long-distance commuting during peak traffic, and other personal matters.

Initiating the Change: The Action Plan

Once unfreezing has been accomplished, the organization is ready for change. Internal or external agents begin to implement the actions planned in previous stages. This stage involves using one or more strategies of intervention. Although writers on the subject have proposed numerous strategies, we will group them under three general headings: force, re-education, and rational appeal.[6]

Force One common approach to implementing change is to use *force.* This strategy is seen, for example, when the Department of

Labor acts as a change agent in enforcing the Occupational Safety and Health Act. Suppose some labor department inspectors discover a violation of the law in a particular plant. Because of their legal authority, they can force the organization to correct the unsafe condition.

The advantage of this strategy is obviously the speed with which a change can be implemented. The disadvantage is that this approach requires compliance but often fails to truly change attitudes, which is necessary for long-lasting results. Thus an agent may resort to another strategy.

Re-education   People usually behave as they do because they have been taught to do so. Education is an important influence on behavior, so why not use it to bring about change? Management training is a good example of *re-education*.

A particular organization may note that worker dissatisfaction is increasing because supervisors lack supportive attitudes. The management of the organization, therefore, decides to offer human relations training to supervisors in an effort to change their attitudes and to reduce employee dissatisfaction.

This approach, if successful, has long-lasting effects. On the other hand, it consumes valuable time and can be expensive.

Rational Appeal   *Rational appeal* can be extremely successful under certain conditions. The agent using this approach is aware of the self-interest motive in people and appeals to it. In other words, an effort is made to show people that it is to their advantage to alter or redirect their behavior in line with the change.

For example, a change agent who wants to redesign an organization may stress to employees how their jobs will be more rewarding and more meaningful when the program is completed. If the logic is acceptable, employees probably will change quickly, and the alteration will be long-lasting.

Proposition 15.2

Three common strategies for implementing planned change are force, re-education, and rational appeal. Force is fast, but it fails to bring long-range changes. Re-education is slow and costly, but it secures long-term commitment. Rational appeal is fast and results in lasting commitment.

Stabilizing and Refreezing

When the change is completed, stability is reintroduced into the system. Evaluation is an important part of this phase and is designed to answer such questions as: How successful is the implementation? Should the change efforts be continued? Should the change efforts be terminated? Figure 15.1 diagrams the change process we have discussed.

Returning to our example of Hartsfield General Hospital's maintenance department, recall that McKinney had recommended a flex-time plan. The program for unfreezing is now complete, and implementation must begin.

McKinney suggested that the change strategy combine rational appeal and re-education. Before implementing the flex-time program, Burkovitch held meetings with all maintenance employees to spell out the advantages of the proposed system. The meetings also provided an opportunity to answer employees' questions, thereby reducing opposition. Finally, when the program is implemented, the commitment of the employees must be developed. The new flex-time program must be stabilized so that it becomes the accepted method of operation. Only then will the change program be complete. However, one other issue needs our attention: resistance to change.

Figure 15.1 The Process of Planned Change

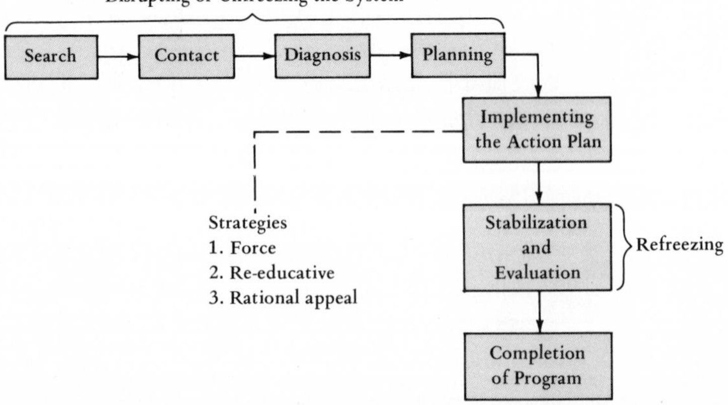

Resistance to Change

Kurt Lewin has presented a useful description of change and of the resistance to it that often develops. In general terms, his concept is referred to as force-field analysis.[7] The concept is illustrated in Figure 15.2.

In this figure, we see the present state of affairs, or the existing balance (B_0). On the left side, are the forces attempting to effect change, represented by DF (driving force). On the right, are the restraining forces (RF) that attempt to inhibit proposed alterations. By increasing the driving forces or reducing the retraining forces, or by some combination of both, a new balance may develop at B_1. Even an apparent equilibrium is really only *quasi-stationary equilibrium* and actually moving.[8]

To illustrate, let us examine the following case. Brakerfield Foundry is considering automating two of its manual casting operations. The main driving force behind this plan is the comptroller, who has calculated that extremely large savings will result from automation.

Figure 15.2   Lewin's Force-Field View of Change

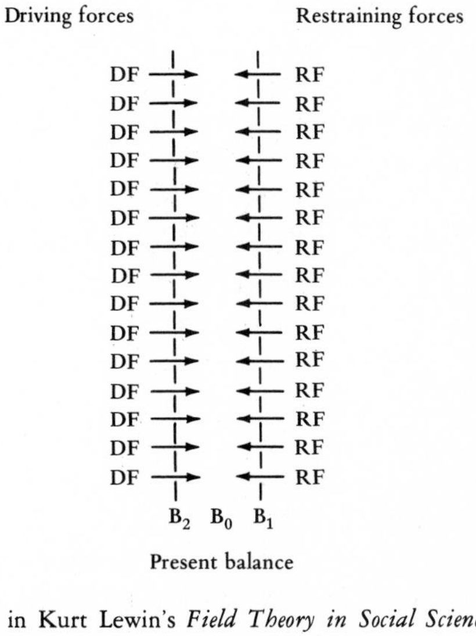

Source: After Figure 31 in Kurt Lewin's *Field Theory in Social Science,* edited by Dorwin Cartwright (New York: Harper & Row, 1951), p. 220.

This view is supported by other people, including the production manager and the supervisor of quality control. Top management is hesitant to finalize the decision because several important restraining forces—including the union and local community action groups—oppose automation, fearing unemployment. Whether or not the operations will be automated depends on the relative strength of the driving and restraining forces.

Thus we see the dynamics of the perceived "steady state." If the comptroller and the other driving forces can make a strong enough argument, automation will result. The approach can be either to strengthen the driving forces or to weaken the restraining forces. The union and community groups can exercise similar options. At a more basic level, there are reasons to expect that employees may resist change. Let us briefly review some of these reasons and suggest some ways that the managers may overcome the resistance.

Why People Resist Change

Assume you are an employee at Brakerfield Foundry and you know about the proposed automation of the casting operations. How might you respond at a personal level?

First of all, you may be skeptical about automation because, from your point of view, there is nothing wrong with manual operations. After all, you have been working at the foundry for twenty years, and castings have always been done manually.[9] At the same time—even though your feelings may be unconscious—you may feel safe and secure with the manual operations and may fear automation.

Such resistance based on fear is not limited to rank-and-file employees. Managers also resist change out of fear. For example, the supervisor in the casting department may be threatened by the proposed automation. He or she may suspect that no supervisor will be needed or that his or her skills may not be adequate for the complex machines.[10]

Any major change is likely to meet resistance from employees and managers. This should not, however, make managers satisfied with the present way of operating. Such satisfaction can be especially troublesome during periods of rapid change.[11]

How Managers Can Ease Change

Perhaps the best thing a manager can do in this situation is to create an environment that encourages creative thought and new ways of doing things. One effective way of creating the proper climate is to ensure free and open communication. Managers should provide opportunities for participation and should build trust and confidence among members of the work group.

Perhaps the most important thing is to share with the employees as much information as possible about the economic and social benefits of the change—and to do this as soon as possible. This sharing is extremely important in ensuring that the expectations of employees, managers, and the public are not greater than can be justified by the success or failure of the change.[12]

Having introduced change, we now can look at an institutionalized concept for implementing change. This concept is known as organization development.

Essentials of Organization Development

The process of applying behavioral science knowledge to problems of organizational change is exciting. Unfortunately, our knowledge about it is far from complete. The literature continues to grow, however, and it is now possible to make certain useful generalizations about organizational change and development.[13]

Organization Development: A Definition

One of the most popular definitions of *organization development* (OD) says that it is a planned, organization-wide effort that has top-management support and is designed to increase organizational effectiveness and health through interventions using behavioral science knowledge.[14] OD interventions are planned, not haphazard. They possess management support to increase the health and effectiveness of the organization, and they use behavioral science knowledge.

These elements imply that organization development is a long-range program designed to use scientific knowledge.[15] It is also normative in that it is clearly goal oriented and is directed toward the goal of improving effectiveness. Frame 15.1 illustrates how one company has used OD.

Frame 15.1

> ### Innovation and Organization Development at B. F. Goodrich
>
> Innovation is not unusual in the automobile tire industry. Goodyear Tire and Rubber Company introduced the elliptic tire as an energy saver that was promoted as a significant improvement over radial tires. However, people at B. F. Goodrich have been asking whether different innovations can be stimulated through OD techniques. Of particular concern is the acceptance of nonproduct or conceptual innovations, such as improvements in financial reporting, strategic planning, information processing, and so on.
>
> To assist in developing this innovation, Goodrich has established a network of staff personnel who are trained in OD techniques. Four objectives are to be accomplished by this network:
>
> 1. To provide management with effective and efficient ways to disseminate and retrieve information
> 2. To provide immediate responses to requests for introducing innovations
> 3. To provide management with the information necessary to "put a finger on the pulse" of the organization
> 4. To provide a link between corporate divisions and site locations for goal setting and other work-flow requirements
>
> Goodrich's concept of the network appears to be useful in creating widespread attention about and understanding of OD throughout the organization.
>
> Adapted from R. J. Howe, M. G. Mindell, and D. L. Simmons, "Introducing Innovation Through OD," *Management Review* 67 (1978): 52–56.

Organization Development and Human Nature

Underlying OD are certain assumptions about human behavior. Bennis has summarized these by discussing the alterations required of postbureaucratic management systems.[16] These are

1. The necessity for developing a new concept of human beings based on new knowledge of the complex and dynamic nature of needs
2. The necessity for a new concept of power formulated around collaboration and reason
3. The development of humanistic-democratic values to replace the mechanistic values of bureaucracy

In other words, OD develops a view of people in organizations that is quite different from traditional assumptions. In the modern view, individuals are assumed to be capable and to desire personal growth and development. They are no longer seen as mechanistic elements in an impersonal organizational structure.[17]

Organization Development and Management Development

Supporters of OD are careful not to confuse it with management training. There is a basic difference between the two. OD attempts to change the total system and to redesign it to fit the individuals within the group. *Management development* accepts the system as it is and attempts to change individuals to fit the structure.[18] Table 15.1 identifies some important areas in which differences are evident.

First, the objective of OD is to change the system. Management development, however, attempts to change individuals so as to achieve a better fit with the system. Thus motivational aspects of the two approaches are different. Improvement in design is the motive of OD; employee training is the motive of management development.

As a general rule, management development relies on the educative change strategy. OD, although educative, is directed more toward problem solving and action. The short run is the main concern

Table 15.1 Comparison of Organization Development and Management Development

Characteristic	Management Development	Organization Development
1. **Objective**	Improve managers' contributions to goal accomplishment.	Alter the organization.
2. **Motive**	Train and equip managers and employees to function better in existing organization.	Improve organizational design. Focus on design, not on the manager.
3. **Change strategies**	Educative or training.	Problem-solving approaches.
4. **Time orientation**	Short range.	Long range.
5. **Specialists required**	No special requirements.	Trained specialists.

Adapted from W. W. Burke and W. H. Schmidt, "Management and Organization Development," *Personnel Administration,* March–April 1971, pp. 46–52, by permission of the International Personnel Management Association, 1313 East 60th Street, Chicago, Illinois 60637. Copyright © 1971 by the Society for Personnel Administration.

of management training, whereas OD is a distinctly long-range concept. The organizational changes visualized are expected to have long-lasting effects, whereas management training must be reintroduced constantly.

Although it is accurate and proper to think of management development as different from organization development, we should recognize that one approach does not preclude the other. In fact, it is most productive to view the two approaches as reinforcing each other.

There is, for example, nothing inconsistent in developing programs to improve the individual manager's skills while implementing a change in the concept and design of the organization. It is also possible, and even desirable, to offer short-term training efforts while longer-range programs are being planned and put into operation.

At the same time, many training activities can be conducted by less specialized personnel while the more comprehensive efforts are being coordinated by specialized change agents. The important thing is for the organization to define and communicate program goals clearly, so that training efforts can make specific contributions to the development program.

Now we have a sufficient view of organization development and planned change to form a foundation for examining and evaluating various OD techniques. This will be done in the following section.

Proposition 15.3

> Organization development is basically different from management training, although the two can reinforce each other. OD is designed specifically to change the organizational system over the long run so as to improve its effectiveness and adaptability.

Some OD Techniques

There are many *OD techniques*, and each has its supporters and critics. We will discuss three broad categories of techniques. The first is the intra- and interpersonal techniques that received much of the attention in the early development of OD. Our illustrations will be built on two cases in point—sensitivity training and encounter groups. Next we will look at techniques directed toward improving the individual's relationship with the organization. As examples, we will review job enrichment and management by objectives. Finally, we will examine a technique that is designed specifically to achieve system-wide changes: the confrontation meeting.

The goal of our discussion is not to present a complete survey of available OD techniques. That is clearly beyond the scope of this test. Nor is our analysis intended to make a person skillful in using any of the techniques discussed. Expertise in this area requires highly trained and qualified specialists. Few managers have such expertise; nor should they be qualified OD practitioners.

Our purpose throughout this book has been to give prospective managers a familiarity with and a basic understanding of the many areas that form the body of knowledge known as organizational behavior. Organization development is only one part of this body of knowledge. Therefore, we will look at a few selected OD techniques to get acquainted with the area. Specialization and competence demand and deserve much more than we can offer here.

Intra- and Interpersonal Analysis

Historically, interpersonal analysis first was applied in the T-group or sensitivity training movement. Team-building concepts, laboratory techniques, and encounter groups also fall under the intra- and interpersonal grouping.

Sensitivity Training   Napier and Gershenfeld point out that the term *sensitivity training* has become too broad to have any real meaning.[19] Although the term has been generalized excessively, there are indeed some specific outcomes expected from sensitivity training. These are:

1. Increased understanding, insight, and self-awareness about our own behavior
2. Increased understanding of and sensitivity to the behavior of others
3. Better understanding and awareness of group and intergroup processes
4. Increased skill at diagnosing group situations
5. Increased ability to transfer learning to action
6. Improved interpersonal relations so that interaction becomes more rewarding and satisfying[20]

Training groups may be composed of strangers, cousins, or family. Stranger groups have had no previous association with one another; cousins may be part of some organization but do not work together; the family group does work together.

To be aware of what happens in a sensitivity session, let us assume that we have a training group of strangers. At the beginning, the trainer probably introduces himself or herself and makes it known that he or she will serve as a resource to the group. After this initial statement, the trainer becomes silent, and the burden of continued interaction is placed on the group.

As training proceeds, participants assume various roles. Some probably withdraw; others become aggressive. The trainer interacts only when necessary to facilitate learning and to ensure that participants understand what is happening in the group.

The success of sensitivity training results from several factors. The trainer's (leader's) style has been shown to be important. Direct or indirect leadership techniques may, among other things, influence whether and how long group skepticism is directed toward the trainer.[21]

Familiarity of the group with the trainer and the trust exhibited among group members also influence the success of sensitivity training. Prior contact with the trainer is associated with the effectiveness of group interaction. Trust among group members is also influential.[22]

Probably everyone who has read and thought about sensitivity training has formed certain opinions about the technique. Some people dismiss it as having little value, whereas others report how their life and work have been changed through participation.

One cannot help but be impressed by the negative reactions often expressed by managers when talking about sensitivity training. There is little sense in denying that numerous large organizations use the technique. Yet, because it probes into the emotions of individuals and encourages openness in groups, many organizations continue— not without justification—to fear possible adverse effects.

For example, Kearney and Martin have reported the results obtained from a survey of 300 relatively large business firms. The 225 respondents indicated that sensitivity training was not an extremely important part of their development efforts, nor did they expect it to be in the future. Although many of these respondents admitted that the sensitivity sessions resulted in permanent changes in their behavior, most stated that they would not recommend use of the technique.[23]

Not all outcomes of sensitivity training can be anticipated when commitments are made to use such a program. Consider the "problem" that developed at Capital Chemical Corporation after a group of executives participated in a sensitivity training program. All the participants appeared to be more conscious of their own behavior and that of other people in the organization. In fact, two executives looked at themselves seriously for the first time and discovered that they did not really want to remain at Capital Chemical. They resigned and sought more personally satisfying careers. Perhaps the executives and the corporation were better off as a result, but the short-run problem of replacing two key executives was serious. Reflecting on the situation, the president of Capital Chemical reported that he was not sure the program was a good idea.[24]

Encounter Groups Although similar to T-groups, encounter groups involve a deeper intervention. Interpersonal dynamics are used as a means of achieving greater individual understanding.[25]

Encounter groups aim at several goals, including building our self-concept and improving the quality of our interaction with others. In some ways, encounter groups seem to operate like T-groups. There is, for example, a small number of participants and a leader who attempts to draw out participants' emotions.[26] The level of personal involvement is what differentiates encounter groups from T-groups.

One development in recent years is known as the trainerless laboratory, which includes the Trust-Openness-Realization-Interdependence (TORI) system.[27] The objective of this and similar systems is to develop a community characterized by interpersonal trust, self-disclosure, and open interaction.

Limited attempts have been made to evaluate the effectiveness of encounter groups. According to one often-cited study, the results of encounter groups in the changed behavior of participants is usually perceived by participants to be greater than can be seen by outside observers.[28]

Proposition 15.4

> Sensitivity training and encounter groups are two methods that were first used as OD techniques. The two methods share many common features. The main difference between them is that encounter groups attempt to achieve deeper personal involvement.

Integrating Individuals and Organizations

Chapter 6 discussed job enrichment and the two-factor theory of motivation from which the enrichment idea evolved. Numerous studies have both confirmed and questioned the usefulness of job enrichment in improving organizational effectiveness.[29]

In job enrichment, jobs are often redesigned. Thus the organization, rather than the individual, is altered.

In recent years, the most discussed OD technique for integrating individual and organizational goals has been management by objectives (MBO). MBO is based on three assumptions. First, people want to know what they are expected to do. Second, they wish to participate in the decisions that influence their lives and careers. Third, individuals want to know how they are doing.[30] From these assumptions we obtain the two related concepts of participative goal setting and evaluation by results.

The MBO process can be illustrated by the case of University Hospital, which recently implemented an MBO system. The administrator began by working with the vice president for medical affairs to obtain a clear statement of the hospital's mission. At the same time, an extensive program of information sharing was initiated through the employee publication. Care was taken to explain the purposes and essential steps involved in MBO.

After the administrator was satisfied that everyone had been informed about the program, a series of meetings was scheduled with the four assistant administrators. At the first meeting, the administrator informed all assistants of the hospital's mission and asked them to think about their own divisions and develop a set of objectives that fit the overall mission. The remaining meetings were used to obtain agreement about the goals, to remove overlap among the divisions, and to ensure that the goals could be measured in quantitative terms so that they could be used to evaluate behavior.

Each assistant administrator then was asked to return with the list of divisional goals, introduce them to his or her department heads, and ask for a similar list of goals for each department. The process was repeated throughout the organization. In this way, all employees were able to participate in goal setting and had an opportunity to integrate their own goals with those of the organization.

The results of MBO programs have been well documented. Raia has noted that improvements in productivity and communication were evident after an MBO program was instituted.[31] Follow-up studies by the same researcher revealed that productivity continued to increase, although managers' attitudes took a change for the worse. For example, complaints arose about such things as having too much paperwork.[32]

Other studies, such as those by Carroll and Tosi at Black and Decker, illustrate that top-management support is critical to the success of MBO.[33] Generally, research indicates that MBO has been quite successful in integrating individual and organizational goals.

MBO has been introduced in nonprofit organizations as well. One example involves the Harris County (Texas) Adult Probation Department.[34] Because of scarce documentation of the use of MBO in law enforcement agencies, the change agents were forced to develop—almost without guidance—their own approach. They decided on a three-stage program. In the first phase, they held meetings with all levels of the organization to explain the concept and method of MBO. Next they conducted departmental workshops designed to build cohesive work groups and teach participants how to write objectives. Finally, they implemented the evaluation and reporting system, along with an ongoing program to assist in updating and defining objectives.

The system brought several important results. Participation increased, and performance was evaluated more realistically against accepted and agreed-upon objectives. The program also emphasized the need for top-management support and for continued developmental efforts in the department. More important, perhaps, is the fact that this experience illustrated the applicability of MBO in organizations other than economic ones.

Similar examples can be found in the health care field. One study reported the results of an MBO program in a state-supported health facility.[35] This study indicated that nonprofit organizations can make use of management by objectives. It also illustrated that the critical factors influencing employee attitudes toward the technique are their perception of how supervisors feel about MBO and the system's ability to contribute positively to communication within the organization. Once again, managerial support emerged as a critical factor in any successful program of planned change.

The Confrontation Meeting

One interesting OD technique that is designed to change an entire organization is the confrontation meeting. This meeting most often is conducted through a one-day program that is designed to assess the organization's strengths and weaknesses as well as its ability to mobilize problem-solving resources.[36] In general this technique is used with management personnel but may have wider applications.

The environment for the confrontation meeting is established by top management and an outside consultant, who state the reason for the meeting and stress the need for openness. Often the meeting is held to address a specific problem that is troubling the organization's management. Individuals usually are assigned to small, diverse groups that include personnel from several functional areas (such as accounting, sales, and so on).

Groups then are separated and concentrate on identifying organizational problems. After a specified length of time, the groups are brought together again to report on the problems they have identified. Problems are categorized, and problem-solving groups are established to rank the importance of identified problems, to devise plans for solving them, and to recommend solutions. Groups continue to work on solutions and to make periodic reports to management.

Since the confrontation meeting is a relatively new concept, not enough information has been developed for a comprehensive evaluation of the technique. In an unsystematic way, however, reports indicate that the meeting is valuable as a technique for identifying and solving problems.[37]

Proposition 15.5

> A variety of OD techniques are available. They focus on intra- and interpersonal improvements and on the integration of individual and organizational goals and/or system-wide alterations.

Obviously, we have been selective in this chapter's coverage of OD techniques. Increasingly, management literature refers to the organizational use of transactional analysis, grid concepts, and so on. Each of these topics deserves attention. However, our purpose is not to explain each of these techniques but to illustrate that OD can be approached in various ways and at different levels.

What Managers Should Know About Planned Change and Organization Development

Organizations are constantly confronted with change, and managers must be prepared emotionally and theoretically to deal with it. Perhaps most important is the manager's need to recognize change as a social process. People change and resist change for a number of reasons. Sometimes they are unsure with existing conditions; at other times they are threatened with any alteration in the status quo. Managers are no different.

Fortunately, managers have an extensive body of theory to assist in managing change. One of the most systematic efforts in this area is known as organization development.

As the name implies, organization development relates to large-scale changes in an entire organizational system. As such, the significance of the decision to participate in an organization development effort is an important one. It may mean in the end that the organization will do things in significantly different ways and that the manager's authority will be greatly altered in the process. For example, when a new managerial system such as MBO is implemented, the managers of an organization will have to commit to more consultation and interaction with employees; performance evaluation will become more predictable; and the formal authority in the system may be substantially redistributed, giving lower-level employees more voice in their own growth and development. If the managers can accept such a design with enthusiasm, however, organizational performance may reach new and higher levels, and many of the problems of hierarchical, authority-based organizations will likely disappear.

Summary

Change can be classified as random change or planned change. In either case, change is inevitable. When one makes no effort to anticipate it, change is said to be random or haphazard. When managers consciously attempt to influence the direction of inevitable alterations, planned change is initiated.

The individuals and groups that attempt to direct change are called change agents. External or internal pressure groups often assume the role. An example of the former type is a conservation or consumer safety group; a local labor union illustrates the internal pressure group.

An organization's management often decides to employ the services of an external consultant trained as a specialist in facilitating planned change. Other organizations may use in-house staff experts. An external consultant may have the advantage of possessing objectivity, but may lack a complete view of the organizational realities. An insider, on the other hand, is likely to understand the organization, but may have difficulty maintaining objectivity.

For simplicity, planned change can be broken down into three stages. First, the change agent must unfreeze the existing system. A need to initiate alterations is perceived and a search for available alternatives is initiated. Next when unfreezing has been accomplished, an action plan must be activated. A key decision at this stage is the proper strategy, or combination of strategies, to use. The agent may use force, legitimate authority, or a rational appeal to individual self-interest. It is also possible to engage in re-education, attempting to redirect values in line with proposed alterations. A comprehensive change effort is likely to involve a combination of all three strategies.

When the action plan is accomplished, the organizational system must be stabilized. This stage is known as refreezing. It is tempting to assume that the stabilized system (or any system, for that matter) is static and fixed. In fact, stabilization is static only at the perceptual level, since the organization is always in a quasi-stationary equilibrium, with driving and restraining forces engaged in a never-ending contest.

Many organizations have recognized the need for change and have established formal development programs. The goal of OD programs is to improve organizational effectiveness and health by applying behavioral science knowledge. Thus OD is a science-based, long-range effort designed to make organizations responsive to change.

Organization development (OD) uses many techniques in facilitating change. Among the most common and controversial techniques are sensitivity training and encounter groups. Other popular efforts involve management by objectives (MBO) and confrontation meetings.

It is important to remember that OD techniques are highly sophisticated behavioral science applications. Thus their use often requires trained specialists who understand and appreciate their dangers as well as their potential value. In this chapter, the goal has been merely to introduce the more familiar techniques—not to train specialists.

Questions for Discussion

1. Explain quasi-stationary equilibrium. Why is this so important for planned change?
2. Compare and contrast organization development and management development. Do you consider either one to be more or less important than the other? How can they be used to complement one another?
3. Based on your personal perception, what do you think about sensitivity training? Have you ever known anyone who participated in sensitivity training sessions? If so, what was his or her reaction?
4. How can MBO help integrate individual and organizational goals? What practical advantages do you see in this approach?
5. List some reasons why people resist change. How can managers overcome such resistance?

Case: Management Development at Bayer Bindery

Bayer Bindery is a large publisher and bindery in a southwestern city. It specializes in printing and binding college catalogs for institutions of higher learning throughout the country. It has grown substantially since its founding about thirty-five years ago. All the management and supervisory personnel worked their way up through the organization and for the most part have little or no formal management training.

John Bayer, Jr., son of the founder, recently assumed the presidency of the firm and is taking a look at the "management team." He is particularly concerned by what he considers to be "a serious lack of human relations skills" among first-line managers.

In response to this perceived problem, Bayer has contacted a national firm that specializes in providing in-house supervisory training programs. He is impressed especially because the firm will provide all necessary materials and will allow the bindery's own managers to function as instructors. Essentially, the material is organized around the following major topics:

1. *Making the transition to manager*—emphasis is on thinking as a manager would, rather than as a rank-and-file employee
2. *Understanding human behavior*—analyzing why employees behave as they do and examining ways to motivate performance
3. *Evaluating employee performance*—a survey of methods for evaluating employee behavior
4. *Effective communication*—an in-depth examination of communication and a review of the barriers to effective communication

Bayer is prepared to begin the program next month. Consider the following questions:

1. Is the program as outlined an example of management or organization development? Explain your response.
2. What do you think is the best result Bayer can expect from the proposed program? Why?
3. What additional measures would you suggest before the program is initiated?

Case: Sally Washington's Battle to the Top

Sally Washington is about to give up on her career. She is an engineer by training but has entered management by choice. When she was hired by the state highway department, she was the first female field civil engineer to be employed as a professional engineer with responsibilities outside the main office. The department had always assumed that no female would be happy to survey through woods in rain, mud, and snow—but Sally was happy.

Not only did Sally enjoy the work, but she was "head and shoulders" above any male engineer, according to Chief Engineer Hal Benson. She was so good that after one year Benson promoted her to head of the survey section and encouraged her to take a leave of absence to complete a master's degree in engineering management. Sally completed the degree with high honors and returned to the survey section. There she has remained for five years.

In the state highway department, no one really believes a woman can function in a technical area like civil engineering. In this view, women supervise large numbers of field engineers who—next to oil field workers—are as "tough as they come." All the standard points have been raised:

A woman head of engineers will adversely influence the morale of male engineers.

The head of engineers is a responsible job, and women require too much sick leave.

What if Sally gets married and decides to start a family?

What if her husband gets transferred to another city or state?

No woman can work for long in the rugged environment of the field civil engineer.

Benson is convinced. He thinks Sally deserves greater responsibility. He continues to recommend her for all the more promising openings, but Sally remains in her position as section head.

1. Why do you think Sally continues to meet reluctance on the part of upper management, even though she has proved her abilities?
2. What are some ways that Benson or Sally could overcome the resistance (consider educative, rational-appeal, and force strategies)?
3. Which strategy do you think will be most effective? Why?

Suggested Readings

Albrecht, Karl. *Successful Management by Objectives*. Englewood Cliffs, N.J.: Prentice-Hall, 1978.

Bowen, D. D. "Value Dilemmas in Organizational Development." *Journal of Applied Behavioral Science* 13 (1978): 543–556.

Chacko, T. I., T. H. Stone, and A. P. Brief. "Participation in Goal Setting Programs: An Attributional Analysis." *Academy of Management Review* 4 (1979): 433–438.

Flaherty, J. E. *Managing Change: Today's Challenge for Management*. New York: Nellen, 1979.

Fowler, Cling, and Eva Schindler-Rainman. "A Communication Workshop: An OD Intervention." *Training and Development Journal* 33 (April 1979): 53–55.

French, W. L., and C. H. Bell, Jr. *Organization Development: Behavioral Science Interventions for Organizational Improvement,* 2nd ed. Englewood Cliffs, N.J.: Prentice-Hall, 1978.

Lewicki, R. "Team Building in the Small Business Community." In *Failures in Organizational Development and Change.* Eds. H. Mirvis and D. N. Berg. New York: Wiley, 1977.

Lien, Lawrence. "Reviewing Your Training and Development Activities." *Personnel Journal* 58 (1979): 791–794.

Schermerhorn, J. R., Jr. "Interorganizational Development." *Journal of Management* 5 (1979): 21–38.

Williams, T. A. "The Search Conference in Active Adaptive Planning." *Journal of Applied Behavioral Science* 15 (1979): 470–484.

Using Behavioral Knowledge to Improve Organizational Performance

To use behavioral science perspectives within enterprises to achieve organizational change requires the development and integration of models of knowledge utilization that will connect the sponsoring enterprise with the full network of institutions concerned in the generation and application of knowledge.

Peter A. Clark,
Action Research and Organizational Change

The end of our study of organizational behavior is near, and it is time for reflection. There does exist a body of behavioral knowledge that managers can use to improve organizational performance. In this chapter, we will look at the manner in which behavioral knowledge becomes organizational practice.

In analyzing the transfer from theory to practice, we must examine a number of topics. First, we will look briefly at the knowledge-flow system. Second, we will examine the barriers that inhibit the efficient transfer of knowledge, and we will point out the linking agents that specifically attempt to overcome the barriers. Finally, we will deal with the complex topic of the ethics involved in using behavioral knowledge to accomplish organizational goals.

Figure 16.1 A Simple Knowledge-Flow System

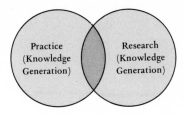

The Knowledge-Flow System

In a most general sense, a *knowledge-flow system* includes all the resource and user subsystems involved in the transfer of behavioral knowledge to its implementation.[1] The relevant subsystems usually are defined as the research and practice components. Figure 16.1 illustrates the system.

Developing Behavioral Knowledge: Research Subsystem

The research subsystem has as its main objectives the description and, if possible, the explanation of organizational phenomena. Individuals involved in this research usually are found in the behavioral science and management departments of colleges and universities.[2]

For example, experimental psychologists may be involved in basic or pure research, studying learning under various reinforcement schedules. The psychologist's objective is to generate new knowledge—with no practical end. The method of communicating this knowledge is customarily through scholarly journals, and the audience is composed of fellow psychologists.

Researchers in professional schools of universities also engage in other research. This group of researchers usually has a more applied orientation; thus, there is an overlap between research and practice. This brings us to the domain of applied research in which new knowledge is not generated but is applied to a relevant organizational problem.[3]

One additional research strategy that is becoming increasingly popular is known as action research. Although there are numerous interpretations of what action research is, its distinguishing characteristic seems to be the active involvement of managers and researchers in the scientific and managerial processes.[4] The frequently mentioned action research program is one that seriously involves managers and researchers in problem definition, research design, and the actual implementation of research findings.

Applying Management Knowledge: Practice Subsystem

The practice subsystem is the point at which managers actually use the knowledge gained from the research stage. Their actions are normative or goal oriented. Research findings are directed toward well-defined ends, emphasizing real-world problem solving.

In practice, decision makers in all types of organizations bring expertise to bear on reducing resistance to change. Consider, for example, an organization that is considering a job enrichment program. The manager's task is to evaluate the research done in motivational theory and to design a program that fits the organization's situation.

A final subsystem that has less relevance to our purpose is the consumption component. Consumption relates to the ultimate benefactor of knowledge use. This may involve the owners, employees, or the community.

Proposition 16.1

> The knowledge-flow system contains all the subsystems involved in the transfer of behavioral theory to management practice. The elements of concern to us are the research and practice subsystems.

A presentation of the knowledge-flow system provides only one aspect of the overall problem. Next we must examine some processes that operate within the system.

Linking Management Theory to Practice

The knowledge-utilization process relates to the actual transfer of theoretical information to a usable form. Linkage takes place when a regular pattern of information flow is established between two subsystems within the larger knowledge-flow system.[5]

For example, a linkage is formed when a business school contacts an organization and receives permission to implement an experimental motivation program. In one case, an automobile dealer worked with a business school to develop a positive reinforcement program for its service department. The department's personnel were rewarded if a customer's car was delivered when promised and if no complaints or adjustments resulted. The program was experimental at first, but after three months it became a permanent part of the firm's operations.

Barriers to Knowledge Flow

One characteristic of systems and subsystems is that they tend to develop boundaries that distinguish their limits from those of other systems. Such boundaries result in barriers that inhibit or make more difficult the easy and efficient transfer of knowledge. Referring specifically to the research-practice linkage, we can note several important barriers.

Value Problems　Much has been written about the motivations and expectations of managers and researchers. The researcher views theory as an end, whereas the manager sees it more as a means to some other practical end.[6] For example, a social psychologist may be content to know what factors lead to group cohesiveness. A manager, however, also wants to know how cohesiveness influences performance so that he or she can use the information to accomplish organizational goals.

Another important value or attitudinal issue has to do with what researchers and managers want regarding the relationship between them.[7] Studies have shown that neither group views theory and practice as separate functions. In fact, they both seek greater understanding.[8] The problem is to obtain this goal.

Interpersonal Barriers   Perhaps the most obvious and important interpersonal barrier separating managers and researchers is the different vocabulary that each party uses. Researchers, because of their concern for scientific validity, insist on precisely defined terms and carefully specified equations. Managers, as practical men and women, have less concern for precise terms and more interest in language that easily conveys meaning to people who must accomplish goals.

Other studies have revealed additional interpersonal barriers to knowledge transfer between researchers and practitioners. Both groups, for example, exhibit a distrust for one another, display a resistance to change, and entertain variations in goal orientation.[9]

External Barriers   Important socioeconomic factors surrounding the knowledge-flow system can slow down information flow between the research and management subsystems. For example, when the first users of developing knowledge are not allowed to reap benefits in proportion to the risk of early implementation, they do not have sufficient incentive to innovate.[10] This is often so in a planned, socialistic society. At the other extreme, if potential benefits are too great, ideas may be put into practice too soon and may have an excessively high failure rate.

The economic circumstances facing an organization often influence how receptive the management is to the theories of researchers. If prosperity exists, resources are available to pursue higher-risk ventures. On the other hand, organizations experiencing very depressed conditions may try new things out of distress and anxiety.[11] Thus knowledge transfer can be stimulated by extremely good or bad economic conditions.

Proposition 16.2

> The barriers that slow down the efficient and effective transfer of behavioral knowledge can be classified under a variety of headings. A few of the more important include value differences between researchers and managers, interpersonal problems, and outside factors (such as socioeconomic forces).

Linking Agents: Overcoming Barriers

If the knowledge transfer from research to practice is to be effective, *linking agents* must overcome or reduce the inhibiting effects of the barriers. These linking agents represent a number of individuals and organizations, as shown in Figure 16.2.

Because of the difficulties in effectively transferring management theory to practice, various organizations have been established with at least one of their objectives being to facilitate the transmission of basic knowledge to applied knowledge. We will describe and briefly discuss some of the most important of these organizations.

Professional schools, such as business and management schools, attempt to conduct research that is useful to practicing professionals. They also attempt to extend the basic research done in areas like psychology and sociology and to apply the knowledge gained to relevant management problems. Thus professional schools occupy a unique position as a linking agent between theory and practice.

Two other important linking agents are academic societies (such as the Academy of Management and the American Psychological and Sociological associations) and professional associations (such as the American Management Association). The Academy of Management,

Figure 16.2 Barriers and Linking Agents Relative to the Research-Practice Subsystems

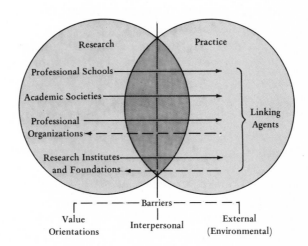

for example, often encourages, through its Institute for Administrative Research, research projects on applied problems that are sponsored by organizations. The American Management Association frequently supports research on questions relating to personnel and policy that are of concern to its membership. Research institutes and foundations also encourage various types of applied research that bring together researchers and practitioners with an interest in managerial problems.

In Figure 16.2, the two-way information flow of professional organizations and research institutes and foundations are included for a specific purpose. One unique characteristic of these organizations is that efforts are made to ensure joint involvement by researchers and managers. In professional organizations, membership of both groups is encouraged. Research institutes and foundations, on the other hand, serve as intermediaries to match funding available for problem-solving research.

Thus all the groups discussed perform important linking functions. Unfortunately, they are rarely completely successful. In recent years, a more promising alternative has developed.

Action Research

Action research is designed to "contribute both to the practical concerns of people . . . and to the goals of social science."[12] In current usage, action research has been visualized as involving researchers and practicing managers in all phases of research design and implementation.

Accuracy requires that, as French and Bell have pointed out, action research must be defined as both a process and an approach. "Action research is the process of systematically collecting research data about an ongoing system relative to some objective, goal or need of that system."[13] Information is fed back into the system, and actions are taken to alter the system and evaluate changes. Figure 16.3 illustrates action research. Notice that the executive perceives a problem and then consults a behavioral scientist. The consultant gathers data, formulates the problem, and gives feedback to the client. Together the consultant and client plan what is to be done, what action is to be taken. The data gathering then begins again, for the process is continuous.

Figure 16.3 The Process of Action Research

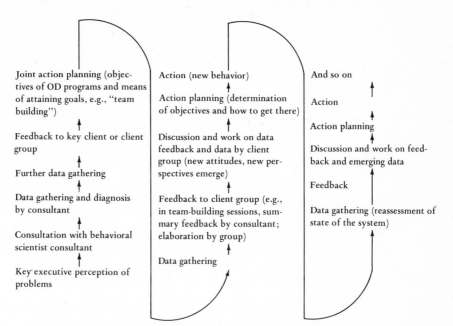

Source: Wendell French, "Organization Development Objectives, Assumptions, and Strategies," copyright © 1969 by the Regents of the University of California. Reprinted from *California Management Review,* volume XII, number 2 (Winter 1969), p. 26, by permission of the Regents.

Action research as an approach "is the application of the scientific method of fact-finding and experimentation to practical problems requiring action solutions and involving the collaboration and cooperation of scientists, practitioners, and laymen."[14] The distinguishing characteristic of action research is that it is not exclusively either pure or applied.

Pure research is oriented toward knowledge building for no specific or practical purpose other than that of acquiring the knowledge itself.[15] Applied research is directed toward solving specific problems. Action research gives equal attention to theory building and its application.[16] The advantages of this approach are a broadening of the researcher's horizons, a reduction of the gap between the view of the theorist and the practitioner, a sharpening of research strategies, and a more accurate selection of relevant problems for examination.[17] The concept of action research is based on the assumption that mutual dependence makes researchers more aware of the manager's problems of implementation, while managers become more aware of the researcher's interest in theory building.

To implement action research, however, a plan must be designed. This plan must consider a variety of factors, such as the problem under examination, the interests of researchers and managers, expected outputs, and so on. To illustrate one possible approach, see Table 16.1 (pages 414–415). The first two columns of the table are designed to highlight the orientations of researchers and managers with respect to important issues in the use of administrative knowledge. The third column pinpoints the major differences between the two groups, whereas the final column suggests action that can be taken to reduce the gap separating the groups.

The rows of the table specify key points on which some agreement must be developed if knowledge is to be transferred efficiently. These points progress through the research formulation, execution, and implementation stages. For example, the question of how one determines a relevant and significant problem for study is first itemized. The second issue relates to where one goes for data or evidence concerning the problem. Then, in accomplishing the research and developing knowledge, issues are raised about what characteristics valid theory must possess and how one proceeds in scientific inquiry. Finally, the results of the process are evaluated, and the question of applicability or practicality is confronted.

In other words, the important questions follow an input-process-output format. The input phase relates to problem definition and information generation. The process step involves analysis of the data generated. (It should be noted that *data* is used as a general term and may include theoretical concepts as well as perceptual phenomena.) The concluding phase involves evaluation of the output. Now we can refer to Table 16.1 to illustrate the proposed plan.

Looking across row 1, we find that the criteria by which a researcher evaluates a problem range from intellectual curiosity to the problem's potential interest for the researcher and his or her colleagues. A manager selects problems on the basis of their relevance to pressing issues for the organization and potential profitability. The involvement of both groups in the initial stages of research formulation ensures that both viewpoints are represented equally.

Row 2, the point of search, or source of information input, reveals similarities and differences. Both researchers and managers rely on observations of real phenomena. However, managers value unsystematically generated experience more than researchers do, whereas researchers place more value on existing research and theoretically oriented literature reporting research results. Since information generation is critical to the outcome, action research is valuable in encouraging systematic data collection and logical analysis of whatever source is utilized.

Row 3 relates to the values used in theory construction. Researchers value empiricism and logical precision, whereas managers look at payoffs and problems. However, mutual understanding is built through cooperative involvement. Researchers, using the methods of science, develop more systematic results, whereas the enthusiasm of practitioners is maintained because the emphasis is on problems with which they can identify. Mutual understanding becomes a reality, because inquiry is relevant to the goals of both groups. As row 4 illustrates, this cooperative orientation is implemented, not just mentioned as a desirable consequence.

Finally, row 5 illustrates how action research results in an expansion of the boundary of existing knowledge (the scientific requirement) while simultaneously addressing realistic concerns of people in organizations.

Thus action research emerges as more than just a means of gaining the commitment of researchers and managers and encouraging their interaction. It also is a practical method for developing meaningful superordinate goals—not an easy task in any setting.

Proposition 16.3	The knowledge-flow problem in organizational behavior is essentially one of linking researchers with practitioners. Action research emerges as an effective means of accomplishing such a linkage, since it acknowledges the problem and proposes means for overcoming it.

Ethical Issues in the Use of Behavioral Knowledge

The behavioral sciences, like the physical and life sciences, have progressed further technically than they have philosophically. Goods

Table 16.1   Comparative Analysis of Investigative Orientations of Researchers and Managers

	Researcher	Manager
1. Criterion of determination of problem significance	Observation of behavior and perceptual phenomena. Empirically based research literature for use in theoretical extensions.	Observation of behavior, recorded information, and perceptual phenomena. Personal experience.
2. Point of search for data evidence	Intellectual curiosity. Potential payoff in continuing research output. Current interest in research and applied communities.	Pressing nature of organizational problem. Potential usefulness in contributing to organizational efficiency and effectiveness.
3. Perceived characteristics of valid theory	Empirical validity. Logical precision. Potential usefulness.	Potential profitability of expected results. Ease of implementation. Relevancy of results to practical concerns.
4. Acceptability of rules of evidence	Structure of experimental design and model construction. Results capable of reproduction	Simplicity of application to specific problems. Ease of communication with groups concerned with implementing outcome.
5. Applicability or practicality of knowledge	Advancement of science. Visibility of results. Potential payoff to client system. Generalization of findings to varied environments.	Solution of problem. Applicability to relevant problems in the local environment.

The author wishes to express appreciation to Professor Paul Gordon of Indiana University, and to acknowledge his contribution in suggesting this matrix form as a means of highlighting the important elements of action research.

Differences in Orientation	Required Intervention
Incongruity in the value of historical, localized, and limited data. Differences in the evaluation of personal experience.	Improved training of managers in the methodology of scientific investigation.
Primary variance relates to the potential outcome of research and its impact on the organization.	Improved quality of interaction to acquaint both parties with the realities of research practice.
Profitability and implementation problems less of a concern to researchers.	Improved quality of interaction to improve mutual understanding.
Conventional rules of science and ability to communicate results to nonscientist occupy less attention in the researcher's mind.	Cooperative involvement by managers and researchers at all phases of the investigative process to ensure participation and commitment to the total research effort.
Researcher's scientific rigor as opposed to manager's interest in problem-solving potential.	Positive efforts on the part of both groups to build enthusiasm for action-oriented research design.

can be produced and distributed efficiently, but little systematic knowledge exists about the adverse effects of this efficiency on the quality of life.

Concern about the *ethical issues* involved in using behavioral knowledge and experimentation is growing. For example, the Department of Health and Human Services has formulated regulations to protect human subjects from physical and psychological risk in all scientific inquiry.

The problem of the behavioral sciences is that they have shown evidence of success—at least limited success. If behavioral knowledge had no potential for influence, no one would be concerned about how it is applied to real-world problems. Specifically, we can say several things about the advancement of behavioral science. Kelman has made the following points:

1. Our knowledge about the control of human behavior is increasing steadily and systematically.
2. Society is more receptive to information and misinformation on behavior control.
3. Behavioral scientists are becoming more respected and accepted in business, government, and other areas.[18]

These observations reinforce the increasing possibility of ethical problems for behavioral scientists. For example, in the area of motivation theory, the knowledge gained tends to be applied and has a greater likelihood of actually producing the expected behavioral outcomes. Because behavioral scientists are commanding greater respect, organizations are more likely to use the course of action that scientists recommend. Thus behavioral scientists, like biologists and physicists, must become increasingly concerned about how developing knowledge is used. The detached, unemotional, logical viewpoint that is so essential in knowledge development may require some tempering in the application of behavioral knowledge, since knowledge may be used for evil as well as for good.

More specifically, it is important to note that value issues become part of the scientist's daily work. In the simplest case, the end toward which the research is directed involves a value judgment. For example, an urban researcher makes a value choice when he or she chooses to study one form of municipal government rather than others. On another level, choosing the means to accomplish established goals involves ethical judgment. In the area of motivation theory, one may choose to redesign a job rather than to modify an individual.

Finally, evaluating the consequences of implemented decisions is characterized by value issues. For example, a manager may evaluate the introduction of a new production process according to its contribution to profit. A researcher might have done well to consider the associated direct and indirect effects that such technology might have on the environment, employment, and so on.[19]

The point of this discussion is not to argue that behavioral research should be constrained because of potential dangers in the use of developing knowledge. Instead, as behavioral science develops, it creates the possibility of a "science of power," which can be used for evil as well as for good.[20] What we know of group dynamics can be used to improve the quality of life in human organizations. At the same time, such knowledge can be—and has been—used for political indoctrination and for brainwashing prisoners of war. Behavioral scientists should recognize the possible uses of knowledge, even though they cannot control these uses. Pethia has shown clearly that values are inherent in the development of administrative theory.[21] The least we can do is to acknowledge their presence.

Proposition 16.4	Behavioral science is developing in both volume and sophistication. As a result, more attention must be given to the ethical implications of the use of the developing knowledge.

Why Managers Should Understand Knowledge Transfer

All managers confront problems that appear so unique they simply do not know where to begin in arriving at a solution. As behavioral science and management knowledge grow in volume and improves in quality, it is highly probable that someone, somewhere has looked already at the issue under discussion. How does a manager get access to the information?

It is extremely valuable for managers to know about the sources of behavioral data and the application of research. For example, *Organizational Dynamics,* published by the American Management Association, is devoted to transferring management theory to practice. Such publications are helpful to any manager. The transfer of good theory into sound practice would be eased and hastened if managers were aware of the linking agents designed to assist them. Moreover, if managers and researchers tried to understand and recognize the barriers separating them, great strides could be made in the application of well-planned, important behavioral research.

Prospects for the Future: Some Speculations

In this book, we have covered the state of the art of organizational behavior. Obviously, our coverage has been selective, but we have sought to make it as objective and as complete as possible. Our emphasis, as we noted in the beginning, has been on the research of the field.

We have attempted to summarize those topics expected to be of increasing importance in the future. The attention we gave to conflict and power relations, as well as our view of complex organizations from the technology-organization-environment perspective, were offered as needed complements to the purely interpersonal orientation.[22]

Future researchers and practitioners of organizational behavior will need to be more than people who have interpersonal skills. Important as these skills are, researchers and practitioners also require a broader and ever-increasing perspective of the whole as well as the parts. This book has attempted to present the essentials that prepare us all for the future. We must prepare on the basis of the best guide we have—our knowledge of the past. Those who will succeed are those who can master existing knowledge and can adapt to future demands. As Will and Ariel Durant so clearly argue: "History smiles at all attempts to force its flows into theoretical patterns or logical grooves; it plays havoc with our generalizations, breaks all our rules; history is baroque."[23]

Questions for Discussion

1. What is meant by the knowledge-flow system? By the knowledge-utilization process? List three ethical problems that can develop in behavioral science at the research and practice stages of the knowledge-flow system.
2. How is action research different from pure research? From applied research? What challenges do you think action research will face in the future?
3. Why, in your opinion, do researchers and managers experience difficulty communicating with one another? How can these problems be reduced?
4. In what ways can the economic environment influence knowledge transfer? Explain.
5. Why do you think society is becoming more concerned with the ethics of behavioral research? Do you think the concerns are valid? Give two examples of ethical issues in organizational behavior.

Case: The Little Red Schoolhouse

The Little Red Schoolhouse is a retail factory outlet for one of the large national manufacturers of children's clothes. It began in a small South Carolina town in an old service station located next to the manufacturer's primary plant facility. Initially, The Little Red Schoolhouse sold only factory seconds and slightly irregular clothing. The business is now located in four states, has twenty-six outlets, handles an entire line of the manufacturer's children's clothing, and relies on its factory-seconds business for less than half of its total revenue.

With growth, however, problems as well as opportunities and challenges have developed. The business has grown while at the same time experiencing higher operating costs and lower levels of profit. Hal Jackson, the owner and operator of the company recently attended a seminar at the state university on managing the small business. While on the campus, he became friends with Dr. Grace Becker, the university's director of management and organization development programs.

Jackson later wrote to Becker asking her if the university could help in solving the profitability crisis at The Little Red Schoolhouse. (His letter is shown in Exhibit 16.1.) It just so happens that Becker has been reading about action research and thinks this may be the perfect opportunity to give it a try.

Exhibit 16.1

The Little Red Schoolhouse, Inc.
P.O. Box 721
Plantville, USA

Dr. Grace Becker
Management and Organizational Development Center
State University
State University, USA

Dear Grace:

As you know, my business is better than ever, but my profits are dropping every year. Frankly, I do not understand how this can be. I believe I need some help. However, a small business such as mine is not like General Motors or IBM, and I am not sure you and your colleagues can understand my problems. The last thing I need is a theoretical analysis of my problem with no recommended solution.

Do you have, in the Management and Organizational Development Center, someone, or a group of persons, who could serve as consultants to a business like the Little Red Schoolhouse? The truth is that I am not at all sure what my problems are or how they might be solved. You could do me a great favor and save us both considerable energy if you would not refer an "ivory-tower researcher" to me. I won't understand such a person, and he or she is unlikely to understand me. If, however, you know of a possible approach to my problems, I would like very much to hear them. I hope you can help.

Sincerely,

Halbert O. Jackson
President

---

1. If you were Becker, how would you approach Jackson concerning the use of action research to solve his problems?
2. What advantages do you think The Little Red Schoolhouse could obtain from participating in such a program? What advantages would be acquired by the university personnel who participate?

Suggested Readings

Bowman, J. S. "Managerial Theory and Practice: The Transfer of Knowledge in Public Administration." *Public Administration Review* 38 (1978): 563–570.

Cass, L. C., and F. G. Zimmer, eds. *Man and Work in Society* (New York: Van Nostrand Reinhold, 1975).

Crowfoot, J. E., and M. A. Chesler. "Contemporary Perspectives on Planned Change: A Comparison." *Journal of Applied Behavioral Science* 10 (1974): 278–303.

Duncan, W. J. "Professional Education and the Liberating Tradition: An Action Alternative." *Liberal Education* 43 (1977): 453–461.

Dunn, W. N., and F. W. Swierczek. "Planned Organizational Change: Toward Grounded Theory." *Journal of Applied Behavioral Science* 13 (1977): 135–157.

Frohman, M. A., M. Sashkin, and M. J. Kavanagh. "Action-Research as Applied to Organizational Development." *Organization and Administrative Sciences* 7 (1976): 129–161.

Heisler, W. J., and J. W. Houck, eds. *A Matter of Dignity* (Notre Dame, Ind.: University of Notre Dame Press, 1977).

Lingwood, D. A. "A Study of Research Utilization in the U.S. Forest Service." In *Technology Transfer in Research and Development.* Eds. J. A. Jolly and J. W. Creighton. Monterey, Calif.: Naval Postgraduate School, 1975), pp. 37–48.

Weick, K. E. "Educational Organizations as Loosely Coupled Systems." *Administrative Science Quarterly* 21 (1976): 1–19.

Chapter Notes

Chapter 1

1. "The Dissatisfaction at AT&T," *Business Week,* June 25, 1979, pp. 91, 94, 96.
2. Adapted from Walter R. Nord, *Concepts and Controversy in Organizational Behavior* (Pacific Palisades, Calif.: Goodyear, 1972), pp. xiii–xiv.
3. See Fred Massarik and Bruce E. Krueger, "Through the Labyrinth: An Approach to Reading in Behavioral Science," *California Management Review*, 13: 72–73.
4. See A. H. Maslow, *Motivation and Personality* (New York: Harper & Row, (1954); and Frederick Herzberg, *Work and the Nature of Man* (New York: World, 1966).
5. J. Fichter, *Sociology* (Chicago: University of Chicago Press, 1957), p. 1.
6. See Max Weber, "Bureaucracy," in *From Max Weber*, eds. H. Gerth and C. W. Miils (New York: Oxford University Press, 1946).
7. Howard M. F. Rush, "What Is Behavioral Science?" *Conference Board Record* 2 (September 1965): 35–41.
8. Stanley Young, "Research Activities and Interests of the Academy of Management," *Academy of Management Journal* 10 (1967): 205–207.
9. Harold M. Rush and Walter S. Wikstrom, "The Reception of Behavioral Science in Industry," *Conference Board Record* 6 (September 1969): 45–54.
10. Marvin D. Dunnette and Zita Marie Brown, "Behavioral Science Research and the Conduct of Business," *Academy of Management Journal* 11 (1968): 177.
11. James D. Thompson, *Organizations in Action* (New York: McGraw-Hill, 1967), p. 4.
12. George H. Rice, Jr., and Dean W. Bishoprick, *Conceptual Models of Organizations* (New York: Appleton-Century-Crofts, 1971), p. 45.
13. Fremont E. Kast and James E. Rosenzweig, "General Systems Theory: Applications for Organization and Management," *Academy of Management Journal* 15 (1972): 450.
14. Fritz J. Roethlisberger, "Contributions of the Behavioral Sciences to a General Theory of Management," in *Toward a Unified Theory of Management,* ed. Harold Koontz (New York: McGraw-Hill, 1964), p. 42.
15. See Peter M. Blau, *The Dynamics of Bureaucracy,* rev. ed. (Chicago: University of Chicago Press, 1963), chap. 1.

16. Warren G. Bennis, *Organizational Development: Its Nature, Origins, and Prospects* (Reading, Mass.: Addison-Wesley, 1969), p. 20.

17. John P. Anderson and W. Jack Duncan, "The Scientific Significance of the Paradox in Administrative Theory," *Management International Review* 17 (August 1977): 99–106.

18. See Paul R. Lawrence and Jay W. Lorsch, *Organization and Environment* (Homewood, Ill.: Irwin, 1969).

Chapter 2

1. *The Republic of Plato,* trans. Francis M. Crawford (New York: Oxford University Press, 1945), pp. 306–307.

2. D. K. Hart and W. G. Scott, "The Optimal Image of Man for Systems Theory," *Academy of Management Journal* 15 (1972), p. 535.

3. Hart and Scott attribute the first three factors to Freud's analysis and add the fourth as their own. See Hart and Scott, "The Optimal Image of Man for Systems Theory."

4. A detailed treatment of the implications is presented in D. E. McFarland and W. J. Duncan, "Humanism and Management Philosophy: A Dialectical View," paper presented to the annual meeting of The Institute for Management Science, October 1979, Milwaukee, Wisconsin.

5. R. P. Calhoon, "Niccolo Machiavelli and the Twentieth-Century Administrator," *Academy of Management Journal* 12 (1969), 210.

6. Gary R. Gemmill and W. J. Heisler, "Machiavellianism as a Factor in Managerial Job Stress, Job Satisfaction, and Upward Mobility," *Academy of Management Journal* 15 (1972): 51–61.

7. Warren Bennis, *Beyond Bureaucracy* (New York: McGraw-Hill, 1966), p. 66.

8. Julian Freund, *The Sociology of Max Weber* (New York: Random House, 1968), p. 234.

9. See Charles Perrow, *Complex Organizations* (Glenview, Ill.: Scott, Foresman, 1972), chap. 1; and Charles Perrow, *Organizational Analysis: A Sociological View* (Belmont, Calif.: Wadsworth, 1970), chap. 1.

10. A. M. Henderson and Talcott Parsons, eds. and trans., *Max Weber: The Theory of Social and Economic Organization* (New York: Free Press, 1947), p. 328.

11. L. F. Urwick, "Papers on the Science of Administration," *Academy of Management Journal* 13 (1970): 362.

12. Luther Gulick and L. F. Urwick, eds., *Papers on the Science of Administration* (New York: Augustus M. Kelley, 1969), p. 119.

13. H. B. Meyers, "A Hell of a Different Way to Run a Railroad," *Fortune,* September 1963, pp. 101–110;, and H. B. Meyers, "The Sweet, Secret World of Forrest Mars," *Fortune,* May 1967, pp. 154–157 ff.

14. Frederick W. Taylor, *Principles of Scientific Management* (New York: Harper and Brothers, 1914), p. 7.

15. Ibid., pp. 128–129.

16. William M. Fox, "Scientific Management: Taylorism," in *The Encyclopedia of Management,* ed. Carl Heyel (New York: Reinhold, 1963), pp. 876–877.

17. W. Jack Duncan, "Engineers and Psychologists of the Scientific Management Period," *Southern Journal of Business* 6 (January 1971): 30–40.

18. Walter Dill Scott, *Increasing Human Efficiency in Business* (New York: Macmillan, 1911), p. 143.

19. Hugo Munsterberg, *Psychology and Industrial Efficiency in Business* (Boston: Houghton Mifflin, 1913), pp. 29–36.

20. See Peter M. Blau, *The Dynamics of Bureaucracy* (Chicago: University of Chicago Press, 1963).

21. Warren G. Bennis, ed., *Changing Organizations* (New York: McGraw-Hill, 1966), pp. 12–13.

22. Peter Drucker, *The Age of Discontinuity* (New York: Harper & Row, 1968), p. 290.

23. T. E. Stephenson, "The Longevity of Classical Theory," *Management International Review* 8 (November 1968): 78–79.

24. Herbert A. Simon, *Administrative Behavior,* 3rd ed. (New York: Macmillan, 1976), p. 240.

25. V. Subramaniam, "The Classical Organization Theory and Its Critics," *Public Administration* 21 (Winter 1966): 436–440.

26. Daniel A. Wren, *The Evolution of Management Thought,* 2nd ed. (New York: Wiley, 1979), p. 325.

27. Lyndal Urwick, *Golden Book of Management* (London: Newman Neame, 1956), p. 133.

28. John F. Mee, "Management Teaching in Historical Perspective," *Southern Journal of Business* 7 (May 1972): 25.

29. W. Jack Duncan and C. Ray Gullett, "Henry Sturgis Dennison: The Manager and the Social Critic," *Journal of Business Research* 2 (Fall 1974): 134.

30. Fritz J. Roethlisberger and William J. Dickson, *Management and the Worker* (Cambridge, Mass.: Harvard University Press, 1939) pp. 86–89.

31. This report of the Hawthorne Studies has been developed from a variety of sources. Because of overlaps and similarities, specific citations are impractical. However, the sources consulted include Roethlisberger and Dickson, *Management and the Worker;* Elton Mayo, *The Human Problems of an Industrial Civilization* (New York: Macmillan, 1933); Elton Mayo, *The Social Problems of an Industrial Civilization* (Boston: Division of Research, Harvard Graduate School of Business Administration, 1945); and T. N. Whitehead, *The Industrial Worker* (Cambridge, Mass.: Harvard University Press, 1938), vols. 1 and 2.

32. Daniel Bell, *Work and Its Discontents* (Boston: Beacon Press, 1956), p. 25.

33. See Barnard Sarachek, "Elton Mayo's Social Psychology and Human Relations," *Academy of Management Journal* 11 (1968): 189–197.

34. Henry A. Landsberger, *Hawthorne Revisited* (Ithaca, N.Y.: Cornell Studies in Industrial and Labor Relations, 1958), IX, 30–35.

35. Alex Carey, "The Hawthorne Studies: A Radical Criticism," *American Sociological Review* 32 (1967): 403–416.

36. J. M. Sheppard, "On Alex Carey's Radical Criticism of the Hawthorne Studies," *Academy of Management Journal* 14 (1971): 23–32.

37. "Famous Firsts: Workers Can Be a Team Too," *Business Week,* May 25, 1963, pp. 49–50.

38. See John G. Kemeny, *A Philosopher Looks at Science* (Princeton, N.J.: D. Van Nostrand, 1959), pp. 247–252; Herbert Feigl, "The Scientific Outlook" in *Readings in the Philosophy of Science,* eds. Herbert Feigl and May Brodbeck (New York: Appleton-Century-Crofts, 1953), pp. 8–20; and Barnard Berelson and Gary A. Steiner, *Human Behavior,* shorter ed. (New York: Harcourt, Brace, 1967), p. 5.

Chapter 3

1. William Litzinger and Thomas E. Schaefer, "Perspective: Management Philosophy Enigma," *Academy of Mangement Journal* 9 (1966): 340–341.

2. May Brodbeck, "The Nature and Function of the Philosophy of Science," in *Readings in the Philosophy of Science,* ed. Herbert Feigl and May Brodbeck (New York: Appleton-Century-Crofts, 1953), p. 5.

3. Arthur Pap, *An Introduction to the Philosophy of Science* (New York: Free Press, 1962), p. 3.

4. Herbert A. Simon, *Administrative Behavior*, 3rd ed. (New York: Macmillan, 1976), p. 249.

5. Donald Butler, *Four Philosophies,* 3rd ed. (New York: Harper & Row, 1968), p. 23.

6. C. West Churchman, *Prediction and Optimal Decision* (Englewood Cliffs, N.J.: Prentice-Hall, 1961), p. 22.

7. Abraham Maslow, *Motivation and Personality,* 2nd ed. (New York: Harper & Row, 1970), chap. 5.

8. This discussion is based on errors presented in D. T. Campbell and J. C. Stanley, *Experimental and Quasi-experimental Designs for Research* (Chicago: Rand McNally, 1963).

9. Fred N. Kerlinger, *Foundations of Behavioral Research,* 2nd ed. (New York: Holt, Rinehart and Winston, 1973), p. 444.

10. See Donald Campbell, "Factors Relevant to the Validity of Experiments in Social Settings," *Psychological Bulletin* 54 (1957): 297–317.

11. See Edwin G. Boring, "The Nature and History of Experimental Control," *American Journal of Psychology* 67 (1964): 573–589.

12. Richard L. Solomon, "An Extension of Control Group Design," *Psychological Bulletin* 46 (1949): 137–150.

13. Campbell, "Factors Relevant to the Validity of Experiments," p. 303.

14. Charles L. Hulin and Milton R. Blood, "Job Enlargement, Individual Differences and Worker Responses," *Psychological Bulletin* 67 (1968): 50; and William E. Reif and Fred Luthans, "Does Job Enrichment Really Pay Off?" *California Management Review* 15 (Fall 1972): 36.

15. F. A. Hayek, "Scientism and the Study of Society—Part 2," *Economica* 9 (N.S.) (1943): 49.

16. Ernest Dale, *The Great Organizers* (New York: McGraw-Hill, 1960), pp. 7–12.

17. Winston Oberg, "Cross-Cultural Perspectives on Management Principles," *Academy of Management Journal* 6 (1963): 142.

18. See Kerlinger, *Foundations of Behavioral Research,* chaps. 20–22.

19. K. E. Weick, "Laboratory Experimentation with Organizations: A Reappraisal," *Academy of Management Review* 2 (1977): 123–128.

20. E. E. Lawler III, "Adaptive Experiments: An Approach to Organizational Behavior Research," *Academy of Management Review* 2 (1977): 576–585.

21. M. G. Evans, "Opportunistic Organizational Research: The Role of Patch-up Designs," *Academy of Management Journal* 18 (1975): 108.

22. Julian L. Simon, *Basic Research Methods in Social Science* (New York: Random House, 1969), chap. 16.

23. J. S. Armstrong and T. S. Overton, "Estimating Nonresponse Bias in Mail Surveys," *Journal of Marketing Research* 14 (1977): 397–402; W. J. Duncan, "Mail Questionnaires in Survey Research: A Review of Response Inducement Techniques," *Journal of Management* 5 (1979): 39–55; and A. S. Linsky, "Stimulating Responses to Mail Surveys," *Public Opinion Quarterly* 39 (1975): 82–101.

24. J. Guilford, *Psychometric Methods,* 2nd ed. (New York: McGraw-Hill 1954), pp. 11–12; and Warren S. Torgerson, *Theory and Method of Scaling* (New York: Wiley, 1958), chaps. 1–2.

25. Donald S. Tull and Gerald S. Albaum, *Survey Research* (New York: Intext, 1973), p. 82.

26. S. S. Stevens, "On the Theory of Scales of Measurement," *Science* 103 (1946): 677–680.

27. Tull and Albaum, *Survey Research,* p. 91.

Chapter 4

1. Robert M. Liebert and Michael D. Spiegler, *Personality* (Homewood, Ill.: Dorsey Press, 1970), pp. 39–40.

2. Ruth L. Monroe, *Schools of Psychoanalytical Thought* (New York: Dryden Press, 1955), pp. 90–93; and Calvin S. Hall, *A Primer of Freudian Psychology* (New York: New American Library, 1955), p. 85.

3. See Sigmund Freud, "The Metapsychology of Instincts, Repressions, and the Unconscious," in *Collected Papers of Sigmund Freud,* ed. Ernest Jones (New York: Basic Books, 1959).

4. J. P. Guilford, *Personality* (New York: McGraw-Hill, 1959), p. 6.

5. See R. B. Cattell, *The Scientific Analysis of Personality* (Baltimore: Penguin, 1965).

6. Roger J. Williams, "The Biological Approach to the Study of Personality," in *Theories of Psychopathology,* ed. T. Milton (Philadelphia: Saunders, 1967), p. 22.

7. John B. Miner, *The Management Process,* 2nd ed. (New York: Macmillan, 1978), p. 616.

8. Liebert and Spiegler, *Personality,* p. 214.

9. Colin Wilson, *New Pathways in Psychology: Maslow and the Post-Freudian Revolution* (New York: New American Library, 1972), pp. 1–2.

10. Abraham Maslow, *Motivation and Personality,* 2nd ed. (New York: Harper & Row, 1970), chap. 5.

11. A. H. Maslow, "Self-Actualizing People," in *The World of Psychology,* vol. 2, ed. G. B. Levitas, (New York: George Braziller, 1963), p. 537.

12. C. P. Alderfer, "A New Theory of Human Needs," *Organizational Behavior and Human Performance* 4 (1969): 142–175; and W. H. Mobley and E. A. Locke, "The Relationship of Value Importance to Satisfaction," *Organizational Behavior and Human Performance* 5 (1970): 463–483.

13. Edward E. Lawler III and J. Lloyd Suttle, "A Causal Correlational Test of the Need Hierarchy Concept," *Organizational Behavior and Human Performance* 7 (1972): 265–287.

14. Clayton P. Alderfer, *Existence, Relatedness, and Growth* (New York: Free Press, 1972), p. 124.

15. David C. McClelland, "Toward a Theory of Motive Acquisition," *American Psychologist* 20 (1965): 322.

16. David C. McClelland, *The Achieving Society* (Princeton, N.J.: D. Van Nostrand, 1961), p. 102.

17. W. Edgar Vinacke, *Foundations of Psychology* (New York: Van Nostrand Reinhold, 1968), pp. 20–21.

18. Harold J. Leavitt, *Management Psychology,* 4th ed. (Chicago: University of Chicago Press, 1964).

19. See Kurt Lewin, *A Dynamic Theory of Personality: Selected Papers* (New York: McGraw-Hill, 1935).

20. William E. Reif and Fred Luthans, "Does Job Enrichment Really Pay Off?" *California Management Review* 15 (Fall 1972): 36.

21. D. O. Hebb, "The Mammal and His Environment," *American Journal of Psychiatry* (1950): 830.

22. Story related in Wilson, *New Pathways in Psychology,* pp. 126–127.

23. Theodosius Dobzhansky, *Mankind Evolving: The Evolution of the Human Species* (New Haven, Conn.: Yale University Press, 1962), p. 41.

24. Edward B. Tylor, *Primitive Culture,* 3rd English ed. (London: Murray, 1891), p. 1.

25. Bernard Berelson and Gary A. Steiner, *Human Behavior,* shorter ed. (New York: Harcourt, Brace, 1967), p. 15.

26. See Blair I. Kolasa, *Introduction to Behavioral Science for Business* (New York: Wiley, 1969), pp. 303–304.

27. Barry M. Richman, "Significance of Cultural Variables," *Academy of Management Journal* 8 (1965): 292–308.

28. See M. H. Segal, D. I. Campbell, and M. J. Herskovits, *The Influence of Culture on Visual Perception* (Indianapolis: Bobbs-Merrill, 1966).

29. Harry Levenson, *The Exceptional Executive: A Psychological Conception* (Cambridge, Mass.: Harvard University Press, 1968).

30. Max Weber, *The Protestant Ethic and the Spirit of Capitalism* (London: George Allen and Unwin, 1930).

31. *Youth in Turmoil* (New York: Time-Life Books, 1969), pp. 31–33.
32. Daniel Yankelovich and Ruth Clark, "College and Noncollege Youth Values," *Change* 6 (September 1974): 45.
33. James V. McConnell, "The College Student 1984: Implications for Booksellers and Publishers," *College Store Journal* 12 (October 1978): 61.
34. Leonard I. Pearlin and Melvin I. Kohn, "Social Class Occupation, and Parental Values: A Cross-national Study," *American Sociological Review* 31 (1966): 466–479.
35. Melvin I. Kohn and Carmi Schooler, "Class, Occupation, and Orientation," *American Sociological Review* 34 (1969): 659–678.
36. Talcott Parsons and Edward Shils, eds., *Toward a General Theory of Action* (Cambridge, Mass.: Harvard University Press, 1959), pp. 76–77.
37. Louis A. Zurcher, Jr., Arnold Meadow, and Susan Lee Zurcher, "Value Orientation, Role Conflict and Alienation from Work," *American Sociological Review* 30 (1965): 539–549.
38. R. T. La Piere, "Attitudes vs. Action," *Social Forces* 13 (1934): 233–234.
39. R. D. Minard, "Race Relationships in the Pocahontas Coal Field," *Journal of Social Issues* 8 (1952): 29–44.
40. See Muzfer Sherif and C. I. Hovland, *Social Judgment* (New Haven, Conn.: Yale University Press, 1956).
41. C. R. Tittle and R. J. Hill, "Attitude Measurement and Prediction of Behavior," *Sociometry* 30 (1967): 199–213.
42. Adapted from Barry Collins, *Social Psychology* (Reading, Mass.: Addison-Wesley, 1970), pp. 82–86.
43. M. A. Hewgill and G. F. Miller, "Source Credibility and Response to Fear Arousing Communication," *Speech Monographs,* no. 32 (1965): 95–100.
44. Leonard L. Mitnick and Elliot McGinnies, "Influencing Ethnocentrism in Small Discussion Group through a Film Communication," *Journal of Abnormal and Social Psychology* 56 (1968): 82–90; and W. Jack Duncan, "Transferring Management Theory to Practice," *Academy of Management Journal* 17 (1974): 724–738.

Chapter 5

1. A. W. Combs, Anne C. Richards, and Fred Richards, *Perceptual Psychology* (New York: Harper & Row, 1976), pp. 16–18.
2. A. T. Welford and L. Houssiados, *Contemporary Problems in Perception* (London: Taylor and Francis, 1970), pp. 5–8.
3. Lewis R. Benton, "The Many Faces of Conflict: How Differences in Perception Causes Differences in Opinion," *Supervisory Management* 43 (March 1970): 7–10.
4. D. C. Dearborn and H. A. Simon, "Selective Perception: A Note on Departmental Identification of Executives," *Sociometry* 21 (1958): 140–144.
5. Floyd H. Allport, *Theories of Perception and the Concept of Structure* (New York: Wiley, 1955), p. 313.

6. Mason Haire, E. E. Chiselli, and Lyman Porter, *Managerial Thinking: An International Study* (New York: Wiley, 1966), p. 16.

7. Lyman W. Porter, "Differential Self-Perceptions of Management Personnel and Line Workers," *Journal of Applied Psychology* 42 (1958): 105–108.

8. John Senger, "Manager's Perception of Subordinates' Competence as a Function of Personal Value Orientations," *Academy of Management Journal* 14 (1971): 422–423.

9. Sheldon S. Zalkind and Timothy W. Costello, "Perception: Some Recent Research and Implications for Administrators," *Administrative Science Quarterly* 6 (1962): 218–221.

10. Bernard Berelson and Gary A. Steiner, *Human Behavior,* shorter ed. (New York: Harcourt, Brace, 1967), p. 158.

11. John Mihalasky and Hugh C. Sherwood, "Dollars May Flow from the Sixth Sense," *Nation's Business* 59 (April 1971): 64–66.

12. Ivan P. Pavlov, *Conditional Reflexes* (New York: Oxford University Press, 1927).

13. B. F. Skinner, *About Behaviorism* (New York: Knopf, 1974), chap. 4.

14. T. George Harris, "All the World's a Box," *Psychology Today* 5 (January 1971): 34.

15. P. S. Hundal, "Knowledge of Performance as an Incentive in Repetitive Industrial Work," *Journal of Applied Psychology* 53 (1969): 224–226.

16. Henry Morlock, "The Effect of Outcome Desirability on Information Required for Decisions," *Behavioral Science* 12 (1967): 296–300.

17. Joan E. Sieber and John T. Lanzetta, "Conflict and Conceptual Structure as Determinants of Decision Maker Behavior," *Journal of Personality* 32 (1964): 622–641.

18. Ibid., pp. 623–626.

19. Ernest H. Weinwurm, "Preliminaries on the Decision Making Process," *Management International Review* 17 (April 1968): 116.

20. See Clyde Hendrick, Judson Mills, and Charles A. Kiesler, "Decision Time as a Function of the Number and Complexity of Equally Attractive Alternatives," *Journal of Personality and Social Psychology* 8 (1968): 313–318.

21. Leon Festinger, *A Theory of Cognitive Dissonance* (Stanford, Calif.: Stanford University Press, 1957).

22. Sadaomi Oshipawa, "Can Cognitive Dissonance Theory Explain Consumer Behavior?" *Journal of Marketing* 33 (October 1969): 44–49; and Sadaomi Oshipawa, "The Measurement of Cognitive Dissonance: Some Experimental Findings," *Journal of Marketing* 36 (January 1972): 64–67.

23. Jack W. Brehm and Arthur R. Cohen, *Explorations in Cognitive Dissonance* (New York: Wiley, 1962), pp. 306–308.

24. Jack W. Brehm and Arthur R. Cohen, "Re-evaluation of Choice Alternatives as a Function of Their Number and Qualitative Similarity," *Journal of Abnormal and Social Psychology* 59 (1959): 372–378.

25. Robert E. Knox and James A. Inkster, "Post-Decision Dissonance at Post Time," *Journal of Personality and Social Psychology* 8 (1968): 319–322.

26. James G. March and Herbert A. Simon, *Organizations* (New York: Wiley, 1958), pp. 137–138.

27. Richard M. Cyert and James G. March, *A Behavioral Theory of the Firm* (Englewood Cliffs, N.J.: Prentice-Hall, 1963), p. 10; and March and Simon, *Organizations.*

28. Rex V. Brown, "Do Managers Find Decision Theory Useful?" *Harvard Business Review* 48 (May/June 1970): 79.

29. Eugene E. Carter, "The Behavioral Theory of the Firm and Top-Level Corporate Decisions," *Administrative Science Quarterly* 16 (1971): 413–428.

30. Cyert and March, *A Behavioral Theory of the Firm*, pp. 146–147.

31. John E. Felming, "Study of a Business Decision," *California Management Review* 9 (Winter 1966): 51–56.

Chapter 6

1. M. R. Jones, ed., *Nebraska Symposium on Motivation* (Lincoln, Neb.: University of Nebraska Press, 1955), p. 14.

2. Victor H. Vroom, *Work and Motivation* (New York: Wiley, 1964), p. 184; and George Strauss, "Human Relations—1968 Style," *Industrial Relations* (1968): 24.

3. See Donald P. Schwab and Larry L. Cummings, "Theories of Performance and Satisfaction: A Review," *Industrial Relations* 9 (1970): 408–430; and George Strauss, "Job Satisfaction, Motivation, and Job Redesign," in George Strauss et al., *Organizational Behavior* (Madison, Wis.: Industrial Relations Research Association, 1974), p. 35.

4. Dennis W. Organ, "A Reappraisal and Reinterpretation of the Satisfaction-Causes-Performance Hypothesis," *Academy of Management Review* 2 (1977): 46–53.

5. See Chester I. Barnard, *The Functions of the Executive* (Cambridge, Mass.: Harvard University Press, 1938); and Herbert A. Simon, *Administrative Behavior,* 3rd ed. (New York: Macmillan, 1976).

6. Vroom, *Work and Motivation;* Victor H. Vroom, "Organizational Choice: A Study of Pre- and Post-Decision Processes," *Organizational Behavior and Human Performance* 2 (1966): 212–225; and John P. Campbell et al., *Managerial Behavior, Performance, and Effectiveness* (New York: McGraw-Hill, 1970), p. 343.

7. See H. G. Heneman and Donald P. Schwab, "Evaluation of Research on Expectancy Theory Predictions of Employee Performance," *Organizational Behavior and Human Performance* 8 (1972): 1–9.

8. J. Stacy Adams, "Toward an Understanding of Inequity," *Journal of Abnormal and Social Psychology* 66 (1963): 422–436; and Paul S. Goodman and Abraham Friedman, "An Examination of Adam's Theory of Inequity," *Administrative Science Quarterly* 16 (1971): 271–288.

9. See B. F. Skinner, "Beyond Freedom and Dignity," *Psychology Today* 4 (August 1971): 26–29.

10. Stephen F. Jablonsky and David L. DeVries, "Operant Conditioning Principles Extrapolated to the Theory of Management," *Organizational Behavior and Human Performance* 7 (1972): 340–358.

11. "New Tool: Reinforcement for Good Work," *Business Week,* December 18, 1971, pp. 68–69.

12. E. R. Hilgard, *Introduction to Psychology,* 3rd ed. (New York: Harcourt, Brace, 1962), p. 614.

13. Fred Luthans and Robert Kreitner, "The Role of Punishment in Organizational Behavior Modification (OB Mod)," *Public Personnel Management* 2 (May/June 1973): 156–161.

14. D. N. Robinson, "Therapies: A Clear and Present Danger," *American Psychologist* 28 (1973): 129–133.

15. Herbert G. Heneman III and Donald P. Schwab, "Evaluation of Research on Expectancy Predictions of Employee Behavior," *Psychological Bulletin* 78 (1972): 1–9.

16. T. R. Mitchell and B. W. Knuden, "Instrumentality Theory of Predictions of Students' Attitudes Toward Business and Their Choice of Business as an Occupation," *Academy of Management Journal* 16 (1973): 41–52; and T. R. Mitchell and D. Albright, "Expectancy Theory Predictions of the Satisfaction, Effort, Performance, and Retention of Naval Aviation Officers," *Organizational Behavior and Human Performance* 8 (1972): 1–20.

17. Edward E. Lawler III, "The Mythology of Management Compensation," *California Management Review* 9 (Fall 1966): 11–22; and Donald P. Schwab and Larry L. Cummings, "Theories of Performance and Satisfaction: A Review," *Industrial Relations* 9 (1970): 420–422.

18. Frederick H. Herzberg, Bernard M. Mausner, and Barbara Snyderman, *The Motivation to Work* (New York: Wiley, 1959), p. 12.

19. Frederick Herzberg, "One More Time: How Do You Motivate Employees?" *Harvard Business Review* 46 (January-February 1968): 53–62.

20. Jack E. Powers, "Job Enrichment: How One Company Overcame the Obstacles," *Personnel* 49 (May/June 1972): 18.

21. L. K. Waters, "An Empirical Test of Five Versions of the Two-Factor Theory of Job Satisfaction," *Organizational Behavior and Human Performance* 7 (1972): 23.

22. Charles L. Hulin and Milton R. Blood, "Job Enlargement, Individual Differences and Worker Responses," *Psychological Bulletin* 69 (1968): 41–55; and William E. Reif and Fred Luthans, "Does Job Enrichment Really Pay Off?" *California Management Review* 15 (Fall 1972): 30–37.

23. L. K. Waters, "An Empirical Test of Five Versions of the Two-Factor Theory of Job Satisfaction," *Organizational Behavior and Human Performance* 7 (1972): 19.

24. R. C. Birney, "Research on the Achievement Motive," in *Handbook of Personality Theory and Research,* eds. E. F. Borgotta and W. W. Lambert (Chicago: Rand McNally, 1968), p. 878.

25. D. C. McClelland, "Toward a Theory of Motive Acquisition," *American Psychologist* 16 (May 1965): 322.

Chapter 7

1. Max Skousen, "Scorekeeping Is the Key to Motivation," *Machine Design*, 14 December 1972, p. 134.

2. Muzafer and Carolyn Sherif, *Groups in Harmony and Tension: An Integration of Studies on Intergroup Relations* (New York: Octagon, 1966), pp. 186–211.

3. Robin M. Williams, Jr., *American Society*, 3rd ed. (New York: Knopf, 1970), pp. 519–520. See also R. H. Hall, J. E. Haas, and N. J. Johnson, "Organizational Size, Complexity, and Formalization," *American Sociological Review* 32 (1967): 903–912.

4. Howard Becker and Ruth Useem, "Sociological Analysis of the Dyad," *American Sociological Review* 2 (1942): 13–26.

5. Theodore Caplow, "A Theory of Coalitions in the Triad," *American Sociological Review* 21 (1959): 489.

6. Charles N. Greene, "Relationships Among Role Accuracy, Compliance, Performance Evaluation, and Satisfaction in Managerial Dyads," *Academy of Management Journal* 15 (1972): 205–215.

7. George Simmel, "The Significance of Numbers in Social Life," in *Small Groups—Studies in Social Interaction*, eds. A. Paul Hare et al. (New York: McGraw-Hill, 1966), pp. 9–15.

8. Theodore Caplow, *Two Against One: Coalitions in Triads* (Englewood Cliffs, N.J.: Prentice-Hall, 1968), p. 489.

9. Adapted from Caplow, *Two Against One*, p. 7.

10. See Raymond V. Lesikar, *Business Communication*, 4th ed. (Homewood, Ill.: Irwin, 1980).

11. W. G. Savage, "Sure, Listen: But Watch Their Gestures Too," *Administrative Management Society Report* (August 1972), p. 33.

12. D. M. Ehat and M. Schnapper, "What Your Employees' Non-verbal Cues Are Telling You," *Administrative Management* 20 (May 1974): 64–65.

13. E. T. Bush, "Clothing Choices of Successful and of Aspiring College Administrators," *Proceedings of the Southeast Division of the American Institute of Decision Sciences* (1976): 239–240.

14. H. J. Leavitt, "Some Effects of Certain Communication Patterns on Group Performance," *Journal of Abnormal and Social Psychology* 46 (1951): 38–50.

15. See summary in G. M. Goldhaber, *Organizational Communication* (Dubuque, Iowa: William C. Brown, 1974), p. 221.

16. Thomas E. Lasswell, "The Perception of Social Status," *Sociology and Social Research* 45 (1961): 170.

17. Adapted from Chester I. Barnard, "Functions and Pathology of Status Systems in Formal Organizations," in *Industry and Society*, ed. William F. Whyte (New York: McGraw-Hill, 1946), pp. 53–58.

18. William F. Whyte, *Street Corner Society* (Chicago: University of Chicago Press, 1943), pp. 17–18.

19. George C. Homans, *The Human Group* (New York: Harcourt, Brace, 1950), pp. 140–143.

20. E. P. Hollander, "Conformity, Status, and Idiosyncrasy Credits," *Psychological Bulletin* 60 (1958): 117–127.

21. E. P. Hollander, "Competence and Conformity in the Acceptance of Influence," *Journal of Abnormal and Social Psychology* 56 (1961): 365–369.

22. See M. H. Fisek and Richard Ofshe, "The Process of Status Evolution," *Sociometry* 33 (1970): 327–343; and Desmond Graves, "Reported Communica-

tion Ratios and Informal Status in Managerial Work Groups," *Human Relations* 25 (1972): 160–165.

23. D. L. Westby, "The Career Experience of the Symphony Musician," *Social Forces* 38 (1969): 225–228.

24. G. I. Susman, "The Concept of Status Congruence as a Basis to Predict Talk Allocations in Autonomous Work Groups," *Administrative Science Quarterly* 15 (1979): 164–166.

25. Leonard Berkowitz, "Social Motivation," in *Handbook of Social Psychology*, eds. G. Lindsey and E. Aronson (Reading, Mass.: Addison-Wesley, 1964), III: 84–85.

26. S. Z. Nagi, "Status Profile and Reactions to Status Threats," *American Sociological Review* 28 (1963): 441.

Chapter 8

1. E. P. Hollander, "Conformity, Status, and Idiosyncrasy Credit," *Psychological Review* 65 (1958): 118.

2. C. A. Kiesler and S. B. Kiesler, *Conformity* (Reading, Mass.: Addison-Wesley, 1969), p. 2.

3. Ibid., pp. 2–3.

4. Louis A. Dow and W. Jack Duncan, "Economic Neoliberalism: A Behavioral View of the Sportsmanship Assumption," *American Journal of Economics and Sociology* 33 (1974): 351–365.

5. Muzafer Sherif, "A Study of Some Social Factors in Perception," *Archives of Psychology,* no. 187 (1935).

6. S. E. Asch, "Effects of Group Pressure upon the Modification and Distortions of Judgments," in *Basic Studies in Social Psychology,* ed. Harold Proshansky and Bernard Seidenberg (New York: Holt, Rinehart and Winston, 1965), pp. 393–401.

7. Bib Latane, Kipling Williams, and Stephen Harkins, "Social Loafing," *Psychology Today* 13 (1979): 104, 106, 110.

8. See C. R. Shepard, *Small Groups* (San Francisco: Chandler, 1964).

9. Leon Festinger, S. Schacter, and K. Back, *Social Pressure in Informal Groups* (New York: Harper & Row, 1959).

10. Stanley E. Seashore, *Group Cohesiveness in the Industrial Work Group* (Ann Arbor, Mich.: Institute for Social Research, University of Michigan, 1954).

11. N. R. F. Maier, "Quality of First and Second Solution Group Problem Solving," *Journal of Applied Psychology* 44 (1960): 27–29.

12. Andrew Van de Ven and André Delbecq, "The Effectiveness of Nominal, Delphi, and Interacting Group Decision Making Process," *Academy of Management Journal* 17 (1974): 605–621.

13. See E. J. Hall, J. S. Mouton, and R. R. Blake, "Group Problem Solving Effectiveness Under Conditions of Pooling Versus Interaction," *Journal of Social Psychology* 27 (1963): 147–157.

14. L. R. Hoffman, "Homogeneity of Member Personality and Its Effect on Group Problem Solving," *Journal of Abnormal and Social Psychology* 54 (1959): 27–32; and L. R. Hoffman and C. G. Smith, "Some Factors Affecting the Behaviors of Members of Problem Solving Groups," *Sociometry* 23 (1960): 273–291.

15. Andrew Van de Ven and André Delbecq, "Nominal Versus Interacting Group Processes for Committee Decision Making Effectiveness," *Academy of Management Journal* 15 (1971): 205.

16. N. Kogan and M. A. Wallach, "Risk Taking as a Function of the Situation, the Person, and the Group," in *New Directions in Psychology III*, eds. G. Mandler et al. (New York: Holt, Rinehart and Winston, 1967); and Rober Brown, *Social Psychology* (New York: Free Press, 1963), chap. 13.

17. S. Schacter, "Deviation, Rejection, and Communication," *Journal of Abnormal and Social Psychology* 46 (1951): 190–207; and B. E. Collins and Harold Guetzkow, *A Social Psychology of Group Processes for Decision Making* (New York: Wiley, 1964), pp. 42–43.

18. M. W. Belovicz, F. E. Finch, and Halsey Jones, "Do Groups Make Riskier Decisions than Individuals?" *Proceedings of the Academy of Management,* December 1969, pp. 73–85.

19. John W. Thibaut and Harold H. Kelley, *The Social Psychology of Groups* (New York: Wiley, 1959), p. 142.

20. See Robert L. Kahn et al., *Organizational Stress* (New York: Wiley, 1964).

21. Robert H. House and John R. Rizzo, "Role Conflict and Ambiguity as Critical Variables in a Model of Organization Behavior," *Organizational Behavior and Human Behavior* 7 (1972): 467–505; and John M. Ivancevich and James H. Donnelly, Jr., "A Study of Role Clarity and Need for Clarity for Three Occupational Groups," *Academy of Management Journal* 17 (1974): 28–36.

22. Kahn et al., *Organizational Stress.*

23. See A. F. Cohen, E. Stotland, and D. M. Wolfe, "An Experimental Investigation of Need for Cognition," *Journal of Abnormal and Social Psychology* 51 (1955): 291–295; T. F. Lyons, "Role Clarity, Need for Clarity, Satisfaction, Tension and Withdrawal," *Organizational Behavior and Human Performance* 6 (1971): 99–110; R. Neel, "Nervous Stress in the Industrial Situation," *Personal Psychology* 8 (1955): 405–416; and D. W. Organ and C. N. Greene, "The Perceived Purposefulness of Job Behavior: Antecedents and Consequences," *Academy of Management Journal* 17 (1974): 69–78.

24. Edmond H. Curcuru and James H. Healey, "The Multiple Roles of the Manager," *Business Horizons* 15 (July 1970): 15–24.

25. Douglas T. Hall and Francine E. Gordon, "Career Choices of Married Women: Effects on Conflict, Role Behavior, and Satisfaction," *Journal of Applied Psychology* 58 (1973): 42–48.

26. Douglas T. Hall, "A Model of Coping with Role Conflict: The Role Behavior of College Educated Women," *Administrative Science Quarterly* 17 (1972): 471–486.

27. C. K. Yun, "Role Conflicts of Expatriate Managers: A Construct," *Management International Review* 13, No. 6 (1973): 105–113.

28. R. A. H. Rosen, "Foreman Role Conflict: An Expression of Contradictions in

Organizational Roles," *Industrial and Labor Relations Review* 23 (1970): 541–552.

29. See Archie Carroll, "Don't Let Role Conflict Get You Down," *Supervisory Management* 18 (April 1973): 17–21.

Chapter 9

1. Kelly Kerin and C. N. Waldo, "NFL Coaches and Motivation Theory," *Michigan State University Business Topics* 26 (Autumn 1978): 15.

2. J. R. P. French and B. H. Raven, "The Bases of Social Power," in *Studies in Social Power,* ed. Darwin Cartwright (Ann Arbor, Mich.: Institute for Social Research, University of Michigan, 1959).

3. B. H. Raven, "Social Influence and Power," in *Current Studies in Social Psychology,* eds. I. D. Steiner and M. Fishbein (New York: Holt, Rinehart and Winston, 1965), p. 373.

4. Max Weber, *From Max Weber,* eds. H. H. Gerth and C. W. Mills (London: Oxford University Press, 1946).

5. Max Weber, "Three Types of Legitimate Rule," in *Complex Organization,* ed. Amitai Etzioni (New York: Holt, Rinehart and Winston, 1961), p. 10.

6. Victor Thompson, *Modern Organization* (New York: Knopf, 1963), p. 114.

7. Winston Oberg, "Charisma, Commitment, and Contemporary Organization Theory," *Michigan State University Business Topics* 29 (Spring 1972): 31.

8. Ralph Stogdill, "Personal Factors Associated with Leadership: A Survey of the Literature," *Journal of Psychology* 25 (1948): 35–71.

9. Stogdill, quoted in Cecil A. Gibb, ed., *Leadership* (London: Penguin, 1969), p. 125.

10. Dorothy M. Kipnis, "Interaction Between Members of Bomber Crews as a Determinant of Sociometric Choice," *Human Relations* 10 (1957): 263–370.

11. A. Bavelas et al., "Experiments on the Alteration of Group Structure," *Journal of Experimental and Social Psychology* 1 (1965): 55–70.

12. See Alex Bavelas, "Communication Patterns in Task-oriented Groups," *Journal of the Accoustical Society of America* 22 (1950): 725–730; and Harold Leavitt, "Some Effects of Certain Communication Patterns on Group Performance," *Journal of Abnormal and Social Psychology* 45 (1951): 38–50.

13. L. Carter, W. Haythorn, and M. Howell, "A Further Examination of the Criteria of Leadership," *Journal of Abnormal and Social Psychology* 45 (1950): 350–358.

14. C. A. Gibb, "The Sociometry of Leadership in Temporary Groups," *Sociometry* 13 (1950): 226–243.

15. Robert N. McMurray, "The Case for Benevolent Autocracy," *Harvard Business Review* 36 (January/Febuary 1958): 82–90.

16. E. A. Fleishman, E. F. Harris, and R. D. Burtt, *Leadership and Supervision in Industry* (Columbus, Ohio: Ohio State University Press, 1955).

17. E. A. Fleishman and E. F. Harris, "Patterns of Leadership Behavior Related to Employee Grievances and Turnover," *Personnel Psychology* 51 (1962): 45–53.

18. See E. A. Fleishman and D. A. Peters, "Interpersonal Values, Leadership Attitudes, and Managerial Success," *Personnel Psychology* 51 (1962): 137–143; and A. K. Korman, "Consideration, Initiating Structure and Organizational Criteria: A Review," *Personnel Psychology* 55 (1966): 349–361.

19. Michael J. Kvanah, "Leadership Behavior as a Function of Subordinate and Task Complexity," *Administrative Science Quarterly* 17 (1972): 591–600.

20. Robert Kahn and Daniel Katz, "Leadership Practices in Relation to Productivity and Morale," in *Group Dynamics,* 2nd ed., eds. Cartwright and Zander (New York: Harper & Row, 1960), pp. 617–627.

21. See Rensis Likert, *New Patterns of Management* (New York: McGraw-Hill, 1961).

22. A. S. Tannenbaum, *Control in Organizations* (New York: McGraw-Hill, 1968).

23. C. G. Smith and O. N. Ari, "Organizational Control Structure and Member Consensus," *American Journal of Sociology* 68 (1964): 624.

24. J. T. McMahon and G. W. Perritt, "Toward a Contingency Theory of Organizational Control," *Academy of Management Journal* 16 (1973): 663.

25. Tannenbaum, *Control in Organizations.*

26. For details on some methodological limitations of control graphs, see J. T. McMahon and G. W. Perritt, "The Control Structure of Organizations: An Empirical Examination," *Academy of Management Journal* 14 (1971): 327–339.

27. Fred E. Fiedler, "The Contingency Model—New Directions in Leadership Utilization," *Journal of Contemporary Business* 3 (1974): 65.

28. See Fred E. Fiedler, "Engineer the Job to Fit the Manager," *Harvard Business Review* 43 (September/October 1965): 115; and Fred E. Fiedler, "Style or Circumstance: The Leadership Enigma," *Psychology Today* 2 (March 1969): 40.

29. Fred E. Fiedler, G. E. O'Brien, and D. R. Ilgen, "The Effect of Leadership Style upon Performance and Adjustment of Voluntary Teams Operating in a Stressful Foreign Environment," *Human Relations* 22 (1966): 504.

30. Fred E. Fiedler and Martin M. Chemers, "Leadership and Management," in *Contemporary Management,* ed. Joseph W. McGuire (Englewood Cliffs, N. J.: Prentice-Hall, 1974), pp. 373–374.

31. Fred E. Fiedler, *A Theory of Leadership Effectiveness* (New York: McGraw-Hill, 1967), pp. 22–23.

32. See J. G. Hunt, "The Validity and Extension of Fiedler's Theory of Leadership Effectiveness," *Academy of Management Journal* 11 (1969): 33–47.

33. J. E. Stinson and Lane Tracy, "The Stability and Interpretation of the LPC Score," *Proceedings of the Academy of Management,* August 1972, pp. 182–184; and Martin Fishbein, Eva Landy, and Grace Hatch, "Some Determinants of an Individual's Esteem for His Least Preferred Co-worker," *Human Relations* 25 (1969): 173–188.

34. A. K. Korman, "Applications of Management Theory: A Review of the Empirical Literature and a New Dimension," *Proceedings of the Academy of Management,* August 1972, pp. 170–173.

35. Robert J. House and Terence R. Mitchell, "Path-Goal Theory of Leadership," *Journal of Contemporary Business* 3 (1974): 81.

36. M. G. Evans, "The Effects of Supervisory Behavior on the Path-Goal Relationship," *Organizational Behavior and Human Performance* 55 (1970): 277–298.

Chapter 10

1. W. M. Evans, "The Organizational Set: Toward a Theory of Interorganizational Relations," in *Approaches to Organizational Analysis,* ed. J. D. Thompson (Pittsburgh: University of Pittsburgh Press, 1966), pp. 177–180.

2. Eugene Litwak and L. F. Hylton, "Interorganizational Analysis: A Hypothesis on Coordinating Agencies," *Administrative Science Quarterly* 17 (1962): 398.

3. For some examples, see Harrington Emerson, *The Twelve Principles of Efficiency,* 6th ed. (New York: Engineering Magazine, 1924); Luther Gulick and L. F. Urwick, eds., *Papers on the Science of Administration* (New York: Harper & Row, 1947). For a notable exception see M. F. Follett, *Freedom and Coordination* (London: Management Publications Trust, 1949).

4. K. E. Boulding, "Two Principles of Conflict," in *Power and Conflict in Organizations,* eds. R. L. Kahn and K. E. Boulding (New York: Basic Books, 1964), p. 76.

5. See Henry Assael, "Constructive Role of Interorganizational Conflict," *Administrative Science Quarterly* 14 (1969): 573–582; and L. R. Pondy, "Varieties of Organizational Conflict," *Administrative Science Quarterly* 14 (1969): 503.

6. The word *ideal* is used in a methodological rather than a normative sense. The ideal bureaucracy is a theoretical abstraction like the perfectly competitive market in economic theory. Ideal does not mean preferred or good. See W. Jack Duncan, "The Concept of the Ideal Type as a Method of Understanding Organizational Behavior," *Management International Review,* no. 1 (1971): p. 19.

7. See Julian Freund, *The Sociology of Max Weber* (New York: Random House, 1968), p. 284; and Max Weber, *The Theory of Social and Economic Organization,* trans. and ed. A. M. Henderson and Talcott Parsons (New York: Free Press, 1947), pp. 330–331.

8. See David Ewing, *The Managerial Mind* (London: Macmillan, 1964), pp. 33–34; and Alexander Winn, "Social Change in Industry: From Insight to Implementation," *Journal of Applied Behavioral Science* 2 (1966): 170.

9. H. A. Simon, *Administrative Behavior,* 3rd ed. (New York: Macmillan, 1976), p. 20.

10. M. P. Follett, *Freedom and Coordination* (London: Management Publications Trust, 1949), p. 64.

11. W. G. Bennis, K. D. Benne, and Robert Chin, eds., *The Planning of Change,* 2nd ed. (New York: Holt, Rinehart and Winston, 1969), p. 152.

12. S. P. Robbins, *Managing Organizational Conflict* (Englewood Cliffs, N.J.: Prentice-Hall, 1974), pp. 13–14.

13. C. F. Fink, "Some Conceptual Difficulties in the Theory of Social Conflict," *Journal of Conflict Resolution* 2 (1968): 412–460.

14. C. G. Smith, "A Comparative Analysis of Some Conditions and Consequences

of Interorganizational Conflict," *Administrative Science Quarterly* 11 (1966): 504–506.

15. These points selectively adapted from R. E. Walton and J. M. Dutton, "The Management of Interdepartmental Conflict: A Model and Review," *Administrative Science Quarterly* 14 (1969): 73–77; and Clark Kerr, "Industrial Conflict and Its Mediation," *American Journal of Sociology* 59 (1954): 230.

16. See L. A. Dow and W. J. Duncan, "Economic Neoliberalism: A Behavioral View of the Sportmanship Assumption," *American Journal of Economics and Sociology* 33 (1974): 351–365.

17. F. S. Haiman, *Group Leadership and Democratic Action* (Cambridge, Mass.: Harvard University Press, 1951), p. 179.

18. R. R. Blake, H. A. Shepard, and J. S. Mouton, *Managing Intergroup Conflict in Industry* (Houston: Gulf, 1964), pp. 86–100.

19. Muzafer Sherif and Carolyn Sherif, *Groups in Harmony and Tension* (New York: Harper & Row, 1953); and Muzafer Sherif, *In Common Predicament: Social Psychology of Intergroup Conflict and Cooperation* (Boston: Houghton Mifflin, 1966).

20. Harold Aldrich, "Organizational Boundaries and Interorganizational Conflict," *Human Relations* 24 (1971): 287.

21. Mary Parker Follett, "Coordination," in *Classics in Management,* ed. H. F. Merrill (New York: American Management Association, 1960), pp. 341–343.

22. Theodore Caplow, "A Theory of Coalitions in the Triad," *American Sociological Review* 21 (1959): 489.

23. W. A. Gamson, "An Experimental Test of a Theory of Coalition Formation," *American Sociological Review* 26 (1961): 565–573.

24. For greater detail see W. J. Duncan, "Organizations as Political Coalitions: A Behavioral View of the Goal Formation Process," *Journal of Behavioral Economics* 5 (Summer 1976): 25–44.

25. See Richard Rose and Derik Urwin, "Social Cohesion, Political Parties, and Strains in Regimes," *Comparative Political Studies* 2 (1969): 19–30.

26. G. W. England, "Organizational Goals and the Expected Behavior of American Management," *Academy of Management Journal* 10 (1967): 110–117. Also see W. J. Duncan, "Organizational Goals and the Value Determination Process in Managerial Decision Making," in *Managing the Changing Organization,* ed. D. F. Ray and T. B. Green (Atlanta: Southern Management Association, 1974), pp. 228, 234.

27. R. E. Walton, J. M. Dutton, and H. G. Fitch, "A Study of Conflict in Process, Structure, and Attitudes of Lateral Relationships," in *Some Theories of Organization*, rev. ed., eds. A. H. Rubenstein and C. J. Haberstroh (Homewood, Ill.: Irwin, 1966), pp. 444–465.

Chapter 11

1. D. S. Pugh, "Modern Organization Theory: A Psychological and Sociological Study," *Psychological Bulletin* 63 (1966): 239.

2. Charles Perrow, *Organizational Analysis* (Belmont, Calif.: Wadsworth, 1970), p. 2.

3. H. M. Trice, James Belasco, and J. A. Alutto, "The Role of Ceremonials in Organizational Behavior," *Industrial and Labor Relations Review* 23 (1969): 42.

4. Max Weber, "Bureaucratic Organizations," in *The Theory of Social and Economic Organization,* trans. and eds. A. M. Henderson and Talcott Parsons (New York: Macmillan, 1947). Reprinted in *Readings on Modern Organizations,* ed. Amitai Etzioni (Englewood Cliffs, N.J.: Prentice-Hall, 1969).

5. Thomas S. Burns, *Tales of ITT—An Insider's Report* (Boston: Houghton Mifflin, 1974), pp. 60–65.

6. Charles Perrow, *Complex Organizations* (Glenview, Ill.: Scott, Foresman, 1972), p. 7.

7. Perrow, *Organizational Analysis,* p. 2.

8. Charles Argyris, *Interpersonal Competence and Organizational Effectiveness* (Homewood, Ill.: Dorsey Press, 1962), p. 5.

9. Chris Argyris, "Personality vs. Organization," *Organizational Dynamics* 3 (1974): 2–5.

10. See Chris Argyris, *Intervention Theory and Method* (Reading, Mass.: Addison-Wesley, 1970), chap. 2.

11. Chris Argyris, "The Individual and Organization: Some Problems of Mutual Adjustment," *Administrative Science Quarterly* 2 (1957): 501–508.

12. Warren G. Bennis, *Beyond Bureaucracy* (New York: McGraw-Hill, 1966), p. 10.

13. Warren G. Bennis, *Organizational Development* (Reading, Mass.: Addison-Wesley, 1969), p. 20.

14. See George Kozmetsky, "The End of the 20th Century," *Bell Telephone Magazine,* March-April 1970, pp. 27–32.

15. Warren G. Bennis, "Organizational Revitalization," *California Management Review* 9 (Fall 1966): 55.

16. B. H. Harvey and Fred Luthans, "Flexitime: An Empirical Analysis of Its Real Meaning and Impact," *Michigan State University Business Topics* 27 (Summer 1979): 31–36.

17. W. F. Dowling and L. R. Sayles, *How Managers Motivate,* 2nd ed. (New York: McGraw-Hill, 1978), pp. 138–139.

18. Fremont E. Kast and James E. Rosenzweig, *Contingency Views of Organization and Management* (Chicago: Science Research Associates, 1973), p. ix.

19. Shirley Terreberry, "The Evolution of Organizational Environments," *Administrative Science Quarterly* 13 (1968): 612; and Charles Perrow, "A Framework for the Comparative Analysis of Organizations," *American Sociological Review* 32 (1967): 194–208.

20. Joan Woodward, *Industrial Organization* (London: Oxford University Press, 1965), p. 36.

21. Joan Woodward, "Automation and Technical Change: The Implications for the Management Process," in *Organizational Structure and Design,* eds. G. W. Dalton, P. R. Lawrence, and J. W. Lorsch (Homewood, Ill.: Irwin, 1970), pp. 298–299.

22. W. L. Zwerman, *New Perspectives on Organization Theory* (Westport, Conn.: Greenwood, 1970), p. 11.

23. See Edward Harvey, "Technology and the Structure of Organizations," *Ameri-

can Sociological Review 33 (1968): 247–259; and W. A. Rushing, "Hardness of Material as Related to Division of Labor in Manufacturing Industries," *Administrative Science Quarterly* 13 (1968): 229–245.

24. Paul R. Lawrence and Jay W. Lorsch, *Organization and Environment* (Homewood, Ill.: Irwin, 1969), pp. 19, 85–87.

25. See T. E. Stephenson, "The Longevity of Classical Theory," *Management International Review* 8, no. 6 (1968): 78–79.

26. R. H. Simonds, "Are Organizational Principles a Thing of the Past?" *Personnel* 26 (January/February 1970): 8–17.

27. See W. G. Scott, "Organizational Theory: A Reassessment," *Academy of Management Journal* 17 (1974): 242–254.

Chapter 12

1. See Jeffery Pfeffer and Huseyin Leblebici, "The Effect of Competition on Some Dimensions of Organizational Structure," *Social Forces* 52 (1973): pp. 269–279.

2. Jay R. Galbraith, *Designing Complex Organizations* (Reading, Mass.: Addison-Wesley, 1973). Also see R. B. Duncan, "Characteristics of Organizational Environments and Perceived Environmental Uncertainty," *Administrative Science Quarterly* 17 (1972): pp. 313–327.

3. James March and Herbert Simon, *Organization* (New York: Wiley, 1958), pp. 36–37.

4. Warren G. Bennis, "Leadership Theory and Administrative Behavior," *Administrative Science Quarterly* 4 (1959): 259–300.

5. See Richard H. Hall, "Professionalism and Bureaucracy," *American Sociological Review* 33 (1968): 92–104; and Edward Harvey, "Technology and the Structure of Organizations," *Administrative Science Quarterly* 13 (1968):247–259.

6. W. G. Bennis, "Beyond Bureaucracy," in *The Temporary Society,* eds. W. G. Bennis and P. E. Salter (New York: Harper & Row, 1968).

7. Chris Argyris, "Today's Problems with Tomorrow's Organizations," in *Tomorrow's Organizations,* eds. J. S. Jun and W. B. Storm (Glenview, Ill.: Scott, Foresman, 1973), p. 63.

8. Harold J. Leavitt, William R. Dill, and Henry B. Eyring, *The Organizational World* (New York: Harcourt Brace Jovanovich, 1973), p. 84.

9. Gloria E. Engle, "Professional Autonomy and Bureaucratic Organization," *Administrative Science Quarterly* 15 (1970): 12–21; and C. G. Smith, "Consultation and Decision Processes in a Research and Development Laboratory," *Administrative Science Quarterly* 15 (1970): 203–215.

10. Leonard R. Sayles and M. K. Chandler, *Managing Large Systems* (New York: Harper & Row, 1971), p. 184.

11. Clayton Reeser, "Some Potential Human Problems of the Project Form of Organization," in *Academy of Management Proceedings,* August 1969, pp. 112–113; and Clayton Reeser, "Some Potential Problems of the Project Form of Organization," in *Academy of Management Journal* 12 (1969): 459–467.

12. Arlyn J. Melcher and Thomas A. Kayser, "Leadership Without Formal Authority," *California Management Review* 13 (1970): 57.

13. David I. Cleland, "Why Project Management?" *Business Horizons* 5 (Winter 1964) 84.

14. Richard M. Hodgetts, "Leadership Techniques in Project Organization," *Academy of Management Journal* 11 (1968): 211–219.

15. Ibid.

16. Harvey F. Kolodny, "Evolution to a Matrix Organization," *Academy of Management Review* 4 (1979): 545.

17. See Norman H. Wright, Jr. "Matrix Management: A Primer for the Administrative Manager," *Management Review* 68 (April 1979): 58–61.

18. See Peter F. Drucker, *Management: Tasks, Responsibilities, and Practices* (New York: Harper & Row, 1974), chap. 35.

19. G. H. Rice, Jr., and D. W. Bishoprick, *Conceptual Models of Organization* (New York: Appleton-Century-Crofts, 1971), p. 88.

20. Jay Friedman and M. I. Roemer, *Doctors in Hospitals: Medical Staff Organization and Hospital Performance* (Baltimore: Johns Hopkins, 1971), p. 8.

21. J. M. Beyer and T. M. Lodahl, "A Comparative Study of Patterns of Influence in United States and English Universities," *Administrative Science Quarterly* 21 (1976): 104–129.

22. See H. H. Hiatt, "Protecting the Medical Commons: Who Is Responsible?" *New England Journal of Medicine,* no. 293, July 31, 1975, 235–241.

23. Henry Mintzberg, *The Structuring of Organizations* (Englewood Cliffs, N.J.: Prentice-Hall, 1979), p. 363.

24. B. L. T. Hedberg, P. C. Nystrom, and W. H. Starbuck, "Camping on Seesaws: Prescriptions for a Self-Designing Organization," *Administrative Science Quarterly* 21 (1976): 41–65.

Chapter 13

1. J. P. Kotler, "Managing External Dependency," *Academy of Management Review* 4 (1979): 87.

2. See S. M. Schmidt and T. A. Kochan, "Interorganizational Relationships: Patterns and Motivations," *Administrative Science Quarterly* 22 (1977): 220–234.

3. This symbolism is adapted from R. M. Emerson, "Power-Dependence Relations," *American Sociological Review* 27 (1962): 32–33.

4. See Gerald Zeitz, "Interorganizational Relationships and Social Structure: A Critique of Some Aspects of the Literature," *Organization and Administrative Sciences* 5 (Spring/Summer 1974): 131–139.

5. H. E. Aldrich, "Resource Dependence in Interorganizational Relations," *Administration and Society* 7 (1976): 419–455.

6. Howard Aldrich and Diane Herker, "Boundary Spanning Roles and Organization Structure," *Academy of Management Review* 2 (1977): 217–230; and Donald Schwartz and Eugene Jacobson, "Organizational Communication Network Analysis: The Liaison Communication Role," *Organizational Behavior and Human Performance* 18 (1977): 158–174.

7. Richard Leifer and André Delbecq, "Organizational/Environmental Interchange: A Model of Boundary Spanning Activity," *Academy of Management Review* 3 (1978): 40–50.

8. R. C. Dailey, "Group, Task, and Personality Correlates of Boundary Spanning Activities," *Human Relations* 32 (1979): 273–285.

9. Richard Leifer and G. P. Huber, "Relations Among Perceived Environmental Uncertainty, Organization Structure, and Boundary Spanning Behavior," *Administrative Science Quarterly* 22 (1977): 235–247.

10. Aldrich and Herker, "Boundary Spanning Roles," pp. 223–224.

11. J. D. Thompson, *Organizations in Action* (New York: McGraw-Hill, 1967), pp. 15–18.

12. Aldrich and Herker, "Boundary Spanning Roles."

13. R. T. Keller, A. D. Szilagyi, and W. E. Holland, "Boundary Spanning Activity and Employee Relations: An Empirical Study," *Human Relations* 29 (1976): 699–710.

14. See R. T. Keller and W. E. Holland, "Boundary Spanning Roles in a Research and Development Organization: An Empirical Investigation," *Academy of Management Journal* 18 (1975): 388–392; and R. T. Keller, "Boundary-Spanning Activity, Role Dynamics, and Job Satisfaction: A Longitudinal Study," *Journal of Business Research* 6 (1978): 147–158.

15. R. C. Dailey, "Group, Task, and Personality Correlates of Boundary Spanning Activities," *Human Relations* 32 (1979): 273–285 and R. C. Dailey and C. P. Morgan, "Personal Characteristics and Job Involvement as Antecedents of Boundary Spanning Behavior: A Path Analysis," *Journal of Management Studies* 15 (1978): 330–339.

16. R. B. Glassman, "Persistence and Loose Coupling in Living Systems," *Behavioral Science* 18 (1973): 83–98; and K. E. Weick, "Middle Range Theories of Social Systems," *Behavioral Science* 19 (1974): 357–367.

17. W. J. Duncan, "Knowledge Transfer in Administrative Science," *Public Administration Review* 40 (1980): 341–349.

18. See K. E. Weick, "Educational Organizations as Loosely Coupled Systems," *Administrative Science Quarterly* 21 (1976): 1–19.

19. See S. W. Becker and T. L. Whisler, "The Innovative Organization: A Selective View of Current Theory and Research," *Journal of Business of the University of Chicago* 40 (1967): 348.

20. Tushman, M. L., "Special Boundary Roles in the Innovation Process," *Administrative Science Quarterly* 22 (1977): 587–605.

21. Edwin Mansfield and Samuel Wagner, "Organizational and Strategic Factors Associated with Probabilities of Success in Industrial Research," *Journal of Business of the University of Chicago* 48 (1975): 179–198.

22. J. V. Baldridge and Robert Burnham, "Organizational Innovation: Individual, Organizational, and Environmental Impacts," *Administrative Science Quarterly* 20 (1975): 165–176; and John Czepiel, "Patterns of Interorganizational Communication and the Diffusion of a Major Technological Innovation," *Academy of Management Journal* 18 (1975): 6–24.

23. D. W. Organ, "Linking Pins Between Organizations and Environment," *Business Horizons* 14 (December 1971): 73–80.

Chapter 14

1. T. K. Reeves and Joan Woodward, "The Study of Managerial Control," in *Industrial Organization,* ed. Joan Woodward (New York: Oxford University Press, 1970), p. 66.

2. Theo Haimann, *Professional Management* (Boston: Houghton Mifflin, 1962), pp. 488–492.

3. T. H. Stone, "An Examination of Six Prevalent Assumptions Concerning Performance Appraisal," *Public Personnel Management* 2 (November/December 1973): 408–414.

4. J. F. Bryan and E. A. Locke, "Goal Setting as a Means of Increasing Motivation," *Journal of Applied Psychology* 51 (1967): 274–277; and E. A. Locke, "Toward a Theory of Task Motivation and Incentives," *Organizational Behavior and Human Performance* 3 (1968): 157–189.

5. A. C. Stedry and Emanuel Kay, "The Effect of Goal Difficulty on Performance: A Field Experiment," *Behavioral Science* 11 (1966): 459–470.

6. H. S. Field and W. H. Holley, "Traits in Performance Ratings—Their Importance in Public Employment," *Public Personnel Management* 4 (March 1975): 327–330.

7. L. C. Lawrence and P. C. Smith, "Group Decisions and Employee Participation," *Journal of Applied Psychology* 39 (1955): 334–337.

8. N. R. F. Maier and L. R. Hoffman, "Using Trained 'Developmental' Discussion Leaders to Improve Further the Quality of Group Discussions," *Journal of Applied Psychology* 44 (1960): 247–251.

9. L. Cronbach and P. Meehl, "Construct Validity of Psychological Tests," *Psychological Bulletin* 52 (1955): 282.

10. Dorothy E. Schneider and A. G. Bayroff, "The Relationship Between Rater Characteristics and Validity of Ratings," *Journal of Applied Psychology* 37 (1953): 278–280.

11. W. K. Kirchner and D. J. Reisberg, "Difference Between Better and Less-Effective Supervisors in the Appraisal of Subordinates," *Personnel Psychology* 15 (1962): 296–301.

12. M. M. Mandell, "Supervisory Characteristics and Ratings," *Personnel* 32 (1956): 435–446.

13. See M. D. Dunnette, *Personnel Selection and Placement* (San Francisco: Wadsworth, 1966).

14. R. M. Guion, *Personnel Testing* (New York: McGraw-Hill, 1965), pp. 103–104.

15. For an example, see L. Fogli, C. L. Hulin, and M. R. Blood, "Development of First-level Behavioral Job Criteria," *Journal of Applied Psychology* 55 (1971): 3–8.

16. M. D. Dunnette, R. D. Avery, and L. W. Hellervik, "The Development and Evaluation of Behaviorally Based Rating Scales," *Journal of Applied Psychology* 57 (1973): 15–22.

17. D. P. Schwab, H. Heneman III, and T. A. DeCotiis, "Behaviorally Anchored Rating Scales: A Review of the Literature," *Academy of Management Proceedings,* ed. A. G. Bedeian et al. (New Orleans: Academy of Management, 1975), pp. 222–224.

18. See J. P. Campbell et al., *Managerial Behavior, Performance and Effectiveness* (New York: McGraw-Hill, 1970); and P. C. Smith and L. M. Kendall, "Retranslation of Expectations: An Approach to the Construction of Unambiguous Anchors for Rating Scales," *Journal of Applied Psychology* 47 (1963): 149–155.

19. See W. C. Borman and W. R. Villon, "A View of What Can Happen When Behavioral Expectation Scales are Developed in One Setting and Used in Another," *Journal of Applied Psychology* 49 (1974): 197–201; and W. E. Williams and D. A. Seller, "Relationship Between Measures of Effort and Job Performance," *Journal of Applied Psychology* 57 (1973): 49–54.

20. L. L. Cummings and D. P. Schwab, *Performance in Organizations* (Glenview, Ill.: Scott, Foresman, 1973), chap. 7.

21. M. S. Klores, "Rater Bias in Forced-Distribution Performance Ratings," *Journal of Applied Psychology* 59 (1974): 445–451.

22. The selection of participants is currently a source of controversy. See W. C. Byham, "Assessment Centers for Spotting Future Managers," *Harvard Business Review* 47 (November/December 1970): 155.

23. I. R. Ginsburg and Arnold Siverman, "The Leaders of Tomorrow: Their Identification and Development," *Personnel Journal* 51 (1972): 663.

24. W. C. Byham, B. M. Cohen, and J. L. Moses, "The Validity of Assessment Centers," *Journal of Industrial and Organizational Psychology* 4 (1973): 32.

25. "How Good Are Assessment Centers?" *Administrative Management* 36 (May 1975): 51–52.

26. R. M. Steers, "Problems in the Measurement of Organizational Effectiveness," *Administrative Science Quarterly* 20 (1975): 546–558.

27. Amitai Etzioni, "Two Approaches to Organizational Analysis: A Critique and a Suggestion," *Administrative Science Quarterly* 5 (1960): 257–278.

28. B. S. Georgopoulos and A. S. Tannenbaum, "A Study of Organizational Effectiveness," *American Sociological Review* 22 (1975): 534–540.

29. R. M. Steers, *Organizational Effectiveness* (Santa Monica, Calif.: Goodyear, 1977), chap. 10.

30. Neil W. Chamberlain, *Enterprise and Environment* (New York: McGraw-Hill, 1968), pp. 8–10.

31. J. R. Hackman and E. E. Lawler, "Employee Reactions to Job Characteristics," *Journal of Applied Psychology* 55 (1971): 259–286.

32. For a detailed discussion of these factors, see E. E. Lawler and J. G. Rhode, *Information and Control in Organizations* (Santa Monica, Calif.: Goodyear, 1976), chap. 6.

Chapter 15

1. M. Sashkin, W. Morris, and L. Horst, "A Comparison of Social and Organizational Change Models: Information Flow and Data Use Processes," *Psychological Review* 80 (1973): 510–526.

2. Robert Chin and Kenneth Benne, "General Strategies for Effecting Change in

Human Systems," in *The Planning of Change,* 2nd ed., ed. W. G. Bennis, K. D. Benne, and Robert Chin (New York: Holt, Rinehart and Winston, 1965), p. 33.

3. C. Ferguson, "Concerning the Nature of Human Systems and the Consultant's Role," *Journal of Applied Behavioral Sciences* 4 (1969): 186–187.

4. Edward Schein, *Process Consultation: Its Role in Organizational Development* (Reading, Mass.: Addison-Wesley, 1969), p. 120.

5. See D. Kolb and A. Frohman, "An Organization Development Approach to Consulting," *Sloan Management Review* 12 (Fall 1970): 51–65.

6. Chin and Benne, "General Strategies," pp. 24–44.

7. Kurt Lewin, *Field Theory in Social Science* (New York: Harper & Row, 1951).

8. K. D. Benne and Max Birnbaum, "Change Does Not Have to Be Haphazard," *School Review* 68 (1960): 285.

9. Gerald Zaltman and Robert Duncan, *Strategies for Planned Change* (New York: Wiley, 1977), pp. 81–86.

10. R. E. Levinson, "How to Conquer the Panic of Change," *Management Review* 66 (July 1977): 20–24.

11. Hazel Henderson, "How to Cope with Organizational Change," *Management Review* 65 (July 1976): 19.

12. W. J. Reddin, "Confessions of an Organizational Change Agent," *Training and Development Journal* 31 (October 1977): 52–57.

13. W. Burke, "Organizational Development Pro and Con II," *Professional Psychology* 16 (1973): 194–196.

14. R. Beckhard, *Organizational Development Strategies and Models* (Reading, Mass.: Addison-Wesley, 1969), p. 9.

15. See W. French and C. Bell, Jr., *Organizational Development: Behavioral Science Interventions for Organization Improvement,* 2nd ed. (Englewood Cliffs, N.J.: Prentice-Hall, 1978), p. 14.

16. See W. G. Bennis, "The Decline of Bureaucracy and Organizations of the Future," in *Changing Organizations,* ed. W. G. Bennis (New York: McGraw-Hill, 1966), pp. 12–13. For another opinion, see R. D. Miewald, "The Greatly Exaggerated Death of Bureaucracy," *California Management Review* 13 (Winter 1970): 66–67.

17. E. F. Huse, *Organization Development and Change* (St. Paul, Minn.: West, 1975), p. 23.

18. J. B. Miner, "The OD-Management Development Conflict," *Business Horizons* 17 (December 1973): 35.

19. R. Napier and M. Gershenfeld, *Groups: Theory and Experience* (Boston: Houghton Mifflin, 1973), p. 277.

20. J. Campbell and M. Dunnette, "Effectiveness of T-Group Experiences in Managerial Training and Development," *Psychological Bulletin* 70 (1968): 73–103.

21. D. Lundgren, "Attitudinal and Behavioral Correlates of Emergent Status in Training Groups," *Journal of Social Psychology* 90 (1973): 141–153.

22. F. Friedlander, "A Comparative Study of Consulting Process and Group Development," *Journal of Applied Behavioral Science* 4 (1968): 375–377; and F. Friedlander, "The Primacy of Trust as a Facilitator of Further Group Accomplishment," *Journal of Applied Behavioral Science* 6 (1970): 387–401.

23. W. J. Kearney and D. D. Martin, "Sensitivity Training: An Established Management Training Tool," *Academy of Management Journal* 17 (1974): 755–760.

24. For an actual argument along these lines see, "Backlash in Sensitivity Training," *Electrical World,* February 15, 1974, p. 83.

25. See M. Lakin, *Interpersonal Encounter: Theory and Practice in Sensitivity Training* (New York: McGraw-Hill, 1972), pp. 2–3.

26. C. Rogers, "The Process of the Basic Encounter Group," in *Challenges of Humanistic Psychology,* ed. J. Bugenthal (New York: McGraw-Hill, 1967), pp. 81–97.

27. J. Gibb, "TORI Theory: Consultantless Team-building," *Journal of Contemporary Business* 1 (1972): 33–42.

28. M. Lieberman, I. Yalom, and M. Miles, "The Impact of Encounter Groups on Participants: Some Preliminary Findings," *Journal of Applied Behavioral Sciences* 8 (1972): 29–50.

29. For example see M. Fein, "Job Enrichment: A Reevaluation," *Sloan Management Review* 15 (Winter 1974): 69–88; and Fred Luthans and William Reif, "Job Enrichment: Long on Theory and Short on Practice," *Organizational Dynamics* 2 (Winter 1974): 30–38.

30. E. F. Huse, "Putting in a Management Development Program That Works," *California Management Review* 9 (Winter 1966): 73–80.

31. Anthony Raia, "Goal Setting and Self-Control: An Empirical Study," *Journal of Management Studies* 2 (1965): 34–52.

32. Anthony Raia, "A Second Look at Management Goals and Controls," *California Management Review* 8 (Summer 1965): 49–58.

33. S. Carroll and H. Tosi, Jr., *Management by Objectives* (New York: Macmillan, 1973).

34. J. E. Taylor and Elizabeth Berinot, "An OD Intervention to Install Participative Management in a Bureaucratic Organization," *Training and Development Journal* 27 (January 1973): 18–21. The discussion of the Harris County System is taken from this source.

35. D. D. White, "Factors Affecting Employee Attitudes Toward the Installation of a New Management System," *Academy of Management Journal* 16 (1974): 636–646.

36. R. Beckhard, "The Confrontation Meeting," *Harvard Business Review* 45 (March/April 1967): 149–154.

37. Warren Bennis, *Organizational Development* (Reading, Mass.: Addison-Wesley, 1969), p. 7.

Chapter 16

1. Ronald G. Havelock, *Planning for Innovation* (Ann Arbor, Mich.: Institute for Social Research, University of Michigan, 1969), pp. 1–12.

2. W. Jack Duncan, "The Knowledge Utilization Process in Management and Organization," *Academy of Management Journal* 15 (1972): 276.

3. P. A. Clark, "The Peak Period Phenomenon: Its Implications for Organizational Design," *Organizational Design: Theory and Practice* (London: Tavistock, 1972), pp. 39–41.

4. R. K. Merton, "The Role Set," *British Journal of Sociology* 8 (1957): 106–120; and W. O. Haagstrom, *The Scientific Community* (New York: Basic Books, 1966).

5. Havelock, *Planning for Innovation,* pp. 2–10.

6. See A. W. Gouldner, "Explorations in Applied Social Science," *Social Problems* 3 (1956): 169–181; and E. A. Ohmann, "Search for a Managerial Philosophy," *Harvard Business Review* 35 (May/June 1957): 41–51.

7. See T. R. Dyckman, "Management Implementation of Scientific Research: An Attitudinal Study," *Management Science* 13 (1967): B-612-B-619; and D. R. Ladd, "Report on a Group's Reaction to 'The Researcher and the Manager: A Dialectic of Implementation,' " *Management Science* 11 (1965): B-23-B-25.

8. C. W. Churchman and A. H. Schainblatt, "The Researcher and the Manager: A Dialectic of Implementation," *Management Science* 11 (1965): B-16-B-87; and W. J. Duncan, "The Researcher and the Manager: A Comparative View of the Need for Mutual Understanding," *Management Science* 20 (1974): 1157–1163.

9. W. J. Duncan, "Management Theory and the Practice of Management," *Business Horizons* 18 (October 1974): 48–52.

10. Yoram Barzell, "Optimal Timing of Innovations," *Review of Economics and Statistics* 50 (1968): 348–355; and J. L. Simon and Leslie Golembo, "The Spread of a Cost-free Business Innovation," *University of Chicago Journal of Business* 40 (1967): 385–388.

11. H. A. Shepard, "Innovation-Resisting and Innovation-Producing Organizations," *University of Chicago Journal of Business* 40 (1967): 470–477.

12. Quoted in P. A. Clark, *Action Research and Organizational Change* (New York: Harper & Row, 1972), p. 23.

13. W. L. French and C. H. Bell, Jr., *Organization Development,* 2nd ed. (Englewood Cliffs, N.J.: Prentice-Hall, 1978), p. 88.

14. Ibid., p. 90.

15. For an example, see A. L. Stinchcombe, "Bureaucratic and Craft Administration of Production: A Comparative Study," *Administrative Science Quarterly* 3 (1959): 168–187.

16. Gerald Zaltman, C. R. A. Pinson, and Reinhard Angelmar, *Metatheory in Consumer Research* (Hinsdale, Ill.: Dryden Press, 1973), p. 4.

17. M. Bunge, *Metascientific Queries* (Springfield, Ill.: Charles C. Thomas, 1959), p. 26.

18. H. C. Kelman, "Manipulation of Human Behavior: An Ethical Dilemma for the Social Scientist," *Journal of Social Issues* 21 (1965): 31–33.

19. D. P. Warwick and H. C. Kelman, "Ethical Issues in Social Intervention," in *The Planning of Change,* 3rd ed., eds. W. G. Bennis et al. (New York: Holt, Rinehart and Winston, 1976), p. 471.

20. Jessie Bernard, "The Power of Science and the Science of Power," *American Sociological Review* 14 (1949): 575–584.

21. Robert F. Pethia, "Some Content Analytic Findings on Values in Normative

Administrative Theory," *Academy of Management Proceedings,* August 1969, pp. 145–153.

22. D. L. Bradford and George Strauss, "O.B. of the Present and Future: Reflections from the S.M.U. Conference," *The Teaching of Organizational Behavior* 1 (1975): 5.

23. Will and Ariel Durant, *The Lessons of History* (New York: Simon and Schuster, 1968), p. 13.

Important Terms

Note—The number in parentheses after each definition indicates the chapter in which the term is first discussed.

Achievement motivation—McClelland's theory that describes behavior primarily in terms of the need to achieve. (6)

Achievement motive—the need for achievement (*n Ach*). This is the basic element of analysis in David McClelland's theory of motivation. (4)

Action research—research designed to contribute to the solution of practical problems and to the goals of science. This research usually encourages the active involvement of researchers and managers at all stages of research and implementation. As a process, action research involves ongoing continuous feedback, monitoring, action, and evaluation. (16)

Administrative organization—the view of administration identified with Henri Fayol. The emphasis is on the process and functions of management (planning, organizing, and controlling). (2)

Ambiguity—the extent to which a person is uncertain about his or her expected behavior in the group. *Role conflict,* on the other hand, does not involve role uncertainty. Individuals in conflict are clear about their roles, but are confronted with inconsistent demands from others. (8)

Appraisal methods—methods of measuring performance. A few techniques discussed include alternative ranking and forced distribution methods, weighted checklists, and behaviorally anchored rating scales. (14)

Assessment center—a method of evaluating managerial potential in which promising individuals are placed in simulated organizational environments and evaluated on their decision-making performances. (14)

Attitude—a predisposition to react in some manner to an attitude object, such as another person or a given situation. (4)

Attitude scale—instrument designed to measure attitudes. (4)

Behavioral alterations—the recognition that conflict, if not excessive, can have favorable behavioral effects such as the stimulating change and innovation. (10)

449

Behavioral decision theory—the decision theory that attempts only to describe human decision making. It does not attempt to prescribe how decisions should be made. (5)

Behavioral design theories—theories of organizational design that emphasize the personalities and human factors in organizational structure. (11)

Behaviorally anchored rating scales (BARS)—appraisal scales that are based on relevantly identified dimensions of performance. The scales are based on performance dimensions that have been identified by people who know about the job under consideration. (14)

Behavioral sciences—disciplines that build knowledge through the application of scientific methods. Organizational behavior involves a variety of disciplines concerned with the psychological, sociological, economic, and political aspects of human behavior. (1)

Behavior modification—an intentional change in the relationship between a stimulus and a response through learning. (6)

Boundary-spanning activities—functions designed to improve the interaction of organizations and environmental forces including other organizations; the tasks accomplished by those in boundary-spanning positions. (13)

Boundary-spanning role—a position or expected behavior pattern that improves the interaction of two or more organizations. (13)

Bureaucracy—the theoretical description of organizational design as popularized by Max Weber. The distinguishing aspect of bureaucracy is its concentration on structural aspects of organization. (2)

Bureaucratic perspective—the perspective developing from the theory of bureaucracy that coordination of intergroup behavior is the natural state of affairs. Conflict is viewed as a breakdown in the efficient management of the organization. (10)

Change agent—any individual or group that attempts to facilitate and direct planned change. (15)

Classical conditioning—a type of learning in which the stimulus occurs before, or simultaneously with, the response (for example, Pavlov's experiments with dogs). (5)

Closed system—an organizational design that emphasizes the precision of internal structure at the expense of external, environmental forces that can influence decision making. (12)

Closed-systems view—a view of organizations concerned with the internal operation of organizations that does not explicitly include environmental factors. (1)

Closure—the tendency of human beings to assume that they perceive the total situation, in spite of selective perception. Stereotyping and the halo effect are examples of closure. (5)

Coalition—an association that frequently arises in triads, when two members align themselves against the third individual. (7)

Cognitive dissonance—the conflict that develops in an individual when a choice is made and the acquired knowledge is not consistent with expectations. Dissonance occurs because people must reject alternative courses of action that have favorable characteristics. (5)

Cognitive process—any thinking process engaged in by human beings. The basic cognitive processes are perception, learning, and problem solving. (5)

Collegial structure—an organizational design characterized by a powerful professional core and an administration developed and maintained to support the core. (12)

Communication barrier—any factor in communication that reduces the accuracy of message transfer. (7)

Competition—the striving of two or more groups for the favors of an outside entity, such as consumers, where the interaction is characterized by well-defined rules of the group. (10)

Conflict—antagonistic and hostile interaction among groups. (10)

Conflict resolution—the reduction of conflict through the use of conscious strategies such as problem solving and superordinate goals. (10)

Conformity—a modification of behavior in line with group norms. Compliance is outward adherence to the norm, whereas acceptance involves the values underlying the norm. (8)

Congruent attitude change—a change in the intensity but not in the direction of an attitude. (4)

Construct—an abstract property or characteristic of an object that is being studied. (3)

Construct validity—the preciseness with which a particular appraisal instrument measures the properties or performance of the phenomenon being examined. (3, 14)

Content theories of motivation—motivation theories based on the presence of needs or motives. Examples include Herzberg's two-factor theory and McClelland's achievement motivation. (6)

Context—the environment within which perception takes place. The context is composed of physical and psychological factors. (5)

Contingency theory—a situational theory of leadership that proposes that no one style of leadership is best in all situations. Rather, leadership style depends on the situation. This theory attempts to explain relationships within and among subsystems of an organization, as well as between the environment and the organization. (9, 11)

Control graph—a pictorial representation of the perceived actual (and perceived desired) amount and distribution of power in an organization. (9)

Coordination—the effective direction of individual and group actions toward some desirable goal. (10)

Culture—the complex whole of learned behavior including law, custom, and so forth. (4)

Deductive model—a method of explanation whereby one moves logically from general premises to specific conclusions. (3)

Defense mechanisms—according to psychoanalytical theory, patterns of behavior designed to reduce an individual's anxiety over the extreme demands of the id and superego. (4)

Dialectical approach—an approach to learning that begins with a proposition or thesis, follows with an examination of the counterposition, and concludes with a synthesis of the views. (1)

Differentiation—in the Lawrence and Lorsch studies, the degree to which managers of functional units differed in their goal orientation, time orientation, and interpersonal orientation, and the degree to which units differed in their formal structure. (11)

Distributive and integrative relationships—terms given to the stereotyped relationships among groups based on (1) the freedom of information exchange, (2) informality of communication, and (3) trust and friendliness. When the relationship is protective, formal, unfriendly, and characterized by mistrust, it is said to be distributive. When it is free, informal, and friendly, it is integrative. (10)

Dyad—a two-person group. (7)

Ethical issues—questions relating, on humanistic grounds, to the advisability of using behavioral science knowledge. (16)

Exchange view—an interorganizational perspective based on equal power among interacting groups that tends to foster cooperation. (13)

Expectancy—an individual's perception of the likelihood that a specific act will result in a specific outcome. (6)

Expectancy theory—a motivation theory proposing that individuals choose a course of action on the basis of expected outcomes. (6)

Experimental variable—a change introduced into an experiment to allow the measurement of differences from another situation. (3)

External validity—relates to the generality of an experimental design, established when results of an experiment are not bound by a specific group of subjects. (3)

Extrasensory perception (ESP)—perception that occurs outside the five senses. The most commonly discussed types of ESP are precognition, telepathy, clairvoyance, psychokinesis. (5)

Feedback control—the process of monitoring actual performance, comparing it with desired performance, measuring variances, and taking corrective action based on the information obtained. (14)

Force—a strategy of implementing planned change through legitimate organizational authority. (15)

Formal group—a group that is created deliberately to accomplish specific goals. Formal groups display specialized roles, rigid norms, and sanctions against noncompliance. (7)

Functional perspective—similar to the bureaucratic view in terms of inter-group behavior. Coordination is viewed as natural and desirable, whereas conflict is seen as dysfunctional in accomplishing goals. (10)

Goal optimization—the position that equates organizational effectiveness with goal accomplishment. (14)

Group—two or more people who interact to accomplish a common goal; group members share common motives, are affected differently by the interaction, and receive varying degrees of status. Group interaction occurs within an established but dynamic structure. (7)

Group cohesion—the ability of a group to think and act as a single unit; the strong "glue" that holds members of a group together. (8)

Haphazard change—alterations in which no attempt is made to anticipate or direct the influence of change. (15)

Hawthorne Studies—extensive management studies conducted by the Harvard Business School in the mid- and late 1920s at Western Electric Company. These studies, although recognized as pioneering investigations, have been the subject of much controversy. (2)

Holistic approach—a systems view that begins with the notion of understanding the system through a macro orientation. This view assumes the whole is more than the sum of the parts. (12)

Human relations—the view of management derived from the Hawthorne Studies. The primary aspect of this view is the concept of the work group as a social phenomenon. (2)

Hygiene factors—in Herzberg's theory, these factors are external to the work itself and are capable only of reducing dissatisfaction (or contributing to its increase if they are not present in the work environment). (6)

Hypothesis—a precisely stated proposition that can be tested logically. (3)

Incongruent attitude change—a change in the direction of an attitude. (3)

Inductive model—a logical method whereby one progresses from actual observations to more general conclusions. (4)

Informal group—a group that is spontaneous, is based on emotional factors, and has little structure. (7)

Innovation—the proposing, creating, and adopting of an idea, concept, product, or service. (13)

Instrumentality—an individual's perception that one outcome or consequence of behavior will assist in achieving another outcome of consequence. A person behaves in a certain way to achieve some outcome. (6)

Instrumental theories of motivation—motivation theories that are based on the principles of instrumental learning. Examples include exchange theory, expectancy theory, and operant conditioning. (6)

Integration—a method of conflict resolution in which the manager, without the use of force or compromise, develops a creative solution to a problem that satisfies all hostile parties. Also, in the Lawrence and Lorsch studies, the state of collaboration among managers of functional units necessary to achieve coordination and unity of direction. (10, 11)

Interacting groups—problem-solving groups brought together in open interaction and face-to-face communication. (8)

Internal validity—the characteristic of an experimental design or deductive argument whereby cause-and-effect relationships are established. (3)

Knowledge-flow system—all the resource and user subsystems involved in the transfer of basic knowledge to implementation. (16)

Law of effect—the proposal that favorable consequences perpetuate a given response, whereas unfavorable consequences discourage the response. (5)

Leadership—an influence process whereby one person obtains control over another individual or group. (9)

Leadership style—the manner in which influence is exercised. Most classification systems range from autocratic to laissez-faire styles. (9)

Levels of measurement—the relative preciseness of various measuring instruments. The preciseness ranges from the classification aspects of nominal scales to the sophistication of ratio scales. (3)

Linking agents—individuals and organizations that assume the role of facilitating the transfer of knowledge. (16)

Loose coupling—a linkage among systems or subsystems in which a change in one unit is not reflected directly in the other units. (13)

Machiavellianism—the practical-political view of organizational and managerial behavior. This orientation is usually thought of as the "end-justifies-the-means" view of decision making. (2)

Management development—an individually oriented training effort designed primarily to change the individual manager rather than the organization. (15)

Managerial authority gap—in project management, the difficulty of managing highly specialized personnel and those over whom the project manager does not have direct functional authority. (12)

Matrix organization—an organizational design that employs a permanent two-dimensional flow of authority. The primary hierarchy is maintained but is supplemented by a series of problem-oriented units. (12)

Membership group—a group to which one belongs but has no more than a minor relationship. (7)

Modern behavioral science view—the analysis of organizational phenomena directed toward the scientific analysis of individual and group behavior. (2)

Motivation—the study of how human behavior is activated, maintained, directed, and stopped. (6)

Motivators—in Herzberg's theory, the factors that are capable of producing job satisfaction. These are considered to be intrinsic to the work itself. (6)

Multiple-factor model of organizational effectiveness—the contemporary view of effectiveness, which considers several factors such as efficiency, responsiveness, and behavioral forces. (14)

Nominal groups—groups in name only. These also are problem-solving entities, but they do not involve open interaction and face-to-face communication. (8)

Nonverbal communication—message transfer that results from body movements and facial expressions without language. (7)

Normative decision theory—decision guidelines proposing how choices should be made to achieve a specific outcome (norm). (5)

Norms—rules or guidelines of accepted behavior that are established by the group and used to control the behavior of its members. (8)

Open system—an organizational design that actively allows for an interaction with the larger environment. (12)

Open-systems view—a view of organizations that examines collective behavior within the environmental context. (1)

Operant conditioning—a type of learning in which the response takes place in anticipation of a consequence (stimulus). (5)

Opinion—an expression of an evaluation or judgment of a situation. (4)

Organic-adaptive (ad hoc) design—an organizational design that maximizes the potential for innovation and encourages the formation of multidisciplinary problem-solving teams. (12)

Organization—a collection of interacting and interdependent individuals who work toward common goals within structured relationships. (1)

Organizational behavior—the field of study concerned with the application of behavioral sciences to management problems in an organizational or group setting. (1)

Organizational design—theories about structuring organizations so as to direct human behavior toward goal accomplishment. (11)

Organizational development—a planned, organization-wide effort to increase organizational effectiveness and health through behavioral science knowledge. (15)

Organizational development techniques—a variety of techniques (such as sensitivity training, encounter groups, and confrontation meetings) designed to effect planned organizational change. (15)

Organizational set—the entire network of interactions and relationships of one group with another. (10)

Path-goal theory—an expectancy, or instrumentality, formulation that emphasizes the leader's role in clarifying employee goals and assigning importance to those goals. (9)

Perceived environmental uncertainty—the extent of uncertainty that the managers of an organization perceive in the external environment. (13)

Personality—a person's unique character, behavior, and temperament. (4)

Personality theory—the study of the formation and development of the human personality. Major traditions of this research include Freud's psychoanalytical analysis, treat theory, and the needs theories of Maslow and McClelland. (4)

Planned change—a conscious and deliberate attempt on the part of some agent to effect change toward a specific goal. (15)

Power—the ability to influence others through some personal or situational characteristic(s). (9)

Power-dependency view—an interorganizational perspective that is based on power relationships. When the relationship is asymmetrical or unequal, conflict is the likely outcome. (13)

Premise—an assumption about the state of nature that is under consideration. (3)

Preventive control—the control process in which major attention is directed toward planning and the prevention of deviations from the standard. Proportionately less attention is directed toward controlling after deviations develop. (14)

Professionalized hierarchy—an organizational design that is formed around a professional core but retains an administrative structure for housekeeping purposes. (12)

Project director—the leader of a project team, who possesses authority for the accomplishment of a specific task or solution of a specific problem. (12)

Project structure—an organizational design that is built around a task force and is directed toward a specific task or problem. This is a temporary design that uses a two-dimensional flow of authority. (12)

Quasi-stationary equilibrium—Kurt Lewin's force-field view of the stationary state, in which the existing state of affairs in a system is seen as a dynamic contest between driving and restraining forces. (15)

Rational appeal—a strategy of planned change that appeals to the self-interest motives of those involved. (15)

Receiver—the object of a message initiated by the source in the communication process. (7)

Re-education—a strategy of planned change in which training is used to redirect values in accordance with the proposed alteration. (15)

Reference group—a group to which a person belongs (or hopes to belong), allowing the group to influence his or her behavior. (7)

Reinforcement schedules—the various patterns in which a consequence follows a response in the operant conditioning model. (6)

Relations orientation—a leadership characteristic that emphasizes interpersonal relations and is less concerned with task accomplishment. (9)

Relevant set—the environmental framework within which intergroup behavior takes place. (10)

Reliability—the consistency of a measurement technique. An instrument is reliable if it consistently measures a specific phenomenon. (3)

Risky-shift hypothesis—the argument that there is an increased tendency to assume risk when an individual is in a group. (8)

Role—an expected behavior pattern for an individual in the group. This pattern may be prescribed formally or imposed informally. (8)

Scientific management—approach popularized by Frederick Taylor that analyzed shop management from a scientific perspective. (2)

Single-factor model of organizational effectiveness—the outdated view of effectiveness, which equated organizational effectiveness with a single broad measure such as profitability or job satisfaction. (14)

Situational view—the argument that the ability to influence arises from impersonal aspects of the circumstance rather than from personal traits. (9)

Source—the initiator of a message in the communication process. (7)

Source-of-leadership controversy—the continuing argument between advocates of the traitist view and the supporters of situational theories. (9)

Status—social ordering, or the position a person holds in a group. (7)

Structural view—the organizational design perspective that stresses positions and roles rather than personalities and human factors. (11)

Systems boundary—the limit or extent of a system or subsystem. Boundaries can be defined accurately only by taking a specified perspective. (13)

Systems coupling—the extent to which two or more systems or subsystems are related. (13)

Systems model of organizational effectiveness—the position that relates organizational effectiveness to the performance of key organizational subsystems or elements. The elements included in our model are efficiency, interpersonal relations, and adaptability. (14)

Task orientation—a leadership characteristic that places primary importance on goal accomplishment and secondary emphasis on interpersonal relations. (9)

Theory—an attempt to associate and integrate in a comprehensive statement the data collected through experimentation and observation. (3)

Tight coupling—a linkage among systems or subsystems in which a change in one unit is reflected directly and promptly in the other units. (13)

Trait theory—the argument that one's ability to influence another arises from some superior physical or psychological characteristic. (9)

Triad—a three-person group. (7)

Valence—according to expectancy theory, the strength of a person's desire, for a specific outcome. (6)

Index

Abilities, and status structure, 179
Absenteeism, and job satisfaction, 47
Academic societies, as linking agents, 409–410
Academy of Management, 10
  Institute for Administrative Research, 409–410
Acceptance theory, of authority, 31
Acculturation, 85
Achievement, as motivation factor, 153
Achievement motivation, theory of (McClelland), 151, 156–157
Achievement motive (*n Ach*) (McClelland), 80
Action
  and attitudes, 92–95
  see also Behavior
Action research, 406
  and barriers to knowledge-flow system, 410–413
Adaptability, and structure, 15
Administration
  authoritarianism in, 21–22
  and collegial structure, 314
  modern thought in, 23 (fig.)
  and professionalized hierarchy, 315–316
  see also Bureaucracy
Administrative organization theory, 26
  criticized, 29–30
Advancement, as motivation factor, 153
Aerodynamic Research Institute (ARI), 317 and *fig.,* 318
Aggression, and psychoanalytical theory, 75–76

Air Defense Command (U.S. Air Force), 347, 348
Alcoholism, 19–20
Alienation, and work values, 89
Alternative ranking, 356
Ambiguity (role), 204–205, 208
  and boundary-spanning behavior, 337–338
American Assembly of Collegiate Schools of Business (AACSB), 338–339, 340
American Civil Liberties Union, 107
American Management Association, 409, 410, 418
American Medical Association, 339
American Motors, 258
American Telephone and Telegraph Company (AT&T), 4, 365 (fig.), 366
  Bell Laboratories, 341
Anxiety, and cognitive dissonance, 132
Appraisal instruments, and performance evaluation, 353–356
Appraisal methods, and performance evaluation, 356–360
Argyris, Chris, view of total personality, 281–284, 282 (fig.)
Asch, S. E., studies of, 195
Assessment centers, 350
  and leadership potential, 364–366
Assimilation, 85
Attitudes, 90–100
  and behavior, 92–95
  change of, 98–100
  development of, 91 and *fig.*
  and environment, 93
  measuring, 95–98

Attitude scales, 95–98
Attractiveness (source), and attitude change, 99
Authoritarianism
  in administration, 21–22
  not related to success, 21
Authority, 48, 311
  and acceptance, 31
  and bureaucracy, 277
  and family structure, 86
  forms of, 25
  and leadership, 223–224
  and power, 215–216
  and professionalized hierarchy, 315
Authority gap, in temporary groups, 309–310
Autocratic style, of leadership, 221–223, 227
Automation, and fear of change, 385–386
Avoidance, and psychoanalytical theory, 76

Bacon, Francis, 20
Barnard, Chester, 31, 32
Barnard-Simon model, see Exchange theory
BARS (behaviorally anchored rating scales), 359–360
Behavior
  analyzing, 40
  and attitudes, 92–95
  causes of, 48
  in groups, 184–185
  normative, 191–192
  and organizational development, 389
  in organizations, 19–20
  and perception, 114
  and status structure, 184
  and structure, 302–303
  systems view of, 81–84
  see also Action; Boundary-spanning behavior; Organizational behavior; Worker behavior
Behavioral assumptions, on performance evaluation, 350–351
Behavioral decision theory, 129–131, 132
Behavioral demands, and boundary-spanning behavior, 337–338
Behavioral design theories, 281–286, 292 (table)

Argyris's hypothesis, 281–284, 282 (fig.)
Bennis on bureaucracy, 284–285
Behavioral foundations, of systematic management, 22–31
Behavioral knowledge, 404–421
  and action research, 410–413
  and barriers to knowledge flow, 407–408
  and ethical issues, 416–417
  and knowledge flow, 405–406
  and linking agents to overcome barriers, 409–413
Behaviorally anchored rating scales (BARS), 359–360
Behavioral measurement, 61–67
Behavioral perspective, and coordination, 253–254
Behavioral process, 108 and fig.
Behavioral sciences, 8–11, 18–44
  and administrative theory and practice, 26
  and bureaucracy, 22–26
  and criticisms of traditions, 28–30
  economic psychology, 10
  economics, 8, 10
  emergence of, 19–22
  and human relations movement, 31–38
  and human understanding, 20–21
  and Machiavellianism, 21
  psychology, 9
  and scientific management movement, 26–27, 30
  social psychology, 10
  sociology, 8, 9
Behavioral scientists (modern), concepts of, 40–41 (table)
Behavior modification, and operant conditioning, 149–150
Belongingness needs, 78
Bennis, Warren, 284–285
Berkeley, George, 21
Blue-collar workers, and job satisfaction, 155, 156
Boulwarism, 245, 249
Boundaries, and systems, 328–329
Boundary-spanning behavior, 327–346
  and behavioral demands, 337–338
  and environment, 335–337
  and innovation, 340–341
  and interorganizational issues, 330–331

Boundary-spanning behavior (*cont.*)
and interorganizational relations,
332–333
systems and boundaries, 328–329
and systems coupling, 338–340
Brakerfield Foundry, 385, 386
Bulova Watch Company, 297
Bureaucracy
ideal, 23, 29
structure of, 23–26, 24 (fig.), 28–29,
251 (fig.)
threats to, 284–285
Weber theory of, 22–26, 28–29, 251,
276–278, 279
see also Administration
Bureaucratic perspective, and coordination, 251–252, 253
Burkovitch, Ruby, 381–382, 384
Burns, Thomas, 278

Calvin, John, 87
Capital Chemical Corporation, 393–
394
Carey, Alex, 37
Center for the Study of Democratic In-
stitutions, 317
Ceremonies, and bureaucracy, 277
Change, 369–370
agent, 379–380
attitude, 98–100
and boundary-spanning behavior, 336
and bureaucracy, 284
easing, 387
Lewin's force-field view of, 385 and
fig.
resistance to, 385–386
and status structure, 184
types of, 379
see also Planned change
Charismatic authority, 25
Charismatic power, 217
Checklists, weighted, 356–359
Childhood, 157
and expectations, 156
Child, John, 115
Choice, nature of, 126, 127
Chrysler Corporation, 258, 299
Clairvoyance, 116
Class (social), and work values, 88–89
Classical conditioning, 117–119, 120
Classifications
of groups, 168–172

of leadership, 228–229
of leadership styles, 221–225
of situation, 229–230
Closed systems, 12, 299–300
Closure, and perception, 111–112,
113, 115
Coalitions, 170, 171, 262–266
formation of, 263–265
and organizations, 265–266
Coals, Benjamin, 4
Codetermination, and worker participation, 154
Coercive power, 216
Cognition, 92
Cognitive dissonance, 126–127, 132
Cognitive processes, 106–136
learning, 9, 106–108, 116–123,
132–136
perception, 106–116, 123, 132–136
problem solving, 106–108, 123–136
Cohesiveness
and coalitions, 263–264
and conformity, 197–199
and performance, 197–199, 198 (fig.),
208
Collective bargaining, and conflict resolution, 245
Collegial structure, 313–318
and organic-adaptive (ad hoc) structure, 316–318
and professionalized hierarchy, 314–
316
Communication, 6–7
barriers, 173–175
interpersonal, 172–176, 173 (fig.),
184–185
nonverbal, 175–176, 185
patterns, 177–178
and performance, 94
person-to-person, 172–176, 184–185
see also Information exchange
Communication networks, 176, 177
and *fig.*
centralized and decentralized, 178
Communication Workers of America, 4
Communicator credibility, and attitude
change, 99
Company policy and administration, as
hygiene factor, 153
Compensation, and psychoanalytical
theory, 76
Competence, and leadership, 181–182

Competition
and conflict, 256–259, 269
and market share, 257 and *fig.*
Compliance
and acceptance, 208
and conformity, 192–193
and status, 180–183
Compromise, and conflict resolution,
261
Compromising, *see* Satisficing
Concurrent validity, 66–67
Conditioning
classical, 117–119, 120
operant, 119–120, 123, 146–150
Conflict, 37
and competition, 256–259
and coordination, 259–260
and intergroup behavior, 247–249
and intergroup relations, 254–262,
269
see also Role conflict
Conflict resolution, 37, 260–262
and collective bargaining, 245
Conformity, 192–199
and acceptance, 192–193
and cohesiveness, 197–199
and group norms, 192–197
and status, 180–183
studies of, 194–197
types of, 192–193
Confrontation meeting, and organizational development, 396–397
Congruent attitude change, 98
Consensus, as means, 31
Consideration, and leadership style,
224–225
Construct validity, 66
and performance evaluation, 353–355
Consumption, 406
Content theories, of motivation, 151–
157
Herzberg's two-factor theory, 151–
156, 157
McClelland's theory of achievement
motivation, 151, 156–157
Content validity, 66
Context, perceptual, 112–113, 114,
115
Contingencies, 304–313
and matrix organization, 311–313
and project structure, 304, 306–309
and temporary groups, 309–310

Contingency theory, of leadership,
228–234, 280
classification of leader, 228–229
classification of situation, 229–230
implications of, 230–234
Contingency theory, of organizational
design, 286–290, 292 (table), 372
Lawrence and Lorsch studies, 288–
290
Woodward's studies, 287–288, 290,
298
Continuous triad, 171
Contraction, and conflict resolution,
261
Control, reactive and preventive,
348–350
Control graph, 226–227
Control processes, 349 (fig.)
Control structure, and leadership,
226–227
Conventional wisdom, and research, 67
Cooperation, and interorganizational
relations, 333
Coordination, 249–254
behavioral perspective, 253–254
bureaucratic perspective, 251–252,
253
and conflict, 259–260, 269
functional perspective, 252–253
Copernicus, Nicolaus, 20
Coupling (systems), and boundary
spanning, 338–340
Coworker, least-preferred, 228–229
Credibility (communicator), and attitude change, 99
Criteria, and performance evaluation,
351–352
Culture, 84–88
characteristics of, 85
influence of, 86
and performance, 86–87
and U.S. youth, 87–88

Darwin, Charles, 20
Data collection and analysis, 67
Decision making, 126, 193
and bureaucratic structure, 25
and cognitive dissonance, 127–128
and information, 47
and professionalized hierarchy, 315
and research methods, 67

Decision making (*cont.*)
  in work groups, 200–203
  see also Problem solving
Decision theory, 128–132
  behavioral, 129–131, 132
  criticized, 131
  normative, 128–129, 131, 132
Deductive model, of knowledge devel-
    opment, 49–50
Defense mechanisms, and
    psychoanalytical theory, 75–76
Democratic style, of leadership, 222,
    223, 227
Dennison, Henry, 31–32
Dennison Manufacturing Company, 32
Dependency imbalance (task), and
    conflict, 255–256
Design, *see* Organizational design
Deviation, and status, 180–183
Dialectical approach, and behavioral
    science research, 14
Differentiation, and organizational de-
    sign contingency theory, 289–290
Dissonance, *see* Cognitive dissonance
Distributions, forced, 356, 357 (table)
Distributive relationships, and informa-
    tion exchange, 267–268
Domination, and conflict resolution, 261
Durant, Ariel, 418
Durant, Will, 418
Dyads, 169, 171–172

Economic psychology, 10
Economics, 8, 10
Educational constraints, 86
Effect (law of), and operant condition-
    ing, 119–120
Efficiency, and organizational effective-
    ness, 369–370
Ego, in psychoanalytical theory, 75
Emotions, and perception, 114
Employee-centered leader, 225
Employees, 73–105
  and attitudes, 90–100
  and environment, 84–90
  and Hawthorne studies, 36
  and managers, 100, 223–224
  personality development of, 74–80
  and systems view of behavior, 81–84
  and Theory X vs. Theory Y managers,
    223–224
  see also Participation; Worker behavior

Encounter groups, 394
Enculturation, 85
England, 278
  family structure in, 86
English philosophers, 40–41
Environment, 84–90
  and attitudes, 93
  and boundary-spanning behavior,
    335–337
  and culture, 84–88
  and design, 298–299
  and heredity, 82–84
  and leadership, 226–227
  and organizational design, 298–299
  and organizational effectiveness, 371,
    372
  social class and work values, 88–89
  and structure, 302–303
Environmental change, and behavior
    modification, 149
Environmental consequences, 146
Environmental distortion, 174–175
Environmental uncertainty, perceived,
    335
Episodic triad, 171
Equilibrium
  and change, 385
  and organizational effectiveness,
    369–370
Equity formulation, 146
Equivalent-forms procedure, 65
Errors, and experimental research de-
    signs, 53–54
Esteem needs, 78
Ethical issues, and behavioral knowl-
    edge, 416–417
Evaluation, 363–364 (table)
  and conflict, 256
  and information, 113
  of organizational effectiveness, 366–
    369
  questionnaire, 96–97 (table)
  see also Appraisal instruments; Ap-
    praisal methods; Performance evalu-
    ation
Exchange theory, 142–143
Existence needs, 79
Existence-relatedness-growth (ERG)
    theory, 79–80
Exorcist, The (film), 106
Expansion, and conflict resolution,
    261

Expectancy theory, 143–146, 150–151
  basic logic of, 144
  expanded view of, 145
  and instrumentality, 235–236
Expectations
  and childhood, 156
  role, 204 (fig.)
Experience, *see* Environment
Experience bypass, 174
Experimental research designs, 52–59
  and errors, 53–54
  recent variations in, 57–59
  and validity, 54–57
Experimentation, and behavioral sciences, 38
Experiments, field, 51–52
Expertise, and boundary-spanning behavior, 336
Expert power, 217
External barriers, to knowledge-flow
  system, 408
External validity, and experimental re-
  search designs, 56–57
Extraorganizational spanning, 341
Extrasensory perception (ESP), 116
Eye movements (oculesics), and com-
  munication, 176

Fairway Materials Company, 329
Family structure, and authority, 86
Fast Market Foods (FMF), 332–333
Fayol, Henri, 2, 22, 26, 31, 251
Federal Metal and Non-Metallic Mine
  Safety Board of Review, 278
Federal Trade Commission, 106
Feedback
  and appraisal methods, 360
  and performance, 123
  and subordinate reviews, 362
Feedback control, 348
Festinger, Leon, 127
Fiedler, Fred E., contingency theory of,
  228–231
Field experiments, 51–52
Field studies, 51
Fixed resources, and conflict, 256
Flex-time, 382
Follett, Mary Parker, 31, 32, 253, 261
Force
  and conflict resolution, 261
  and planned change, 382–383
Forced distributions, 356, 357 (table)

Force-field view, of change (Lewin),
  385 and *fig.*
Ford Motor Company, 27, 258
Forgetting, and learning, 122 and *fig.*
Formal groups, 168, 171
Formal structure, and contingency
  theory, 289
Formal system, of status structure,
  179–180
Freud, Sigmund, 20, 75, 80
Functional approach, to administration,
  26
Functional perspective, and coordina-
  tion, 252–253

General Electric Company, 245, 248–
  249, 275–276
Generality-specificity, and attitude-
  action, 93–94
General Motors, 4, 5, 114–115, 258,
  275, 290
Germany, 22
  family structure in, 86
Goal attainment, and path-goal theory,
  235–236
Goal conflict, 248
Goal optimization, 367
Goal orientation, 94
  and contingency theory, 288–289
Goals, superordinate, 260
Goal setting
  and MBO programs, 395–396
  and performance evaluation, 351–352
Goodrich, B. F. (company), 388
Goodyear Tire and Rubber Company,
  388
Greek philosophers, early, 19
Group norms, 167, 191–192
  and conformity, 192–197
Groups, 8, 166–189, 214
  characteristics of, 167–168
  classifying, 168–172
  and communication networks, 177 and
    fig., 178
  control vs. comparison, 59
  experimental vs. control, 55–56
  formal, 168, 171
  heterogeneous, 200, 263–264
  homogeneous, 200, 201, 263–264
  informal, 168, 171
  interacting, 199–200, 201–202,
    208–209

Groups (*cont.*)
  and interpersonal communication,
    172–176
  nominal, 199–200, 201–202, 208–
    209
  normative behavior in, 191–192
  power and leadership in, 214–237
  reference, 168–169, 171, 193
  and risk, 202–203
  social behavior in, 184–185
  and social psychology, 10
  and sociology, 9
  and status structures, 179–184
  temporary, 309–310
  see also Encounter groups; Membership
    groups; Pressure group; Research
    groups; Work groups
Growth, as motivation factor, 153
Growth needs, 80
Growth orientation, 94

Halaby, Najeeb E., 214
Halo effect, 355
  and perception, 111–112
Haphazard change, 379
Harris County (Texas) Adult Probation
  Department, 396
Harris Drapery, Inc., 368–369
Harrison, Betty, 3
Hartsfield General Hospital, 381–382
Harvard Business School, 32, 33
Hawthorne effect, 33
Hawthorne Studies, 32–36, 180
  criticisms of, 36–38
Health care field, MBO programs in,
  396
Heredity, and environment, 82–84
Herzberg, Frederick, 57
  two-factor theory of motivation,
    151–156, 153 (table), 157
Hester Institute of Science and
  Technology, 327
Heterogeneous groups, 200, 263–264
High performers, attitudes of, 94–95
Historical perspective, 18–44
  behavioral foundations of systematic
    management, 22–31
  emergence of behavioral sciences,
    19–22
  human relations movement, 31–38
History errors, 53
Holistic approach, 302 and *fig.*

Homogeneous groups, 200, 201,
  263–264
Horizontal interactions, 246
Horizontal relationships, 266–268
Hospital
  and boundary-spanning behavior, 336
  as professionalized hierarchy, 314–315
Hostility
  and competition, 258–259
  and conflict, 254–255
Human nature, assumptions about, 40
Human relations movement, 31–38
  Hawthorne Studies, 32–38
Hume, David, 21
Hygiene factors, in two-factor theory,
  152–154
Hypothesis, defined, 47

Iacocca, Lee A., 258
IBM, 137
Id, in psychoanalytical theory, 75
Ideal bureaucracy, 23, 29
Ideological differences, and coalitions,
  264
Imaginativeness, and performance, 94
Incongruent attitude changes, 98–99
Independence, and social class, 89
Individual
  and group, 166–167, 195–197
  vs. organizations, 281–284
  and organizational effectiveness, 371,
    372
Individual differences, and Hawthorne
  studies, 36
Individuality, 150
Inducement techniques, in mail sur-
  veys, 60, 62–63
Inductive method, 20–21
Inductive model, of knowledge devel-
  opment, 50–51
Informal groups, 168, 171
Informal relationships, 34–35
  and bureaucratic structures, 29
Information
  and decision making, 47
  and evaluation, 113
Information control, and situational
  theories of leadership, 219–220
Information exchange, distributive vs.
  integrative, 267–268
Information generation, and action re-
  search, 412–413

Information search, 124–125, 127
Initiating planned change, 382–383
Initiating structure, and leadership
style, 224–225
Innovation
and boundary-spanning behavior,
340–341
and organizational development, 388
Input-process-output view, 301
Inputs, and systems view, 81–82
Instrument (appraisal), for performance
evaluation, 353–356
Instrumentality, 141–142
and expectancy theory, 143–144,
235–236
Instrumental learning, 120 (fig.)
Instrumental theories, of motivation,
141–151
exchange theory, 142–143
expectancy theory, 143–146
implications of, 150–151
operant conditioning, 146–150
Instrument construction, 67
Instrument decay errors, 54
Integration
and conflict resolution, 261
and contingency theory, 289
of individual and organizational goals,
394–396
Integrative relationships, and information exchange, 267–268
Intensive technology, 336–337
Interacting groups, 199–200, 201–202,
208–209
Interaction, 92
horizontal and vertical, 246–247
and status structure, 183–184
Interactive errors, 54
Interdependence
and conflict, 255
and interorganizational relations, 333
Intergroup behavior, 246–249
and complexity of interactions, 246–
247, 249
and conflict, 247–249
and coordination, 249–254
Intergroup relations, 245–274
and coalitions, 262–266
and conflict, 254–262, 269
and coordination, 249–254, 269
and horizontal relationships, 266–268
and intergroup behavior, 246–249

Internal validity, and experimental re-
search designs, 54–56, 57
International Telephone & Telegraph
Corporation (ITT), 278
Interorganizational issues, 330–331
Interorganizational relations, 332–333
exchange view, 333
power dependency view, 332–333
Interpersonal analysis, 392–394
encounter groups, 394
sensitivity training, 392–394
Interpersonal barriers, to knowledge
flow, 408
Interpersonal communication, 172–
176, 173 (fig.), 184–185
Interpersonal orientation, and contin-
gency theory, 289
Interrole conflicts, 207
Intersender conflicts, 207
Interval scale, 64
Intraorganizational spanning, 340
Intrapersonal analysis, 392–394
encounter groups, 394
sensitivity training, 392–394
Intrasender conflicts, 207
Intraunit spanning, 340
Iran, 335
hostage crisis in, 249

Japan, 57
management philosophy vs. U.S. philosophy, 73–74, 85
Job-centered leader, 225
Job enrichment, 83, 155, 156, 371,
394–395
Job performance, see Performance
Job satisfaction, 83
and absenteeism, 47
and boundary-spanning behavior,
337–338
and dissatisfaction, 152, 154, 155–156
and motivation, 139–141
and participation, 352
and performance, 150–151
Job stress, and Machiavellianism, 21
Joyfulness, and performance, 95

Kinesics, and communication, 175–176
Knowledge, 48
and collegial structure, 313–314
see also Behavioral knowledge

Knowledge development models,
48–51
deductive model, 49–50
inductive model, 50–51
Knowledge-flow system, 405–408
barriers to, 407–408
overcoming barriers to, 409–413
practice subsystem, 406, 409 (fig.)
research subsystem, 405–406, 409
(fig.)
Kyocera International, 73
Kyoto Ceramic Company of Japan, 73,
74, 84–85, 90

Labor-management conflicts, 245
Labor specialization, and bureaucratic
perspective, 251
Laissez-faire style, of leadership, 222–
223
Lakeville, 250
police department, 369
Law of effect, and operant conditioning,
119–120
Lawrence, Paul R., 288–290
Leader, job-centered vs. employee-
centered, 225
Leader-follower relations, and contingency theory, 229–233
Leadership, 178, 214–215, 217–241,
280–281
and assessment centers, 364–366
and authority, 223–224
and competence, 181–182
contingency theory, 228–234
and Hawthorne studies, 36
measuring styles of, 225–227
path-goal theory, 235–236
and power, 217–221
research on, 224–225
situational theories, 219–221, 229–
234
styles of, 221–227, 228
in temporary groups, 309–310
trait theory, 218–219, 220–221
Learning, 9, 106–108, 116–123, 132–
136
and classical conditioning, 117–119,
120
and forgetting, 122 and fig.
instrumental, 120 (fig.)
measurement of, 121–122

and operant conditioning, 119–120,
123
selected patterns, 121 (fig.)
and training, 123
Legitimate power, 216
Lewin, Kurt, 82
force-field view of change, 385 and fig.
Lighting, and output, 32–33
Likert scale, 95–98
Linkage, and knowledge-flow system,
407
Linking agents, and barriers to
knowledge-flow system, 409–413
Locke, John, 20–21
Long-linked technology, 336
Loose coupling, 339–340
Lorsch, Jay W., 288–290

McClelland, David, 87
achievement motive (n Ach), 80
theory of achievement motivation,
151, 156–157
McGregor, Douglas, 223–224
Machiavelli, Niccolo, 21, 40–41
Machiavellianism, 61
and job stress, 21
McKinney, Charlotte, 381–382, 384
Magnavox, 377, 378
Mail surveys, 60
and response rates, 62–63 (table)
Management development, and organi-
zational development, 389–391
Management-by-objectives (MBO)
programs, 58–59, 353, 395–396
time-series data for, 58 and fig.
Managerial behavior, and bureaucracy,
285
Managers
and employees, 100
vs. researchers, 414–415 (table)
Theory X vs. Theory Y, 223–224
Market share, and competition, 257 and
fig.
Mars Candy Company, 26
Maslow, Abraham, 83, 151
needs hierarchy, 49–50, 77–80
Mass production, and contingency
theory, 287–288
Matrix management, at Steller International Corporation, 311 (fig.)
Matrix organization, vs. project structure, 311–313

Maturity errors, 54
Mayo, Elton, 32, 37, 40–41
Measurement, behavioral,
  61–67
  of attitudes, 95–98
  errors, 93
  and interval scale, 64
  of leadership styles, 225–227
  of learning, 121–122
  levels, 61–63
  and nominal scale, 63
  and ordinal scale, 63–64
  and ratio scale, 64
  reliability and validity, 64–67
Media, and attitude change, 99
Media selection, 174
Mediating technology, 336
Membership (group), 167
  and status, 180
Membership groups, 168–169, 171,
  193
Messages, 178
  misunderstanding of, 174–175
  subliminal, 106–107, 114
Middle class
  and job satisfaction, 83, 155, 156
  and work values, 89
Midwestern Research Center, 368
Minimum-size principle, of coalition
  formation, 263
Miscommunication, 174
Mortality error, 54
Motivation, 56–57, 137–162
  content theories, 151–157
  and goal setting, 351–352
  instrumental theories, 141–151
  and job satisfaction, 139–141
  and learning, 132
  and participation, 353
  process of, 138–139
  two-factor theory, 151–156, 153
  (table), 157
  see also Scientific management movement
Motivators, in two-factor theory, 152–
  155
Motives, and groups, 167
Motorola (company), 377, 378
Movies, and subliminal messages,
  106
Munsterberg, Hugo, 28
Murphy, Thomas, 154

National Aeronautical and Space Ad-
  ministration (NASA), 307
National Research Council (National
  Academy of Sciences), 32
National Rifle Association, 337
Needs
  categories of, 78–79
  and culture, 85
Need satisfaction, and path-goal theory,
  235–236
Needs theory, 77–80
  McClelland's achievement motive (n
  Ach), 80
  Maslow's needs hierarchy, 49–50,
  77–80
Networks, communication, 176, 177
  and $fig.$
  centralized and decentralized, 178
Newman, J. W., Corporation, 94
Nominal groups, 199–200, 201–202,
  208–209
Nominal scale, 63
Noncompliance, and status, 180–183
Nonprofessional staff, and collegial
  structure, 314
Nonverbal communication, 175–176,
  185
Normative behavior, in groups, 191–
  192
Normative decision theory, 128–129,
  131, 132
Nowness, and performance, 95

Occupational Safety and Health Act,
  383
Oh, Tai K., 73n
Ohio State leadership studies, 224–225
OPEC nations, 335
Open systems, 12–13, 300–302
Operant conditioning, 119–120, 123,
  146–150
Opinion, defined, 91
Optimism, and performance, 94
Ordinal scale, 63–64
Organic-adaptive (ad hoc) structure,
  304, 316–318
Organizational behavior, 3–17
  analyzing, 13–15, 48
  and behavioral sciences, 8–11
  historical perspective of, 18–44
  and organizations, 4–7
  see also Behavior

Organizational design, 93, 275–296
  behavioral design theories, 281–286
  contingency theory, 286–290
  and environment, 298–299
  structural design theory, 276–281
  see also Structure
Organizational development (OD),
    387–403
  and behavior, 389
  and confrontation meeting, 396–397
  integrating individual and organiza-
    tional goals, 394–396
  intra- and interpersonal analysis,
    392–394
  and management development, 389–
    391
  techniques, 391–394
Organizational development consultant,
    as change agent, 379–380
Organizational Dynamics (publication),
    418
Organizational effectiveness, 366–376
  descriptive measure of, 369–370
  evaluation of models, 366–369
  model of, 370–372
Organizational set, 246
Organizational size, and bureaucracy,
    284
Organizations
  alternative views of, 11–13
  behavior in, 19–20
  closed systems, 12, 299–300
  and coalitions, 265–266
  vs. individual, 281–284
  open system, 12–13, 300–302
  and organizational behavior, 4–7
  structure of, 6–7
  see also Bureaucracy
Outcomes, and expectancy theory, 144
Output
  and lighting, 32–33
  and systems view, 81–82
  and wave incentives, 33–34
  see also Productivity
Outsiders, and performance evaluation,
    363, 364
Owen, Robert, 166

Participation, and performance evalua-
    tion, 352–353
  see also Worker participation

Participative approach, to management,
    227
Path-goal theory, of leadership, 235–
    236
Pavlov, Ivan, 117–118
Peer reviews, and performance evalua-
    tion, 361, 363
Perceived environmental uncertainty,
    335
Perception, 106–116, 123, 132–136
  characteristics of, 110 (fig.)
  and closure, 111–112, 113, 115
  and culture, 86
  extrasensory, 116
  selective, 109–111, 113, 115
  and subliminal messages, 106–107, 114
Perceptual context, 112–113, 114, 115
Performance
  and attitudes, 94–95
  and cohesiveness, 197–199, 198 (fig.),
    208
  and culture, 86–87
  and feedback, 123
  individual vs. group, 195–197
  and job satisfaction, 150–151
  and leadership styles, 225
  and pressure, 95
  and reinforcement, 148
  see also Task performance
Performance evaluation, 347–366,
    372–376
  and appraisal instruments, 353–356
  and appraisal level, 360–364
  and appraisal methods, 356–360
  assessment centers, 364–366
  and behavioral assumptions, 350–351
  and goal setting, 351–352
  and organizational control, 348–350
  and participation, 352–353
Perkins, Barry, 3
Perrow, Charles, structural view of,
    279–281
Personal acceptance
  and compliance, 208
  and conformity, 192–193
Personal factors, and perception, 114
Personality, Argyris view of total,
    281–284, 282 (fig.)
Personality development, 74–80
  needs theory, 77–80
  psychoanalytical theory, 75–76
  trait theory, 76–77

Person-to-person communication, 172–176, 184–185
Philosophy, and science, 45–48
Physical appearance, and communication, 176
Piece-rate system, 27
Planned change, 377–384, 398–403
  agents of, 379–380
  initiating, 382–383
  process, 384 and *fig.*
  stabilizing and refreezing system, 384
  unfreezing system, 381–382
  see also Change
Plato (Greek philosopher), 19
Political science, areas of, 10
Positioning (proxemics), and communication, 176
Position power, and contingency theory, 229–233, 280
Power, 214–221, 236–241
  and authority, 215–216
  and collegial structure, 314
  and leadership, 217–221, 227
  position, 229–233, 280
  types of, 216–217
  see also Leadership
Power dependency, and interorganizational relations, 332–333
Practicality, vs. humanistic ideals, 22
Practice subsystem, 409 (fig.)
  and knowledge-flow system, 406
  see also Linking agents
Precognition, 116
Predictive validity, 66–67
Prejudice, 91, 92, 93
  and perception, 114
Premise, defined, 47
Pressure, and performance, 95
Pressure group (external and internal), as change agent, 379
Preventive control, 348–350
Primary effects, and reinforcers, 146
Principles of Scientific Management (Taylor), 27
Problem definition, and action research, 412
Problem solving, 106–108, 123–136
  and cognitive dissonance, 126–127, 132
  and communication networks, 178
  and conflict resolution, 260
  and decision theory, 128–132
  and information search, 124–125, 127

in work groups, 199–203
  see also Decision making; Project structure
Process production, and contingency theory, 287–288
Productivity
  and cohesiveness, 197–199, 208
  and status, 180
  see also Output
Professional associations, as linking agents, 409–410
Professionalized hierarchy, as collegial structure, 314–316
Professional schools, as linking agents, 409
Project structure, 304–313
  advantages of, 307–308
  and contingencies, 304, 306–309
  disadvantages of, 308–309
  vs. matrix organization, 311–313
  at Sigma Systems, 305 (fig.)
Psychoanalytical theory, 75–76
  and defense mechanisms, 75–76
Psychokinesis, 116
Psychology, 8, 9
Punishment, as negative reinforcer, 146

Quasi-experimental designs, 57–59
Quasistationary equilibrium, 385

Rand Corporation, 190, 200
Ranking techniques, 356
Rational appeal, and planned change, 383
Rationalization, 76, 127–128
Rational-legal authority, 25, 26
Ratio scale, 64
Reactive control, 348–350
Recognition, as motivation factor, 153
Re-education, and planned change, 383
Reference groups, 168–169, 171, 193
Referent power, 217
Refreezing system, and planned change, 384
Regional differences, and coalitions, 264–265
Reinforcement, 146–148
  continuous, 148
  fixed and variable, 147–148
  partial, 147–148
  positive and negative, 146, 148
Relatedness needs, 80

Reliability, in measurement, 64–67
Research Associates (R.A.), 303
Researchers, vs. managers, 414–415
  (table)
Research foundations, as linking agents,
  410
Research groups
  control vs. comparison, 59
  experimental vs. control, 55–56
Research institutes, as linking agents,
  410
Research methods, 45–70
  behavioral measurement, 61–67
  experimental research designs, 52–59
  field experiments, 51–52
  field studies, 51
  models of knowledge development,
    48–51
  and science and philosophy, 45–48
  survey research, 59–60
  and understanding organizational be-
    havior, 48
Research subsystem, 409 (fig.)
  and knowledge-flow system, 405–406
  see also Linking agents
Response rates, in mail surveys, 60,
  62–63
Responsibility
  as motivation factor, 153
  and performance, 94
Reward power, 216
Reward system, and status system, 183
Risk taking, and performance, 95
Risky-shift hypothesis, 202–203
Role, defined, 203
Role ambiguity, 204–205, 208
  and boundary-spanning behavior,
    337–338
Role clarity, in work groups, 204–205,
  207–208
Role conflict
  and boundary-spanning behavior,
    337–338
  types of, 207
  in work groups, 205–208
Role expectations, 204 (fig.)
Role relationships, in work groups,
  203–205, 209

Safety needs, 78
Sample selection, for surveys, 60, 67
Satisficing, 130

Science, 46–47
  advances in, 20–21
Science and philosophy, 45–48
  and scientific inquiry, 46–47
Scientific inquiry, 46–48
  hypothesis, 47
  premise, 47
  and science, 46–47
  theory, 47
Scientific management movement,
  26–27
  criticized, 30
  see also Motivation
Scientific mentality, 46–47
Scientific method, 38
Scott, Walter Dill, 28
Secondary effects, and reinforcers,
  146–147
Selection errors, 54
Selective perception, 109–111, 113,
  115
Self-actualization needs, 78–79
Self-direction, and social class, 89
Self-evaluation, and performance evalu-
  ation, 361, 364
Self-image, 20
  and performance, 94
Sensitivity training, 392–394
Sherif, Muzafer, 92, 194–195
Sigma Systems, 304, 306, 309, 311, 312
  project structure at, 305 (fig.)
Silence (chronemics), and communica-
  tion, 176
Simulation, and preventive control,
  349–350
Situational design theory, see Contin-
  gency theory
Situational factors
  and attitude change, 99
  and contingency theory, 228–234
Situational theories, of leadership,
  219–221, 229–234
Size, and group classification, 169–172
Skinner, B. F., 20, 119, 146, 157
Sloan, Alfred P., Jr., 252–253, 275,
  290
Small businesses, 298
Social class, and work values, 88–89
Social dimension
  and administrative theory, 30
  and bureaucratic structure, 29
  and worker behavior, 34–35

Social equilibrium, 369–370
Socialization, defined, 88–89
Social psychology, 10
Social system, and status structure, 179–180
Sociological constraints, 86
Sociology, 8, 9
"Solomon four-group" design, 56
Soul (human), divisions in, 19
Source attractiveness, and attitude change, 99
South Essex studies (Woodward), 287–288, 290, 298
Spanning, levels of, 340–341
  see also Boundary-spanning behavior
Specialization, and bureaucracy, 251, 285
Specificity-generality, and attitudes-action, 93–94
Split-half technique, 65
Stabilizing system, and planned change, 384
Staff expert, as change agent, 380
Standardization, and bureaucracy, 285
Status, 167, 185
  and compliance, 180–183
  congruency, 183
Status structure, 179–184
  compliance and noncompliance, 180–183
  formal and social systems, 179–180
  and interaction patterns, 183–184
Status system, and reward system, 183
Stein, Rachel, 3–4
Steller International Corporation, 311–312
  matrix management at, 311 (fig.)
Stereotyping, 111–112, 355
Stimulus (unconditioned), in classical conditioning, 118
Structural design theory, 276–281, 292 (table)
  Perrow's structural view, 279–281
  Weber's theory of bureaucracy, 22–26, 28–29, 251, 276–278, 279
Structural formality, and contingency theory, 289
Structure, 14, 297–323
  and adaptability, 15
  and behavior, 302–303
  of bureaucracy, 23–26, 24 (fig.), 28–29, 251 (fig.)

closed systems, 299–300
collegial, 313–318
and contingencies, 304–313
environment and design, 298–299
open systems, 300–302
and organizational effectiveness, 371–372
of organizations, 6–7
see also Initiating structure; Organic-adaptive (ad hoc) structure; Project structure; Status structure; Task structure
Subliminal messages, 106–107, 114
Subordinate reviews, and performance evaluation, 361–362, 364
Success, not related to authoritarianism, 21
Summed-rating measure, 96
Superego, in psychoanalytical theory, 75
Superordinate goals, and conflict resolution, 260
Supervision, as hygiene factor, 153
Supervisors
  and performance evaluation, 355, 361, 363
  relations with, as hygiene factor, 153
Survey research, 59–60
Systematic management, 22–31
  criticisms of, 28–31
System stabilizing and refreezing, 384
System unfreezing, 381–382
Systems, open and closed, 299–302
Systems boundaries, 328–329
Systems coupling, and boundary-spanning behavior, 338–340
Systems view, 81–84
  heredity and environment, 82–84
  inputs, transformations, outputs, 81–82

Task complexity, and contingency theory, 280
Task forces, see Project structure
Task performance
  and path-goal theory, 235–236
  and status, 179–180
Task structure, and contingency theory, 229–233
Taylor, Frederick W., 22, 27, 28, 30, 31, 40–41, 56–57
Teamwork, vs. individual performance, 195–197

Technical terms, use of, 174
Technology
  and boundary-spanning behavior,
    336–337
  and bureaucracy, 284
  and contingency theory, 287–288
Telepathy, 116
Telephone surveys, 60
Tension, and cognitive dissonance, 132
  see also Job stress
Terminal triads, 171
Testing errors, 53
Testing reliability, 65
Test-retest approach, 65
T-groups, vs. encounter groups, 394
Theory, defined, 47
Theory building, and action research,
    411–412, 413
Theory X and Y managers (McGregor),
    223–224
Thorndike, E. L., 83
Tight coupling, 338–339
Time orientation, and contingency
    theory, 289
Time-series analysis, 57–59
Time study, 27
Toffler, Alvin, 316
Tradition
  and bureaucracy, 277
  and collegial structure, 314
Traditional authority, 25
Training, and learning, 123
Trait theory, of leadership, 218–219,
    220–221
Trait theory, of personality, 76–77
Traits, hereditary, 82–83
Transformations, and systems view,
    81–82
Trans World Airlines (TWA), 85
Triads, 169–172
  continuous, 171
  episodic, 171
  possible structure of, 170 (fig.)
  terminal, 171
Trust, and performance, 95
Trust-Openness-Realization-Interde-
    pendent (TORI) system, 394
TV commercials, and subliminal mes-
    sages, 106
Two-factor theory, of motivation
    (Herzberg), 151–156, 153 (table),
    157

Unconditioned stimulus, in classical
    conditioning, 118
Unconscious factors, and perception,
    114
Understanding, human, 20–21
Unfreezing system, 381–382
United States, 22, 190
  energy crisis, 330–331
  family structure in, 86
  investments in Germany, 154
  and Iran hostage crisis, 249
  management philosophy vs. Japanese
    philosophy, 73–74, 85
  youth in, 87–88
United States Chamber of Commerce,
    154
United States Department of Health,
    Education, and Welfare, 5, 416
United States Department of Labor,
    382–383
U. S. Steel, 331
Unit production, and contingency
    theory, 287–288
Universal Industries, 380
University Hospital, 395

Valence, and expectancy theory, 143
Validity, 64–67
  concurrent, 66–67
  construct, 66
  content, 66
  of evaluation instruments, 353–356
  and experimental research designs,
    54–57
  predictive, 66–67
Value problems, as barriers to
    knowledge-flow system, 407–408
Values, 41, 167
  and culture, 86, 87–88
  see also Work values
Value systems, and achievement moti-
    vation, 156
Vertical interactions, 246–247
Vertical specialization, and bureaucratic
    perspective, 251
Volvo (Swedish company), 137–138,
    156

Wage incentives, 146
  and Hawthorne studies, 37
  and output, 33–34
Warner Brothers, 106

Watergate scandal, 279
Watson, Thomas, 137
Webb, James E., 307
Weber, Max, 14, 31, 40–41, 87, 216
  theory of bureaucracy, 22–26, 28–29,
  251, 276–278, 279
Weighted checklists, 356–359
Western Electric Company, 32
West Germany, codetermination in,
  154
White-collar workers, and job enrich-
  ment, 156
Whyte, William, 180
Woodrow Wilson Center for Interna-
  tional Scholars, 317
Woodward, Joan, South Essex studies,
  287–288, 290, 298
Words, abstract nature of, 175
Work, as motivation factor, 153
Worker behavior, and social dimension,
  34–35
  see also Blue-collar workers; White-
  collar workers

Worker participation, and codetermination, 154
Work groups, 190–213
  conformity and cohesiveness, 197–
  199
  group norms and conformity, 192–
  197
  and normative behavior, 191–192
  problem solving in, 199–203
  role ambiguity in, 204–205, 208
  role conflict in, 205–208
  role relationships in, 203–205, 209
Working conditions, as hygiene factor,
  153
Work performance, *see* Performance
Work values, 100
  and social class, 88–89

Yankelovich, Daniel, 87
Youth, in United States, 87–88

Zenith (company), 377–378